Holding Television Accountable

ALSO OF INTEREST
AND FROM McFARLAND

Badass Women and Hashtagged Zombies: Gender in The Walking Dead *from Screen to Social Media*
(Allison Christina Budaj, 2024)

All Kinds of Scary: Diversity in Contemporary Horror
(Jonina Anderson-Lopez, 2023)

Holding Television Accountable

Essays on Audience Demands in the Social Media Age

Edited by
ALLISON CHRISTINA BUDAJ *and*
JONINA ANDERSON-LOPEZ

McFarland & Company, Inc., Publishers
Jefferson, North Carolina

This book has undergone peer review.

LIBRARY OF CONGRESS CATALOGING-IN-PUBLICATION DATA

Names: Budaj, Allison Christina, 1985– editor. | Anderson-Lopez, Jonina, 1986– editor.
Title: Holding television accountable : essays on audience demands in the social media age / edited by Allison Christina Budaj and Jonina Anderson-Lopez.
Description: Jefferson, North Carolina : McFarland & Company, Inc., Publishers, 2025. | Includes bibliographical references and index.
Identifiers: LCCN 2024056256 | ISBN 9781476691589 (paperback : acid free paper) ∞
ISBN 9781476654492 (ebook)
Subjects: LCSH: Audience participation television programs—Social aspects. | Television viewers—Social aspects. | Television programs—Social aspects. | Online social networks—Social aspects. | LCGFT: Television criticism and reviews. | Essays.
Classification: LCC PN1992.8.A83 H65 2025 | DDC 791.45/6—dc23/eng/20250121
LC record available at https://lccn.loc.gov/2024056256

ISBN (print) 978-1-4766-9158-9
ISBN (ebook) 978-1-4766-5449-2

© 2025 Allison Christina Budaj and Jonina Anderson-Lopez. All rights reserved

No part of this book may be reproduced or transmitted in any form or by any means, electronic or mechanical, including photocopying or recording, or by any information storage and retrieval system, without permission in writing from the publisher.

Front cover image: © Alano Design/BrightRainbow/urfin

Printed in the United States of America

*McFarland & Company, Inc., Publishers
Box 611, Jefferson, North Carolina 28640
www.mcfarlandpub.com*

Acknowledgments

Allison Christina Budaj would like to thank:
 My very supportive family and friends. I never get tired of hearing your words of encouragement and for allowing me the space to write.
 R.J. Lambert. It has been a pleasure working with you and seeing this idea come to life.
 Our contributors. I very much appreciate your thought-provoking work and dedication to this project.
 My colleague and good friend, Jonina Anderson-Lopez, the best co-editor, research partner, and collaborator this scholar could have!

Jonina Anderson-Lopez would like to thank:
 My family and friends, who keep me sane and happy.
 R.J. Lambert, who helped jumpstart this endeavor.
 My partner in crime through this process, Allison Christina Budaj. Your work ethic is amazing, and you're an even better friend than I could have ever asked for!

Table of Contents

Acknowledgments v

Introduction
    Jonina Anderson-Lopez *and* Allison Christina Budaj 1

Part 1: Reality Television

Audience Interventions and the Plight of Systemic Racism on *Big Brother*
    Ragan Fox 17

Canceling CBS: Black Alliances and Diversity on Reality TV's *Survivor* and *Big Brother*, 2021–22
    Christina S. Walker, Esq., J.D. 35

"You don't work for me anymore": Race, Cancel Culture, and *Vanderpump Rules*
    Camille S. Alexander 53

Just Change the Channel? Analyzing Bravo's Response to Online Calls for Cancellation
    Rosemarie Jones 64

The Role of Crisis in Online Audience Participation's Influence on Television Content: A Case Study of *The Activist*
    Lukasz Swiatek, Marina Vujnovic, Chris Galloway, *and* Dean Kruckeberg 81

Part 2: Network and Cable Television

Tug of War: Social Media, Cancel Culture, and Diversity for *Girls* and *The 100*
    Jonina Anderson-Lopez, R.J. Lambert, *and* Allison Christina Budaj 95

Black Dude Dies First: Portrayals and Casting Choices in *Fear the Walking Dead*
    Juanita "Tico" Tenorio 120

Some Kind of Wonderful: An Analysis of Audience Reaction for *The Wonder Years* 2021 Reboot
    Erin E. Gilles *and* Saleema Mustafa Campbell 130

#TheySilencedThem: The Strange Case of *Supernatural*'s Queerbaiting
    ANNA CATERINO   148

Celebration and Mourning: Audience Reception of Queer Relationships
    in *Schitt's Creek* and *The 100*
    CHANDRAMA BASU   172

Part 3: Streaming Television

The Races and Genders of Jarl Haakon: Historical Fiction Caught
    Between Accuracy and Authenticity in *Vikings: Valhalla*
    PAUL CSILLAG   193

The Marketing of Fictional Portrayals of Real-World Social Causes
    on Broadcast and Streaming Networks
    RONEN SHAY *and* ARIEN ROZELLE   210

"An absolute travesty": Probing Parasocial Relationships and Audience
    Negativity in HBO's *And Just Like That…*
    ERIN E. GILLES   223

Ms. Marvel Beyond Cancel Culture: Multicultural Casting
    and Mixed Reviews
    FARHA B. TERNIKAR   243

Streaming and Video-on-Demand (SVOD) Has Become
    the "New Queer Cinema"
    VICTOR D. EVANS   255

Conclusion
    JONINA ANDERSON-LOPEZ *and* ALLISON CHRISTINA BUDAJ   275

About the Contributors   281

Index   285

Introduction

JONINA ANDERSON-LOPEZ
and ALLISON CHRISTINA BUDAJ

Hate the most recent season of a television show? Create a viral petition! Better yet, find an old tweet of a cast member from that show to publicly shame them. In other audience spheres, "cancel culture" has been derided for critiquing Dave Chappelle, Roseanne Barr, and *The Mandalorian*'s Gina Carano. Interestingly, the idea of "cancel culture" has even been self-consciously explored within television plotlines for *Younger* and *The Good Fight*. On shows like *Girls* and *The 100*, audience reception and protest influenced creative decisions for plotlines and characterization. These are but a few examples of audience participation's influence on television content in a social-networked age. Examples like these have resulted in collaborative articles such as "Tug of War: Social Media, Cancel Culture, and Diversity for Girls" (which included the two volume editors, and was originally published in *KOME*). Examples of audience reception have also led to the creation of volumes like this one.

Audiences are not a new constraint on creative content. Take Henry Jenkins's analysis of *Star Trek: The Next Generation* fans as an example. Claiming a "'moral right' to criticize the program's producers," Jenkins (1992) noted the strength of fans to complain not only as sole viewers of a series but as a like-minded community manifested through on-going discussion and debate (p. 88). Audiences increasingly communicate demands on television writers and studios to shape productions. The reach and effectiveness of such demands is, in part, the result of social media platforms that allow for opinions to quickly spread and gather mainstream attention among news outlets and critics. This dynamic relationship between creators, audiences, and critics can help boost or sink shows. Although creators and commercial distributors have always considered audience desires to some degree, the online visibility of contemporary audience feedback regularly impacts television entertainment. Sometimes dismissed as "cancel culture" or "snowflakes," the amplification of user sentiment nonetheless advocates effectively for increased diversity and inclusion on TV.

With this collection, we wish to highlight the import of the editors' original article ("Tug of War," mentioned above), and how each part was integral to founding this book (i.e., audience reception/cancel culture/diversity), and the academic support for each. In building the three parts of the collection, we cultivated submissions from an array of voices drawing on diverse scholarly topics related to television and audience reception. Through this collection, we argue how the relationship between audience reception has evolved, creating a modern landscape that includes culture and diversity as a result. Online spaces have and are still evolving—in between the time of drafting and editing these essays, Twitter and HBO changed their names, but certain essays may still refer to these titles. When online audiences criticize a television show, if their comments point out cultural, racial, gender, or other points of diverse representation or marginalization, these comments can gain wider recognition among other fans and even showrunners. For this reason, many of the essays review television show incidents revolving around an issue of diverse character depiction or marginalization as pointed out by online fans. In some of these cases, members of the cast or crew may have been put on notice by the network or fired altogether. The timing of the consequences or firings have persuaded critics and fans to refer to this treatment as cancel culture (a term mired in various definitions, to be explained in various contexts across essays), which is why this is another topic some of the essays explore in relation to case studies of television shows.

We've edited a collection grounded primarily in audience reception as an interpretive lens. A rift between traditional criticism and popular receptions of media "raises a key issue regarding the use of film criticism in reception studies: to what extent can the critics' views be taken as representative?" (Chapman et al., 2007, p. 195). In an age of new "media citizenship" and "the ethics of performativity" (Elsaesser, 2004, p. 76), this question may be extended to revise (and re-envision) the very function of the critic, getting to the heart of contemporary reception studies.

Audience Reception

Reception Theory

Why apply reception theory to television? This question seems easy to answer. After all, television is a visual medium meant for audiences to watch and consume. However, connecting what initially appears to be a theory applied primarily to texts warrants a deeper conversation. By definition, reception theory refers to the various theoretical methodologies with "potential implications" for visual arts and their context (Kaufman, 2003, para. 1). There is specific interest in the reaction or response of readers or beholders to those works (Kaufman, 2003, para. 1). In essence, this theory shifts from the production or creation of literary or artistic works to focus on how readers or observers understand or interpret these works. Considering the value of reception theory beyond its initial definition helps to elucidate the symbiotic relationship between the audience and the various televised or streamed narratives presented throughout this text.

While agreeing with Wolfgang Iser (2006) about the perceptible duality of reception theory in considering both the reception of literary texts and the effects on their audience, this theory extends far beyond its preliminary academic use (p. 57). If, as he asserts, "what literature brings into the world can only reveal itself by means of questioning what it reproduces from the world," the subsequent conversations of both the receiving or rejecting of televised or streamed narratives by audiences in the following essays undoubtedly applies (Iser, 2006, p. 67). Though, as Thomas Dacosta Kaufmann (2003) reminds us, conventional reception theory misses the ontological complexities of interpreting visual arts. The reception of a visual image is not the same as the reception of a written text (para. 15). Despite this difficulty, an argument can be made for visual narratives because these works should not be considered just by their producers. Instead, these visual narratives are part of an enduring historical and interactive process (Kaufmann, 2003, para. 17).

Additionally, visual narratives may result in responses from critics and audiences based on meaning, or what is signified. Iser (1993) describes "the semiotic difference between signifier and signified," and how "splitting the signifier doubles that difference and, in consequence, allows the signifier to be used in other ways" (p. 248). With a particular show (or text), the meaning can vary from audience to audience. They choose to convey their perceptions (i.e., social media posts, petitions, and more) in various online spaces, thus creating a link between their viewership and interactions. Through what Iser (1993) refers to as "text play," television audiences engage in performative spectatorship through social actions in relation to their own understanding with the show they're viewing, and then discussing (p. 274).

Implied Viewer

In the same way that texts are meant to be read, television is intended to be watched. Put differently, as Neil Postman (2006) urges, "the single most important fact about television is that people watch it, which is why it is called 'television'" (p. 93). Unique to television is its ability to incorporate all forms of discourse by providing varied content depending on what viewers seek (Postman, 2006, p. 93). When audiences engage in watching, this engagement calls into question the impact of this varied content on the audience. According to Shi (2013), the entire reading practice becomes "an evolving process of anticipation, frustration, retrospection, reconstruction, and satisfaction" (p. 985). The medium of television lends itself to this cycle thanks to its serialized nature, one that streaming and reality television disrupt, but more to come on that later. In this interface and considering how viewers bring their perceptions and experiences, reactions to these works inexorably and continuously change and are reconstructed (Shi, 2013, p. 985). The interactive nature of viewing does not leave the author or creator as the sole producer of meaning. Instead, a dynamic relationship between viewers and narratives contributes to making new meaning and continues to create new meaning as new readers engage with the work.

Watching a visual narrative on television or streaming is a communal meaning-making process. To contemplate the ability of televised and streamed narratives to become part of an interactive process, we must first consider their creation. In the production stage, those involved (i.e., writers, actors, producers, directors, and the like) are all participants in the creative development of the eventual product. Though each category of participant brings differing contributions to the development of the eventual outcome, according to Stuart Hall (1973), the final product of this creation essentially passes through various modes of language until its transformation is eventually accomplished (p. 3). Per Hall (1973):

> Before this message can have an "effect" (however defined), or satisfy a "need" or be put to a "use," it must first be perceived as a meaningful discourse and meaningfully de-coded. It is this set of de-coded meanings that "have an effect," influence, entertain, instruct or persuade, with very complex perceptual, cognitive, emotional, ideological or behavioural consequences [p. 3].

As Hall describes, progressing through a series of determinate moments motivates this process of encoding and eventually decoding messages through communicative events. However, before communicative events occur, the events must become stories (Hall, 1973, p. 2). The stories encompassed in these visual narratives provide audiences with ways to become active participants in understanding and reconstructing meaning.

Social Television

Though it is possible to watch visual narratives on television (or by streaming) without others, the engagement with its content is by no means a solitary process. Unlike the restrictive nature of the theater, where talking or using devices such as cell phones is vehemently prohibited, television presents a social viewing experience. Within the home, groups may converse about visual narratives between commercial breaks or during the telling of the story itself with little worry about interjecting into the viewing experience of another. Even still, the social viewing experience is not relegated to just one location at a time. Maria Jose Arrojo (2015) points to how viewers can actively comment on this accessible audiovisual content thanks to technology such as social media (p. 37). As Arrojo (2015) claims, social viewing "creates a new framework of social relations between these individuals; and on the other hand, it allows for a new communication channel between users and the entity transmitting audiovisual content" (p. 37). In view of this perspective by Arrojo, social television is not just about the communication between the various parties receiving the same broadcast content. As Yun Jung Choi (2017) concludes, "where people with diverse backgrounds are watching visual content together in a mediated environment and exchanging diverse ideas related to the program, which can lead to more analytical and critical viewing" (p. 1060). So, social viewing facilitates a multitude of interpretations by its varied and wide-reaching viewing audience.

Platforms such as X, formerly known as Twitter, allow for social co-viewing, which allows viewers to "observe, feel a part of, and share experiences with a much larger community without necessitating any direct socializing" (Cohen & Lancaster, 2014, p. 512). However, this engagement with other viewers is not the only communication social television permits. Instead, viewers can voice their opinions (both in support and in dissent) of the viewed content that the producers of the content can easily access. In essence, social viewing provides a plethora of instances for viewers to express their delight or extreme displeasure in selecting actors, specific character portrayals, representations of diversity, plot development, and so on. Still, the social viewing experience is not restricted to the parameters of just when a television show airs live. Thanks to on-demand viewing, streaming services, and other means such as purchasing content, viewers can return to their favorite series time and time again while also communicating with other fans through platforms such as Reddit. Unlike X, where users are limited to a specific number of characters, Reddit is comprised of millions of communities or "subreddits," where users can discuss, at great length, their favorite hobbies, interests, and yes, even television shows (Widmann, 2022). Outside of fan debates, floating possible theories, or speculating about outcomes, users can also use Reddit as a sounding board for their dissent (or approval) of changes to said beloved series.

For example, Jacquelyn Arcy and Zhana Johnson (2018) describe how combinations of fan fiction and social media campaigns focused on the series *Sleepy Hollow* (2013–2017), bringing attention to the stereotypical treatment of Black women in television (para. 1.2). In particular, the hashtag #AbbieMillsDeservesBetter critiqued the treatment (and later killing off) of main protagonist Agent Grace Abigail "Abbie" Mills (played by Nicole Beharie). Throughout her tenure in the series, Abbie routinely sacrifices her well-being to help her partner Ichabod Crane (played by Tom Mison) fight against the forces of evil and prevent the apocalypse (Arcy & Johnson, 2018, paras. 4.1–4.4). On the other hand, Eleanor Patterson (2018) highlights the more positive use of the live tweet campaign surrounding a series of television shows produced by Shonda Rhimes. Using the hashtag #TGIT (representing the "Thank God It's Thursday" programming block), ABC amassed 1.3 million reactions out of 5.2 million tweets, consistently attained high ratings, and carried the network to number one place with 18- to 49-year-old viewers throughout the fall of 2014 (Patterson, 2018, para. 1.2).

Other considerations for the impact fans extend to the influence fan demands have on the decisions made by producers. As Hansel Chang (2022) points out, director Sam Raimi acknowledged the casting of John Krasinski to play Reed Richards in *Doctor Strange: Multiverse of Madness* thanks to fan demand (para. 1). However, films take longer to see change come to fulfillment, unlike television, which can make changes during the production of a series. For instance, the reboot of *Roseanne* (2018) experienced a tremendous change due to a discriminatory tweet sent by the show's namesake. Firing Rosanne Barr after her fateful tweet, the show rebranded to become *The Conners* (2018–present). Blaming a lethal combination of botched knee surgery and opioid addiction, viewers learned of her noticeable absence from the narrative. Using social media platforms like Reddit to follow up with fans about the change, comments run the gamut from several expressions of approval to indifference and even a more minor gripe conveying how the show is missing out without the actress (Shoaff, 2022, para. 2–6).

Despite its somewhat extensive history since the first television sets became a prevalent form of at-home entertainment, watching visual narratives experienced quite the revolution due to tremendous technological advancements. Visual narratives can be streamed on-demand, thus eliminating the extensive waiting time between episode releases and season premieres. With social media, multi-screening allows viewers to follow the desired programming and share related content and reactions, and connect with other viewers at various times before, during, and after watching a program (Lin et al., 2015, p. 171).

For such narratives to exist without any audience reception goes against the very nature of television (and, by extension, streaming) as a form of popular culture. As Tim Delaney and Tim Madigan (2016) note, popular culture lacks a universal definition; we can generally discuss popular culture as encompassing the "most immediate and contemporary elements" of daily life (p. 1). Continuing with this thought about daily life, Postman (2006) points out how "[t]elevision is our culture's principal mode of knowing about itself" (p. 92). Thus, if people (specifically here in the United

States) ages 15 and older spend more than half of their leisure time watching television, then watching television is unquestionably America's preferred form of entertainment (Krantz-Kent, 2018, para. 4). In determining meaning and "knowing about itself" through television, U.S. culture has also engaged in cancel culture.

Ties to Cancel Culture and Television

The topic of cancel culture has large appeal in the discussion of politics and social movements, which is discussed in more detail below. Additionally, there seems to be a connection between cancel culture and religious speech as evidenced by *Uncanceled Finding Meaning and Peace in a Culture of Accusations, Shame, and Condemnation* by Phil Robertson of *Duck Dynasty* fame who quoted from Scripture while being interviewed for a national magazine and subsequently "canceled" by audiences due to this reference.

This book differs from others (such as *Cancel This Book: The Progressive Case Against Cancel Culture* by Dan Kovalik, *Cancel Culture: The Latest Attack on Free Speech and Due Process* by Alan Dershowitz, *Canceling Comedians While the World Burns: A Critique of the Contemporary Left* by Ben Burgis, and *We Will Not Cancel Us: And Other Dreams of Transformative Justice* by adrienne maree brown) in its overarching analysis of scripted televised or streamed visual narratives that are meant for audience entertainment rather than primarily focusing on political commentary or political figures. While Kovalik (2021) speaks openly about the increased ease of being "canceled" in recent years, the focus of this work is on the political discussions surrounding the 2020 election of President Joe Biden and Vice President Kamala Harris. Specifically, Kovalik concludes how those deemed as being transgressive do not realize or know the latest trends or norms in language or current topics. Similarly, Dershowitz focuses primarily on politics but with specific attention paid to free speech. In his work, Dershowitz (2020) openly advocates for cancel culture and its efforts to defend certain rights. Both works are strongly political in focus but differ in their arguments about the need for canceling culture. For Kovalik, cancel culture might be causing more harm than good when it comes to making progress toward the efforts of those calling for such cancellations to happen. For Dershowitz, cancel culture is necessary in protecting the rights to free speech and due process. Unlike the other two authors, Burgis advocates for a smarter approach in a time when leftism is often thought of as a performative exercise in expressing political commitments. However, more aligned with the focus of this book is *We Will Not Cancel Us: And Other Dreams of Transformative Justice* by adrienne maree brown, which approaches the discussion of cancel culture through the lenses of Black, queer, and feminist viewpoints. Despite this similarity, brown (2021) more so focuses on cancel culture and the recent wave of various social movements rather than audience reaction and reception of scripted visual narratives made available on television and streaming services.

Diversity and Television

Television has been, as Rebecca Feasey (2016) mentions, a traditionally homogenous landscape of White males. Over the last twenty years, television has been reshaping the homogeneity of the past to embrace the diverse populations of the present and future. This change could be in part due to an increase in diverse casting on television, coupled with the availability of online spaces, creating more opportunities for diverse creators. Thus, this next section will discuss how diversity on television is constantly changing because of the portrayals influencing audience perception, streaming platforms, and how online spaces are creating unique opportunities for content creators.

Audience Perceptions of Diversity

Based on how a group, culture, or minority is portrayed, the audience may be influenced in their perception of this type of character. Outside of the U.S., viewer perceptions of characters have been interpreted using questionnaires or analysis of immigrant experiences.

Rebecca Feasey conducted a series of questionnaires to determine how mothers in the U.K. perceived the portrayal of motherhood in series like *Supernanny* and *Gilmore Girls*. Feasey (2016) observes how "it can be argued that television plays a part in upholding the 'good' mother myth, it has also been seen to present mothers as inept, ineffectual and fragile" (p. 2). Many of the women in Feasey's questionnaire expressed discontent with how parenthood was depicted on television. For instance, they "felt that there were very few characters that they could relate to and that those women who were regularly and routinely seen on screen played to narrow and divisive extremes of parenting" (Feasey, 2016, p. 4). Though viewers in the U.K. may have drawn different interpretations of parenting ("good" mother versus "inept" mother) based on the character portrayals, they seemed to ultimately be hoping for characters they could connect with.

Immigrants viewing television series are likewise hoping to identify with on-screen characters. Ien Ang (2009) concludes that her interest in diverse television arose from her experiences as a Swedish migrant living in Australia (p. 6). Over the last thirty years, Ang believes that Australian television has diversified. She explains, "Australia's multicultural broadcaster has translated the abstract idea of 'multiculturalism' into concrete radio and TV practices" (Ang, 2009, p. 6). For Ang, television reaches into everyone's homes daily. Television reflects culture because "it is one of the routines through which television binds the nation symbolically together [...] though less and less so because of the internet" (Ang, 2009, pp. 11–12). In striving to reflect culture for several different types of audiences, national and international, what the Australian SBS (or news station) decides to show first is often up for debate. Ang (2009) describes "[the broadcast] doesn't try to transcend differences but tries to cater for as many of them as possible, it will always attract and repel different people at different times" (p. 14). Ultimately, Ang thinks that migrants might be repelled by nationalist news versus news with an international appeal because like all viewers, they're attracted to news about or for them. Ang's immigrant experience of television mirrors the U.K. viewers from Feasey's questionnaire: they wanted to identify with characters that reminded them of their experiences. This longing may be similar for U.S. audiences and their perspectives on character portrayal on television.

In the U.S., perceptions of immigrants may be influenced due to television portrayals. Largely, the U.S. television narrative about immigration has been two-fold: the news covers immigration as an abstract concept, whereas fictional depictions humanize the issue. Sowards and Penada (2013) argue that "audiences may interpret these stories in positive ways that evoke sympathy for the plight of the undocumented immigrant in the United States" (p. 73). Their research studied three facets of television related to audience reactions: *Ugly Betty* (2006–2010), *CNN Presents "Immigrant Nation: Divided Country"* (2006), and Los Lobos's album *The Town and the City* (2006). Even as "these grand narratives" portray the Latinx community in a positive light, they may also "reinforce the Latina/o threat narrative" (Sowards & Pineda, 2013, p. 74). In general, their research highlights how the Latinx community has been negatively portrayed ("as rapists, thieves, and murderers"), and how it's hard to deflect these tropes in the media. The three artifacts examined often over-simplified immigration, stressed accented participants (who didn't know English), and portrayed many characters under economic distress. All these conditions, "even as told to generate audience sympathy, reinforce the constructed threat and hatred of such immigrants" (Soward & Pineda, 2013, p. 79). Analyzing impacts of cultural and minority portrayals is important, as audiences can be positively or negatively impacted by what they see as an imitation of their lives (or what their lives could be like).

Streaming Platforms and Diversity

Streaming platforms strive to distance themselves from the network practices of the past, in particular concerning diversity on television. Platforms like Netflix, Showtime, and HBO "have adopted a similar stance in order to cement their reputations as broadcasters of progressive 'quality' programming and prove their relevance within the new media ecosystem" (Boisvert, 2020, p. 184). Even so, the way audiences react to such promises and displays cannot be fully measured, or understood. Stefany Boisvert's (2020) research explores the discourse surrounding LGBTQ characters on Facebook fan pages for *Sense8* (2015–2018) and *Billions* (2016–). Boisvert notes the difference in sentiment for both shows. With *Sense8*, many of the viewers expressed a solidarity with the characters in an emotional sense, whereas with *Billions*, "the majority of fans expressed either hate/discrimination against [the non-binary] character or, at the very least, a discomfort with non-binary identities" (Boisvert, 2020, p. 192). The use of online discussion spaces can help platforms like HBO and Showtime with advertising and building fan bases for their series. Boisvert explains how with *Sense8*, Netflix "might encourage the creation of closed 'taste communities' that are more interested in bonding over a similar passion for a series than in queering normative discourses surrounding social categories and identities" (p. 191). Rather than truly caring about diversity, streaming companies are more interested in aligning themselves with viewer expectations.

Additionally, these companies wish to distinguish themselves from the other, and so may continue to promote diverse casts and themes as a way to "frame or influence […] readings of fictional characters who challenge normative notions of identity"

(Boisvert, 2020, p. 197). Though streaming platforms tout diverse opportunities for characters and creators, their models might also encourage "a renewed emphasis on fixed notions of identity, because of the necessity to attract clearly targeted audiences" (Boisvert, 2020, p. 198). Though streaming platforms seek out and then encourage niche audiences, they are reaching out to a more diverse audience than traditional television networks. The availability of online spaces like social media have displayed the usefulness of niche audience appeal.

Online Spaces and Diverse Opportunities

Online spaces are useful in generating crowdfunding opportunities for unknown television writers hoping to create diverse content. Aymar Jean Christian (2018) details how writers like Adam Goldman discovered this phenomenon well before others like Zach Braff and Spike Lee tried to popularize it (p. 3). Christian (2018) argues that "the Internet brought innovation to television by opening mass distribution to those excluded from legacy development processes, fostering new ways of creating and marketing series" (p. 4). Even if streaming platforms like Netflix and HBO are cultivating diverse marketing campaigns and curating likeminded fandom discussion boards, their models are also being challenged by open content television opportunities from "YouTube […] Vimeo and Funny or Die and multichannel networks like Maker, Machinima, and Fullscreen" (Christian, 2018, pp. 5–6). While Feasey took more of an analytical approach to understanding streaming platforms and their intentions, Christian seems to have more of a neutral approach in terms of its applications. Christian suggests, "Innovation is never all good or all bad, progressive or regressive" (p. 6). Though audiences rely on online platforms to create and release most content, these products are most likely "shaped by the cultural, political, and organizational realities of the early-twenty-first-century media" (Christian, 2018, p. 7). The wide availability of online spaces may increase casting opportunities for diverse populations.

While this collection discusses a multitude of ways social media use led to drastic changes within televised narratives, it is essential to note that social media is not a threat to serialized television. Rather, social media provides an outlet for viewers to advocate for change, express their disapproval, or bring awareness to specific issues such as a lack of representation. Iser (2006) even noted how "no story can ever be told in its entirety" as texts or, in this case of this book, television series are "punctured by blanks and gaps that have to be negotiated in the act" of viewing (p. 65). Social media provides viewers with a space to bridge these blanks (i.e., opportunities) or gaps (i.e., omissions) in the storyline. Of course, viewers can choose to negotiate these blanks and gaps in isolation, or they can turn to online communities to seek dissenting or favoring opinions. Pointing to the democratic power of public access television, Ross and Spitzer (1994) insist that "television must be more than a one-way funnel of status quo platitudes and advertising" but "must begin to incorporate the voices of those communities marginalized by the mainstream media" (p. 42). In its own way, social media opens up the conversation between viewers and creators, offering a place for both parties to make their voices heard.

Methods

This work will review the relationship between the audience and how that may influence television producers. The way that relationship manifests can take various forms, which each essay will explore in a particular way. The theories of Iser and Hall were instrumental in developing this work, specifically in reference to Hall's (1973) discussion of meaningful discourse being meaningfully de-coded, and Iser's (1993) theories on text play in connection with audience participation and viewership. The way audiences share their opinions has changed over time, being more accessible and prone to viral-ability via social media channels. Thus, television producers seem more sensitive to the demands of the audience. In response to audience demands, they sometimes go as far as apologizing, delaying release dates, firing actors and directors, and sometimes changing characterizations. In this way, we have structured our research about audience reception and television production using three frameworks: social media, cancel culture, and diversity initiatives. By analyzing these frameworks, we will identify their import in content creation and possible impacts. The ultimate purpose of the text is to outline how the impetus and application of fan criticism varies and impacts television productions.

Most notably, the work reviews what, if any, tangible production changes (i.e., new or revised plots or characters) result in response to audience reception. Iser (1993) describes how the reader must "play" the "text game" individually because "while the text plays the changeability of what has been brought into play, the reader can join in the game of transformations only to the extent that it will permit a result" (p. 274). In this work, "readers" become the viewers, the "text" becomes the television shows they are discussing, leading to interconnected results of audience spectatorship. However, the individual social media posts about one television show can combine into a unified message (i.e., hashtags, viral posts, trending words), at times followed by a response from a creator or television studio. Producers also capitalize on the hype surrounding a series and actively encourage viewers to tweet or post questions on Facebook along with the live airing of an episode. Case in point, the television series *48 Hours* (1988–present) often poses a question about a case to the audience during the running of an episode, prompting them to respond with their observations or theories on Facebook. In doing so, viewers move beyond mere spectating to become part of a larger community invested in a common interest in true crime narratives.

Part of audience expectations includes assessing diverse character portrayals or phenomena in the modern television landscape, such as queerbaiting, token casting, diversity in VOD (video-on-demand), and ableism. In assessing these phenomena, the research may refer to how X and other social media became more influential from 2012 onward, lending audience opinion and increased presence and influence (and, as a byproduct, increased diversity). Additionally, audience reception will be analyzed in various forms (as the types are constantly evolving), to include X, Cameo, YouTube, social media campaigns, and more. This work will differ from others by analyzing recent television productions, such as *And Just Like That...*, *The Wonder Years* (reboot), *Ms. Marvel*, *Girls*, *The 100*, *Schitt's Creek*, *Supernatural*, *Big Brother*, *Survivor*, and more.

The basics of each essay will start with a brief introduction, purpose statement, then will break down components of the purpose statement through sub-headers and reliance on what researchers have said (past and present). To exemplify the points made, case studies of television fictions are detailed. In certain essays, the authors overview larger trends by way of charts (or figures), and analysis of figures. The essays then close with a brief conclusion.

Scope/Rationale

While audiences react to several genres of fictional and nonfictional entertainment, the editors invited essay proposals that investigate (primarily) online audience reception of recent or current U.S. television shows.

We hoped to explore perspectives on these two research questions:

- *How does the viewing public perform the role of critique through new media participation?*
- *How may we understand internet fandom and social media campaigns in the context of reception studies and audience analysis?*

With these questions in mind, prospective contributors were encouraged to draw on any aspect of reception theory (broadly conceived or theorized) as it related to the influence of online and social media audience participation on television shows, including plots, characterization, cancellations, reboots, or casting and other production issues. We explicitly encouraged a diversity of voices drawing on differing scholarly traditions to submit essay proposals. We also welcomed submissions from scholars at any stage of their career, whether graduate students, independent scholars, or appointed faculty members. Of note, several contributors cited the editors' original article ("Tug of War") which launched the call for proposals for this project. This citation was not required, encouraged, or expected. The editors were surprised to find the citation in any of the subsequent essays, and hope they are viewed as helpful rather than self-serving.

Ultimately, the editors believe that analyzing audience and critical reception of TV shows may reveal motivations for subsequent creative decisions by the creators. On shows like *Girls* and *The 100*, audience reception has influenced decisions concerning creative control. Audience reception may have impacted "cancel culture" and diversity initiatives. As previously noted, the idea of "cancel culture" has been used in plotlines for *Younger* (2015–2021) and *The Good Fight* (2017–2022), and in context with off-screen acts from producers and actors, such as Dave Chapelle's Netflix specials. Additionally, audience demands help sway the market and have opened diversity initiatives in speculative media. The theoretical basis for this collection uses reception theory to inform content analysis of illustrative cases of audience influence on television plots and characterization. To further explore the phenomenon of audience sway over artistic ownership, certain television shows will be examined in context with audience and critical reception, cancel culture, and diversity initiatives across media.

To narrow the focus, the editors have broken down the collection to three relevant categories of television such as reality television, network televisions, streaming television, and a brief afterward.

In Part 1, we begin with reality TV, arguing that it's the least diverse form of television. By "reality TV," we only include network and cable titles, leaving out reality television shows from streaming platforms like Netflix or Hulu. However, several shows reviewed by contributors (like *Big Brother*, *Survivor*, *The Activist*, and *Southern Charm*) have been swayed by audience reception, cancel culture, and diversity initiatives.

In Part 2, we move to scripted network and cable TV shows. Partially because the editors believe it is becoming more diverse, but only because it's in competition with arguably the most diverse form of TV: streaming shows. This could be due to the effect of audience reception, which is reflected in casting choices and diversity initiatives. The contributors analyze titles such as *The 100*, *Schitt's Creek*, *The Wonder Years*, *Fear the Walking Dead*, and *Supernatural*.

With Part 3, we consider how streaming TV is becoming more experimental. This could be due to the need to gain subscribers, and so creators hope to add more and more niche shows both as a response to audience reception and primarily in the pursuit of economic gains. The essays review impacts of audience reception with streaming TV shows like *Vikings*, *And Just Like That...*, and *Ms. Marvel*.

Finally, in the conclusion, the editors discuss how the streaming format is possibly replacing interest in traditional films. Streaming TV is becoming very competitive, which is why some major media companies (Disney+, Paramount, and Peacock included) have launched their own platforms. This wide-open market, which can account for audience reception more quickly than film (as production takes longer), allows for new characterizations and greater inclusion.

Overall, our premise is to detail audience reception for television shows, analyzing how this may have affected production or characterization. Participatory culture reflects established online practices and may be used to sustain media projects, end them, or to invite revision and the production of new media content. Thus, the analysis of television production and audience reception will include essays on the role of social media, cancel culture, and diversity initiatives. Creativity and authorship are always about reception and pleasing the audience; in a networked media age, the audience simply has more immediate and wide-reaching means to make their perspectives heard.

Our interest in diversity stemmed from our research into character representations for television shows like *Girls*, *The 100*, *Big Brother*, *The Activist*, *Vanderpump Rules*, and more. With those case studies, it seemed several factors fostered an exclusion of characterization for diverse races and points of sexuality. Therefore, many of the essays throughout this work may assess television depictions of diverse characters (or suppression of diversity), online fan criticism, and what seemingly results from online fan criticism: cancel culture.

References

Ang, I. (2009). Henry Mayer Lecture 2009 from Dallas to SBS: The popular, the global and the diverse on television. *Media International Australia*, *131*(1), 6–15. https://doi.org/10.1177/1329878X0913100103.

Arcy, J., & Johnson, Z. (2018). Intersectional critique and social media activism in *Sleepy Hollow* fandom. *Transformative Works and Cultures, 26*.
Arrojo, M. (2015). Social television as new relationship between conventional TV and the audience: An analysis of its aims, processes, and results. *International Journal of Social Science Studies, 3*(4), 37–49. http://dx.doi.org/10.11114/ijsss.v3i4.854.
Boisvert, S. (2020). "Queering" TV, one character at a time: How audiences respond to gender-diverse TV series on social media platforms. *Critical Studies in Television, 15*(2), 183–201. https://doi.org/10.1177/1749602020914479.
brown, a.m. (2021). *We will not cancel us: And other dreams of transformative justice*. AK Press.
Chang, H. (2022, June 29). *Kevin Feige cast John Krasinski as Reed Richards because of fan demands*. Hypebeast. https://hypebeast.com/2022/6/kevin-feige-cast-john-krasinski-as-reed-richards-fan-demands.
Choi, Y.J. (2017). Emergence of the viewing public: Does social television viewing transform individual viewers into a viewing public? *Telematics and Informatics, 34*(7), 1059–1070. https://doi.org/10.1016/j.tele.2017.04.014.
Christian, A.J. (2018). *Open TV: Innovation beyond Hollywood and the rise of web television*. New York University Press. https://doi.org/10.18574/9781479814909.
Cohen, E.L., & Lancaster, A.L. (2014, August). Individual differences in in-person and social media television coviewing: The role of emotional contagion, need to belong, and coviewing orientation. *CyberPsychology, Social Networking, and Behavior, 17*(8), 512–518. doi: 10.1089/cyber.2013.0484.
Delaney, T., & Madigan, T. (2016). *Lessons learned from popular culture*. State University of New York Press.
Dershowitz, A. (2020). *Cancel culture: The latest attack on free speech and due process*. Hot Books.
Feasey, R. (2016). *Mothers on mothers: Maternal readings of popular television* (First edition). Peter Lang.
Fedorak, S. (2009). *Pop culture: The culture of everyday life*. University of Toronto Press.
Hall, S. (1973). *Encoding and decoding in the television discourse*. ePapers Repository. http://epapers.bham.ac.uk/2962/.
Iser, W. (1993). *The fictive and the imaginary: Charting literary anthropology*. Johns Hopkins University Press.
_____. (2006). *How to do theory*. Blackwell.
Jenkins, H. (1992). *Textual poachers: Television fans & participatory culture*. Routledge.
Kaufmann, T.D. (2003). Reception theory. *Grove Art Online*. https://doi.org/10.1093/gao/9781884446054.article.T071032.
Kovalik, D. (2021). *Cancel this book: The progressive case against cancel culture*. Hot Books.
Krantz-Kent, R. (2018, September). Television, capturing America's attention at prime time and beyond. *Beyond the Numbers: Special Studies & Research, 7*(14). https://www.bls.gov/opub/btn/volume-7/television-capturing-americas-attention.htm.
Lin, J.S., Sung, Y., & Chen, K.J. (2016). Social television: Examining the antecedents and consequences of connected TV viewing. *Computers in Human Behavior, 58*, 171–178. https://doi.org/10.1016/j.chb.2015.12.025.
Patterson, E. (2018). Must tweet TV: ABC's #TGIT and the cultural work of programming social television. *Transformative Works and Cultures, 26*. https://doi-org.ezproxy.snhu.edu/10.3983/twc.2018.1147.
Postman, N. (2006). *Amusing ourselves to death: Public discourse in the age of show business*. Penguin.
Ross, J.M., & Spitzer, J.A. (1994). Public access television: The message, the medium, & the movement. *Art Papers, 18*, 41–44.
Shi, Y. (2013). Review of Wolfgang Iser and his reception theory. *Theory and Practice in Language Studies, 3*(6), 982–986. https://doi.org/10.4304/tpls.3.6.982-986.
Shoaff, B. (2022, June 27). *How fans of* The Conners *really feel about the lack of Roseanne*. Looper. https://www.looper.com/908616/how-fans-of-the-conners-really-feel-about-the-lack-of-roseanne/.
Sowards, S.K., & Pineda, R.D. (2013). Immigrant narratives and popular culture in the United States: Border spectacle, unmotivated sympathies, and individualized responsibilities. *Western Journal of Communication, 77*(1), 72–91. https://doi.org/10.1080/10570314.2012.693648.
Weingartner, S. (2021). Digital omnivores? How digital media reinforce social inequalities in cultural consumption. *New Media & Society, 23*(11), 3370–3390. https://doi-org.ezproxy.snhu.edu/10.1177/1461444820957635.
Widman, J. (2022, December 28). *What is Reddit?* Digital Trends. https://www.digitaltrends.com/computing/what-is-reddit/.

Part 1
Reality Television

Audience Interventions and the Plight of Systemic Racism on *Big Brother*

RAGAN FOX

Premiering in summer 2000, *Big Brother* is one of network television's longest-running reality programs. *Big Brother* is set on a soundstage designed to look like a home. Fifty-two cameras and ninety-five microphones record ten to sixteen strangers living in the *Big Brother* house. Each week, the houseguests compete in a Head of Household contest. The person who wins the Head of Household competition nominates two players for eviction. Contestants vote on one of the two nominated players to be evicted from the house and, subsequently, eliminated from the competition. The process restarts each week until the last person standing wins a half-million dollars. *Big Brother* airs three times a week on CBS and 24 hours a day on a live internet feed. *Big Brother*'s live feed permits viewers to compare CBS's slickly produced edits to more unfettered events they witness online.

"Expect the unexpected," is *Big Brother*'s unofficial motto. Host Julie Chen utters the phrase when she introduces one of the program's overwrought gameplay twists, such as twins playing as the same person. "Expect the unexpected" belies *Big Brother*'s predictability, from the same character archetypes cast each summer to individual challenges recycled from one season to the next. "As a TV show," wrote TV critic Andy Denhart (2020), "*Big Brother* is in a well-worn rut. Players are so familiar with the structure that they know when to expect … frequent eruptions of racism and bigotry or twists that go nowhere" (pp. 23–26). The show's formula is perhaps most obvious when CBS reveals the cast at the start of each summer. Most seasons feature a few racial, ethnic, and sexual minorities embedded in a predominantly White, heterosexual cast. *Big Brother*'s racial and sexual demographics have resulted in a slate of winners who are overwhelmingly White and heterosexual.

A racist structure undergirds the dynamics of many competition-oriented reality programs. Shows like *Big Brother* are a "microcosm of American values" insofar as they celebrate self-interest and rugged individualism (Foster, 2004, p. 279). TV critics have likened *Big Brother* to a "cutthroat, strategic game of social chess" (Caruso, 2020, para. 3). The "social chess" metaphor bolsters a meritocracy myth that the "best" player wins the game. The chess analogue fails to illustrate the multiple ways that *Big Brother*'s structure significantly benefits straight, White men. *Big Brother*'s executive producers Alison Grodner and Rich Meehand have historically proven unwilling to address racism on the program. *Big Brother* producers have treated racism as "exceptional or an aberration, rather than as a normative practice structuring Western societies through the differential allocation of resources (to the privileged) and the ongoing impact of racist policies and practices (upon those who are racially marginalized)" (Riggs & Due, 2010, p. 258). In the last ten years, fans of the program have used social media to perform critical interventions that challenge CBS's racially evasive modes of representation. Anderson-Lopez, Lambert, and Budaj (2021) contended that "audience demands help sway the market and have opened diversity initiatives in speculative media" (p. 64).

In this essay, I underscore how racism is "baked into" the competition before contestants enter the *Big Brother* house. This research strives to address key questions: (1) What sustained patterns call attention to systemic, or institutional, racism on *Big Brother*? (2) How have audiences used social media sites like *Survivor* Sucks, YouTube, and Twitter to intervene on *Big Brother*'s culture of racism? I first consider common motifs of racism in the context of reality television. I then note some of the ways that *Big Brother*'s audience uses social media to call attention to and challenge structural racism on the program.

Theorizing Race and Sexuality on Reality Television

Racism on *Big Brother* takes two primary shapes: individual and systemic. Individual racism focuses on "individual whites acting against individual blacks" and other people of color (Ture & Hamilton, 1992, p. 4). Take, for example, racism that emerged in *Big Brother 21* when contestant Jack Matthews referred to an Asian American houseguest as "rice pudding" (Ross, 2019); or when season 19 competitor Paul Abrahamian applied Black facial cosmetics in self-described blackface while targeting a Black player (Hautman, 2020). Systemic racism describes a more covert system of racial injustice that "originates in the *operation* of established and respected forces in society" (Ture & Hamilton, 1992, p. 4). Institutional racism proves especially insidious on competition-oriented reality TV shows like *Big Brother*, where color-blind "notions of meritocracy, of achieving success purely through hard work are post-racial, post-feminist fallacies [that ignore] racial hierarchy, patriarchy, and structural inequality" (Joseph, 2009, p. 249). Examples of systemic racism throughout *Big Brother*'s run include producers encouraging Black houseguests to "use a stereotypical Black accent for [soundbites] in the show's confessional 'diary room'" (Braxton, 2019, para. 4) and production's tendency to omit racism from its network broadcasts (Fox, 2019).

Systemic racism on *Big Brother* often takes the form of racist casting practices designed to promote racial conflict. Reality TV has "borrowed from broadcast television's history and techniques of integration," where one person of color is surrounded by White men and women; and the illusion of multiculturalism gives way to a "racial conflict script" (Squires, 2017, p. 268). Reality TV producers value racial diversity because their programming relies on the sort of "human drama that unfolds when people from diverse backgrounds—based on race, ethnicity, socioeconomic, age, religion, and sexual orientation—interact with one another" (Orbe, 2008, p. 349). Unfortunately, racial diversity on reality TV programming rarely results in nuanced narratives about racism.

In her textual analysis of representations of race on *Survivor: Cook Islands*, *Black. White.*, and *The Real World: Denver*, Bell-Jordan (2008) outlined five primary ways that race, and racism are narratively brought to life on reality TV programs. She argued that the shows

> (1) dramatize race and racial issues by juxtaposing opposing viewpoints; (2) promote conflict in the framing of race and racial issues; specifically in terms of interracial and interracial conflict; (3) perpetuate hegemonic representations of race by emphasizing violence and anger; (4) personalize racism by privileging individual solutions to complex social problems; and (5) leave conflict and contradictions unresolved [p. 369].

When producers tackle racist subject matter, they "repeatedly depict racism as a matter of personal belief situated in rural conservatives, which downplays structural aspects of racism and suggests that its solution is to be found in the education of ignorant individuals" (Kraszewki, 2009, p. 207). Portraying racism as a character flaw enables producers to sidestep serious conversations about the myriad ways in which racism is systemic and bolstered through the so-called "reality" TV production teams manufacture.

In this study, I reflect on *Big Brother*'s twenty-two years of production and twenty-three seasons to illustrate the ways in which institutional racism structures the network program and competition. For instance, how might casting choices illuminate *Big Brother*'s investment in structural racism? How do story editors reinforce institutional racism by perpetuating the myth that racism on *Big Brother* exists solely in individual players and not in structural factors controlled by the program's producers? Although I reference examples from several seasons to illustrate *patterns* of racist behavior, I focus largely on Season 15 and Season 22.

I concentrate on Season 22 for a few reasons. First, CBS filled the *Big Brother* house exclusively with returning players, or "All Stars." Season 22 marks the second time in *Big Brother*'s twenty-one-year run that only returning players competed. The "All Stars" label suggests that contestants invited back are among the most exemplary contestants to play the game. The moniker sets the season up to function as a "representative anecdote," a term Kenneth Burke (1969) uses to characterize synecdoche, or a part of symbolic action (e.g., one season of *Big Brother*) meant to represent the whole (e.g., larger patterns of behavior that run across multiple seasons). Wess (2004) explains that "Burke's synecdochic logic works by presupposing a reality larger than the scope of any anecdote. A particular part of reality (anecdote, test case) is evaluated on the basis of how well it represents this reality in general" (p. 19). I reference examples from other seasons to further substantiate the extent to which patterns of racism emergent in Season 22 provide a "faithful reflection" (Burke, 1969, p. 59) of *Big Brother*'s sustained and manufactured "reality." Second, the "All Stars" conceit makes it difficult for producers to claim ignorance about each player's strategy and prejudices. Producers can feign shock and dismay when a *new* player enters the house and fails to work with or denigrates houseguests from historically marginalized groups; but production's veil of ignorance vanishes when they *invite back* players who only worked with other White players their initial season. Inviting these houseguests to return illustrates structural racism at the heart of *Big Brother*'s first twenty-two seasons.

I also explore the ways in which production handles individual acts of racism in the *Big Brother* house. Season 15 includes some of the most unabashed racism that has emerged in the *Big Brother* house. Racism on Season 15 proved so egregious that outraged fans like Ed King (2013) and Robin Humphrey (2013) created online petitions calling for CBS to intervene. Over the last seventeen years, *Big Brother* has amassed a loyal and passionately engaged fanbase. Casual viewers watch the CBS broadcast of *Big Brother*, which is aired three times a week. The "super fan" label is reserved for people who spend a significant part of their summers glued to CBS's 24-hour live Internet feed of the show and see controversial exchanges left out of the CBS broadcast. Fan response to racism in the house provides a critical entryway to examine how some audience members have turned to social media to intervene on the show's production. Reality TV shows represent sites of rhetorical "struggle and negotiation over the meanings of race"; audience members performatively spectate race "in ways that reinforce or correspond to [their] own social and cultural reality" and predispositions (Bell-Jordan, 2008, p. 354).

I use performative intervention as a primary anchoring concept in this essay. The term theorizes what transpires when audiences create secondary texts in response to a primary text, like *Big Brother*. Audience response often guides interpretations of a primary text. *Performative spectatorship* theorizes how audience members create YouTube videos, commentary, and online petitions to actively participate in a television program's narrative rendering of race and racism. Performative spectatorship takes into consideration audience-text intertextuality by focusing on secondary texts audience members share on social media platforms. The method calls attention to how peripheral materials (e.g., audience commentary) work in conjunction with a primary performance text (e.g., a TV show) to alter, challenge, and build upon its meaning.

Performative Spectatorship in Season 15

Big Brother's fifteenth season offers a compelling entryway to investigate individual acts of racism on the show, as well as production's racist complicity. Season 15 featured sixteen houseguests, including two Black competitors, one Korean contestant, and thirteen White players. The season took an early and uncomfortable turn in the game's first week when Internet viewers reported multiple instances of racist speech uttered by several of the season's White participants. Three White women named Aaryn, GinaMarie, and Amanda were among the season's worst offenders. Aaryn called a Korean player named Helen "Asian eyes," made racist statements like "Shut up and go make some rice," and used a hyperbolized Korean accent in yellow-face impersonations of Asian women. Aaryn's ally GinaMarie suggested punching Helen in the face might "make her eyes straight." Aaryn also engaged in racist acts of provocation when she moved a Black houseguest's mattress from its frame to the floor. When Candice, the only Black woman in the house, confronted Aaryn about the prank, the White woman snapped her fingers, rolled her shoulders, and mimicked Black speech dialects. She mockingly asked Candice, "Whatchu gon' du, gurl? Where's yo' class?" (Grodner & Meehan, 2013).

Producers unfortunately failed to tackle the use of racist slurs from cast members in the early weeks of CBS's *Big Brother* broadcast. Casting people of color and sexual minorities but failing to include moments of racism and homophobia they endure in the *Big Brother* house exemplifies structural prejudice. Reality competition series often invite viewers "to consider race within the logic of relational choice, rather than within the logic of representation or production" (Dubrofsky, 2006, p. 42). Producers initially neglecting to include racial prejudice in *Big Brother*'s primetime narrative functions as structural, or institutionalized, racism. CBS's strategic erasure of racism and tokenization of players from historically marginalized groups reveal the program's implicit racial/racist bias. In this section, I first call attention to the show's history of erasing racism. I then discuss some of the ways in which fans have turned to social media to intervene on CBS's strategies of racial evasion.

Big Brother has a history of erasing racism from its broadcast edit. Executive producer Allison Grodner has previously defended cutting racism from the program's CBS edit, claiming that "it would be irresponsible to put hate on the airwaves just for hate's sake" (Stelter, 2013, para. 10). Grodner also admitted that she "would rather not have *those* headlines," implying stories about racism mar the production's reputation (Braxton, 2019, para. 16). In 2019, CBS Entertainment President Kelly Kahl even refused to answer whether *Big Brother*'s primary production team included people of color (Braxton, 2019). Grodner's and Kahl's positions advance a color-evasive approach to racial issues. Their sentiment suggests race and racism are both too immaterial and dangerous to address on the CBS broadcast and in production workrooms.

Grodner's and Kale's color-evasiveness may also be interpreted as racist erasure. In the context of this essay, *erasure* plays on the race/erasure homonym and characterizes the production team's deliberate act of excluding racism and homophobia minoritized players experience in the house. My use of the term minoritized is deliberate. People with power minoritize populations through interconnected speech acts and policies. Minority implies subjection implicitly resides in an individual. Minoritized underscores that marginalization/minoritization is something one group does to another to strip their power and minimize their oppression. For instance, eliminating racism or homophobia from the CBS broadcast functions as a manufactured and "strategic absence" on the program (Fox, 2013, p. 194). One example of erasure emerged in the first week of Season 11, when a White, heterosexual player named Braden used racist slurs to attack a Latina named Lydia. In a fit of rage, Braden called Lydia "a fucking Mexican from San Diego. You're a fucking beaner. I'm fucking white and American. You're all beaners!" Braden also told the season's sole gay competitor to "stick a banana up [his] ass." The footage aired on the internet live feed but not on the network broadcast. Rightfully anticipating Braden's homophobic and racist remarks would not air on CBS, a Black houseguest named Chima used Thursday's live show to call out Braden's hateful remarks only minutes before his eviction. During live shows, the two players nominated for eviction make cases for why they should stay in the house. Chima passionately revealed that Braden "called both of my very good friends [censored] so a vote for Braden is a vote for a bigot. He called you a whore, Julie, yes he did!" (Grodner & Meehan, 2009). TV critic Andy Denhart (2009) pointed out that "the most despicable part of the episode was the producers' editing and manipulation of the backyard fight between Braden, Lydia, and Kevin, which skipped over all of Braden's racism" (p. 7).

CBS's most high-profile act of racist erasure occurred Season 15. Along with Aaryn's above-mentioned racist aggressions, she complained that the solitary gay player would likely win a special power because "people love the queers" (Davies, 2013, para. 4). She also demanded that a Black woman say "asked, not axed." As a former *Big Brother* competitor, I was shocked by production's choice to omit these racist and homophobic speech acts from its network broadcast. Outraged, I penned an open letter to *Big Brother*'s production team and posted it on my blog on June 30, 2013. I wrote:

> Houseguests GinaMarie, Aaryn, and Katlin referred to historically marginalized players as "tokens." Sadly, they aren't too far off in their assessment. Characters like Andy, Candice, Howard, and Helen are reduced to mere tokens when production fails to include micro-aggressions that they endure on a day-to-day basis. What's the point of casting racial, ethnic, and sexual minorities if production's going to edit out the racism, ethnic discrimination, and homophobia that these people encounter inside the house? What makes Aaryn's homophobia and racism especially insidious is that it comes packaged in a bright-eyed, pageant-like exterior. How can somebody so sweet looking spew so much venom? Viewers would have to see it to believe it [Fox, 2013].

Within a week, the *New York Times*, the *Los Angeles Times*, *People*, and the *Hollywood Reporter* featured portions of my critique in stories about *Big Brother 15*'s manufactured absence of racism and homophobia. Brian Stelter (2013) of the *New York Times* spoke to production's contrived omission of hate speech when he explained that

> the slurs were shown on the Internet (where paying subscribers watch live feeds from the house around the clock—"See what we can't show you on TV," the CBS Web site says) but were not immediately on the television version of the show, whose producers distill the action into three hourly episodes each week. This troubled some loyal followers of *Big Brother*, because television viewers were seeing an incomplete picture of the participants. On a show with a $500,000 grand prize, perceptions and reputations are important [para. 3].

The longer CBS ignored the controversy in *Big Brother*'s narrative, the larger viewer outrage grew. *Big Brother* is in part remarkable because it is one of the rare programs that allows its audience to view hundreds of hours of unaired footage every season. *Big Brother*'s live feed provides audiences a partial glance into what Goffman (1973) might describe as reality TV's backstage performances, engendering a sort of voyeurism. Backstage voyeurism enables *Big Brother*'s audience to intervene when its broadcast narrative becomes problematic. Twenty-seven thousand fans of the program signed an online petition asking CBS to expel Aaryn from the house. The network finally acquiesced and aired Aaryn's comments on its July 7 *Big Brother* broadcast. Soon thereafter and for the first time in the show's 15-season history, each episode started with a disclaimer that read:

> *Big Brother* is a reality show about a group of people who have no privacy 24/7. At times, the houseguests may reveal prejudices and other beliefs that CBS does not condone. Views or opinions expressed by a houseguest are those of the individuals speaking and do not represent the views or opinions of CBS [CBS, as cited in Hibberd, 2013].

One can only speculate whether CBS would have included racism in its Season 15 narrative had fans of the show and journalists not intervened and pressured them to do so. It is, however, undeniable that, in the summer of 2013, *Big Brother*'s spectators proved to be more than passive consumers of entertainment. Thousands of Internet viewers actively participated in the show's production by highlighting hateful comments CBS left on the cutting-room floor for two weeks.

Several other *Big Brother 15* houseguests engaged in acts of racist and homophobic antagonism, yet their vitriol was largely left unaired on CBS. *Big Brother 15* contestant Amanda, for instance, called gay competitor Andy "faggoty Ann," said Candice's hair is "greasy and nappy," characterized Helen (a Korean) as "the fucking Chinaman," and referred to "the black guy, the Asian, and the gay guy" as the "three outcasts." Grodner and Meehan shockingly made Amanda the primary narrator and in-house critic of Aaryn's racism. Producers even edited and broadcast a package where Amanda confronted Aaryn about her racist animus. CBS failed to air footage where Amanda backpedaled and told Aaryn that she is not racist and claimed Candice and Howard played the "race card" to get ahead in the game. After producers had Amanda narrate Aaryn's racism, one live-feed viewer posted a six-minute YouTube video of Amanda's numerous racist and homophobic moments. In the montage, Amanda claimed the shower reserved for competition-related punishments was the "Puerto Rican shower" because "Puerto Ricans are smelly," referred to Black contestant Howard as Black Mamba, suggested Candice smells like watermelon and Helen likes eggrolls, and called Andy "Kermit the fag" when he wore green shorts and an emerald shirt. By crafting narratives where racism is depicted as rare and relegated to a single person in the house, *Big Brother* obscured the ways in which racism is often commonplace and structural.

Season 15's controversy provided an opportunity for fans to create art to highlight racism they witnessed on the internet live feed. Their art and commentary act as performative spectatorship, or secondary texts that aid in the interpretation of a primary text like *Big Brother*. Throughout the season, for example, many fans pointed out that Aaryn is an anagram for Aryan and described her as "KKK Barbie." Calling Aaryn Aryan reconfigures her name so that it is linked to Nazi ideologies of White supremacy. Fans titled her *Survivor* Sucks thread, "Aryan: Racist Narcissist with a Busted Hat: 'Who Wants to See my KKK Room?'" One viewer active on the forum asked, "Was she raised by neo–Nazis? I wonder if the whole Aaryn=Aryan anagram was a subtle reference by her parents when naming her" (Zingbot9000, 2013). Another user wrote, "Aryan's a pretty girl. She can certainly find a rich Klan daddy" (Edgar, 2013).

Fans of the show also created numerous Photoshopped images of the more overtly racist *Big Brother 15* houseguests. *Survivor* Sucks user Django (2013) posted Figure 1.a to the season's "Photochop" thread. Aaryn's head is placed on the body of World War II icon Rosie the Riveter. Django (2013) altered Rosie's famous catchphrase, "We can do it!" so that it reads, "We Klan do it!" Klan is, of course, a synecdochical reference to the U.S.-based White supremacist group, the Ku Klux Klan. The Klan's emblem is pasted to the lapel of Aaryn's shirt. Figure 1.b is a fan-produced image of GinaMarie and Aaryn as a team on the CBS reality series *The Amazing Race*. The viewer reworked the show's title so that it reads, "The Amazing Racists" (PassThePaxil, 2013). In Figure 1.c, *Survivor* Sucks participant ArtMaggot (2013) reimagined an oft-referenced scene

24 Part 1: Reality Television

from 1957, when nine high school students were among the first Black people to integrate into Little Rock's public school system. One of the more prominent photos from the event features a group of White men and women trailing behind a Black high school student named Elizabeth Eckford.

A 15-year-old White woman named Hazel Massery screams at Eckford. Reporters at the event noted that the White demonstrators behind Eckford yelled racist epithets and screamed, "Lynch her! Lynch her!" Aaryn's face is placed over Massery's in the digitally manipulated image. ArtMaggot (2013) joked that the picture is one of "Aaryn's family photos." Figure 1.d includes GinaMarie and Aaryn standing in front of a sign that reads, "We want White tenants in our White community" (Talk, 2013). Aaryn's face is covered by a Ku Klux Klan hood. A Nazi arm patch wraps around her left bicep.

The images shown in Figure 1 are parodied allusions that "direct the audience's attention by the addition, omission, substitution, and/or distortion of visual elements"

Figure 1. Clockwise: "We Klan do It!"; "The Amazing Racists"; "Aaryn Family Photos"; and "We Want White Tenants in Our White Community."

(DeLuca, 1999, pp. 21–22). Big Brother viewers act as cultural critics when they add a Klan emblem to Rosie the Riveter's shirt, substitute Aaryn for Hazel Massery, and distort the name The Amazing Race so that it reads "The Amazing Racists." The art functions as a performative intervention insofar as it reminds other viewers that racism is not only an act of personal prejudice but also systemic and intertwined in a socio-historical web of meaning and violence. Images that parody iconic photographs potentially transcend their historical allusions and gain "meaning from subsequent symbolic associations" (Edwards & Winkler, 1997, pp. 302–303). Images that comprise Figure 1 situate Aaryn's and GinaMarie's racist speech acts in a larger field of historically significant and culturally recognizable images of U.S.-based racism. The secondary texts work together to frame Aaryn's and GinaMarie's behavior as regressive and inconsistent with today's cultural values. To modify Figure 1.d, some Big Brother fans do not want racist houseguests in their virtual community.

Fan-produced art calling attention to unaired racism fills a lacuna, or racism void, Big Brother's producers intentionally manufactured. Although reality TV's "two-way, participatory medium is by no means an inherently progressive one" (Andrejevic, 2002, p. 268), the abovementioned audience-initiated interventions exemplify a few ways that CBS's viewers weaponized interactivity and disrupted white supremacist and capitalist impulses to short-circuit discussions about racism. Big Brother's viewers inverted the program's titular panoptic gaze by amplifying live-feed footage CBS initially refused to air. These fans watch the watchers and police the program's producers. Their work helped generate publicity, or news items, about hate speech on the Big Brother set and perhaps influenced an initially reluctant major media conglomerate to address racist and homophobic behavior among the fifteenth season's participants.

White Racial Bonding and Big Brother's Systemic Racism

From 2000 until 2020, the Big Brother soundstage has provided a temporary home to 269 people; 208 White contestants, twenty-seven Black men and women, nineteen Latin@ players, ten Asian American participants, three Middle Eastern houseguests, and three multiracial competitors have played the game. Each season features a few people of color competing against a cast of primarily White, heterosexual players. Take, for example, Season 2, in which eleven White players, one Black contestant, and one Latina houseguest competed to be the last person standing; or Season 4, where twelve White people and two Asian American contestants vied for the half-million-dollar prize. Big Brother's illusion of democracy obfuscates White supremacist dynamics that favor White houseguests. The program's superficial investment in democracy includes a majority vote to determine each week's evicted player and a cast that includes "everyday people" who are not professionally trained to be on television. Much like U.S. democracy, Big Brother's racism infuses the game's structure.

The racial composition of Big Brother's cast animates institutional racism by promoting White racial bonding. Sleeter (1994) defined White racial bonding as the linguistic and behavioral tendency for White people to form communicative bonds with one another. Fasching-Varner (2013) compared White racial bonding to "alliance building" (p. 22). He argued that

> one may tend to only think of this bonding in large-scale virulent racism such as the KKK or other racial pride groups. In only understanding white racial bonding from that limited perspective, one misses the opportunity to understand everyday racism and the bonding of those implicated by whiteness [Fasching-Varner, 2013, p. 22].

Fasching-Varner's description of racial bonding as "alliance building" proves especially salient on *Big Brother*, where "alliance" is a native-language term that characterizes strategic bonds players form to make it further in the game. For example, the Brigade was an alliance three White, heterosexual men used to make it to the end of Season 12. Other notable groupings include Season 10's White and male duo named the Renegades that resulted in a first and second-place finish; Season 14's exclusively White Quack Pack, which included the two last players standing; Season 15's exclusively White Exterminators that resulted in first and second-place accolades; and Season 16's exclusively White and male duet named the Hitmen, both of whom advanced to the final two. Burtyn (2002) contended that White racial bonding is magnified in games and sports, contexts where competition operates under the false pretense of meritocracy and a so-called color-blind approach to gamesmanship.

White racial bonding's racist implications unmistakably materialized in summer 2020 during the second All-Stars season. Eleven White players, three Black contestants, one interracial houseguest, and one Middle Eastern competitor comprise Season 22's cast. Six White players made up the season's dominant alliance called the Committee. One need only review the list of each week's nominees to appreciate White racial bonding's racist repercussions. In the first nine weeks of *Big Brother 22*, houseguests of color accounted for a staggering fourteen of the season's first eighteen nominees. An exclusively White group of heads of household targeted every player of color. Twitter user Brian Scally (2020) used a series of cast photos to illustrate White Heads of Household targeting contestants of color in All Stars 2 (see Figure 2). The fan's Twitter post was liked 3869 times and retweeted by 793 people. Social media posts calling attention to racism in the house function as performative spectatorship, where viewers create secondary texts (tweets) that guide interpretations of a primary text (*Big Brother*).

Production is complicit in the season's racist machinations. Not only did the production team pack the house with eleven White players but CBS overwhelmingly cast straight, White players who only played with other heterosexual, White contestants their initial seasons. Of the eleven White competitors invited to return for All Stars only three had a history aligning with houseguests of color in previous seasons. The most insidious part of production's Faustian bargain with White players is that gameplay results perpetuate a myth of meritocracy, where straight, White men and women are painted as "naturally" better at the game and minoritized houseguests are mere tokens and "bad" at the game.

Houseguests of color confronted with in-game racism are placed in a double-bind. Remaining silent in the face of racism ensures that racial prejudice will not be thematically represented in CBS's broadcast narrative. Conversely, addressing racism in the *Big Brother* house ensnares houseguests implicated by hate speech. A Black woman

Figure 2. Thirteen of *Big Brother 22*'s first sixteen nominees were people of color (Scally, 2020).

calling out racial prejudice may perceptually engender stereotypes, such as the "angry Black woman." A heartbreaking moment from Season 22 illustrates my point. In week five of the game, a White woman named Christmas nominated two Black women, Da'Vonne and Bayleigh, for eviction. Da'Vonne's and Bayleigh's nominations were part of nine consecutive weeks in which White players targeted contestants of color for eviction. Christmas joked to members of her all-White alliance that she feared "getting shot" by the women after they learned their fate (Sim, 2020). After Christmas quarreled with her nominees, Da'Vonne removed herself from the emotionally heightened situation and calmly walked to the backyard. "I hate this game," Da'Vonne cried to the camera (*Big Brother*, 2020). She continued:

> Why does she get to talk to me like that, but if I respond everyone's going to look at me crazy? She's talking to me like I'm her child. "There goes Da'Vonne. That's the eruption we were waiting for." That felt like a set up. I was having a calm conversation. The more people who

came into the kitchen, she kept getting louder and louder. She kept talking to me crazy [*Big Brother*, 2020].

Da'Vonne's tears and frustration remind me of a poetic moment from Boylorn's (2008) autoethnographic account of audiencing Black women on reality TV. She wrote: "I watch her/like watching myself/crying my damn eyes out/being judged without/the ability to defend myself/assumptions you make/the way you look down on me/with the things you say" (pp. 426–427). Da'Vonne's backyard narration of the interaction performs a critical intervention in guiding viewers to (1) locate her interaction with Christmas in a history of mediated interracial scripts where White women are victims and Black women are aggressors and (2) appreciate that a Black woman's response—no matter how benign—to aggression is often coded as angry and extreme. *Big Brother* contestants are not professional actors. Producers pull cast members like Da'Vonne from the ranks of everyday viewers. Prior to entering the *Big Brother* house, Da'Vonne likely witnessed Black reality show players fall into a racial trap she evaded by calling attention to its machinations *in situ*. Her interpretive lens as a viewer enabled her to short-circuit a racist trope of representation while she was embedded in TV's representational machine.

As Da'Vonne expertly narrated the racist trap, Bayleigh stayed inside and talked to Christmas. Christmas began crying over the situation. Christmas's White tears implicitly cited hundreds of years in the United States where White women have hijacked conversations about racism and used tears to recast themselves as the true victims of racial tension and prejudice. Christmas's tears quickly turned to aggression when Bayleigh stated that she would not accept Christmas playing victim. Christmas yelled at Bayleigh, waved fingers in her face, loudly clapped at her, and told her to "fuck off." Bayleigh noted that if she responded with a similar aggression she would be labeled "crazy."

To review, (1) a White woman nominated two Black women for eviction, (2) provoked (e.g., clapped, used a raised voice, wagged fingers in face) two women of color after their nominations, and (3) used White tears to play victim after her antagonism. Both Bayleigh and Da'Vonne deftly pointed out Christmas' performative trap. Responding emotionally to Christmas's provocation would lead viewers to cast Bayleigh and Da'Vonne as angry, crazy Black women. Da'Vonne and Bayleigh have likely witnessed countless televised narratives where White people provoke women of color and then play victims after racially minoritized women respond in kind. Pickens (2015) argued that

> Black women reality–TV stars contend with larger discussions about their behavior as representative of all blackness and a general anxiety about how their images circulate within the public sphere. Some censorship and disciplining of black women's performance comes from the characters on reality TV (i.e., they avoid specific behaviors on camera or reframe their behavior in the confessional moment taped days later) [p. 42].

Fans held Christmas' feet to the proverbial fire when she conducted an Instagram Live after Season 22's finale. One viewer pretended to be a former *Big Brother* houseguest and asked to join the Instagram broadcast. Christmas quickly learned the viewer was a disgruntled fan when she asked, "Why'd you say that Da'Vonne and Bayleigh were going to shoot you, you racist piece of shit?" (Sim, 2020).

CBS's rhetoric of tokenization becomes clearer when considering summer 2020's racial politics. Only two months before *Big Brother 22*'s premiere, three Minneapolis police officers pinned a 46-year-old Black man to the ground. Officer Derek Chauvin dug his knee into George Floyd's neck for over eight minutes, as he cried, "I can't breathe." The officers' actions resulted in Floyd's death. Two months prior, three White, plainclothes officers fatally shot a 26-year-old Black woman named Breonna Taylor in her own home. Taylor's and Floyd's deaths brought heightened attention to the #BlackLivesMatter movement, which resulted in numerous months of people protesting anti–Black police brutality. Tapped into the United States zeitgeist, *Big Brother*'s production team cast four Black contestants, which, at the time, marked the series' highest number of Black players in a single summer. Season 22 proved to be an empty-hearted attempt to cash in on Black suffering highlighted by the Black Lives Matter movement. Placing five players of color in a cast with eleven White players—eight of whom only had a history of working with other White players—is a cruel act of tokenization. A player like Da'Vonne can say, "Justice for Breonna Taylor" in the season's first live show but she plays a game so implicitly racist that she has little opportunity to competitively thrive. *Big Brother*'s rhetoric of tokenization explains why Da'Vonne and Bayleigh did not have the same agency to perform aggression and why Da'Vonne's anti-racist commentary largely focused on events *outside* the *Big Brother* house. *Big Brother*'s production team tends to sentimentalize oppression people of color experience outside the game, such as a Middle Eastern contestant named Kaysar sharing anti–Islam prejudice he has encountered. Unfortunately, CBS fails to narrate bigotry contestants like Kaysar, Da'Vonne, and Bayleigh experience playing the game.

White racial bonding during Season 22 incited fans of the show to create online petitions calling for CBS to radically modify its casting process. One petition authored by Briana_BB (2020) highlighted that *Big Brother* seasons "typically see one Black female, one Black male, and possibly one race other than White. In Season 22, every BIPOC [Black, Indigenous, and person of color] has been nominated. The casting process needs to change." Another petition created by viewer Evan Quinones (2020) implored *Big Brother* executive producer Allison Grodner to "feature more houseguests of color going forward—perhaps eight houseguests of color and eight houseguests that are not of minority background." Another petitioner claimed that viewers are "tired of the consistent bullying of minority players in the house and insist that underrepresented communities [make] up at least half of the cast in the *Big Brother* house" (Vasquez, 2020).

Fan backlash proved so significant that CBS announced that they planned to significantly change *Big Brother*'s casting process to level the playing field for contestants of color. First, two months after Season 22's finale, CBS announced a diversity pledge focused primarily on its reality shows. CBS president George Cheeks declared in a press release that "the reality TV genre is an area that's especially underrepresented, and needs to be more inclusive across development, casting, production, and all phases of storytelling" (as cited in Huaser, 2020, para. 4). Cheeks promised that, moving forward, at least half the cast of CBS's unscripted shows would include people of color. Journalists noted that past contestants of color on *Survivor* played an integral role in CBS's decision. Backdropped by #BlackLivesMatter protests, previous Black *Survivor* competitors including Dr. J'Tia Taylor Hart, Jamal Shipman, Julia Carter, and Brice Johnston formed a group called the Soul Survivors Organization. Hart created a petition that urged CBS to feature people of color "in their full breadth and depth" (qtd. in Hauser, 2020). Hart's activism complements the audience-reception/onscreen-talent dualism showcased when Da'Vonne refused to fall into the "angry Black woman" trap. Like Da'Vonne, Hart used her platform as a reality TV participant and standpoint as a Black *consumer* of reality TV to start a consciousness-raising campaign about representations of racially minoritized reality TV participants.

Second, *Big Brother*'s executive casting director, Robyn Kass, announced in a tweet that *Big Brother 22* would be her last season. Kass had cast twenty-one of the program's twenty-two seasons. Although Kass worked in conjunction with the show's executive producers and high-level CBS executives in charge of reality programming, many viewers primarily blamed her for *Big Brother*'s white-washed casts and storylines. For twenty-two years, *Big Brother*'s production team rhetorically situated racism as a problem located in individual houseguests. Kass's departure from the show signaled that CBS had finally turned inward and planned to address systemic racism behind the scenes. Delighted fans responded to Kass's tweet with messages like "We won" (Colesahh, 2021); "Hopefully the change in casting will lead to a more diverse cast" (Lowrimore, 2021); and "KKKasting is finally gone" (Alfeó, 2021). One person asked, "Was it the new diversity rule? Be honest for once" (@BobbyHill80, 2021).

Season 23 featured the most racially diverse cast in *Big Brother* history. The cast of sixteen included eight people of color. For the first time in the show's twenty-two-year run, an alliance composed exclusively of Black players made it to the final six contestants standing. Viewer-produced secondary texts aided in the peri-performative dynamics that set the stage for Season 23's players of color. Peri-performativity characterizes rules that establish permissible speech acts and performances in a given context, or the structural elements that constrain and enable alliances on a show like *Big Brother*. Fan interventions during seasons 15 and 22 illustrate the extent to which "the viewing public come to *perform* the role of critic through new media participation" (Anderson-Lopez, et al., 2021, p. 67). The performative spectatorship outlined in this essay demonstrates some of the ways in which audience members may co-produce televised media they consume.

Conclusion: The Power of Performative Spectatorship

Big Brother is commonly referred to as a game of social chess, in which players must strategize moves in advance and use one another as pawns. Producers have celebrated the social chess analogue in two ways. First, every season includes a chess board in the house. The chess board is one of the few staples present every season. Second, Seasons 3, 6, 16, and 22 featured a Head of Household competition called Knight Moves, where houseguests stood on a huge chess board and played a modified version of the game. The chess metaphor implies an equal playing field structured by egalitarianism. The comparison fails to capture significant ways in which structural racism favors White players in the *Big Brother* house. Instead of a game of chess, *Big Brother* is like a video game where straight, White competitors play on the "easy" setting while minoritized houseguests are forced to win the game on "hard" mode. Capitalism's illusion of "fair" competition is largely premised on a racially evasive consensual hallucination that merit determines success. This game show mirage of meritocracy downplays structural privilege, which places players from historically minoritized populations at a distinct disadvantage. The repetition of *Big Brother*'s racist structure is consistent with Jameson's (1991) notions of late capitalism, where television programs result in the replication of an "increasingly essential structural function to aesthetic innovation and experimentation" (p. 5). In its first two decades of production, *Big Brother* experimented with the "aesthetic innovation" of reality television to dress old modes of racist representation in new clothes. CBS simply found a new way to commodify individual racism while obfuscating structural racism at the heart of its production practices. Programs like *Big Brother* have allowed everyday consumers to "participate in the production process without controlling the means of production, which is just another way of describing the category of wage labor" (Andrejevic, 2002, p. 265). This conundrum, or illusion of democratic participation, illustrates racism's deep entrenchment in late capitalism's corporate power.

Nuanced stories of racism and homophobia prove few and far between on reality TV shows like *Big Brother*. Noting how a production team tackles prejudice or repeatedly fails to do so reveals the structural, or institutional, trappings of racism on a reality TV program. Squires (2008) contended that reality TV manufactures a world where "racial conflict is the norm" but "whites are only implicated in race when they say or do something exceedingly racist" (p. 435). Reality TV critics are uniquely positioned to point out the ways in which producers avoid substantive conversations about prejudice and frame racism as "individuals in conflict, rather than as emblematic of a nation shaped by practices of colonization" (Riggs & Due, 2010, p. 259). More often than not, *Big Brother*'s producers erase and diminish racism minoritized houseguests experience in the house. For 22 years, CBS failed to acknowledge or rectify the ways in which systemic racism affected gameplay, casting, characterization, and narratives.

Systemic change only emerged after viewers utilized social media to textualize their discontent. It is no accident that the above-mentioned audience demands for structural change, as well as CBS's pledge to modify its practices, coincided with temporally adjacent social movements, such as Black Lives Matter and #MeToo. Social justice causes have increasingly turned to social media to (1) point out myths that perpetuate structural abuse, (2) call attention to specific instances of mistreatment, and (3) offer practical ways for everyday people to request meaningful remedies. Anderson-Lopez, Lambert, and Budaj (2021) claimed that "the very act of watching may engender a feeling of possession for the audience, a feeling nurtured by online spaces" (p. 65). Fan-generated secondary texts posted on Twitter, Change.org, and fan forums modified *Big Brother*'s DNA, or components that comprise its basic structure. John Fiske (2013) so perfectly elucidated the importance of secondary texts in today's mass-mediated climate that I quote him at length. He wrote:

> The excessiveness and openness of primary texts in our culture have produced a huge industry of secondary texts that advertise, promote, criticize, and respond to the primary texts of television, film, literature, and so on. Relations between these and the primary texts are direct and specific: secondary texts relate to specified primary ones and these intertextual relations are their sole *raison d'être*. They work to activate certain meanings rather than others, to legitimate certain pleasures rather than others. There is also a sense in which those secondary texts provide a "ghost text," like the ghost image on a television set with poor reception. These secondary texts increase the viewer's sense of power over the meanings and pleasures offered by the primary texts because they grant them access to, and thus allow them to participate in, the mode of representation. The pleasure of making meanings is greater by far than that of finding them ready-made [Fiske, 2013, pp. 65–66].

Reality TV's audience interactivity provides a "promise of 'power' [that] clearly has political significance" (Holmes, 2004, p. 214). Audience-text intertextuality is especially important to explore in the context of reality TV because the mode of entertainment is premised upon the genre's audience acting as eventual on-screen participants.

As reality TV competitions march into their third decade, media studies scholars should increasingly call attention to erasure tactics that *cut across seasons—even decades*—of reality TV programming. Erasure's repetition greases up the machine that renders structural racism unintelligible. Critical interventions by fans of the genre short-circuit erasure's repetition and cause its machinery to stutter and stumble. This study offers a model for how other media scholars might use performative spectatorship to theorize fan interventions via secondary texts shared on social media.

References

Alfeó. [@alfredosauce28]. (2021, Jan. 22). *The kkkasting is finally gone maybe this year of bb won't be so bad after all* [Tweet]. Twitter. https://twitter.com/alfredosauce28/status/1352676605852741632.

Anderson-Lopez, J., Lambert, R.J., & Budaj, A. (2021). Tug of war: Social media, cancel culture, and diversity for *Girls* and *The 100*. *KOME—An International Journal of Pure Communication Inquiry, 9*(1), 64–84.

Andrejevic, M. (2002). The kinder, gentler gaze of Big Brother. *New Media & Society, 4*(2), 251–270.

ArtMaggot. (2013, July 12). BB15 official Photochop thread. *Survivor Sucks*. http://survivorsucks.yuku.com/topic/114201/BB15-OFFICIAL-Photochop-Thread?page=14.

Bell-Jordan, K.E. (2008). *Black.White.* and a *Survivor* of *The Real World*: Constructions of race on reality TV. *Critical Studies in Media Communication, 24*(4), 353–372.

Big Brother. (2020, Sept. 10). *Da'Vonne, Bayleigh, and Christmas have it out on* Big Brother: All Stars [Video]. YouTube. https://www.youtube.com/watch?v=fr0OdbzAQuo.

@BobbyHill80. (2021, Jan. 22). *Was it the new diversity rule? Be honest for once* [Tweet]. Twitter. https://twitter.com/BobbyHill80/status/1352678790615494656.

Boylorn, R.M. (2008). As seen on TV: An autoethnographic reflection on race and reality television. *Critical Studies in Media Communication, 24*(4), 413–33. https://doi.org/10.1080/15295030802327758.

Braxton, G. (2019, Sept. 25). *Big Brother's* season was marred by allegations of racism. It's not the first time. *Los Angeles Times*. https://www.latimes.com/entertainment-arts/tv/story/2019-09-24/cbs-big-brother-racism-controversy-context.

Brianna_BB. (2020). Change the casting process of *Big Brother* US. *Change.org*. https://www.change.org/p/cbs-change-the-casting-process-of-big-brother-us.

Burke, K. (1969). *A grammar of motives*. University of California Press.

Burtyn, T.M. (2002). Critically examining white racial identity and privilege in sport psychology consulting. *The Sport Psychologist, 16*(3), 316–336. https://doi-org.csulb.idm.oclc.org/10.1123/tsp.16.3.316.

Caruso, N. (2020, Sept. 27). *"Big Brother": 10 ways to fix the reality competition's 'new school' slump*. TVLine. https://tvline.com/2020/09/27/big-brother-all-stars-review-bb22-ways-to-improve-cbs/.

@Colesahh. (2021, Jan. 22). *We won* [Tweet]. Twitter. https://twitter.com/colesahh/status/1352671650790187009.

Davies, M. (2013, July 1). The contestants of *Big Brother* are horrifying racist. *Jezebel*. https://jezebel.com/the-contestants-of-big-brother-are-horrifyingly-racist-639129718.

DeLuca, K.M. (1999). *Image politics: The new rhetoric of environmental activism*. The Guilford Press.
Denhart, A. (2009). Braden evicted after tie despite producers' pathetic sanitizing of his bigotry. *Reality Blurred*. https://www.realityblurred.com/realitytv/2009/07/big-brother-11-braden_out_producers_censor/.
Denhart, A. (2020). Is *Big Brother's* format broken? *Reality Blurred*. https://www.realityblurred.com/realitytv/2020/08/big-brother-format-broken/.
Django. (2013, July 18). BB15 official Photochop thread. *Survivor Sucks*. http://survivorsucks.yuku.com/topic/114201/BB15-OFFICIAL-Photochop-Thread?page=18.
Dubrofsky, R. (2006). *The Bachelor*: Whiteness in the harem. *Critical Studies in Media Communication, 23*(1), 39–56. https://doi.org/10.1080/07393180600570733.
Edgar, M. (2013, July 13). Aryan: Racist narcissist with a busted hat: "Who wants to see my KKK room?" *Survivor Sucks*. http://survivorsucks.yuku.com/search/ topic/topic/114198/q/aryan?page=5.
Edwards, J.L., & Winkler, C.K. (2013). Representative form and the visual ideograph: The Iwo Jima image in editorial cartoons. *Quarterly Journal of Speech, 83*(3), 289–310. https://doi.org/10.1080/00335639709384187.
Fasching-Varner, K.J. (2013). "Uhh, you know, don't you?": White racial bonding in the narrative of white pre-service teachers. *Educational Foundations*, 21–41.
Fiske, J. (2013). Moments of television: Neither the text nor the audience. In E. Seiter, H. Borchers, G. Kreutzner, & E. Warth (Eds.), *Remote control: Television, audiences, and cultural power* (pp. 65–66). Routledge.
Foster, D. (2004). "Jump in the pool": The competitive culture of *Survivor* fan networks. In S. Holmes & D. Jermyn (Eds.), *Understanding reality television* (pp. 270–289). Routledge.
Fox, R. (2013, June 30). An open letter to *Big Brother's* production team. *Ragan Fox*. https://ragan.wordpress.com/2013/06/30/an-open-letter-to-big-brothers-production-team/.
Fox, R. (2019). *Inside reality TV: Producing race, gender, and sexuality on "Big Brother."* Routledge.
Goffman, E. (1973). *The presentation of self in everyday life*. Overlook.
Grodner, A., & Meehan, R. (Executive Producers). (2009, July 14). *Big Brother* (Season 9, Episode 3) [TV series episode]. Fly on the Wall Productions.
Grodner, A., & Meehan, R. (Executive Producers). (2013, July 5). *Big Brother* (Season 15, Episode 5) [TV series episode]. Fly on the Wall Productions.
Halberstam, J. *The art of queer failure*. Duke University Press.
Hauser, C. (2020, Nov. 11). Survivor and other reality shows will feature more diverse casts, CBS says. *The New York Times*. https://www.nytimes.com/2020/11/11/business/media/cbs-reality-tv-diversity.html.
Hautman, N. (2020, Nov. 17). *Big Brother* controversies through the years. *US Magazine*. https://www.usmagazine.com/entertainment/pictures/big-brother-controversies-through-the-years/.
Hibberd, J. (2013, July 14). *Big Brother* adds disclaimer for prejudice. *Entertainment Weekly*. https://ew.com/article/2013/07/14/big-brother-disclaimer-prejudice/.
Holmes, S. (2004). "But this time *you* choose!" Approaching the "interactive audience" in reality TV. *International Journal of Cultural Studies, 7*(2), 213–231.
Humphrey, R.E. (2013). *Remove Amanda Zuckerman from the "Big Brother" house*. [Online petition]. Change.org. https://www.change.org/p/cbs-remove-amanda-zuckerman-from-the-big-brother-house.
Jameson, F. (1991). *Postmodernism, or the cultural logic of late capitalism*. Duke University Press.
Joseph, R.L. (2009). "Tyra Banks is fat": Reading (post-)racism and (post-)feminism in the new millennium. *Critical Studies in Media Communication, 26*(3), 237–254.
King, E. (2013). *CBS television network: To expel current contestant of "Big Brother"* 15 Aaryn Gries. [Online petition]. Change.org. https://www.change.org/p/cbs-television-network-to-expel-current-contestant-of-big-brother-15-aaryn-gries.
Kraszewski, J. (2009). Country hicks and urban cliques: Mediating race, reality and liberalism on MTV's *The Real World*. In S. Murray and L. Ouellette (Eds.), *Reality TV: Remaking television culture* (pp. 205–222). New York University Press.
Lowrimore, M. [@gomichaelgo]. (2021, Jan. 22). *I love BB, and hopefully the change in who is casting will lead to a more diverse cast, and not just Instagram influencers in the making* [Tweet]. Twitter. https://twitter.com/gomichaelgo/status/1352675742400700416.
Orbe, M. (2008). Representations of race in reality TV: Watch and discuss. *Critical Studies in Media Communication, 25*(4), 345–352.
PassThePaxil. (2013, July 18). BB15 official Photochop thread. *Survivor Sucks*. http://survivorsucks.yuku.com/topic/114201/BB15-OFFICIAL-Photochop-Thread?page=39.
Pickens, T.A. (2015). Shoving aside the politics of respectability: Black women, reality TV, and the ratchet performance. *Women & Performance: A Journal of Feminist Theory, 25*(1), 41–58. http://dx.doi.org/10.1080/0740770X.2014.923172.
Quinones, E. (2020). CBS's *Big Brother*, cast more racial minorities going forward. *Change.org*. https://www.change.org/p/cbs-cbs-s-big-brother-needs-to-cast-more-racial-minorities.
Riggs, D.W., & Due, C. (2010). The management of accusations of racism in *Celebrity Big Brother*. *Discourse & Society, 21*(3), 257–271.

Ross, D. (2019, Aug. 8). Julie Chen grills Jack Matthews about offensive *Big Brother* comments. *Entertainment Weekly*. https://ew.com/tv/2019/08/08/big-brother-julie-chen-jack-matthews-racist-comments/.

Scally, B. (2020) *The #BB22 HOHs. Their nominees* [Photograph]. Twitter. https://twitter.com/Brian_Scally/status/1310390680318029826/photo/2.

Sim, B. (2020, November 20). *Big Brother:* Fan interrupts Christmas' Instagram live and calls her racist. https://screenrant.com/big-brother-22-allstars-christmas-abbott-instagram-racist/.

Sleeter, C. (1994). White racism. *Multicultural Education, 1*(4), 5–8.

Squires, C. (2008). Race and reality TV: Tryin' to make it real—but real compared to what? *Critical Studies in Media Communication, 25*(4), 434–440.

Stelter, B. (2013, July 8). Reality show contestants pay a real-world price: On *Big Brother*, racial and gay slurs abound. *New York Times*. www.nytimes.com/2013/07/09/business/media/on-big-brother-racial-and-gay-slurs-abound.html.

Talk. (2013, July 14). BB15 official Photochop thread. *Survivor Sucks*. http://survivorsucks.yuku.com/topic/114201/BB15-OFFICIAL-Photochop-Thread?page=14.

Ture, K., & Hamilton, C.V. (1992). *Black power: The politics of liberation in America*. Vintage.

Vasquez, K. (2020). CBS casting more minority players on *Big Brother. Change.org.* https://www.change.org/p/cbs-cbs-casting-more-minority-players-on-big-brother.

Wess, R. (2004). Representative anecdotes in general, with notes toward a representative anecdote for Burkean erocriticism in particular. *K.B. Journal: The Journal of the Kenneth Burke Society, 1*(1). https://www.kbjournal.org/wess.

Zingbot9000. (2013, July 4). Aryan: Racist narcissist with a busted hat: "Who wants to see my KKK room?" *Survivor Sucks*. http://survivorsucks.yuku.com/search/ topic/topic/114198/q/aryan?page=2.

Canceling CBS

Black Alliances and Diversity on Reality TV's
Survivor *and* Big Brother, *2021–22*

CHRISTINA S. WALKER, ESQ., J.D.

Discrimination, racism, and lack of representation in America are not new occurrences. However, during former president Trump's administration from 2017 to 2021 and thereafter, America has seen emboldened displays of racism and hate speech, political attempts to ban Critical Race Theory (CRT) at state and federal levels, and heightened critiques targeting recently established social movements and campaigns intended to advocate against racial atrocities and injustices (e.g., Black Lives Matter) (Butcher & Gonzalez, 2020; Schaffner, 2020). Consequently, there has been immense pressure for big name brands, corporations, and media to partake in socially responsible actions and messaging demonstrating commitment to furthering diversity, equity, and inclusion (Maiorescu-Murphy, 2022). For example, in November 2020, CBS, a major media network, publicly displayed its commitment to diversity by creating an initiative to increase diversity and representation within its cast members and content creators/producers (Ramos, 2020). Among several commitments, in a partnership with the National Association for the Advancement of Colored People (NAACP), CBS vowed that "starting in the 2021–22 season, at least half of the cast members of its unscripted programs will be people of color" (Hauser, 2020, para. 3; Ramos, 2020). The manifestation of this initiative was shown during the most recent seasons of two highly popularized reality TV shows: *Big Brother*, season 23 (Grodner & Meehan, 2000–2022), and *Survivor*, season 41 (Probst, 2000–2022). In these historical seasons, people of color (particularly Black players), teamed up to create alliances to assist them in furthering their chances of remaining on the show and ultimately winning each show's competition (Boyd, 2021; Braxton, 2021). Though this historic feat was perceived by many viewers as long overdue and necessary, many other viewers perceived CBS's actions and the emerging alliances between Black cast members unfavorably (Boyd, 2021; Braxton, 2021; Dehnart, 2021). Among much negative and hateful online commentary, social media posts from these viewers included statements concerning reverse racism, micro assaults and microinvalidations, and threats to boycott or cancel CBS all together due to CBS's supposed role in perpetuating such environment where these alliances could form (Boyd, 2021; Braxton, 2021). Nevertheless, such statements only present very limited perspectives while offering simplistic assessments of a much more complex issue.

Very little of these viewers discussed the ways in which people of color, other minorities and underrepresented players have been historically excluded from previous seasons of *Big Brother* and *Survivor* (Bell-Jordan, 2008; Falconer, 2020; Perrett, 2021). In particular, these shows have been compared to social experiments in which cool kid cliques form as if in high school settings, while "others" not conforming to racial, beauty, ableist, and body-type norms are isolated and picked off one by one (Bell-Jordan, 2008; Braxton, 2020; Perrett, 2021; Timmermans, 2012). Furthermore, and arguably, in each season race has been the number one disqualifier, causing Black players to be eliminated extremely early, if not first (Braxton, 2020; Dehnart, 2016; Falconer, 2020; Iannucci, 2019; Perrett, 2021; Pittman, 2020). With this in mind, this essay seeks to explain viewers' negative receptions of racial diversity on the latest seasons of *Big Brother* and *Survivor* by exploring two theories central to mass media communication, Reception Theory and Uses and Gratifications Theory.

The content of this essay is presented in five sections. First, I provide an overview of the shows including their sociocultural aspects. Second, I explain Reception Theory and Uses and Gratifications Theory as they relate to *Big Brother*, season 23 and *Survivor*, season 41. Third, I will explain the diversity related changes that occurred during these seasons. Fourth, through a Reception Theory and Uses and Gratification Theory lens (Hall, 1973; Herzog, 1944; Katz et al., 1973), I dissect viewers' internet posts, revealing statements that imply that viewers' motivations for watching these reality TV shows has historically stemmed from their desire to consume media that reinforces dominant-hegemonic messages, yet because the latest seasons deviated from these narratives, this caused a backlash. Finally, in light of the negative receptions, I conclude by briefly offering best practices grounded in proven crisis communication theory and methodology to mitigate cancel culture while simultaneously enabling CBS to remain committed to furthering its diversity initiative.

Section 1: CBS's Big Brother *and* Survivor

To fully understand audience receptions and reactions to *Big Brother*, season 23, and *Survivor*, season 41, readers must have knowledge surrounding the history of each show, including the purposes of each show and how each show operates. I make no assumptions that all readers have watched CBS's *Big Brother* or *Survivor*. Therefore, to ensure readers have sufficient background information, in this section I provide a brief overview of each reality TV show while also providing a synopsis of the intertwined sociocultural aspects. This will enable readers to better understand how CBS's diversity initiative is a major shift from the historical traditions of CBS's *Big Brother* and *Survivor* that viewers have grown accustomed to.

Big Brother: An Overview

Big Brother, introduced over twenty years ago (Brizzee, 2021), is a reality TV show competition or game in which strangers live together in a home while their every move, conversation and interaction is broadcasted to the world via TV and internet (Fox, 2018). House guests (i.e., participants) must compete in competitions to win the opportunity to be designated "Head of Household," which provides immunity from elimination while equally providing power to put two (sometimes three) other houseguests on the block (i.e., to nominate them for eviction). Generally, house guests put on the block can be taken off by winning a separate small competition (i.e., the veto competition), or alternatively, someone else who wins may save them. If this occurs, a replacement nominee is chosen by the Head of Household (Fox, 2018). In any case, because evictions are ultimately determined by majority vote of all house guests, social alliances form, requiring guests to be on the right side of the numbers to remain in the house (Fox, 2018). House guests are voted off one by one until a final three remain. In the end, all finalists must convince the evicted house guests (i.e., the jury) to select them as the winner. The person with the most votes receives an award ranging from $500,000 to $750,000 (Fox, 2018).

Survivor: An Overview

Survivor, also a reality TV competition and game show, has aired on CBS for over twenty years (CBS, n.d.). The game requires players to live together while stranded on an island within harsh conditions. Specifically, players do not eat consistently, are unable to shower, and must live, sleep and function off the land. Players begin the game in teams or tribes which determines where and who they live with and compete in difficult competitions to earn both rewards for luxury items (e.g., food, correspondence from home, sleeping supplies, etc.) and immunity to remain in the game (Karlan, 2017). Winning teams obtain reward or immunity, depending on the challenge. Players also have other limited opportunities to obtain immunity or other benefits that may increase their chances of staying in the game, such as locating hidden immunity idols or other game advantages or powers (Karlan, 2017). Losing teams attend what is referred to as a tribal council where players vote to eliminate a player. When teams merge, the game becomes an individual game and only individuals can be safe from elimination. Throughout the game players need to join alliances to ensure they have numbers to avoid being voted out. In the end, two to three finalists answer questions presented by eliminated players (i.e., the jury) who decide which player "outplayed, outwitted, and outlasted" all others, leading to a one-million-dollar award along with the title of "sole survivor" (CBS, n.d., para. 1; Karlan, 2017).

History of Sociocultural Influences and Race on *Big Brother* and *Survivor*

The history of sociocultural influences and races may impact productions of *Big Brother* and *Survivor* and are worthy of analysis. Historically marginalized persons cast on both *Big Brother* and *Survivor* have repeatedly faced rejection and, at times, even hostility (Dehnart, 2016; Iannucci, 2019). For example, despite these shows being categorized as reality TV, producers frequently reject to document truly authentic versions of such cast members, and instead depict fabricated "tropes of representation" (i.e., normalized characterizations) (Fox, 2013, p. 193). Moreover, strict expectations producers place on historically marginalized casts members requires these cast members to play into racialized, gendered, and sexually oriented stereotypes (Fox, 2018; Quail, 2011). In turn, producers edit these shows to not only demonstrate such tropes and stereotypes, but to capitalize off them (Fox, 2013; Park, 2009). To cast members, this communicates that there are distinct roles and that each cast member should "stay in their lane" by taking on the behaviors and attributes of the character whom they are assigned (Miller, 2007). Resultantly, this creates a pecking order that is unmistakably clear from the onset of each game, thereby setting the stage for the very same social hierarchies in everyday society to be replicated (Apple & Beers, 2007). Sadly, this does not merely influence game strategy, but it equally influences cast members social interactions and connections made in the game.

Other examples of rejection on *Big Brother* and *Survivor* include social rejection of minority and underrepresented players, specifically constant othering and ostracism. More specifically, the formulation of interpersonal relationships and alliances are based on in-group and out-group membership; and voting based on social norms (Drew, 2011). Likewise, an instance when a cast member belonging to a historically marginalized group experienced hostility was shown in 2017 during season 34, *Survivor: Game Changers* (Roberts, 2018). During tribal council, it was revealed that the player, Zeke Smith, was transgender. The player who outed Smith claimed that Smith's decision to keep this information private was a clear indication of Smith's deception and untrustworthiness (Roberts, 2018). The player was voted out during the same tribal council and terminated from employment upon returning home, indicating *Survivor* players' denouncement of such behavior while equally showing others in everyday society also opposed the behavior (Roberts, 2018). Nonetheless, recurring stereotypical portrayals of *Big Brother* and *Survivor* LGBTQIA+ players and the constant othering of them confirms much work is still needed to combat hegemony and bias that spills over from everyday norms into these reality TV games (Roberts, 2018).

Big Brother and *Survivor* have been perceived as shows lacking diversity of cast members. Failure to embrace people of color (POC) through diverse representation in casting and treatment among cast members has been evident across *Big Brother* and *Survivor* seasons (Brizzee, 2021; Falconer, 2020). Throughout *Big Brother*'s more than twenty-one-year history across twenty-two seasons, there has been no Black winners and only one Black player was included in a final six. In contrast, White males have dominated the game, winning the show more than fifty percent of the time, with White females being the second most winningest population and only three winners identifying as POC (Brizzee, 2021; Espada, 2021; Perrett, 2021). Moreover, in multiple *Big Brother* seasons, Black and other POC house guests were subjected to racism and racist attacks involving use of racist insults and slurs by other house guests, while POC house guests and most notably, Black house guests, have repeatedly been evicted first and or very early throughout the competition (Braxton, 2020; Iannucci, 2019; Perrett, 2021).

As for *Survivor*, CBS went as far as creating themes based on the idea of testing racial and cultural biases and stereotypes (Bell-Jordan, 2008; Bresnahan & Lee, 2018; Drew, 2011; Peers, 2019). For instance, in previous seasons, players were divided by age, race and ethnicity, and stigmas and stereotypes (i.e., *Brawns vs. Brains vs. Beauty*) (Bell-Jordan, 2008; Peers, 2019). Sadly, though CBS producers submit their intent was to refute misconceptions premised on race, gender and generation, selectively editing content and giving more camera time to focus on stereotypical narratives (rather than counter-stereotypical ones) had the opposite effect. Most noticeably, it further segregated and stigmatized such groups, subjecting players to toxic environments all for the sake of entertainment (Bresnahan & Lee, 2018). Like *Big Brother*, in comparison to White players, POC players have been voted out early at disproportionate rates across the majority of *Survivor* seasons (Dehnart, 2016; Falconer, 2020; Pittman, 2020). In a similar manner, Black *Survivor* players have equally endured racism and racist slurs by other players (Moorhouse, 2012). Black players even alleged producers engaged in racism by deliberately editing footage to convey racially charged portrayals of Black players in order to increase ratings, so much so that these players formed the Black Survivor Alliance (BSA) and the Soul Survivors Organization to address these actions in addition to issues of underrepresentation (Falconer, 2020; Ross, 2021).

Section 2: Reception Theory and Uses and Gratifications Theory

Reception Theory

As readers have already ascertained from reading this book, Hall's (1973) Reception Theory helps to explain how viewers come to understand and derive meaning from the media they consume. This meaning is heavily influenced by sociocultural background (Martin, 2007; Morley, 1992). Viewers' interpretations may be completely or partially aligned with media's intentions, or alternatively, in total opposition (Hall, 1973; Morley, 1992; Martin, 2007). In either case, viewers tend to be more receptive to media when content produced aligns with their own sociocultural perspectives and values (Morley, 1992).

Research has focused on the ways in which hegemonic norms may impact viewers' reception of media (Martin, 2007; Morley, 1992). Hegemonic norms include societal expectations that have become prevalent and normalized (Martin, 2007). For example, the idea that beauty is limited to certain representations of race, skin complexion, hair texture, or body type. Also, ideas that people should be limited to certain traditional sexual orientations and gender roles; and that people historically in power and people historically oppressed should remain in such hierarchical structures (Kwan & Trautner, 2009).

Research suggests people with cultural identities and beliefs that align with hegemonic norms often willingly accept dominant media messages (Martin, 2007). Historically, media messages that dominate society include those that are produced by the privileged and powerful, particularly, media conglomerates primarily managed and owned by White males who traditionally use media as a forum to express cisgender values (Corey & Shivers, 2016; Martin, 2007; U.S. Commission on Civil Rights, 1977). These limited perspectives shape normative ideas about race and race relations which impact racial judgements, stereotypes and prejudices (Corey & Shivers, 2016).

Likewise, because people's exposure to others outside their race and culture is typically restricted, viewers routinely rely on racial portrayals in the media to gather information, which can lead to flawed judgment (Cox et al., 2016). Simply put, media messages can reinforce and perpetuate certain racial biases and stigmas (Corey & Shivers, 2016). Viewers who are receptive to willingly consuming such messages without questioning their validity are referred to as dominant or dominant-hegemonic viewers or audiences (Martin, 2007).

On the other hand, people with cultural identities and belief systems that align with minority perspectives may be resistant to consuming dominant media messages (Martin, 2007). Such viewers often include racial minorities, ethnic minorities, LGBTQIA+ individuals, religious minorities, individuals with disabilities, and other viewers of historically oppressed or underrepresented backgrounds (Low & Forsey, 2012). These viewers are categorized as oppositional viewers or audiences. They tend to "oppose, contest, or question" dominate media messages (Low & Forsey, 2012, p. 6), while "challenging the allegedly hegemonic 'wisdom' of the message's producers" (Low & Forsey, 2012, p. 2). Lastly, viewers may take on a negotiated viewpoint by not merely accepting or rejecting media messages outright. Alternatively, when interpreting media messages, they rely on their own experience, background and knowledge along with knowledge gained from other sources (Martin, 2007).

Uses and Gratifications Theory

Uses and Gratifications Theory (UGT) was developed to study and identify reasons people consume and interact with different media, like radio, TV, internet including social media, and TV genres such as reality TV (Herzog, 1944; Katz et al., 1973; Mcguire, 1974; Zhao, 2014). According to UGT, people have certain psychological and social needs and look to different media to gratify these needs (Herzog, 1944; Katz et al., 1973; Mcguire, 1974). Viewers become motivated to consume media to gratify five different needs: cognitive needs, affective needs, personal integrative needs, social integrative needs, and tension free needs (Handfield, 2012).

Cognitive needs describe the need for knowledge or information (Handfield, 2012). Examples of media that may gratify these needs include educational TV documentaries or radio podcasts. Affective needs include the need to garner an emotional connection or feel an emotional mood (Handfield, 2012; Zhao, 2014). Examples of media consumption to fulfill affective needs include listening to music to derive or recall certain emotions, or watching a scary movie to trigger fear. Personal integrative needs describe needs for affirmation and self-confidence (Handfield, 2012). For example, watching a reality TV show because cast members are relatable and inspiring may improve viewers' perceptions of themselves. Social integrative needs describe viewers' needs for social interaction, like using social media to connect with others. Finally, tension free needs include viewers' needs to escape or seek relief or relaxation, such as seeking to escape reality by playing video games (Zhao, 2014).

Handfield (2012) finds most people watch reality TV because it allows them to pass time and connect with cast members. Zhao (2014) agrees, stating viewers' underlying motivations for consuming reality TV stem from "entertainment, relaxing, habitual pass time, companionship, social interaction, and surveillance (information seeking)" (p. 15); all reasons that can be categorized within the five different gratification needs. To this end, there are several justifications that explain why reality TV captivates viewers. First, it enables them to identify with and see themselves in similar cast members (Handfield, 2012; Zhao, 2014). Second, it enables viewers to consume media that relates to them by depicting normalized societal roles and expectations (Handfield, 2012). Third, the vast array of reality TV genres allows viewers to seek out content that supports their previously held ideologies (Handfield, 2012). Last, reality TV allows viewers to seek out content they perceive to be most valuable to them; this creates the expectation that their needs will be gratified. Thus, depending on viewers' reception of a reality TV show, expectations may or may not be met (Zhao, 2014).

Theories in Context of *Big Brother* and *Survivor*

While reception theory helps to elucidate the role of sociocultural differences in interpreting media messages, by explaining underlying motivations for why viewers consume reality tv in the first place, UGT can work with reception theory to reveal potential conflicts that can arise when media messages are irreconcilable with viewers' goals and expectations. Regarding *Big Brother*, season 23, and *Survivor*, season 41, these theories assist in understanding the following:

- the role sociocultural differences play in how viewers interpret media messages on these seasons, and whether negative receptions incite opposition
- the viewers' overall reception of these seasons (particularly focusing on integration of diversity initiatives)
- the viewers' underlying motivations for watching *Big Brother* and *Survivor* and the needs they seek to gratify
- the general perceived value garnered from watching these shows, and in light of this value, whether expectations were met by watching these seasons

Section 3: Past Versus Present, Big Brother *and* Survivor *Diversity Related Changes*

In 2020, during season 23 of *Big Brother* and season 41 of *Survivor*, viewers saw a shift from the reality TV shows that they were accustomed to. First, participants included the most diverse players ever cast (Boyd, 2021; Braxton, 2021; Hauser, 2020). Diversity representation increased to include varying personalities and body types and players with varying types of sexual orientations and gender identities and players with disabilities (Boyd, 2021; Braxton, 2021). Most conspicuously, the greatest pivotal and deliberate change by CBS was inclusion of more POC players—50 percent, to be exact (Hauser, 2020).

Some viewers argue that *Big Brother* and *Survivor* always included diverse representation (CBS Survivor, 2021; CBS Survivor, 2021a). It is true, *Big Brother* and *Survivor* have previously included LGBTQIA+ players, players with disabilities, players not reflecting popularized social roles, and racial minorities (Peers, 2019). Nevertheless, and as noted in section one, it cannot be denied that inclusion of these players was always conditioned on producers' ability to create stereotypical narratives, capitalizing off caricature types and tropes to play into viewers' expectations and increase ratings (Fox, 2013; Park, 2009). Additionally, though different types of players were included, prior to these seasons, players from majority backgrounds and or those viewed more favorably in the social hierarchy (e.g., White males, cisgender players, White females, physically fit players, etc.) were disproportionately cast, while rates at which other players were injected into each game and their subsequent treatment from other cast members suggest these players were cast only to be tokens, enabling producers to check off diversity boxes on their demographic questionnaires (Fox, 2013; Park, 2009).

The second noteworthy change that took viewers by surprise during these *Big Brother* and *Survivor* seasons was the content producers chose to focus on and promote, and the narratives highlighted (Hauser, 2020; Ramos, 2020). Because casts included an unprecedented amount of POC players, players tended to engage in conversations about race and related issues, such as challenges of being Black or a POC in America, turmoil between law enforcement and Black and Brown communities, current events, and systemic racism (Brizzee, 2021; CBS Survivor, 2021). Further, producers' deliberate focus on these conversations and intentional effort to make them part of the core narratives were in support of honoring CBS's commitment to diversity in solidarity with the NAACP (Ramos, 2020).

The third, and arguably the most discussed change emerging in season 23, *Big Brother*, and season 41, *Survivor*, was the alliances that formed on the basis of racial affinity and the consequent power shift from majority to minority players (Boyd, 2021; Braxton, 2021; Perrett, 2021). As overviewed in section one, formation of alliances based on social hierarchy has been an integral part of these shows (Bell-Jordan, 2008; Braxton, 2020; Perrett, 2021; Timmermans, 2012). Cool kid majority alliances were created while excluding minority players, and most markedly, Black players (Falconer, 2020; Perrett, 2021). Again, even *Survivor* producers separated players by race, ethnicity, stereotypes, and stigmas, giving players no choice in the tribes they were assigned, rather than allowing alliances to form naturally (Bell-Jordan, 2008; Bresnahan & Lee, 2018; Peers, 2019). Yet, in the discussed *Big Brother* and *Survivor* seasons, instead of being relegated to the confines of typical social circles and their ensuing inferior roles, Black players took matters into their own hands, having the power of numbers to create majority alliances and arguably control each game (Boyd, 2021; Braxton, 2021; Perrett, 2021). These alliances formed differently because rationale originated from the duties that Black players felt obligated to perform that extended far beyond each game (Boyd, 2021; CBS Survivor, 2021; Perrett, 2021). Specifically, this included the duty to bond and come together during a historic season of unparalleled diverse representation, despite not always liking another alliance member or agreeing with another member's gameplay. Also, the duty to sacrifice individual gameplay for a greater cause, and finally, the duty to represent for the Black Culture in light of ongoing racial atrocities and systemic racism that was taking place in the U.S. leading up to and during the filming and airing of *Big Brother*, season 23 and *Survivor*, season 41 (Boyd, 2021; CBS Survivor, 2021; Perrett, 2021). This included the Black Lives Matter (BLM) Movement; the January 6 insurrection; and the overall surge of emboldened displays of racism, hate crimes, and discrimination under former President Trump's administration (Braxton, 2021).

Section 4: Dissecting Viewers' Receptions

Now that readers have a thorough understanding of how *Big Brother* (season 23) and *Survivor* (season 41) compare to past seasons, it is time to explore the resulting backlash from viewers. This following section will explore three key themes: the viewers' general motivations for watching *Big Brother* and *Survivor*, the viewers' negative reception to these seasons, and the viewers' resulting engagement in cancel culture. I will achieve this by focusing on excerpts of social media posts in response to video clips, photos, and content covering *Big Brother*, season 23, and *Survivor*, season 41.

Due to the volume, I used only a limited number of posts as examples. However, recurring sentiments were found across both sources. Finally, for each theme, I use the excerpts as evidence to theorize the following: (1) viewers generally watch these shows due to the entertainment and escapism factors garnered from consuming dominant-hegemonic messages, (2) the messages included in these *Big Brother* and *Survivor* seasons deviated from viewers' expectations and thus were not gratifying, and (3) non-gratification of viewers' needs led to the desire to cancel CBS.

Underlying Motivations: Why They Watch

Excerpts from thousands of social media posts demonstrate much of *Big Brother* and *Survivor* audiences are dominant-hegemonic viewers. This was illustrated when viewers revealed hegemonic perspectives, reinforced social hierarchy, and condemned conversation about race or diversity efforts or promoted removing this content from these seasons and retaining old narratives. For instance, in showing discontent with the racial discourse and narratives, a *Big Brother* audience member stated:

> Just like the BS of black parents have to have a "special" talk on how to deal with police, white parents and every ethnicity have the same talk OR Black kids aren't listening. The fact that you think color has anything to do with anything is your racial bias, racism, and white privilege. It's a scam brought on by the rich to have me and you fighting all the time.

This comment is not only insensitive and undermines racial issues and the injustices endured by Black people but advocates disregarding conversations that address these issues, while asserting the world is a color-blind society.

Next, in support of UGT, many of these excerpts hint that some viewers watch *Big Brother* and *Survivor* for its entertainment value and to escape, or seek relief or relaxation (i.e., to gratify tension-free needs). Most importantly, some viewers make vividly clear that they do not seek to gratify cognitive needs, in particular, to be educated or become knowledgeable about race, diversity and inclusion. In fact, many viewers stated they believed such knowledge has been largely politicized. Viewers also clarified that they did not seek to gratify affective needs, or more explicitly, to experience emotional empathy from learning of POC player's experiences and challenges facing systemic racism. For example, a *Survivor* audience member revealed:

44 Part 1: Reality Television

Whenever something doesn't go your way, you just pull the race card, so everyone will have sympathy for you. You want to victimize yourself and pretend like it's impossible for people of color to win. See what I mean, I watch TV as an escape from life and actual reality. Bringing in race and genders and what-not is just exhausting. Keep it as a game show.

Another *Survivor* audience member expressed the same sentiment, stating "for decades people knew you did not bring religion or politics into entertainment because you would end up offending a portion of the audience." People look to entertainment to escape not to be lectured. Likewise, a *Big Brother* audience member revealed "this was never talked about even just a few years ago because politics didn't infest everything. I would rather have a cast that is very smart and fights for their lives than a diverse cast that is boring." These revelations augment reception theory research which explains that people with cultural identities and beliefs that align with hegemonic norms often willingly accept dominant media messages (Martin, 2007).

Negative Receptions: The Backlash

Excerpts from the thousands of social media equally revealed that media messages on *Big Brother*, season 23, and *Survivor*, season 41, were surprising to viewers and were unwelcomed. Because viewers became accustomed to the previous seasons and their dominant-hegemonic content, viewers developed certain expectations. However, CBS's integration of diversity narratives deviated from viewers' expectations, and therefore, some viewers did not perceive these seasons to be gratifying. These revelations augment research findings on UGT which explain that standards for meeting media expectations are determined by viewers' own subjective perceptions of value (Zhao, 2014). For example, a *Big Brother* audience member explained:

Okay, good for them, very happy the mission was accomplished and the history of big brother has forever been changed BUT can we please go back to the lying, manipulating, backstabbing big brother that we all fell in love with next season??? Idc what nationality or race the contestants are as long as they are awful human beings to each other on the show!!!

Likewise, a *Survivor* audience member stated, "CBS and Probst have ruined a tradition by not only allowing politics, critical race theory, alternative lifestyles and just plain insane thoughts to be the show's new norm but not only allowing but pushing it to the forefront." These excerpts support the reception theory research which explains that viewers tend to be more receptive to media when content produced aligns with their own sociocultural perspectives and values (Martin, 2007; Morley, 1992).

Canceling CBS: Too Woke for Reality TV

Social media excerpts also show that many viewers' overall negative reception of *Big Brother*, season 23, and *Survivor*, season 41, led to the viewers' desire to engage in cancel culture. Viewers expressed dissatisfaction with CBS's diversity related changes. Moreover, some viewers were explicit in expressing that CBS failed to gratify their needs and meet their expectations to such a level that they vowed to discontinue watching *Big Brother* and *Survivor* in the future, not just during the seasons discussed. Some even discussed canceling CBS altogether. For example, a *Big Brother* audience member stated

"I'm a super fan and this is the worst season ever. Race agenda." Agreeably, another audience member voiced similar disdain for *Survivor*, stating, "we always record the show to watch due to work schedules and we fast forwarded through all of them. Both choices at tribal told us how unqualified these survivors are. Count us as part of the million lost viewers." These statements tend to show that even viewers once loyal and devoted to watching these shows were highly enraged about CBS's new direction.

The Evidence: Social Media Excerpts

Table 1 and 2 include all social media posts, with most being posted during the airing of these shows from July 2021 to March 2022. Social media posts were gathered from on CBS's Facebook (CBS Survivor, 2021; CBS Big Brother, 2021a, 2021b, 2021c, 2021d), and popularized YouTube videos (Sci All, 2021; The Russell Hantz Show, 2021; Totally Tanya Vlogs, 2021). All demonstrate negative receptions.

These social media pages and videos were selected due to the volume of attention and interaction from viewers they accumulated, as evidenced by the amount of posts, shares, mentions in other articles or websites, and comments from viewers. In sum, the attention and interaction received in response to these pages and videos was greater than what was received elsewhere. Additionally, negative receptions were focused on because the purpose of this essay is to focus on negative backlash and resulting cancel culture in response to *Big Brother*, season 23, and *Survivor*, season 41, rather than all and any type of reception to these seasons.

Based on rhetoric, column 1 identifies whether each post illustrates that the viewer is dominant-hegemonic, their motivation (or lack of motivation) for consumption, and or whether each post reflects engagement in cancel culture. Sometimes posts demonstrate one of these factors or receptions. However, rhetoric showed that factors or receptions often overlapped.

The categorizations or codes (i.e., dominant-hegemonic, motivation, and cancel culture) were developed through an iterative analysis. More specifically, I used findings and explanations from Reception Theory and UGT to interpret social media posts and subsequently assign a category (Bowen, 2006). I adopted this method because I conducted this research alone and therefore could not compare my interpretations of each post with another researcher to achieve similarity or intercoder reliability. Because iterative analysis requires making interpretations based on explanations grounded in sound research findings and evidence (Bowen, 2006), this is a trusted methodology that is commonly used.

Table 1. *Big Brother* Posts (Dominant-hegemonic Viewers, Motivations, Cancel Culture)

Viewer, Motivation, Cancel Culture	Example Post/Excerpt
Dominant-hegemonic Cancel Culture	Another CBS show with this blatant racism. This show is done. This woke nonsense is unwatchable. The producers and the network set this all up just like they did on BB. Time to move on. R.I.P.

46   Part 1: Reality Television

Viewer, Motivation, Cancel Culture	Example Post/Excerpt
Dominant-hegemonic Anti-cognitive Cancel Culture	I'll NEVER watch it again. I have better things to do than get more politics pushed on me.
Dominant-hegemonic Cancel Culture	I'm a super fan and this is the worst season ever. Race agenda. I was looking forward to BB23 but I can't even watch it.
Cancel Culture	I hope CBS ratings go down because of this nonsense.
Dominant-hegemonic Cancel Culture	Every single genre of entertainment is dealing with this shamelessly hypocritical and bigoted nonsense. And every aspect of society is dealing with the same, which is why more and more need to boycott all of these industries.
Dominant-hegemonic Cancel Culture	They should send Big Brother to BET television.
Dominant-hegemonic Anti-affective Anti-cognitive	Whenever something doesn't go your way, you just pull the race card, so everyone will have sympathy for you. You want to victimize yourself and pretend like it's impossible for people of color to win. See what I mean, this was never talked about even just a few years ago in BB, because politics didn't infest everything. I would rather have a cast that is very smart and fights for their lives in BB, then a diverse cast that is boring and only one alliance rules the house. The content of the contestants character is more important than race, which is a principle conceptionalized by MLK.
Dominant-hegemonic	It was their celebration of their accomplishment that has everyone upset. Have you ever once seen a white group bring up anything like that? NO ... and God help us all if they ever would.
Dominant-hegemonic Tension free needs Anti-affective	Okay, good for them, very happy the mission was accomplished and the history of big brother has forever been changed BUT can we please go back to the lying, manipulating, backstabbing big brother that we all fell in love with next season??? Idc what nationality or race the contestants are as long as they are awful human beings to each other on the show!!!
Dominant-hegemonic Cancel Culture	Yup just hoping this was an off season because of agenda, been a fan since day one, but this year I just read the spoilers mostly. Not good for sponsors.
Dominant-hegemonic Anti-affective	Everyone faces that ... no matter what color you are. Just like the high school clicks ... jocks look for jocks, stoners look for stoners and hippies ... the nerds with the nerds.... It's always been that way no matter who you are. Just like the BS of black parents have to have a "special" talk on how to deal with police ... white parents and every ethnicity have the same talk.... OR.... Black kids aren't listening.... The fact that you think color has anything to do with anything is your racial bias ... racism and white privilege. It's a scam brought on by rich dems to have me and you fighting all the time.

Viewer, Motivation, Cancel Culture	Example Post/Excerpt
Dominant-hegemonic Tension free needs	One of the biggest problems in the world is we care more about making history than we do about just playing the game. If everything has to be about making history or breaking barriers or pushing our beliefs on everyone else we Will always have turmoil.
Dominant-hegemonic Cancel Culture	Big big racisme !!!!! I hate that et i stop to look this emission in 20 years. Too much racisme, the black take control the Big Brother and the production let do this
Dominant-hegemonic Cancel Culture	Not watching this year, need more common people, just can't relate to this cast.
Dominant-hegemonic Tension free needs	I don't care to watch to the end. .. this season sucks, I don't need this racial tension on one of my favorite tv show…
Dominant-hegemonic Anti-cognitive	they have ruined a good show where people just competed against people. I never even thought of rates being an issue on the show until they brought up but they perceive as past racism that none of us ever saw.
Dominant-hegemonic Tension free needs	Well unfortunately I have to turn off BB I can't stand by and watch a show that I loved since season one turn into a race war. You have done this purposely and it sickens me…. This isn't about outwit, out sneak, out play other players it's just about race. Not the show I loved. Goodbye BB you will not be on my tv tonight or ever. Do better.

Table 2. *Survivor* Posts (Dominant-hegemonic Viewers, Motivations, Cancel Culture)

Viewer, Motivation, Cancel Culture	Example Post/Excerpt
Dominant-hegemonic Anti-affective needs	I couldn't listen to all the BS talk I'm sorry. Black culture. Keep together. Brotherhood…. Can we drop this vulnerable Crap out and go back to how it used to be ?? A GAME WITHOUT AN AGENDA ??
Dominant-hegemonic Anti-cognitive needs Cancel Culture	this season was our last. We have watched every season … but this was the end of our tradition. CBS and Probst have ruined a tradition by not only allowing politics, critical race theory, alternative life styles and just plain insane thoughts to be the shows new norm but not only allowing but pushing it to the forefront. After 21 years we say goodbye Survivor!
Dominant-hegemonic Anti-cognitive needs	>says we shouldnt focus on race, like MLK said we should>You say this is why we need to have these conversations. Naw, how much melanin someone has is irrelevant to character, attitude, game play. Its literally not needed.

48   Part 1: Reality Television

Viewer, Motivation, Cancel Culture	Example Post/Excerpt
Dominant-hegemonic *Cancel culture*	Instead we got a preachy dose of woke garbage that doesn't even feel like the game…. This mess was just pitiful and I hope it fails miserably.
Dominant-hegemonic *Anti-affective needs* *Tension free needs*	Agreed. I'm all for a good game. Outwit, Outlast and Outplay the best Wins the prize. Pretty simple but when we have to stop and all bow our heads for a long stand up and now you are self nominated as the representative of your entire culture and or race I'm not sure where this applies to the game. When people like this and the viewers who are on board with this type of change to the game do they play games at home with friends where they stop the game to completely talk about the difference and challenges and struggles in different Races? … Will a blind side not be allowed or will we stop the show to draw a parallel to reality so we can all just think about that … but Survivor is not real life, it's a game. Maybe the TV show game has changed to part time education and so be it, but sometimes I just tuned in to see if I could have Survived on the tv show GAME….
Dominant-hegemonic *Anti-affective needs* *Tension free needs*	This show has turned from a very entertaining one to a racist one and everyone is getting sick and tired of it. Enough is enough. When are people of color going to realize that we are all people with color because the last time I checked WHITE is a color too or have whites turned into ghosts and don't exist anymore???
Tension free needs	… They've over engineered it with gimmicks and lost what is entertaining about the show. Now people will conflate diversity and inclusion with bad entertainment.
Anti-cognitive needs *Tension free needs*	I had to fast forward it. I feel like it's forced into everything we see now a days. Can't I just watch survivor and relax. Why does everything have to do with race. We're all human beings here if you want to stop the divide stop dividing us !
Anti-cognitive needs *Tension free needs* *Cancel culture*	now, I'd literally rather watch the news at this point. I watch TV as an escape from life & actual reality. Bringing in race & genders and what-not is just exhausting. Keep it as a game show.
Anti-affective needs	It's not uncomfortable it's boring. In good ole USA everyone can go after that brass ring. There's nothing stopping you! My neighborhood is over half black and no one complains. We walk into each other houses borrow coffee sugar and stamps. We even share BBQ … so get out of here!
Dominant-hegemonic *Anti-affective needs* *Anti-cognitive needs* *Cancel Culture*	they purposefully picked these players based on woke culture criteria alone, and that nobody nobody nobody wants to watch or cares about their woke home lives montages. We always record the show to watch due to work schedules and we fast forwarded through all of them. Both choices at tribal told us how unqualified these survivors are to be there. Count us as part of million lost viewers.

Viewer, Motivation, Cancel Culture	Example Post/Excerpt
Dominant-hegemonic Tension free needs	For decades people knew you did not bring religion or politics into entertainment because you would end up offending a portion of the audience. People look to entertainment to escape not to be lectured.
Dominant-hegemonic Tension free needs	Just check out their programming and politics permeates their shows. It's everywhere from Hawaii 5–0 to Big Brother. You're right. All we want is to close the curtains on the world at night and relax with some tv. But we have to get politics and indoctrination shoved down our throats like some goose being force fed for foie gras.
Dominant-hegemonic Tension free needs Cancel culture	Racism, ethnocentrism, cultural bias, gender supremacy or the like, shouldn't be a part of a family show, especially now, when it's such a volatile topic. To me, Survivor was one of those shows that bonded people rooting for a particular contestant, not because of race, sexual orientation, financial status, ethnicity, looks, mental abilities, etc. Now, it just divides…. No fun watching it, unless you support that frame of mind, … Watching Survivor this season has been a sad disappointment. It doesn't help me relax and escape into the la-la land of reality television where I rooted for my favorite, not knowing if he/she'd be the next to go. If so, then, I would root for the next in line. Dislike most of the cast, dislike Jeff's grandiose stance, dislike the idols and the looooong annoying councils, etc. I started watching Survivor from its beginning. In the last 8 years it's has been the only program I watch on tv. Not sure if I'll be watching my favorite program, anymore
Anti-cognitive needs Tension free needs	Never ever missed an episode. Now I wonder why I'm bothering. I don't need a lesson on race relations or civics when I just want to be entertained. How silly and ridiculous this has become.
Tension free needs	… This is the worst SURVIVOR ever. I watch this show for entertainment. It no longer is.
Dominant-hegemonic Cancel culture	All this has made me sick to my stomach. It's really a shame what survivor has become. This season has what seems to be a very solid cast, but wokeness is a cancer that does way more harm than good and I refuse to support it. These people are in a cult, brainwashed into thinking that they're doing good for the world. It's sick.

Section 5: Best Practices to Mitigate Cancel Culture Against CBS

As demonstrated, social media posts may illustrate many viewers' discontentment, and at times, utter fury in response to the latest *Big Brother* and *Survivor* seasons. Research exploring diversity and crisis communication campaigns indicates the best way CBS can engage in reputational repair while still furthering its diversity initiatives is through communicating in ways that are relatable and sincere, being prepared to confront and work through conflict, and by clearly defining its position and role to viewers (Wei & Bunjun, 2020; Veil & Waymer, 2021). This means media messages must be personalized for CBS viewers and diversity initiatives should not be perceived as a mere quick fix (Wei & Bunjun, 2020).

CBS might achieve such communication by editing successive seasons in ways that show conversations and issues of diversity and race unfolding more naturally, rather than dramatizing or sensationalizing them. When brands seemingly engage in diversity initiatives for strategy (e.g., for ratings), viewers do not believe these messages (Wei & Bunjun, 2020). In a like manner, race is often considered the "elephant in the room" and it is inevitable that effort to address race will lead to conflict, but the subject must not be avoided and highlighting it as a niche or seasonal topic is equally harmful because it further de-normalizes these necessary conversations (Phillips et al., 2014). Thus, CBS must not concede in its efforts despite tension, rather finding ways to make diversity and race commonplace will be most effective (Wei & Bunjun, 2020). Finally, CBS should spread further awareness of its initiative and partnership with the NAACP. Social media posts indicated most viewers did not know about this initiative. When brands publicly champion the historically marginalized and underrepresented communities whom they claim to advocate for, they share the burden with these communities which may lessen criticism of these individuals and further public understanding of the brand's related initiatives (Veil & Waymer, 2021).

Other TV networks can also learn from these best practices and CBS's recent diversity efforts by first and foremost assessing their current practices to determine if they communicate a clear and permanent commitment to diversity and inclusion. If history has taught us anything, it is that it will repeat itself unless deliberately examined and subsequently interrupted. Thus, although some viewers may initially be uncomfortable with TV networks engaging in change, sincere efforts to publicly denounce and dismantle non-inclusive practices is a process that can be achieved, when done consistently and openly, and in a way that relates to viewers.

REFERENCES

Apple, K.J., & Beers, M.J. (2007). The power of the situation. In R.J. Gerrig (Eds.), *The psychology of survivor: Leading psychologists take an unauthorized look at the most elaborate psychological experiment ever conducted ... Survivor!* (pp. 47–56). BenBella.
Bell-Jordan, K.E. (2008). Black. White. And a survivor of the real world: Constructions of race on reality TV. *Critical Studies in Media Communication, 25*(4), 353–372. https://doi.org/10.1080/15295030802327725.
Bowen, G.A. (2006). Grounded theory and sensitizing concepts. *International Journal of Qualitative Methods, 5*(3), 12–23. http://dx.doi.org/10.4135/9781526421036.
Boyd, J. (23, December 2021). All I want for Christmas is an un-woke 'Survivor' season. *The Federalist.* https://thefederalist.com/2021/12/23/all-i-want-for-christmas-is-an-un-woke-survivor-season/.
Braxton, G. (2020, November 10). On reality tv shows like 'Big Brother' and 'The Bachelor,' race becomes impossible to ignore. *Chicago Tribune.* https://www.chicagotribune.com/entertainment/tv/ct-ent-race-reality-tv-1112-20201110-flugbogvnfe77odsq7bl56rffa-story.html.
Braxton, G. (2021, August 19). A 'Big Brother' alliance could make history. Not everyone is thrilled. *Los Angeles Times.* https://www.latimes.com/entertainment-arts/tv/story/2021-08-19/big-brother-23-cast-the-cookout.
Bresnahan, M.J., & Lee, C. (2011). Activating racial stereotypes on Survivor: Cook Islands. *The Howard Journal of Communications, 22*(1), 64–82. DOI:10.1080/10646175.2011.546746.
Brizzee, J. (21 July 2021). *Is Big Brother's racial equity hurting reality tv? Houseguests form all Black alliance in woke attempt to make history.* California Globe. https://californiaglobe.com/hollywood/is-big-brothers-racial-equity-hurting-reality-tv/.

Butcher, J., & Gonzalez, M. (2020). Critical race theory, the new intolerance, and its grip on America. *Heritage Foundation Backgrounder, 3567*, 2020–12. https://www.heritage.org/civil-rights/report/critical-race-theory-the-new-intolerance-and-its-grip-america.
CBS. (n.d.). *About us.* https://www.cbs.com/shows/survivor/about/.
CBS Big Brother. (2021, August 15). *Let's hear it America! who do you think is playing the best game so far and why? tell us your thoughts!* [Photo]. Facebook. https://www.facebook.com/BigBrother/photos/10158974335894473
CBS Big Brother. (2021, September 9). *We want to hear your predictions for tonight's double eviction!* [Photo]. Facebook. https://www.facebook.com/BigBrother/photos/10159016821154473
CBS Big Brother. (2021, September 10). *Tiffany's grand jury entrance* [Video]. Facebook. https://www.facebook.com/watch/?v=235343648553871
CBS Big Brother. (2021, September 24). *The final 6 houseguests* [Video]. Facebook. https://www.facebook.com/watch/?v=4679077968810596.
CBS Survivor. (2021, December 9). *Vulnerable conversations* [Video]. Facebook. https://www.facebook.com/Survivor/videos/491207975528265.
Corey, D.H., & Shivers, K. (2016). *Shot in the foot: Why media diversity starts with rejecting neoliberalism* [Undergraduate manuscript]. Department of Marketing and Journalism & Media Studies, Rutgers University.
Cox, D., Navarro-Rivera, J., & Jones, R.P. (2016). Race, religion, and political affiliation of Americans' core social networks public religion research institute. *Public Religion Research Institute*. Retrieved April 24, 2022, from https://www.prri.org/research/poll-race-religion-politics-americans-social-networks/.
Dehnart, A. (2016, October 19). On Survivor, early votes against people of color are increasing. *Reality Blurred*. https://www.realityblurred.com/realitytv/2016/10/survivor-racial-bias-early-votes/.
Dehnart, A. (2021, December 8). How responsible is *Survivor* for its fans' racism? *Reality Blurred*. https://www.realityblurred.com/realitytv/2021/12/survivor-41-racist-fan-response/.
Drew, E.M. (2011). Pretending to be "postracial": The spectacularization of race in reality TV's *Survivor*. *Television & New Media, 12*(4), 326–346. DOI: 10.1177/1527476410385474.
Espada, M. (2021, September 30). How Big Brother finally got its first Black winner after more than 20 years on the air. *Time*. https://time.com/6103015/big-brother-first-black-winner/.
Falconer, S. (2020, August 31). Survivor's race problem: How the odds are stacked against BIPOC players. *Sean Falconer*. https://thefalc.com/2020/08/survivors-race-problem-how-the-odds-are-stacked-against-bipoc-players/.
Fox, R. (2018). *Inside reality TV: producing race, gender, and sexuality on Big Brother*. Routledge.
Fox, R. (2013, February 21). "You are not allowed to talk about production": Narratization on (and off) the set of CBS's *Big Brother*. *Critical Studies in Media Communication, 30*(3), 189–208. https://doi.org/10.1080/15295036.2012.755051.
Grodner, A., & Meehan, R. (Executive Producer). (2000–2022). *Big Brother* [TV Series]. CBS.
Hall, S. (1973). *Encoding and decoding the TV message*. CCCS Mimeo.
Handfield, C.N. (2012). *How do reality television genres relate to collectivistic vs. individualistic values among light and heavy reality television viewers* [Doctoral dissertation, Florida International University]. FIU College of Communication, Architecture + The Arts.
Hauser, C. (11 November 2020). 'Survivor' and other reality shows will feature more diverse casts, CBS says. *The New York Times*. https://www.nytimes.com/2020/11/11/business/media/cbsreality-tv-diversity.html.
Herzog, H. (1944). What do we really know about day-time serial listeners? In P.F. Lazarsfeld and F.N. Stanton (Eds.), *Radio research 1942–1943*. Duel, Sloan and Pearce.
Iannucci, R. (2019, August 8). Big Brother season 21 evictee apologizes for derogatory comments: 'if I could take them back, I would.' TVLine. https://tvline.com/2019/08/08/big-brotherrecap-jack-matthews-evicted-racist-comments-apology-video/.
Karlan, D. (2017). Survivor: Three principles of economics lessons as taught by a reality television show. *The Journal of Economic Education, 48*(3), 224–228.
Katz, E., Blumler, J.G., & Gurevitch, M. (1973). Uses and gratifications research. *The Public Opinion Quarterly, 37*(4), 509–523. https://www.jstor.org/stable/2747854.
Kwan, S., & Trautner, M.N. (2009). Beauty work: Individual and institutional rewards, the reproduction of gender, and questions of agency. *Sociology Compass, 3*(1), 49–71. DOI: 10.1111/j.1751-9020.2008.00179.x.
Low, M., & Forsey, M. (2012). Situating meaning: Reception theory and north American perceptions of Australia. In *2012 Australian Sociological Association Conference: Emerging and Enduring Inequalities* (pp. 1–8). The Australian Sociological Association.
Maiorescu-Murphy, R.D. (2022). Business-centered versus socially responsible corporate diversity communication. An assessment of stakeholder (dis)agreement on twitter. *Public Relations Review, 48*(1), 102138. https://doi.org/10.1016/j.pubrev.2021.102138.
Martin, J. (2007). Audiences and reception theory. *Sociology Made Simple*. https://www.sociologymadesimple.com/papers/.

McGuire, W.J. (1974). Psychological motives and communication gratification. In J.G. Blumler and E. Katz (Eds.), *The uses of mass communications*. Sage.

Morley, D. (1992). *Television, audiences and cultural studies*. Routledge.

Park, J.H. (2009). The uncomfortable encounter between an urban Black and a rural White: The ideological implications of racial conflict on MTV's The Real World. *Journal of Communication, 59*(1), 152–171. doi:10.1111/j.1460-2466.2008.01409.x.

Peers, M. (2019, October 6). *Survivor: 5 season themes we loved (& 5 we hope to never see again)*. ScreenRant. https://screenrant.com/survivor-best-worst-season-themes/.

Perrett, C. (2021, September 29). *A Black contestant will win 'Big Brother' for the first time because the show finally faced the 'monster that racism festered in,' a former contestant said*. Insider. https://www.insider.com/all-black-alliance-the-cookout-dominated-big-brother-23-2021-9.

Phillips, K.W., Medin, D., Lee, C.D., Bang, M., Bishop, S., & Lee, D.N. (2014). How diversity works. *Scientific American, 311*(4), 42–47.

Pittman, J. (2020, July 31). *Survivor and the problem with the first vote*. True Dork Times. https://www.truedorktimes.com/s40/recaps/bipoc-stats.htm.

Probst, J. (Executive Producer). (2000–2022). *Survivor* [TV Series]. CBS.

Quail, C. (2011). Nerds, geeks, and the hip/square dialectic in contemporary television. *Television & New Media, 12*(5), 460–482. DOI: 10.1177/1527476410385476. http://tvnm.sagepub.com.

Ramos, D.R. (2020, July 15). NAACP and CBS enter multi-year partnership to develop diverse and inclusive content. *Deadline Hollywood*. https://deadline.com/2020/07/naacp-cbs-television-studios-deal-diversity-inclusion-representation-1202985862/.

Roberts, R.J. (2018). *Temporarily machiavellian: Performing the self on "Survivor"* (Publication No. 166501) [Undergraduate research scholar's thesis, Texas A&M University]. Texas A&M University Libraries. OAKTrust.

Ross, D. (2021, January 29). Survivor quarantine questionnaire: Phillip Sheppard on being 'traumatized' by his experience. *Entertainment Weekly*. https://www.newsbreak.com/news/2154130691222/survivor-quarantine-questionnaire phillip-sheppard-on-being-traumatized-by-his-experience.

The Russell Hantz Show. (2021, September 28). *The new WOKE survivor! I'm so upset with Jeff!!I told you this was going to happen!!!* [Video]. YouTube. https://www.youtube.com/watch?v=w93SY-0d9ms.

Schaffner, B.F. (2020). *The acceptance and expression of prejudice during the Trump era*. Cambridge University Press.

Sci All. (2021, July 28). *Big Brother 23 diversity cast = Most racist season ever + BB fans ready to slur Xavier + BB19 Cody* [Video]. YouTube. https://www.youtube.com/watch?v=dz5JixfYadw.

Timmermans, M. (2012). *Gender in reality television: A semiotic analysis of masculinity and femininity in the survivor franchise* (Publication No. 920707-0146) [Master's thesis, Stockholm University]. DiVA.

Totally Tanya Vlogs. [Username] (2021, August 21) *BB23: Racism in the house have many fans upset. the cookout alliance on shaky ground* [Video]. YouTube. https://www.youtube.com/watch?v=W746r0d2NWk.

U.S. Commission on Civil Rights. (1977). *Window dressing on the set: Women and minorities in television*. U.S. Government Printing Office.

Veil, S.R., & Waymer, D. (2021). Crisis narrative and the paradox of erasure: Making room for dialectic tension in a cancel culture. *Public Relations Review, 47*(3), 102046. https://www.sciencedirect.com/science/article/abs/pii/S0363811121000382?via%3Dihub.

Wei, M.L. & Bunjun, B. (2020). "We are not the shoes of White supremacists": A critical race perspective of consumer responses to brand attempts at countering racist associations. *Journal of Marketing Management, 36*(13–14), 1252–1279. https://doi.org/10.1080/0267257X.2020.1806907.

"You don't work for me anymore"
Race, Cancel Culture, and Vanderpump Rules
Camille S. Alexander

In December 2020, several cast members from the hit reality series, *Vanderpump Rules* (*VR*) (2013–), were terminated from the show for placing racially problematic or overtly racist posts on social media. However, these terminations do not indicate that the show production team was suddenly invested in taking social responsibility. Instead, the dismissals are manifestations of their fear that audiences might object to *VR* and Bravo employing racist cast members. To mitigate any possible fallout, the network and the show publicly canceled the offending cast members by terminating their contracts. Cast members Stassi Schroeder and Kristen Doute were the first high profile contract terminations, and their dismissals were a direct result of their use of social media to racially profile a former cast member. This essay will analyze how *VR* has consistently avoided race by marginalizing or excluding minorities, much like other Bravo shows and other Hollywood productions.

Background on Schroeder, Doute, and Stowers

To better understand the showrunners decision concerning Schroeder and Doute, background on their social media dealings and on-screen portrayals of Stowers will help. To start, Schroeder and Doute first attempted to report former *VR* cast member Faith Stowers to the police for a crime she did not commit. Stowers, who was a recurring cast member in Season 4 (S4), admitted to engaging in a consensual, brief, sexual relationship with another cast member, Jax Taylor. Stowers, an African American woman, faced immediate backlash from online fans for the onscreen affair with Taylor, who is White, male, and in a long-term relationship with another cast member, Brittany Cartwright.

While Stowers's and Taylor's sexual relationship was problematic on several levels, they were not criminal. Yet, Schroeder and Doute, after failing to have Stowers arrested, resorted to posting harassing messages to social media, encouraging their substantial numbers of followers to harass Stowers. These posts, while childish, were also malicious and could have placed Stowers in significant physical danger and at possible legal risk given the racial tensions permeating American society, the criminal justice system, and social media. Schroeder and Doute attempted to call out Stowers—not for committing an actual crime but for daring to disrupt Taylor and Cartwright's White, cisgender, heteronormative relationship. The racial element of Schroeder and Doute's social media attacks is apparent, further complicating their actions and motives while also illustrating a diversity issue problematizing the entire series.

Monk-Turner et al. (2010) found overall that African American representations on television, including roles and their portrayed behaviors, were generally negative (p. 102). While Latinos were rarely portrayed in entertainment media, African Americans were portrayed more often but as the laziest of the characters in a narrative, given the least respect, and were typically provocatively attired (Monk-Turner et al., 2010, p. 102). Although these images may be included for comic relief, they can also lead to viewers' skewed perception of minorities in the real world. Media images have the power to reinforce stereotypes, leading to how the Other is ultimately treated (Monk-Turner et al., 2010, p. 103). The far-reaching social implications of these stereotypes and false perceptions can impact real lives when minorities apply for jobs, housing, or healthcare. It is possible that *VR* and the Bravo network chose to portray Stowers in a negative manner—as the disrupter of a solid relationship between two (White) cast members. In fact, Stowers became Taylor's victim as he misled her into believing that he and Cartwright were no longer a couple. This portion of the narrative was downplayed, and Taylor's deception was de-emphasized. In contrast, Stowers's actions became the focal point of the narrative, and Schroeder and Doute continuously used social media to drag and harass her prior to their terminations.

VR Cast Member Dismissals and Reactions

Schroeder and Doute's terminations trumpeted the first of several from the *VR* cast, leading to several online reactions. Boyens and Brett Caprioni, new S8 cast members, were also dismissed, but these terminations were based on past actions. Both Boyens and Caprioni were terminated for posting racially offensive comments to social media in their teens—as minors and years before joining the *VR* cast. The timing of the original posts in relation to Boyens's and Caprioni's appearances on *VR* are problematic, raising questions about the logic supporting the decision to terminate these cast members for events so far removed from their current behavior.

In addition to Schroeder, Doute, Boyens, and Caprioni, Jax Taylor and his wife, Brittany Cartwright, were also discharged from *VR*. Cartwright was likely dismissed to completely sever the show from any further relationship with Taylor, negating the possibility that he could appear on screen even in a minor role. Taylor was let go for a host of reasons, the most pressing being a 2017 post supporting the false narrative promoted by Schroeder and Doute about Stowers on social media. In his post, Taylor goes further, accusing Stowers of being AWOL from the military and wanted by the police for grand theft auto; neither claim was remotely accurate. Taylor has also been caught on camera fabricating information about other cast members, stealing from work, cheating on ex-girlfriends, displaying both transphobia and toxic masculinity, and being physically aggressive and emotionally abusive. When considering the entirety of Taylor's behavior, it is difficult to understand why he remained on the show for eight seasons. The timing of his dismissal, like that of the other terminated cast members in December 2020, raises questions as the terminations appear reactive—like responses to fear rather than proactive choices meant to improve the show or make a positive contribution to public discourses on race in American society. The sudden decision by *VR*'s production team to terminate four historically problematic cast members, in addition to two new cast members, for discriminatory social media posts within six months of the Black Lives Matter (BLM) protests in the summer of 2020 is questionable.

The timing of these dismissals is highly suspect as Bravo, prior to the summer of 2020, rarely focused on racially dynamic casting or hiring racially sensitive or socially conscious cast members. On the contrary, *Real Housewives* franchise cast members Vicki Gunvalson and Ramona Singer have, like many other Bravolebrities, made racist, homophobic, politically obtuse, and/or outright rude comments about anyone differing from them economically, socially, or racially. Additionally, they have been guilty of targeting anyone appearing on their respective shows who holds views differing from their own. In recent years, both the network and executive producer, Andy Cohen, have been castigated for casting solely White housewives to represent cities, like New York, which are demographically diverse. The *VR* firings, which are not entirely unwarranted in some cases, signify knee jerk reactions to the BLM protests while also ignoring the racially motivated social imbalances necessitating them. The root cause of the protests rested on more than 500 years of racial discrimination, manifesting in social, political, and economic disenfranchisement. The immediate tipping points leading to the protests were the unjustified murders of two African Americans within months of each other by police. The execution-like murder of Breonna Taylor (1993–2020) and George Floyd (1973–2020) prompted the BLM protests in the summer of 2020, leading to a social backlash in the form of pseudo-racial equity hyperawareness in U.S. media culture. *VR*, as one of Bravo's most profitable series, was trapped in this wave of faux social consciousness, and the offending cast members were removed from the show and publicly canceled to mitigate any discriminatory fallout for the franchise and the network.

VR *and Cancel Culture*

Though the cast members of *VR* were dismissed, it can be argued that they were canceled, as this next section will explore. Clark (2020) defines canceling as a manifestation of agency exercised when one makes a conscious decision to withdraw attention from a person or thing propagating unethical values, questionable actions or inaction, or offensive speech when "one no longer wishes to grace them with their presence, time, and money" (p. 88). When discussing access to media and having the social capital to use it, there is an "unequal distribution of the power to speak, write, be heard, be seen, and be published" (Thiele, 2021, p. 52). The inequality of power dynamics places canceling firmly in the hands of people who do not necessarily need access to more power over others. Cancel culture is a "mediated process ... limited ... by factors of structural power, time, and access to resources" (Clark, 2020, p. 89). Thus, cancel culture is a process that remains in the hands of the most powerful members of society, leading to questions about its efficacy and egalitarianism as a tool of social justice in societies already troubled by power imbalances.

In the past, cancel culture was as detrimental as it is today—even without the added benefit of social media interventions. Events like the Army–McCarthy hearings in the 1950s led to the Red Scare and, subsequently, to the Hollywood blacklist, which placed numerous actors, writers, and other Hollywood employees out of work. These historical incidents demonstrate the power of public shaming, fear, and can be coded as an early instance of cancel culture in the U.S. While there are many parallels between the act of canceling in the past and today, the origins of cancel culture were and are lost. At times, cancel culture can devolve from its initial purpose of accountability, shifting to a public electronic flogging on social media that may cause permanent harm to the offender in the social and economic sphere.

The roots of "accountability practices, including reading, dragging, calling out, in and even canceling, are the creations of Black counterpublics," which Clark (2020) notes are some of the very same "marginalized people" subjected to silencing devices (p. 89). Calling out was originally a social experience isolated to "queer communities of color" that was appropriated by observers from outside of these communities, who then transformed the offending behavior and the person committing this act "into a moral panic" similar to physical harm (Clark, 2020, p. 89). Canceling was initially meant to make certain members of specific, socially marginalized communities accountable for their behavior within those communities. However, Clark (2020) believed that cancel culture has been appropriated by outside elitists—this may include production companies like Bravo, showrunners, journalists, or anyone with the ability to wield power and with a belief in their own moral prerogative over others who they deem less aware or simply too weak to respond and defend themselves (p. 89). To that end, Thiele (2021) observes that "cancel culture is not a new phenomenon" as the need to suppress a person or piece of information has always existed in any given society (p. 53). What is new is using the media for these public, representational floggings. Ross (2019) contends that perhaps the media feeds "the cannibalistic maw of the cancel culture" (para. 17). For the duration of this essay, when referring to cancel culture, I will be using it in the context of a call out, as referenced by Clark.

In the case of *VR*'s dismissed cast members, canceling should have been a call out—an opportunity for the cast members to reflect on their behaviors and possibly make amends and/or restitution to anyone who was victimized by their actions. The argument cannot be made that these young men and women acted appropriately or that they should not be held accountable for their behavior. In fact, the argument could be made that they acted abhorrently and should be held accountable. However, the terminations and public canceling in response to their behavior—particularly in the cases of Boyens and Caprioni—seem extreme. Canceling these *VR* cast members for past racist or insensitive social media posts seems severe for some showrunners and fans. In fact, when the dismissals were announced, Lisa Vanderpump, the show's title character and executive producer, issued multiple statements opposing the decision. Vanderpump believes in second chances, which she demonstrates by rehiring former cast members at her restaurant, like James Kennedy, a *VR* cast member who suffers from alcoholism, and by opening a dog rescue. Yet, Vanderpump's optimistic attitude may not apply to the cast members' recent posts and their possibly damaging consequences—particularly to Stowers, who likely suffered physically and mentally in the aftermath of Schroeder's and Doute's social media posts. Some viewers may judge Vanderpump for allowing the terminations to proceed—particularly in the case of Boyens and Caprioni—but this would be a hasty assumption. Vanderpump was vocal in her support of Boyens and Caprioni during the S8 three-part reunion in June 2020; however, she did reiterate that the posts were inappropriate while also noting that these events occurred in the past and that both men had grown and matured since making those mistakes.

As *VR* fans are aware, cast members are, like every other person, susceptible to human frailties. Their flaws, and the pleasure of watching them played out on the small screen, increase the show's appeal. Audiences essentially watch *VR* to be entertained by a group of 20- and 30-somethings publicly debasing themselves, knowing that they make the same mistakes in private. Suddenly in 2020, the murders of Taylor and Floyd as well as the BLM protests may have transformed some of those same, flawed audiences into a quasi-moral police force, necessitating the offending cast members' immediate terminations. Ross (2019) notes that the internet amplifies call outs, which are "louder and more vicious" in this medium and proliferated by "the 'clicktivist' culture that provides anonymity for awful behavior." Essentially, researchers like Ross (2019) note how armchair moralists use the anonymity of the internet to encourage an electronic feeding frenzy against anyone who does or says anything that these individuals believe to be offensive. Ross (2019) observes that in this "'clicktivist' culture," there is a tendency to view others "as disposable people," leading to violations of their "right to due process." To that end, Bouvier observes that a tweet's "ephemeral nature" may account for the "incivility, aggression and insults" found in posts as social media users may not consider "the consequences and results of what they post, and ... have a shallower level of commitment to what they say" (as cited in Foxman & Wolf, 2013, p. 3). Social media users can type and post without carefully considering the nature or vitriolic tone of their messages, further contributing to the propagation of online cancel culture as well as its sometimes unfortunate outcomes. While many of these netizens believe that they are contributing to a public dialog and engaging in activism through social media use, they may be promoting a social narrative of punishment and eventual banishment for flawed human behavior with their posts—particularly when the poster's race is considered.

In addition, minorities can sometimes be impacted most by online posts. Florini (2014) contends that Black users engage in performances of their identities and Black subjectivities on social media (p. 224). In light of Florini's theory, then the converse can also be considered, indicating that social media can become the space in which users engage in demonstrations of Whiteness. The common theme with the dismissed *VR* cast members who posted racially problematic information to social media is that they were engaged in social activism by issuing call outs—pointing out either an injustice, such as Stowers "criminal" acts, or a glaring flaw—for example, African Americans engaging in questionable behavior. Yet, upon closer examination, their social media posts were actually practices of Whiteness in which their privilege and power afforded them the right to engage in call outs. As mentioned prior, a combination of power, a conviction of one's moral superiority, and a belief that the target is incapable of responding leads to the mainstream social media call out (Clark, 2020, p. 89). In this case, the *VR* cast members' flawed perceptions of people of color as well as their own inclinations towards online harassment and bullying contributed to their decisions to make the original posts. Sometimes, online bullying and call-outs merge to create a harassment campaign rather than acting as a chance to hold someone accountable.

In the wake of the events of the spring and summer of 2020, some of the dismissed cast members' flaws became the untenable reasons for their terminations. Although, during the S8 reunion, some of these issues were addressed—particularly Boyens' and Caprioni's social media posts from their teen years. As Boyens and Caprioni were legally children when they posted racially insensitive comments, Bouvier's (2020) concept applies more to them than to the other dismissed cast members, yet they were the only offenders who were confronted about their actions at the reunion show. In response to an inquiry about the exposure of these posts, Boyens and Caprioni made a few *mea culpas* and generally looked uncomfortable with the public dissemination of this information. While Boyens and Caprioni were placed firmly in the hot seat for a few minutes about their questionable social media posts, none of the other cast members' posts were exposed. Schroeder, Doute, and Taylor are problematic cast members who repeatedly make questionable decisions, and Cartwright is well-known for taking Taylor's side even when he is clearly wrong, yet Boyens and Caprioni were tarred with the same brush when their offenses were committed when they were minors and well before they entered a contract with Bravo.

Bravo responded like many other organizations did in 2020: remove the problems. Yet, this response should not be interpreted as the network making any efforts to "do" the right thing for society or to right past racist wrongs. Rather, the terminations were Bravo's attempt at staunching a possible wound, leading to a financial bleed out that the network could ill afford. The terminations could be viewed as a knee jerk reaction to a social media fallout, which could cost the network money in the form of possible lost viewership. In the aftermath of Covid-19 when so many production and writing teams were forced out of work, Bravo could not risk producing a show that no one would pay to watch, leading to a loss of advertising dollars and possibly ending the show entirely. Although Bravo's response could be attributed to greed, a few executive producers losing their salaries are only some of the components to consider. Ending *VR* would put many people out of work, including the cast members, who are not by any standards wealthy. However, while the financial outcome to many average people working on the *VR* production team and cast was a concern, Bravo's response should not be interpreted as altruistic. By the measure of some critics and fans, Bravo's response to the cast members' social media posts lacked authenticity. If the network was truly concerned, that concern would have been demonstrated earlier during casting.

VR, *Casting, and New Media*

At first glance, one of the most glaring issues with *VR* is that in Los Angeles, which is arguably one of the most diverse cities in the U.S., the main cast is all White with the occasional inclusion of racial minorities in recurring roles. While showrunner Vanderpump employs various racial, ethnic, and queer minorities in her restaurants, these employees are rarely promoted past recurring roles, propelling a "Whites only," cisgender narrative on the show. The racial element to *VR*'s casting practices is not isolated to Bravo shows but extends throughout the entertainment industry and has done so since the industry's inception, occurring largely in boardrooms where major decisions about who is portrayed on screen are made. This "Whites only" casting issue rests with producers and casting directors, who are positioned in the entertainment industry to function in a capacity that offers them the privilege of unconditionally denying certain people employment opportunities (Clark, 2020, p. 89). These stakeholders and decision makers are entirely responsible for the all–White casting practices that continue to haunt the entertainment industry. While multiculturalism has become a catchphrase and practice, finding its way into every aspect of American society from employment to education, the entertainment industry continues to trail its business and instructional counterparts in diversity initiatives. Warner (2016) found a significant effort to "resist multiculturalism" in many feature films and in several television productions, denoting the film and television industries unwillingness to enact substantial measures to "correct the staggering lack of diversity in their labor force" (p. 175).

Bravo's troubling history of uniformly casting Whites to its shows is glaring. The Beverly Hills and NYC iterations of the *Real Housewives* franchise's previous all–White casting displays a marked effort to solely depict Whites as wealthy, elite Americans. The casting of women of color, such as Joyce Giraud de Ohoven in Beverly Hills and Eboni K. Williams in NYC, can be interpreted as reactive measures aimed at preventing the network and its shows from falling prey to cancel culture rather than as authentic efforts to add more dimension to either show. A perusal of both Giraud's and Williams's experiences on their respective shows indicates that, in maintaining all–White casting on many *Real Housewives* shows, Bravo did women of color a disservice as both women were frequently racially profiled and victimized by other cast members. Specifically, cast member Brandi Glanville made offensive comments about Black people not being able to swim to explain why Giraud would not get into a pool on camera. Glanville later stated that she has Black friends onscreen, which was aimed at excusing her appalling behavior. Williams experienced similar issues in NYC—specifically with longtime cast member, Ramona Singer. Singer, who is known for making insulting and/or obtuse comments on the show and on social media, reportedly made a racially offensive comment about having Black people on the show when Williams was asked to leave the home of Luann de Lesseps. While Singer was cleared of all wrongdoing in this incident, a perusal of old and new episodes suggests that she is neither racially egalitarian nor self-aware. In fact, in S14, E14 and E15, Singer made a series of dismissive and/or obtuse comments in addition to behaving disrespectfully at a Shabbat dinner, offending the Jewish and African American community in the process. Yet, Singer is still employed by Bravo while a group of young cast members, who are neither wealthy nor powerful, were terminated.

On the surface, cancel culture seems like a reasonable response to problematic behavior, but as the case study of *VR* highlights, it can lead to negative outcomes for those who are least powerful. To that end, Ross (2019) notes that "one of the best ways to make a point is to ignore someone begging for attention." Reality stars choose an onscreen career that publicizes their personal lives most likely because it suits their personalities, which probably veer more towards the public than the private, and because they intend to segue these television appearances into advancing their careers. A critical part of the job is to maintain a social media persona; therefore "reality stars are increasingly turning to new media to share details of their 'real lives'" (Arcy, 2018, p. 1). Arcy (2018) notes that "reality stars are unique because their online identity must reflect the 'real' lives they lead on TV," which has the dual benefit of promoting their shows and professional careers (p. 1).

When Bravo terminated Schroeder, Doute, and Taylor for victimizing Stowers, the network acted appropriately because Schroeder, Doute, and Taylor violated that fundamental rule of sharing details about *their* real lives. Instead, they chose to fabricate stories about Stowers, and Schroeder and Doute admitted on social media that they attempted to have Stowers arrested by approaching the police with their false information. Essentially, Schroeder, Doute, and Taylor did not adhere to the basic tenets of transmedia storytelling, which involves creating ongoing narratives across multiple media platforms, allowing the storytellers to perform additional "amplified versions of their private lives" (Arcy, 2018, p. 2). The reproduction and widespread use of transmedia storytelling allows storytellers to create open-ended, continuous narratives using various media sources, revealing "how the television industry is using new media to keep viewers engaged between broadcasts" (Arcy, 2018, p. 2).

Despite the benefits of transmedia storytelling to the network and to cast members, there is another element to this practice that is not necessarily beneficial to the storyteller. Arcy (2018) notes that while new media offers more "freedom and flexibility" in telling stories, media organizations do attempt to control their stars' activities on social media (p. 5). Reality shows and their parent companies encourage their stars to utilize social media, which helps brand the shows, making them more marketable (Arcy, 2018, p. 5). These forays into social media can be quite productive, allowing the stars to publicize the shows while also branding themselves and promoting their personal business endeavors. However, reality stars' use of social media can take an unpleasant turn, leading to problematic behaviors, including engaging in online arguments, bashing other cast members, and occasionally engaging in whipping audiences and netizens alike into acts bordering on the harassment of their target. These negative social media patterns are not solely the fault of reality television stars, who are often encouraged to engage in this behavior. Bravo is guilty of pitting the network's stars against each other to motivate their participation in social media use (Arcy, 2018, p. 5). Yet, there are penalties for straying too far from the network's authorized message, including not renewing contracts for reality stars "who went too far off message" (Cohen as cited in Arcy, 2018, p. 5).

Schroeder, Doute, and Taylor were utilizing transmedia storytelling; sometimes, their posts related glimpses into their personal lives, which were not seen on television; however, they occasionally used social media in a manner that did not present information about their authentic selves. In addition, these three *VR* stars clearly went "off message" by providing false information about a former, marginal cast member whose narrative was no longer remotely relevant to the show, which had long-since moved away from the Taylor-Stower affair narrative and was then focused on Taylor and Cartwright's engagement, wedding, and marriage. Schroeder, Doute, and Taylor did not use social media in a manner consistent with the network's goals of promoting the show; instead, social media was utilized to harass a woman whose only crime was having a sexual encounter with Taylor, who was then dating Cartwright. One might question why Stowers, whose narrative was falsified, and then amplified, by Schroeder, Doute, and Taylor, needed a "storyline" when she was no longer on the show and had been a minor cast member when she was on screen. Yet, knowing that Schroeder, Doute, and Taylor were harassing Stowers, Bravo failed to act for the two years between Schroeder initially discussing her and Doute's actions on her podcast and later reposting this information on Twitter, now known as X.

The network's silence on Stowers' treatment on and off screen is glaring as the corporate stance Bravo previously took in this situation was to leave the resolution of the matter to someone else because Stowers was essentially a nobody—a marginalized person lacking the social capital to fight back or defend herself. In addition, Stowers was no longer employed as a recurring cast member; therefore, defending her was most likely deemed unnecessary in the network's estimation. The issue was not directly faced until Schroeder and Doute used social media in support of BLM in 2020, leading some netizens and supersleuths to further investigate their dedication to social equity. On the one hand, neither Schroeder nor Doute can claim prior support of civil rights in a real and meaningful way. It was not until the summer of 2020 that Schroeder and Doute, like many public figures, decided to post sympathetic messages in support of the BLM protests to their social media pages. Observers might note that it is highly unlikely that Schroeder, Doute, or any other celebrity who is both privileged and far removed from these issues placed these posts on social media out of actual concern but that these posts represented calculated moves to garner some positive publicity—to ride the wave, so to speak, of public awareness and social consciousness. The fact that celebrities, including Schroeder and Doute, are business owners and significantly engaged in branding themselves and their products, should be considered when addressing the timing of the posts and their virtual silence on these critical social matters in the past.

Bravo's response to the public revelation that Schroeder and Doute harassed and racially profiled Stowers while other cast members made racially offensive posts to social media in the past was severe, considering the personal losses the cast members endured as a result of their very public terminations. While the *VR* cast members did fulfill their obligation to the network and the show by engaging in transmedia storytelling and showing support for the BLM protests in the summer of 2020, which was a positive contribution to the narrative at the time, the fact remains that their troubling posts about Stowers appeared online two years prior to their terminations. The timing of the initial posts in relation to the dismissals is problematic, demonstrating that Bravo was neither acting in good faith nor in the interest of social justice. There was another, more self-serving reason for the network's response.

The decision to dismiss the offending cast members cannot be interpreted as Bravo's dedication to social awareness or racial equity. Rather, their behavior only garnered any official response from Bravo because the network was afraid. Bravo seemed to be afraid of facing a very public cancellation, which could lead to a significant loss in advertising dollars and other sources of corporate income. In the wake of the BLM protests, the U.S., as a nation, was forced to face its troubling past of racial discrimination, leading to social, educational, housing, healthcare, and economic inequities. This centuries-long situation is not an issue that can be corrected in one summer or by a tweet. Yet, to do nothing—to say nothing—would have been detrimental to the network's corporate bottom line. Financially, Bravo could not afford to remain silent—particularly with its onscreen history of marginalizing racial, ethnic, and queer minorities in the past while promoting the very people who work tirelessly to silence these groups. Jax Taylor was a *VR* cast member who spent a considerable amount of time silencing and/or harassing the Other on the show and whose behavior Bravo ignored for years.

Taylor, whose behavior and romantic relationships are at the center of the Schroeder-Doute termination narrative, also engaged in using social media to harass Stowers. He most likely posted his fabricated story about Stowers to further distance himself from cheating on his then-girlfriend, Cartwright, with Stowers. Although Schroeder and Doute likely viewed their participation in using social media to harass Stowers as an act justified by their love of their friend Cartwright, Taylor engaged in his social media harassment for self-serving reasons. Regardless of the reasons behind their actions, the outcome was the same. Schroeder, Doute, Taylor, and Cartwright have been banned from *VR*, lost other sources of income, and have been brought to their financial knees in the fallout of their terminations, begging the question of whether losing everything for being an obtuse racist or a habitual liar is the best outcome for these former *VR* cast members.

Schroeder, Doute, and Taylor's social media racism likely led internet's morality police to old posts by Boyens and Caprioni, and, because of ridiculous, mindless mistakes made in the past, these two, new *VR* cast members are now unemployed and likely unemployable for the foreseeable future. If contrasted from Schroeder, Doute, and Taylor's outcomes, dismissing Boyens and Caprioni seems excessive. The network's decision to terminate Boyens and Caprioni also sets a dangerous precedent in employment practices moving forward, indicating that any and everything said online—regardless of when it was posted in relation to the user's employment status—is not only fodder for the morality police gristmill but can be used in making future employment decisions. Dismissing employees for past social media posts could be a logical outcome if, for example, Boyens and Caprioni worked for an organization that directly impacts the lives of others, such as a non-profit or a government, or if their Bravo contracts included a morality clause extending to past behavior. As they were employed on a reality television series that encourages questionable behavior and social media hot takes, it is difficult to understand why these two cast members were canceled simply for being immature, oblivious, and unrestrained, which are traits that can typically persist well into adulthood. The question remains whether continuing to bend to public opinion and audience input, by utilizing cancel culture propagated through social media to resolve racism and other social issues, is the most viable solution.

Conclusion

Previously, Thiele's (2021) "unequal distribution of power" was mentioned (p. 52). When this power imbalance is combined with the ease of accessing social media, the use of cancel culture among *VR* cast members is further problematized. The initial tweets/posts—particularly by Boyens and Caprioni—were quick and thoughtless, but one might argue that, in their situations, the response was equally speedy and insensitive. With Boyens and Caprioni, canceling was used as a form of "public shaming," and it was horizontally enacted "by those who believe they have greater integrity or more sophisticated analyses" of the situation at hand (Ross, 2019). Cancel culture functions on the basic principle of "Shaming people" for when the accusers "woke up," making it an unsuitable solution to holding people accountable (Ross, 2019). Canceling is no longer about holding people accountable for their actions but rather engaging in punishing them in perpetuity for their mistakes, whether those errors in judgment were made in the present or the past. In addition, cancel culture no longer functions as a remediation performed by others who are positioned to objectively judge a situation but has become a form of finger pointing at those who continue to err by those who no longer make the same mistakes.

The act of canceling should be a last-ditch effort—one that is enacted when the offending person refuses to heed the warnings of the call-out. Instead, canceling has become the go-to—the first response to any slip of the tongue, or finger, that a person might commit out of insensitivity or simply because the person lacks the restraint to stop and think. This pattern of enacting social justice, which was never meant for mainstream American society, has morphed into a way of using the media to berate others—forcing them into submission and punishing them indefinitely for occasionally being clueless. Rather than acting as a site for self-reflection and improvement, mainstream canceling offers no room for change, leading one to question its long-term purpose and efficacy.

References

Arcy, J. (2018). The digital money shot: Twitter wars, *The Real Housewives*, and transmedia storytelling. *Celebrity Studies, 9*(4), 487–502.

Bouvier, G. (2020). Racist call-outs and cancel culture on Twitter: The limitations of the platform's ability to define issues of social justice. *Discourse, Context & Media, 38*, 1–11.

Clark, M.D. (2020). DRAG THEM: A brief etymology of so-called 'cancel culture.' *Communications and the Public, 5*(3–4), 88–92.

Florini, S. (2014). Tweets, tweeps, and signifyin': Communication and cultural performance on "Black Twitter." *Television & New Media, 15*(3), 223–237.

Langworthy, B., Stewart G., Vanderpump, L. (Executive Producers). (2013–). *Vanderpump rules* [TV series]. Evolution Media; Bravo!

Monk-Turner, E., Heiserman, M., Johnson, C., Cotton, V., & Jackson, M. (2010). The portrayal of racial minorities on prime time television: A replication of the Mastro and Greenberg study a decade later. *Studies in Popular Culture, 32*(2), 101–114.

Ross, L. (2019, August 17). Call-out culture is toxic. *The New York Times*. www.nytimes.com/2019/08/17/opinion/sunday/cancel-culture-call-out.html.

Thiele, M. (2021). Political correctness and cancel culture—A question of power! *Journalism Research, 4*(1), 50–57.

Warner, K.J. (2016). Strategies for success? Navigating Hollywood's 'postracial' labor practices. In M. Curtain and K. Sanson (Eds.), *Precarious creativity: Global media, local labor* (pp. 172–185). University of California Press.

Just Change the Channel?
Analyzing Bravo's Response to Online Calls for Cancellation

ROSEMARIE JONES

Reality television provides a unique landscape to better understand society's constructions of identities, relationships, and markers of success. Reality television also seeks to involve audience participation and feedback in ways that traditionally scripted television shows do not. For example, shows such as *Dancing with the Stars* and *American Idol* invite viewers at home to vote for their favorite contestants to continue in their competitions. With the growing popularity of social media, network executives have experienced additional, more interactive and public methods of audience feedback that they often take into consideration when making casting and production decisions. Social media, in tandem with the recent "social justice awakening," have necessitated reality television to more deeply consider audience reception in casting and storyline decisions (Parks, 2021).

Bravo, an American television network, has positioned itself as a reality television powerhouse. Originally focused on fine arts and film, over the past two decades the network has developed cultural hallmarks in reality television programming. According to The Nielsen Company, an organization that measures exposure to various audience demographics, the network is rated 12th by adults 18–49 and is the 24th most watched by the same demographic (Schneider, 2021). Additionally, in 2019 Bravo ranked first in primetime for women ages 18–29 and 35–54 in cable, for the third year in a row (NBCUniversal, n.d.). As the network's audience continued to grow, so did the power and number of its stars. Of course, it's difficult to be a true celebrity in the twenty-first century without a robust social media presence, and Bravolebrities, a term used by fans to describe Bravo-based celebrities on the network, have been quick to make their social media presence known. However, Bravolebrities often are not famous before starting on the network, and thus do not have media training before their rise to fame. As a result, their social media presence can be damaging to the carefully curated brands they've developed on television (Hearn, 2011). This damage can come in two main forms: (1) exposure of past behavior online and/or (2) problematic posts and interactions with other accounts. Additionally, cast members may try to "defend" their problematic behavior in real time online.

After the murder of George Floyd in 2020, Bravo began to review its programming and cast members in a new light. The network directly addressed racism as a social problem in a statement on May 31, 2020:

Bravo stands in solidarity with the Black community against systemic racism and oppression experienced every day in America.... We owe it to our Black staff, talent, production partners & viewers to demand change and accountability. To be silent is to be complicit. #BlackLivesMatter [Staff, 2020].

However, there was significant problematic behavior exhibited before 2020 that had been addressed in ranging ways (Dominguez, 2015). The reality shows on the network often leaned into racialized tropes and stereotypes, alienating people of color. Because reality television is located within a racist society, we may logically conclude that notes of racism will clearly be present in media "regardless of how positive a spin is put on representation, the work of white supremacy is already done" (Warner, 2015, p. 140). Yet, 2020 seemed to be a turning point in the Bravo-verse in addressing problematic behavior of cast members, which might have occurred on and/or off screen. Social media accounts calling for the "canceling" of shows and stars seemingly began to influence network decisions in more meaningful ways than previously exhibited.

This essay seeks to explore how Bravo has responded to audience calls for re-casting after exposure and discussion of cast members past alleged racist, sexist, and homophobic acts. Additionally, Bravo community discussions online (e.g., Facebook groups, Instagram posts, and tweets) will be analyzed to better understand calls for cast members and/or shows to be "canceled" due to harmful, problematic behaviors perpetrated by cast members, either before or during their tenures on their respective shows. Upon reviewing recent trends, "cancelable" behaviors include allegedly committing sexual assaults, promoting racist rhetoric online, perpetrating microaggressions against fellow cast members, and sharing misinformation about the Covid-19 pandemic. Because social media allows for cast members to interact with audience members calling for their "cancellations," this essay will analyze the unique multi-directional interactions that Bravolebrities can have in the public eye in an attempt to avoid "cancellation." Finally, this essay will discuss the approaches Bravo has taken to "re-boot" shows in the face of calls for change. Overwhelmingly, these decisions appear symbolic in nature and often actually reinforce existing social, political, and historical social structures regarding race, gender, sexuality, ability, age, and other identity markers. The following discussion will incorporate several case studies regarding Bravo cast members and storylines, ultimately underscoring an intersectional, feminist analysis of how Bravo's audience members provide feedback on social media and the resulting casting and production decisions made by network executives.

Bravo Programming: Online Audience Reactions and Relationships

There has been significant research on the effect of reality television's presence within popular culture (Hearn, 2017; Jahng, 2019). The genre of reality television that Bravo programming often falls into is aspirational, meaning their programs highlight individuals with great wealth and status. Examples of these programs include the various *Real Housewives* franchises. This type of aspirational reality television offers a behind-the-scenes view into the glitz and glamor of wealth, which is often hidden behind private gates and exclusive country clubs. It should be noted that in some Bravo programs (e.g., *Vanderpump Rules* and *Below Deck*) there is another dimension to the aspirational model; these shows contrast the aspirational wealth of some characters to the conditions of the workers serving them. For example, *Below Deck* and its multiple spin-offs, highlight both the parties staying on luxurious mega yachts and those in deck and stew positions working on the yachts.

Bravo's current signature programming is its multiple franchises of *The Real Housewives*. The original franchise, *The Real Housewives of Orange County*, gave way to eleven different series in the United States and multiple international and spin-off series. The shows feature the lives of women (who are not actually bound by a requirement to be housewives), wherein viewers can see "behind the gates" of some of the country's most exclusive and wealthy communities (Breitfeller et al., 2022). With the immense wealth and luxury featured on the shows, viewers may feel an initial distance between themselves and the featured housewives. However, the shows also work to limit that distance and provide "relatable moments" for viewers to feel connections with the cast. The distance between cast and audience is then further reduced through the use of social media. For the purpose of this discussion, three main ways social media operates within the Bravo-verse have been identified: (1) Fans interacting with other fans online, (2) Fans interacting with Bravolebrities, and (3) Influential Bravo-centered social media accounts.

Fans may interact with other fans through a variety of social media mechanisms. Multiple social media platforms, such as X, Facebook, Instagram, and Reddit, offer interaction around shows, casting, production, and updates. While Twitter and Instagram allow for conversations in more one-off formats, Facebook and Reddit offer Bravo fans communities to interact with one another. For example, Facebook groups and Reddit threads devoted specifically to discussion of Bravo-related content offer a space for fans to discuss shows, post memes, and take part in debates. Typically, live-threads are created during a show's initial airing time to discuss fan reactions and create an "imagined community" (Stewart, 2019, p. 352). Additionally, these spaces serve as a site for debate over the potential "cancellation" of Bravolebrities, with fans weighing in on alleged toxic behaviors. Often, these spaces are created by fans and only include fans. This is in contrast to how Bravolebrities operate on social media when interacting with fans.

The second identified use of social media as related to Bravo is when Bravolebrities interact with fans online. Opposed to the section above, this interaction typically takes place on Twitter and Instagram. Bravolebrities may take to their Twitter and Instagram pages to defend themselves during and after episodes and apologize for behaviors. However, not all comments are apologetic; often these spaces serve as sites for cast members to reinforce their behavior and defend their actions. In doing so, they regularly interact with supportive fans, thanking them for their appreciation. They also can engage with critical fans who chastise the cast member's behaviors both on-screen and off. Bravolebrities might defend themselves directly to the posters or use their platform to make Instagram stories and/or full tweet threads in defense of their actions.

Finally, notable Bravo fan accounts exist on social media. These accounts have built masses of followers who tune in to their profiles to see commentary, memes, and original content as reactions to Bravo programming. Often, Bravo fan accounts on social media have parallel podcasts dissecting episodes after they air on television. These fan accounts have a larger presence and more influence online than regular fans. They are often sent screeners of episodes to review for their podcasts before they air and are routinely followed by Bravolebrities on their social media accounts. However, as the accounts criticize the cast members, it is commonplace for the Bravolebrities to block the fan accounts online so that account holders can no longer see their posts. Fan accounts serve as fan representatives in the Bravo-verse, as each fan account has its own views on programs and rankings of housewives. There might also be tension among fan accounts online. It should be noted that fan accounts have been invited to participate in Bravo programming, such as *Watch What Happens Live*, Bravo's own late-night show that centers on its programming and other pop-culture topics. Therefore, it is reasonable to assume that the reactions of fan accounts to cast members' toxic behaviors is considered in determining audience feedback.

Fans interacting within the fan community, Bravolebrities interacting with fans, and fan accounts interacting with Bravolebrities and Bravo itself all have influence in who is called upon to be "canceled." Cast members' reactions to their own behaviors on social media (e.g., apologizing or defending their toxic behaviors) also influence these calls. Fan communities might use Reddit and Facebook spaces to try to convince other fans to call on problematic cast members to be canceled from their respective shows. Fan accounts can have similar influence on fans, but have a greater influence on the network, as they "speak" for their followers online and serve as a litmus test of audience reception and reactions.

The following sections of this essay will work through various case studies of Bravolebrities being canceled and the role social media played in specific circumstances. This is not meant to be an exhaustive list of problematic or toxic Bravo cast members, storylines, and production choices. Rather, it seeks to highlight the variety of overarching themes that seem to be reasons for Bravo to "cancel" their employees.

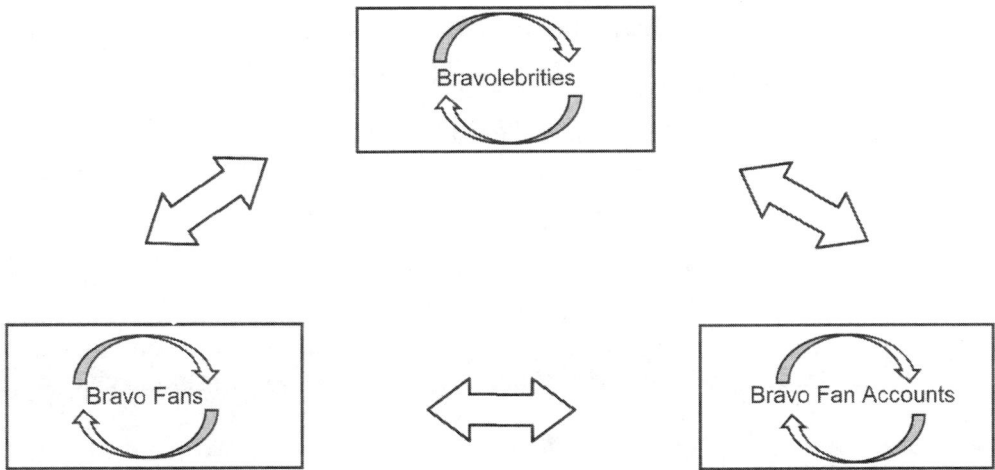

Figure 1. Diagram of Bravo audience relationships.

Additionally, it will highlight how social media might influence these decisions and audience reception to behavior labeled as toxic and/or problematic. Because so many of the problematic behaviors audience members identify are intertwined (e.g., racism, sexism, homophobia, and more), the case studies are categorized together by Bravo's reaction to the behavior and social media exchanges, instead of categorization of the behavior itself. A deeper discussion of the network's reactions, including what it means for diversity and audience reception as a whole, will be covered in the final section.

Reacting to Audience Feedback through Casting Decisions

Though racism existed on Bravo programming well before 2020, after the murder of George Floyd the network made its most notable change in casting in response to cast members' off-screen racist actions and the resulting audience response. Stassi Schroeder and Kristen Doute, two of the centerpieces of *Vanderpump Rules*, which follows the life of servers at Lisa Vanderpump' restaurant, named SUR (Sexy Unique Restaurant), were fired after it surfaced that they called the police to accuse their co-star Faith Stowers of stealing. Stowers explained "that the duo called the police on her after reading a news story about a Black woman committing robberies in the area. Per Stowers, the woman allegedly committing the crimes didn't resemble her, but also happened to be Black" (Desta, 2020). Additionally, two other recently added cast members were fired when their racist tweets resurfaced. In June of 2020, Bravo released a statement that "Bravo and Evolution Media confirmed today that Stassi Schroeder, Kristen Doute, Max Boyens and Brett Caprioni will not be returning to *Vanderpump Rules*" (Aurthur & Wagmeister, 2020). Fans seemed encouraged by the network's actions, tweeting "Bravo finally did the right thing. I never thought I'd see the day" (mainlyraven, 2020) and "Bravo just gave walking papers to Stassi, Kristen, Brett and Max for their racism. 2020 is a cultural reset and I stan #vanderpumprules" (Chenault, 2020). Surveying the Bravo landscape since June of 2020, the network's firing of four cast members after audience calls and negative feedback, empowered audience members to use their power to call for others to be sanctioned. The examples below highlight select cast members, their online interactions, and how audience reception influenced the network's decisions in relation to casting.

There are a few different transgressions that fans seemingly have deemed as "cancelable" behaviors for Bravolebrities. Reality television, a space which some view as an escape from their real-world problems, has not evaded the heightened political tensions brought forward by Donald Trump's "America's first" agenda. Bravo argues that it seeks to show a variety of lifestyles, meaning that a variety of political views might also be represented. However, with both the 2016 and 2020 elections, Bravolebrities began being judged on their political affiliations, in addition to their humor, clothing, relationships, and other status symbols. Certain franchises, such as *The Real Housewives of New York City*, featured the 2016 election and resulting Women's March in the season as a storyline and point of tension between women with conflicting political views. Throughout Bravo programming, multiple housewives and Bravolebrities engaged in political actions online, with Bravo fan accounts taking note. In tandem with their support for the "Make America Great Again" rhetoric and policies, cast members' views on the Covid-19 pandemic were also examined and discussed online. The following two examples discuss circumstances surrounding Kelly Dodd's (*The Real Housewives of Orange County*) and Ramona Singer's (*The Real Housewives of New York City*) political affiliations and personal choices in the pandemic, and the resulting social media interactions with individual fans and Bravo fan accounts.

Kelly Dodd's public political leanings, which she showcased visibly online include criticisms of the Black Lives Matter movement, proliferation of Covid-19 misinformation, and support for Donald Trump, led Bravo fans and fan accounts to call on Bravo to "fire" Dodd in 2020. It is important to note that most housewives who don't return to future seasons are not fired. Rather, their contracts are not renewed. Often, Bravo lets the former cast members make announcements, claiming they are leaving the show of their own volitions because they are "ready to move on." Additionally, in these calls for firings, Andy Cohen, who is often regarded as the face of the network and hosts the pop-culture late show, *Watch What Happens Live*, may also be called on online to step-in and exert what power he has over contracts.

While Dodd, like a substantial number of housewives, has been controversial on her show, her social media interactions caused more significant backlash. Notably, at her bachelorette party, she posted a photo on Instagram wearing a "Drunk Wives Matter" hat, which can be argued belittles the Black Lives Matter Movement. Instagram users commented that in addition to the lack of Covid protocols followed at the 2020 party, the hat was "insensitive." Dodd responded directly to fans online, writing, "[M]y girlfriend bought it for me as a gift. It's a play on words. Some people aren't that smart" (Chung, 2020). Later, Dodd continued her response in an Instagram video, saying, "You know what, all lives matter" and "People that can't get a joke, go f— yourselves" (Chung, 2020). Dodd's spreading of Covid misinformation has also been a contentious topic on her Instagram. In April of 2020, Dodd posted a picture inside of an airplane with her then fiancé Rick Levanthal, a former reporter for Fox News. Fans questioned why she was flying at the beginning of the pandemic, to which she responded in her Instagram comments that COVID was God's way of thinning the herd:

> "Do you know how many people died from the H1N1, the swine flu or SARS?" Dodd continued, writing, "It's 25% get your facts straight you are only hearing numbers not the reality! It's God's way of thinning the herd! If you are vulnerable or compromised stay inside. If you don't protect others by wearings [sic] masks and gloves keep your distance and don't go out if you are ill!! It's common sense!" [Merrett, 2020].

Dodd later apologized in a series of Instagram videos, noting she meant to phrase the question in a philosophical sense. During a promotional tour for *The Real Housewives of Orange County* in December 2020, Andy Cohen asked Dodd about her recent behavior online and interactions with fans on his talk-show *Watch What Happens Live*. Dodd apologized if her words caused harm: "It was a stupid thing for me to say. It was insensitive and I apologize if I hurt or offended anybody, 'cause that wasn't really my intention" (Callahan, 2020). It should be noted that in the Bravo-verse, an apology regarding if someone was hurt or harmed, is often perceived as fake or empty by others on the cast, as it doesn't appear that the person apologizing is recognizing that harm was an outcome of their actions. Cohen noted that fans have reached out to him about Dodd's problematic behavior and she should think before she posts.

This interaction on *Watch What Happens Live with Andy Cohen* serves as a quasi-meeting with "Human Resources" that fans were meant to witness. Andy Cohen, as the essential face of Bravo, wanted fans to see that the network was noting Dodd's behavior as problematic to fans. In other words, fans were supposed to see this interview as Bravo taking Dodd's problematic actions and comments seriously. However, many fans and fan accounts did not think this interaction underscored the harm Dodd caused and could continue to cause while being a public figure supported by Bravo. Fan pages with followers ranging from 10,000 to 40,000 called on Bravo viewers to boycott the upcoming season of *The Real Housewives of Orange County* (Zaragoza, 2020). After the airing of the already filmed season 14, Dodd's contract was not renewed for the next season. After the news became public, Dodd posted a screenshot of a text exchange with another housewife who would not be returning for the new season. In the text, she blamed her for their contracts not being renewed: "This was your fault. We'd still be on the show if you didn't make things so dark and ugly and brought all that political 'woke' BS" and "Your lies about me, calling me a racist and a homophobe were horribly destructive and your phony storylines didn't help either" (Witter, 2021). However, Dodd changed her tone in an interview on SiriusXM's *Jeff Lewis Live*, noting, "Listen, ultimately, I got fired because of myself. I'm the one who got myself fired. And, you know, I'm sorry about that. I feel bad" (Witter, 2021). While fans cannot be certain, it might be speculated that Dodd's response here is an effort to regain Bravo's trust, should an opportunity arise for her to work with the network again.

Similar calls for "cancellation" have been made for other Trump-supporting Bravolebrities. Ramona Singer, an original cast member from *The Real Housewives of New York City*, has faced likewise criticisms from audiences based on her political affiliations and behaviors during the beginning of the Covid-19 pandemic. For example, the 13th season of the franchise featured its first Black housewife, Eboni K. Williams. Williams hosted a Black Shabbat dinner, highlighting her intersecting experiences of marginalized communities. However, during the event Singer detailed experiences of what she claimed was racism directed toward her (Karasin, 2021). Fans took to Twitter, writing, "How can you allow this behavior?! How do you stand behind her?! She is taking #RHONY down single handed" and "Not everything is about you, Ramona! @Andy FIRE RAMONA!!!" (Karasin, 2021). As in the case of Dodd above, fans directed their outrage toward the network and its face, Andy Cohen. Interactions like these are different from simply live-tweeting during a show because they break the barrier between the viewer and the creator, in an effort to influence future casting decisions. Singer, like Dodd, was questioned about her behavior on *Watch What Happens Live* and said she was "mortified" by her behavior and should have spent more time listening to others' experiences that evening. She said she sent an apology text to Cohen, who is Jewish, in addition to many other people. However, from comments on the clip's YouTube page, many fans were not convinced by Singer's authenticity:

> She isn't even capable of reciting her memorized text without sounding like a piece of rehearsed insincere bologna
> LMAO RAMONA IS LITERALLY READING A SCRIPT IM DYING

These comments highlight the lack of sincerity fans noted from her interaction on the talk show (Miller, 2022). In fact, many fans theorized that Singer (and the network) knew she needed to apologize, as she was already cast in a future housewives spin-off, *Real Housewives: Ultimate Girls' Trip*. Additionally, there was no reunion for this season of *The Real Housewives of New York City*. Reunions generally serve as a space for the cast to mend their friendships and apologize for their behavior in the past season. Without this space there was little closure around the situation for fans, in addition to minimal accountability facilitated by the network.

In March of 2022, Bravo announced that *The Real Housewives of New York City* would be splitting into two casts—a housewives first for the network. One cast would be completely new housewives, while another cast would be former housewives. In an interview with *Variety*, Cohen said the new configuration "takes into account everything that our passionate audience has really been telling us over the last year" (Aurthur, 2022). Thus, showing fans that their interactions online truly did influence the network's decision in majorly revamping a foundational series. Cohen noted:

> This is the most multicultural, diverse, and energetic and exciting city in America: We are searching for a multicultural group of friends who really best reflect the most exciting city in the country. We're looking for a group of women who are real friends, and who are of diverse backgrounds, races and religions [as cited in Aurthur, 2022].

Essentially, this is signaling that Bravo isn't only looking to social media reactions and interactions to inform one-off decisions. Rather, the network is recognizing the overall calls on social media for Bravo to do a better job of highlighting diverse groups of women; essentially the network is listening to fans and fan accounts when making programmatic decisions at the highest levels.

The network ultimately decided to cast Singer in *The Real Housewives Ultimate Girls Trip: Real Housewives of New York City Legacy*. However, before the series aired, details of an HR investigation involving Singer were exposed. A *Vanity Fair* article on the working conditions for Bravo cast members found that evidence was inconclusive on whether Singer used the n-word during the previous season. In an exchange with Page Six, Singer addressed the allegations by using a shortened form of the word (Lincoln and Yee, 2023). As a result, Singer was removed from the 2023 BravoCon line-up, which routinely features stars from across the network and draws thousands of fans share in the Bravo-verse. Singer is still slated to appear in the series, as it has already filmed (Lee, 2023).

While Dodd and Singer's political leanings and racist undertones, combined with fans' social media interactions, influenced casting decisions, there are two examples of very overt racist social media usage that affected casting: Jenny Nguyen from *The Real Housewives of Salt Lake City* and Peter Hunziker from *Below Deck Mediterranean*. In both of these examples, Bravo took swift action, when compared to Dodd and Singer, in its response to social media engagement from fans and fan accounts.

Nguyen, who joined *The Real Housewives of Salt Lake City* in its second season, was filming the beginnings of the third season when racist posts from her social media accounts surfaced. Over a six-month span in 2020 amid the ongoing Black Lives Matter protests, Nguyen allegedly posted and reposted memes and photos, including ones which mention phrases like "BLM Thugs" and "Violent Gangs" (Blaire, 2022). One post shared on her Facebook page reads:

> Hundreds of [B]lacks shot and many killed (including children) by other [B]lacks every week. Over a thousand Officers violently injured, some permanently, by rioters. Anarchists rioting in major cities every night, which has caused billions of dollars of destruction to private and public property. And you still think Police Officers [sic] are the problem. You are an idiot [Blaire, 2022].

Another shows a cartoon of a White woman with decals of stick-people on the back of a car typically used to show a family, with the caption "No, that's not my family, that's how many rioters I've hit!" (Blaire, 2022). The racist posts caught attention on January 19, 2022, and fan response was immediate. Fans started tweeted, using hashtags for both the network and the show:

> Me sitting here while the rest of y'all just now realizing Jennie is anti-black #RHOSLC #bravo
> Not Jennie getting exposed for being racist, anti [B]lack and anti-vaxx. Plus the blaccent and racist microaggressions towards Mary AND being a trumper. Her snowflake has officially melted. #RHOSL [Blaire, 2022].

Not only did fans comment on the situation, but fellow *The Real Housewife of Salt Lake City* cast members expressed their outrage online, too. Meredith Marks, another cast member on *Salt Lake City*, posted multiple tweets and Instagram posts about the situation: "I stand with and support the communities affected and targeted by this…. I am deeply disturbed and outraged by her actions. Black Lives Matter" (Jackson, 2022).

Bravo did not release its statement about Nguyen' posts until six days after they surfaced. Their Instagram statement read:

> Bravo has ceased filming with Jennie Nguyen and she will no longer be a cast member of *The Real Housewives of Salt Lake City*. We recognize we failed to take appropriate action once her offensive social media posts were brought to our attention. Moving forward, we will work to improve our process to ensure we make better informed more and more thoughtful casting decision [Sollosi, 2022].

The last sentence of their statement likely refers to fans questioning how the network didn't know about these posts when Nguyen was cast. Fans responded to the statement questioning Bravo's seemingly double standards in holding a woman of color accountable, but not White women. Particularly, posts referencing Ramona Singer, who was discussed above, called for equal accountability among the network stars. One tweet noted that the network's response came after lower ratings, but still commended fans in joining together to call for action: "Bravo CONVENIENTLY released a statement about Jennie's departure AFTER seeing the low viewership #'s. They're not slick BUT we still [heart emoji] to see! This is what happens when people band together & follow through with letting their voice be heard" (Wehniainen, 2022).

It wasn't until ratings suffered that the previously discussed recasting of *The Real Housewives of New York City* was announced, as well. Thus, audience reception in the form of declining viewership clearly has drastic impacts on network decisions. Social media, when used to call for boycotting of shows in the face of problematic behavior from cast members, allows fans to learn of controversies faster and more effectively than ever and lead unified calls for the network to respond accordingly.

Ultimately, the online outrage gave way to season three of *Real Housewives of Salt Lake City* without Nguyen as a cast member. A similar circumstance occurred on *Below Deck* with season five deckhand Peter Hunziker, who had also posted racist memes online before filming. After the season's premiere the posts circulated, and three episodes into the season, Bravo announced that "Bravo and 51 Minds are editing the show to minimize his appearance for subsequent episodes" (as cited in Guglielmi, 2022). While Hunziker was edited out, there was never an announcement on the show, using title cards for example, to explain to viewers why one deckhand was suddenly dropped from the show. This lack of clarity contributes to racism, sexism, homophobia, and other oppressive forces and their ability to continue to perpetuate harm; if they are not called out directly to viewers, thus noting how prevalent these forces continue to be in society, they can continue to exist covertly. However, it should be noted that in response to the previously discussed "great racial awakening" of 2020, Bravo programming has included storylines that discuss issues of diversity, equity, inclusion, and justice. The next section unpacks these discussions and the resulting audience reception and interactions.

Reacting to Audience Feedback through Storylines

One of the most overt storyline arcs, in response to the racial awakening of 2020, was *Southern Charm* season seven. *Southern Charm*, which is based in Charleston, South Carolina, follows a group of relatively wealthy southern socialites. *Southern Charm* presents its connections to racism and patriarchy fairly obviously. For example, events are often held on plantations owned by the White cast members and others brag about their Confederate lineage. During the summer of 2020, Bravo actually removed four episodes from its streaming platform "as part of a review the network [was] doing to flag potentially offensive content" (Aurthur, 2020). However, this removal wasn't announced publicly until a Bravo fan-account created a series of TikToks investigating why certain episodes were missing (Kiki Monique, 2020). In her videos she notes that one of the episodes removed features a cast member showing a "slave cemetery" on her family's property. Since the removal, Bravo has rereleased the episode without said scene (Anquilina, 2020). The other episodes have been restored without edits to streaming platforms. One of these episodes still contains racist gestures, such as "a scene where ex-cast member Thomas Ravenel has lunch with his father, Arthur. In the scene, Arthur—a former South Carolina congressman and state senator—tells Thomas he likes to get rid of $5 bills because of Abraham Lincoln's picture on them, then smirks at the camera" (Aquilina, 2020). The storyline in season seven became much more socially aware in response to cultural conversations brought forward by the Black Lives Matter movement.

In season seven, Leva Bonaparte was added to the cast. Bonaparte was the first person of color on the all–White cast (Moore, 2020). Early in the season she called out other cast members for their White privilege and noted that her business's windows, which had been broken as part of a Black Lives Matter protest could be replaced, while lives can't (Moore, 2020). As the season progressed, storylines continued to be more explicitly racially sensitive. One of the main arcs involved the removal of a Charleston statue of John C. Calhoun, who is the ancestor of Kathryn Dennis, one of the show's main cast members. During the season, Bonaparte served as a social justice guiding force for cast members. For example, after Dennis sent a monkey emoji to a Black woman who was criticizing Dennis' friends for attending a MAGA parade, Bonaparte served as the "facilitator" for Dennis's accountability conversations (Merrett, 2020). However, during the reunion, Bonaparte is positioned as the villain by many cast members for calling out others' problematic behaviors (Guglielmi, 2021).

A similar dynamic was presented on season 13 of *The Real Housewives of New York City*. As previously mentioned, Eboni K. Williams joined the show as the first Black housewife for the franchise. In her joining, conversations about race, social justice, and inclusion were more heavily represented during the season. In addition to the dinner mentioned earlier, other storylines and conversation revolved around race: Williams discussed the angry Black woman trope; a fellow cast member called her "articulate"; and Williams hosted a Harlem Renaissance party to highlight Black culture and history. Singer accused Williams of being "preachy" during a conversation about White fragility. Because there was no season 13 reunion, the women performing these harmful behaviors and microaggressions did not have a space to "redeem" themselves in the eyes of fans. Audience feedback for both *Southern Charm* and *The Real Housewives of New York City*'s race discussions showed displeasure with storyline choices. Fans tweeted to Williams comments that she "made everything about race" and was "too woke" in her discussions (Wright, 2021). Ratings for the season of *The Real Housewives of New York City* reached an all-time low for the franchise, and many blamed Williams as the reason (Wright, 2021). Similar discussions surrounded *Southern Charm*, with fans using the #SouthernCharm hashtag to note their displeasure with the discussions Bonaparte was leading: "Leva was annoying at first but by the end of the season I truly didn't want her back for another season. And I 100% agree that she race baits. #southerncharm" (Jones Foster, 2022). Bonaparte has been cast in additional seasons of *Southern Charm* and received a spin-off show about her various restaurants and bars in Charleston, titled *Southern Hospitality*. This may signal that the network believes there is space and desire for Bonaparte's perspective to be showcased on their network. Alternatively, it may also signal to viewers who positively received Bonaparte's presence that the network supports these conversations.

However, it should be noted that some more recent conversations around race have been better received by the Bravo audience. *Summer House*, which showcases a group of friends who rent a summer house in the Hamptons, tackled race in their most recent season. Mya Allen and Cierra Miller, the only Black women on the show, spoke with their fellow castmates about being Black in the Hamptons and joining a new friend group. The conversation was sparked after a fellow cast mate called Allen by the wrong name. Fellow White cast members reacted to their experiences with compassion and validated that they needed to listen to them and recognize their experiences as Black women would be different from theirs. Fans reacted extremely positively to this conversation, with one Reddit user noting:

> I thought it was a great conversation, and the best race-related conversation I can remember seeing on Bravo.... And I know it's a very low bar, but I was impressed that no one in the group got defensive or tried to interrupt. It's not necessarily the cast I would have expected this from but I am happy it happened the way it did [livieleanor, 2022].

At the reunion, cast members spoke about the differences in microaggressions experienced by an Asian cast member and Latina cast member. The conversations on *Summer House* were perhaps more successful in the eyes of the audience because the fellow cast members were willing to listen and engage. The race-based conversations were seemingly not performed in an effort to create drama or stir tension. Rather, the *Summer House* cast members appeared to genuinely want to include their Black cast mates as their most authentic selves. This is in contrast to the conversations on *The Real Housewives of New York City* and *Southern Charm*, as the White cast members appeared defensive, and perhaps viewed the conversations as a way to elicit drama.

Summer House cast members may have been able to facilitate much more meaningful conversations around power and privilege for a variety of reasons. First, while many of the casts of other shows (e.g., *Housewives*) are displayed as friends, they are often cast into these roles without foundational relationships or ties to the other women. Cast members on *Summer House* appear to have genuine friendships that were established before the show began. Thus, there may be more willingness to engage in productive and empathetic dialogue. Cast members on this show case generally younger than those on Housewives franchises, too. Their positionality within social movements, particularly Black Lives Matter, may help them to recognize how power and privilege operate in their own lived experiences.

Reacting to Audience Feedback through New Programming

In addition to cast changes and storyline decisions, Bravo has had a third approach to reconciling its programming with social conversations around diversity, equity, and inclusion—especially in relation to race: directly talking with cast members about social issues. In the summer of 2020, while Bravo was reviewing its catalog of shows, they developed new programming to address issues of representation in the form of a web-series that was hosted via Instagram live (and available to stream later) and a 90-minute special. The web-series, titled *Amplify Our Voices*, featured Bravo cast members in short, five- to 10-minute segments discussing topics related to race, sexuality, politics, the Covid-19 pandemic, and voting. Typically, these conversations were one on one with Bravo cast members who held minoritized identities (Amplify Our Voices, 2022). In August of 2020, Bravo aired a 90-minute special entitled *Race in America: A Movement Not a Moment* with 10 Bravolebrities to discuss racism and social justice. Of the 10 featured speakers, two were White. The host, Nina Parker from E!, introduced concepts such as White privilege, racism in healthcare, the harm of colorblindness, and the use of social media in political movements. The Bravolebrities then responded with their own experiences and takeaways. When analyzing the content discussed, it can be seen that the Black cast members display very vulnerable experiences of racism, such as racial profiling by the police or experiencing colorism.

However, Braunwyn Windham (a White housewife from *The Real Housewives of Orange County*), noted that she has only recently become aware of the full realities of racism in the United States. While it is commendable that she was transparent in her experience, it might also lead viewers to wonder how Bravo could not find any other White representatives from the network to speak from a place of greater education and knowledge. Though many Bravolebrities supported Blacks Lives Matter during the summer of 2020, posting Instagram stories and tweeting support, having candid conversations might be viewed as much "riskier" if one says the wrong thing. Yet, the Black folks in conversation on the special were asked to display their painful experiences in exchange for recognition of humanity. Dorothy Toran, an executive producer of the special, noted in an interview:

> Bravo was incredibly supportive, of not just being preachy or talking about race in a way that makes people think that you are lecturing them or it's truly a historical lesson. We really wanted to make the issue of race be personal to everyday lives because we think that is a really helpful tool in helping people to understand racism [as cited in Palmieri, 2020].

Though sharing personalized experiences and connecting faces to movements can be important social justice tools, it is equally—if not more—important to ask whether Black and Brown folks' experiences are being used as "trauma porn" for White audiences. Moreover, as in the cases of Leva Bonaparte and Eboni K. Williams, there is mention that they avoid being "too preachy" with their message. Therefore, in addition to sharing painful stories of racism, discrimination, and prejudice, Black and Brown cast members (and production in editing) felt the need to police their own choices so as to appear amenable to White audiences, in an effort to not be "canceled" by them.

Using Reality Programming as a Transformational Space

Ultimately, Bravo as a network and Bravolebrities as individuals have made many strategic choices to "avoid" cancellation. Bravolebrities use social media engagement to apologize for problematic behavior, and the network allows them to use its platform of *Watch What Happens Live with Andy Cohen* to speak directly to a mass number of fans. On the other side, Bravo fans and fan-accounts circulate information related to the problematic behavior and have called for boycotting of shows and individuals. Additionally, fans may seek out diverse fan accounts to better understand how viewers of all backgrounds experience programming. These spaces and relationships can then serve as a site of listening for White audiences (Hockin-Boyers & Clifford-Astbury, 2021). Ultimately, it seems that fans and fan-accounts do hold significant power in driving narratives and casting decisions. Storyline decisions that involve more discussions around racism, inclusion, and representation appear to have mixed reactions from fans. Cast members of color must navigate these conversations in ways that don't appear to be forced, indignant, or preachy so that not only will their White cast members listen to their experiences, but they will also avoid turning off fans. Clearly, these social power dynamics result in difficult terrain to navigate, that may result in fans from multiple "sides" calling for cancelation of all parties involved; in other words, fans might call for the conservative cast members to be canceled due to their inability to listen and recognize humanity, while other fans might call on the cast members driving the conversations around diversity, equity, and inclusion to be canceled because they are promoting a "political agenda." However, even in situations where the conversations were productive and fans felt all cast members were engaged respectfully and meaningfully (e.g., *Summer House* example above and Bravo special programs around representation) there was an unequal burden placed on people of color to drive the conversation and share their pain in ways that White cast members weren't asked to do. The responsibility to explain experiences of oppression fell on those most oppressed. In conversations around "cancel culture" as a whole within society, it doesn't appear that Bravo fans' primary concern is canceling Bravolebrities for their problematic behavior. Rather, it might be analyzed that they feel Bravo as a network has a responsibility to use their platform to showcase proper representation of all identities and experiences, and at a baseline cast members must recognize the humanity in all people. Online spaces, primarily where audience members can interact in more thoughtful ways—for example, message boards compared to character limited posts—can also provide a site for growth, exploration, collaboration, and other empathy-building skills (Ng, 2020).

While highlighting aspirational lifestyles for many, reality television also seeks to connect with audiences and provide moments of similarity to viewers' personal lives. Conversations around race, sexuality, gender, identity, and other politics clearly take place in everyday life. Yet, when they occur on reality television as a tool to stir drama, there is little room for productive conversations. Conversations wherein humanity is recognized, active listening is centered, and thoughtful reflection and education are required are a starting place for change. Under this thought, fans are holding Bravolebrities accountable, not canceling them for their behavior (Ng, 2020). As conversations continue and the social and political landscapes shift, methods on "returning from cancellation" should also be examined in this space. Possible mechanisms for allowing spaces of cancellation to gesture toward growth might be (1) naming harms perpetuated on the show and toward fans, especially in cases of casting decisions; (2) showing authentic diversity in casting, instead of tokenism; and (3) placing the responsibility of these conversations on those who have the most political and social power (e.g., not asking the oppressed to be the educators of the oppressors). Consistently, audience reception favors authentic conversations and connections both on screen among cast members and with fans online.

Though often posited as vapid, reality television holds an important mirror to society; perhaps viewers, in the future, might be able to see reality television as a space for learning skills around growth, listening, and shared experiences to enhance our conversations around diversity, equity, inclusion, and justice in society. In order for this to be a productive site of learning, the network must treat viewers with respect and note their potential to understand complex social dynamics within a landscape created by White supremacist capitalist patriarchy. Networks, such as Bravo, would also need to take accountability for their role in perpetuating racist, sexist, homophobic, and other harmful ideologies through their programming. This level of institutional accountability may be unimaginable under the current matrix of power and privilege in society. Yet, with the ever-increasing importance placed on audience reception and interaction, large-scale change on an institutional level may be possible through boycotting and a reduction in ratings. Notably, this requires viewers to maintain long-term collective memories and hold their convictions so that social movements do not fall into a cycle that (1) pushes for social change, (2) achieves real or symbolic social change, (3) loses momentum as a result of the seeming accomplishment, and (4) dissipation of energy and conviction. The very features of social media, which encourage us to remember our previous posts, may help to disrupt this cycle. Until the aforementioned productive space is achieved, we may all benefit from seriously looking into society's reflection as presented in reality television.

References

Amplify Our Voices. (2022). *Bravo TV*. https://www.bravotv.com/amplify-our-voices.
Aquilia, T. (2020, August 21). *Bravo temporarily pulls Southern Charm episodes due to racially insensitive moments*. Entertainment Weekly. https://ew.com/tv/bravo-southern-charm-episodes-temporarily-pulled/.
Aurthur, K. (2020, August 20). *'Southern Charm' episodes temporarily taken down due to racial sensitivities*. Variety. https://variety.com/2020/tv/news/bravo-southern-charm-missing-episodes-race-1234740793/.
Aurthur, K. (2022, March 23). *Bravo to reboot 'Real Housewives of New York City' with new cast—and launch second 'RHONY' with ex-stars*. Variety. https://variety.com/2022/tv/news/real-housewives-of-new-york-city-reboot-new-cast-rhony-throwback-1235211905/.
Aurthur, K., & Wagmeister, E. (2020, June 9). *'Vanderpump Rules' fires Stassi Schroeder and Kristen Doute for racist actions*. Variety. https://variety.com/2020/tv/news/stassi-schroeder-kristen-doute-fired-vanderpump-rules-1234629172/.
Blaire, C. (2022, January 19). *'RHOSLC' star Jennie Nguyen faces backlash for controversial posts*. Page Six. https://pagesix.com/2022/01/19/rhoslc-star-jennie-nguyen-faces-backlash-for-controversial-posts/.
Breitfeller, T., Burger, M.A., & Murphy, C. (2022, January 28). *'Real Housewives': A beginner guide*. Vanity Fair. https://www.vanityfair.com/hollywood/2022/01/real-housewives-a-beginners-guide.
Callahan, C. (2020, December 3). *'Real Housewives' star Kelly Dodd addresses her COVID-19 'thinning the herd' comment*. Today. https://www.today.com/popculture/kelly-dodd-addresses-her-controversial-covid-19-comment-t202528fg.
Chenault, J. [@JoshualChenault1]. (2020, June 9). *Bravo just gave walking papers to Stassi, Kristen, Brett and Max for their racism. 2020 is a cultural reset and I stan #vanderpumprules* [Tweet]. Twitter. https://twitter.com/joshuachenault1/status/1270431242614460418.
Chung, G. (2020, October 5). *RHOC's Kelly Dodd responds to backlash over 'drunk wives matter' hat and lack of masks at bridal shower*. People. https://people.com/tv/kelly-dodd-responds-backlash-bridal-shower-drunk-wives-matter-hat/.
Desta, Y. (2020, June 9). *Vanderpump Rules: Stassi Schroeder, Kristen Doute fired after racist false police report*. Vanity Fair. https://www.vanityfair.com/hollywood/2020/06/stassi-schroeder-kristen-doute-vanderpump-rules-fired.
Dominguez, P. (2015). "I'm very rich, bitch!": The melodramatic money shot and the excess of racialized gendered affect in the Real Housewives docusoaps. *Camera Obscura, 30*(88), 155–183. https://doi-org.library3.webster.edu/10.1215/02705346-2885486.
Guglielmi, J. (2020, June 17). Bravo fires Below Deck Mediterranean's Peter Hunziker after alleged racist social media posts. *People*. https://people.com/tv/bravo-fires-below-deck-mediterraneans-peter-hunziker/.
Guglielmi, J. (2020, December 3). Southern Charm: Leva Bonaparte supports the removal of Kathryn Dennis' ancestor's statue. *People*. https://people.com/tv/southern-charm-leva-bonaparte-supports-removal-kathryn-dennis-ancestor-statue/.
Guglielmi, J. (2021, February 4). Kathryn Dennis accuses Leva Bonaparte of using her racism scandal to 'come up' on Southern Charm. *People*. https://people.com/tv/kathryn-dennis-accuses-leva-bonaparte-of-using-her-racism-scandal-to-come-up-on-southern-charm/.
Hearn, A. (2011). Confessions of a radical eclectic: Reality television, self-branding, social media, and autonomist Marxism. *Journal of Communication Inquiry, 35*(4), 313–321. https://doi-org.library3.webster.edu/10.1177/0196859911417438.
Hearn, A. (2017). Witches and bitches: Reality television, housewifization and the new hidden abode of production. *European Journal of Cultural Studies, 20*(1), 10–24. https://doi-org.library3.webster.edu/10.1177/1367549416640553.
Hockin-Boyers, H., & Clifford-Astbury, C. (2021). The politics of #diversifyyourfeed in the context of Black

Lives Matter. *Feminist Media Studies, 21*(3), 504–509. https://doi-org.library3.webster.edu/10.1080/14680777.2021.1925727.

Jahng, M.R. (2019). Watching the rich and famous: the cultivation effect of reality television shows and the mediating role of parasocial experiences. *Media Practice & Education, 20*(4), 319–333. https://doi-org.library3.webster.edu/10.1080/25741136.2018.1556544.

Jackson, D. (2022, January 24). RHOSLC's Meredith Marks calls out Jennie Nguyen''s past 'racist' posts: 'I am sickened.' *People*. https://people.com/tv/rhoslc-meredith-marks-calls-out-jennie-nguyen-racist-posts/.

Jones Foster, L.D. [@fdarlene491]. (2022, June 22). *Leva was annoying at first but by the end of the season I truly didn't want her back for another season. And I 100% agree that she race baits. #southerncharm* [Tweet]. Twitter. https://twitter.com/fdarlene491/status/1539622644609327104.

Karasin, E. (2021, August 18). REAL OUTRAGE RHONY fans demand Ramona Singer be fired or show be CANCELED after star's 'racist' behavior at Eboni K Williams' dinner. *The Sun*. https://www.the-sun.com/entertainment/3495851/rhony-ramona-singer-fired-racist-eboni-williams-dinner/.

Kiki Monique [@thetalkofshame]. (2020, August 12). *Did #Bravo think we wouldn't notice the missing #SouthernCharm episodes? #bravotv*. [TikTok]. https://www.tiktok.com/@thetalkofshame/video/6860233781018643717?source=h5_m&lang=en.

Lincoln, R. & Yee, L. (2023, October 31). *Ramona Singer removed from BravoCon after text exchange about racist slur*. The Wrap. https://www.thewrap.com/ramona-singer-bravocon-2023-racial-slur-accusation/.

Livieleanor [@livieleanor]. (2022, February 17). *Summer House airing their race conversation was needed*. [online forum post]. Reddit. https://www.reddit.com/r/BravoRealHousewives/comments/suxfi0/summer_house_airing_their_race_conversation_was/.

Merrett, R. (2020, April 21). RHOC's Kelly Dodd says Coronavirus is 'God's way of thinning the herd' before apologizing. *People*. https://people.com/tv/kelly-dodd-says-coronavirus-gods-way-of-thinning-the-herd-before-apologizing/.

Merrett, R. (2020, May 11). Kathryn Dennis apologizes for using racially insensitive emoji: 'I know and will do better.' *People*. https://people.com/tv/kathryn-dennis-apologizes-for-using-racially-insensitive-emoji/.

Miller, V. (2022, June 7). Ramona Singer 'mortified' by her behavior at RHONY Black Shabbat. *Heavy*. https://heavy.com/entertainment/real-housewives/ramona-singer-black-shabbat-apology-rehearsed/.

Moore, T. (2020, November 20). The tacky charms of Southern Charm. *Vanity Fair*. https://www.vanityfair.com/hollywood/2020/11/southern-charm-bravo-season-7.

NBCUniversal. (n.d.). *2019 Bravo success*. https://together.nbcuni.com/bravo-success-2019/.

Ng, E. (2020). No grand pronouncements here...: Reflections on cancel culture and digital media participation. *Television & New Media, 21*(6), 621–627. https://doi-org.library3.webster.edu/10.1177/1527476420918828.

Palmieri, L. (2020, August 7). Bravo's 'Race In America: A Movement Not A Moment' special is the most important thing you can watch this weekend. *Decider*. https://decider.com/2020/08/07/bravo-race-in-america-a-movement-not-a-moment-special-preview/.

Parks, G.S. (2021). "When they see us" the great white awakening to Black humanity. *University of Maryland Law Journal of Race, Religion, Gender & Class, 21*(1), 1–22. https://digitalcommons.law.umaryland.edu/cgi/viewcontent.cgi?article=1355&context=rrgc.

Schneider, M. (2021, December 30). *Most-watched television networks: Ranking 2021's winners and losers*. Variety. https://variety.com/2021/tv/news/network-ratings-2021-top-channels-1235143630.

Sollosi, M. (2022, January 25). *Bravo fires Jennie Nguyen from The Real Housewives of Salt Lake City after discovery of racist posts*. Entertainment Weekly. https://ew.com/tv/bravo-fires-jennie-nguyen-real-housewives-of-salt-lake-city-racist-posts/.

Staff. (2020, May 31). *Bravo "stands in solidarity with the Black community": "Black Lives Matter."* Bravo TV. https://www.bravotv.com/the-daily-dish/george-floyd-protests-black-lives-matter-bravo-network-responds.

Stewart, M. (2020). Live tweeting, reality TV and the nation. *International Journal of Cultural Studies, 23*(3), 352–367. https://doiorg.library3.webster.edu/10.1177/1367877919887757.

Unfriendly Black Hottie. [@mainlyraven]. (2020, June 9). *Bravo finally did the right thing. I never thought I'd see the day* [tweet]. Twitter. https://twitter.com/mainlyraven/status/1270414044768407554.

Warner, K.J. (2015). They gon' think you loud regardless: Ratchetness, reality television, and Black womanhood. *Camera Obscura, 30*(88), 129–153. https://doi-org.library3.webster.edu/10.1215/02705346-2885475.

Wehniainen, Grace. (2022, January 25). *Jennie Nguyen was fired from RHOSLC after offensive posts*. Bustle. https://www.bustle.com/entertainment/memes-tweets-about-jennie-nguyen-fired-from-rhoslc-bravo.

Witter, B. (2021, December 1). *Kelly Dodd blamed "cancel culture" & a former RHOC star for her firing*. Bustle. https://www.bustle.com/entertainment/why-did-kelly-dodd-leave-rhoc.

Wright, T. (2021, July 7). *RHONY star Eboni K. Williams accused of making 'everything about race' and being too preachy by fans slamming her 'woke' approach*. Daily Mail. https://www.dailymail.co.uk/tvshowbiz/article-9765307/RHONYs-Eboni-K-Williams-accused-making-race-fans-slamming-woke-approach.html.

Yee, L. (2023, November 5). *'The Real Housewives: Ultimate Girls Trip': Ramona Singer front and center *in 'RHONY Legacy' trailer.* The Wrap. https://www.thewrap.com/the-real-housewives-ultimate-girls-trip-rhony-legacy-trailer-ramona-singer/.

Zaragoza, A. (2020, October 20). *Real Housewives fan accounts are boycotting the new season of 'RHOC.'* Vice. https://www.vice.com/en/article/dy8gax/rhoc-kelly-dodd-trump-covid-blmboycott?utm_content=1603378166&utm_medium=social&utm_source=VICE_twitter.

The Role of Crisis in Online Audience Participation's Influence on Television Content

A Case Study of The Activist

Lukasz Swiatek, Marina Vujnovic,
Chris Galloway, *and* Dean Kruckeberg

In an age of flourishing online participatory cultures, television content creators and executives are increasingly wary of the influence that social media users exert on television programming. At best, these users become enthusiastic devotees or followers of content; at worst, they become agitators and adversaries (Hutchins & Tindall, 2016). At times, audience members' hostile responses to television content escalate into crises for those involved with the shows, leading to alterations in content or cancellations of whole shows, among other impacts. Decades ago, observes Anders (2014), most audience members did not know who produced the shows that they watched; these days, though, audiences are "hyper-conscious" of the individuals working behind the scenes (para. 1). Both experienced and (in particular) inexperienced staff involved in the production of television shows, as well as the creative choices made by those staff, now "regularly inspire online rage" (Anders, 2014, para. 3) that often escalates into crises, usually in very short timeframes.

Crises themselves are also becoming increasingly complex, with this complexity being driven by media, especially social media. Sheppard (2020) writes that globally, people are becoming more worried, and perceive that the world is in a very precarious state. His acronym ADAPT summarizes the four major processes that are contributing to this sense of worry, and to the feeling of living in a constant state of crises: asymmetry, referring to increasing wealth disparity and the erosion of the middle class; disruption, relating to technology and its impact on society, climate and our individual lives; age, referring to demographic pressures on businesses, social institutions, and economies; polarization, referring to a fracturing world consensus, as well as the growth of nationalism and populism; and, lastly, trust, referring to declining confidence in social institutions. While these processes show that the world itself is in a state of flux, media, particularly social media, tend to amplify crises and create further tensions.

This essay argues that crises lead television content creators and executives to accommodate audience members' wishes, in order to ease tensions, minimize reputational damage and mitigate financial damage (to the creators, studios, and other parties involved). In the age of social media, the polyvocality of voices that contribute to crises are making these intensely destabilizing situations even more complex (Chewning, 2015). This situation is due to the fact that social media enables individuals and groups, especially stakeholders implicated in the crises, to co-create crisis messages and then observe the ways in which crisis managers respond to the crises (Bukar et al., 2022, p. 799). As such, television content creators and executives responding to crises driven by disgruntled online audiences face increasingly complex challenges the likes of which their peers in previous decades never needed to tackle.

To illustrate this argument, the essay uses the crisis that engulfed the television show *The Activist* as its case study in order to provide a detailed demonstration of these crisis dynamics. *The Activist*, originally due to be launched in late 2021, had to be re-imagined following "rampant criticism" by online audiences and critics (Legaspi, 2021). These criticisms particularly targeted the show's "tone-deaf" format, involving a "crass" *X-Factor*–style competition between activists that gave them the potential chance to lobby world leaders at the G20 (Davies, 2021). The furor that engulfed the show provides a rich way of understanding crisis dynamics in connection with television content and online audience critiques.

The essay fills a gap in knowledge about the influence exerted by audiences on television content production in relation to crises. Although a growing amount of scholarship is shedding light on the dynamics of online audience participation in relation to television shows (see, for example, Guerrero-Pico, 2017; Ng, 2020), little scholarship exists about crises as part of these dynamics (see, for example, Foss, 2020). The essay draws on crisis communication theory, as well as reception theory, to provide a rich elucidation of the dynamics of crises in relation to online audiences' often-significant influence on television content (see, for example, Coombs, 2012). In terms of its focus, the essay considers the vigilance of audiences, but it does not contribute to the literature on "vigilant audiences," which engage in digitally mediated vigilantism in response to moral and criminal offenses (Trottier et al., 2020).

The remainder of the essay is divided into six sections. An outline of today's online participatory cultures provides context for understanding the crises, sparked by audiences, in which television show producers can find themselves. Next, the nature of crises themselves is discussed, shedding light on the dynamics of these intense social phenomena. After that, the essay's case study, *The Activist*, is unpacked in greater detail, with a focus on the crisis that overwhelmed the show. Insights from that crisis are then extrapolated to other television shows that are likely to find themselves beset by crises, given today's growing participatory cultures. Afterwards, the broader implications of the crisis for activism, in relation to media corporations, are discussed. Finally, the conclusion offers closing insights and avenues for further research.

Participatory Cultures

Individuals in online spaces, as Henry Jenkins (2006) influentially noted almost two decades ago, have not simply been passive consumers; rather, they have also been creators of meaning, and have been playing important roles in shaping content. This increased engagement with online content has led to convergence and, ultimately, to "participatory culture." In this view, citizens take part in different communities in a selfless way, giving their free time to enhance collaboration, communication and even democracy. For Jenkins (2006), participatory culture "contrasts with older notions of passive media spectatorship"; he further explains that "[r]ather than talking about media producers and consumers as occupying separate roles, we might now see them as participants who interact with each other" (p. 3). Scholars such as Kelty (2013) have built on Jenkins's original notion by arguing that there is no one, single participatory culture; rather, there are multitudes of these cultures, all with their own "practices, tools, ideologies, and technologies" (p. 29).

Over time, interactions across all kinds of participatory cultures have become increasingly intense. Hutchins and Tindall (2016) have observed that groups of individuals, or publics, now enjoy "seemingly unlimited opportunities to become engaged with organizations, content, and each other" (p. 4). Concerningly, growing numbers of "extreme publics" have come to exhibit very high levels of either supportive or hostile behavior online, especially toward organizations (Krishna & Kim, 2016, p. 23). Lee et al. (2014) have noted that extreme publics are more likely to express their opinions about issues or problems; as such, troublingly, these groups engage freely in active communication without fearing backlashes.

Examples of such active online publics, and their impacts on television show programming, abound. Publics have both halted and saved shows. Recently (at the time of writing), online social media users' criticisms brought about the cancellation of *Resident Evil*, with Pitman (2022) noting that "almost the instant *Resident Evil* came out, viewers took to social media to ridicule the series." By contrast, fans led an "impressive effort" (Venable, 2022) to save the reboot of *Magnum P.I.*, an effort that resulted in the show being saved. In terms of publics' hostile communication activities, two ongoing challenges for professional communicators, including television content creators, involve (1) understanding the motivations behind such antagonistic publics' communication behaviors and (2) developing more effective approaches for proactively decreasing publics' hostile reactions (Krishna & Kim, 2016), so that they do not spiral into crises.

The optimistic view of participation has also come under scrutiny for reasons tied to self-centeredness. Growing amounts of evidence have pointed to participation becoming darker; as Quandt (2018) argues, "dark participation" is a "bleak flip side to the utopian concept of selfless participation" (p. 40). This view has been driven by the realization that individuals online are not always driven by altruism. Sometimes, they are driven by economic concerns; at other times, they are driven by destruction; at yet other times, they are driven by a desire for disruption and the injection of "pollution" into online environments. This type of participation is characterized by "sinister" practices such as trolling, strategic piggy-backing and the large-scale dissemination of disinformation; it also appears to be tied to the growing recent waves of populism in Western democracies (Quandt, 2018).

In this respect, disinformation, misinformation, malinformation and polluted information are as characteristic of today's participatory cultures as any remnants of the selfless altruism so characteristic of our thinking 20 years ago. In fact, as Phillips and Milner (2021) starkly warn, "polluted information is a public health emergency" (p. 5). As participation wanes in some cases, and ramps up in others, it is important—more than ever—to consider who creates content online, as well as to examine the very processes of meaning-creation through the sharing of online content. Building this understanding of online dynamics can help other content creators, such as television producers, better predict online behavior, as well as prepare responses to crises when they arise. In this respect, it is increasingly vital to understand the dynamic nature of modern crises themselves.

Modern Crises

In an interconnected world facing growing numbers of challenges, crises are becoming ever more complex. For this reason, researchers have been paying steadily larger amounts of attention to crises, their causes, dynamics, and after-effects. Indeed, crisis communication has become widely recognized as a salient area of scholarship. Contemporary textbooks (for example, Newsom, Turk, & Kruckeberg, 2013) discuss crisis communication at length, and theoretical monographs devote considerable attention to crises and crisis communication (for example, Brunner & Hickerson, 2019; Brunner, 2019; George & Pratt, 2012). Public relations reference books invariably have a substantial entry for crisis communication (see, for example, Heath, 2013). Scholars such as Valentini and Kruckeberg (2015) have examined both crises and crisis communication extensively.

Among the leading contemporary theorists and researchers of crises are W. Timothy Coombs and Sherry Holladay. These scholars define a crisis as the perception of an unpredictable event that threatens important expectations of stakeholders and that can not only seriously impact an organization's performance but also generate negative outcomes (Coombs & Holladay, 2014). They also define a paracrisis as "a publicly visible crisis threat that charges an organization with irresponsible or unethical behavior" (Coombs & Holladay, 2012, p. 409), noting that a paracrisis can turn into real crises if not promptly resolved.

Social media has considerably changed the dynamics of crises. For this reason, a particular current focus in the scholarship is the role of social media in crisis communication (see, for example, Austin & Jin, 2018; Schwarz, Seeger & Auer, 2016). Valentini, Romenti, and Kruckeberg (2018) note the growing consensus that social media are speeding the development of critical situations and potentially forming new types of crises. The implications of this increasing speed, they explain, are that the managers of organizations that are affected by crises "have less time to plan and to implement actions to solve these crises and, thus, to restore their reputations, with even less time to monitor how publics perceive and discursively talk about these organizations' actions in their online networks" (Valentini, Romenti, & Kruckeberg, 2018, p. 59).

Despite the changes being driven by social media, the major types and phases of crises remain consistent. Crises can be categorized, using Pauchant and Mitroff's (1992) classic taxonomy, into six clusters:

- external economic attacks (such as boycotts and extortion),
- external information attacks (including copyright infringement and loss of information),
- internal breaks or malfunctions (such as recalls and operational errors),
- "megadamage" (caused by major accidents and environmental disasters),
- psycho (including terrorism and kidnappings), and
- occupational health diseases (brought about by working in unsafe environments).

Naturally, some crises—especially new crises—fall outside of these clusters (For an overview of other crisis typologies, see, for example, Harrison, 2011).

The progression, or "life cycle," of a crisis is also generally consistent across the different crisis types (digital, non-digital or semi-digital). A wide variety of crisis life cycle types, from the straightforward to the complex, has been outlined in the scholarship (for an outline, see, for example, Coombs, 2022). A synthesis of the different types is provided by Howell (2012), who draws on the work of other scholars to divide a crisis into five key stages:

- the prodromal or signal detection stage (featuring events that could trigger a crisis),
- the preparation, prevention and probing stage (involving organizations preparing for, and trying to prevent, a full-blown crisis, as well as probing by media),
- the acute or containment stage (featuring critical events, as well as crisis containment measures, in the most serious phase of the crisis),
- the chronic or learning stage (involving an audit or post-mortem by affected organizations, individuals and groups, as well as ongoing media coverage), and
- the resolution or recovery stage (featuring management actions to bring a crisis to a close and to learn from it) [pp. 324–327].

Howell's framework is particularly useful given the fact that it incorporates media activities into the crisis stages. As with the crisis types, the stages of some crises fall outside of these typical life cycle stages.

The responses of social actors to crises—especially the responses of actors at the center of crises—have also been categorized in a systematic way, given the fact that a consistent "repertoire" of responses has been taken by actors over time. The responses have been grouped into four categories: deny, diminish, rebuild, and bolster crisis response strategies (Coombs, 2007). The first three of these categories are often seen to be primary response strategies, while the final one is secondary. The deny strategies include attacking the accuser, denying the crisis, and scapegoating (actors outside of the organization). The diminish strategies involve excusing the organization (in order to minimize responsibility), and justifying the perceived damage caused by the crisis. The rebuild strategies encompass compensations and apologies. The bolster strategies include reminding stakeholders about an organization's past good works, ingratiating the organization with stakeholders, and highlighting the organization's victimhood in the crisis (Coombs, 2007). In each crisis, the crisis management team selects the most appropriate strategy (or strategies) based on the circumstances. These responses, as well as the other crisis dynamics outlined in this section, can significantly impact the creation of creative content, including the content developed by television producers, as the following case study illustrates.

Case Study: The Activist

The crisis that engulfed the television show *The Activist* in 2021 provides a robust, up-to-date way of understanding the impacts of such crises, generated by active online publics, on television shows and television content creators. This single instrumental case study (Stake, 1995) serves as an effective way of understanding principles in other settings (Yin, 1981): namely, the components of crises that engulf television shows (of various kinds) and their creators as a result of the communicative behaviors of individuals and groups online. Original research, of (publicly available) online media commentary and news reports written during the crisis, were analyzed using directed qualitative content analysis (following Hsieh & Shannon, 2005). This analysis approach enabled the components of the crisis, as it unfolded at the time, to be unpacked. The method was suitable for this purpose, as its goal involves validating or conceptually extending theoretical frameworks or theories (Hsieh & Shannon, 2005). A set number of news reports and media commentaries was not analyzed; rather, as many texts as possible were found and examined in order to gain the fullest comprehensive and detailed understanding of the crisis.

Trouble began to brew soon after the television series—due to be produced by CBS, Global Citizen, and Deviant Media—was announced (on September 9, 2021), marking the start of the prodromal or signal detection stage of the crisis. Criticisms of the show began to be published soon after details were released. For instance, in an opinion piece for *Forbes*, published the day after the announcement, Asare (2021) provided the standard details about the show, noting that it "pairs advocates from the worlds of health, education, and the environment with famous figures in a series of competitions that'll take the winners—and their ideas of seismic world change—to the G20 Summit in Italy." However, Asare's (2021) piece quickly turned more critical, with the writer noting that

> a show that has activists compete in a series of competitions to essentially determine who can be the "better activist" centers the individual and not the most marginalized groups that the activists are supposedly advocating for. It's likely that there are some people who are coming on the show for money, fame, clout, and notoriety.

These emblematic comments illustrate a brief signal detection period, given the fact that media outlets rapidly latched onto the problems confronting the show and the critiques being made about it.

The preparation, prevention and probing stage of the crisis was similarly brief and intense. Amid the growing furor, the show's developers attempted to defend their premise and tried to mount rhetorical defenses to probes being made by media. One illustrative example is Cordero's (2021) article, which contained a neutral overview of the show (published on September 9), and an "update" (published on September 10) in response to the backlash. The update featured a statement from Global Citizen, trying to defend the idea's premise:

> After the format for The Activist drew some blowback on social media, *Deadline* reached out to Global Citizen for a statement. "The Activist spotlights individuals who've made it their life's work to change the world for the better, as well as the incredible and often challenging work they do on the ground in their communities," a spokesperson for the group said.

This defense underscores the producers' early awareness of the issues confronting the show. It also highlights the speed at which the crisis developed.

In the acute or containment stage, outrage about the show steadily intensified and online critiques proliferated, with the producers "bow[ing] to pressure" (Milton, 2021) after eight days in an effort to end the crisis. Hibberd's (2021) compilation of condemnations—from both Twitter users and critics "slamming" the show—highlights the negativity of the reactions at the height of the crisis. The censure included remarks such as the following:

> This is truly horrific
> Such obscene shows make total sense in a disconnected, elite world where activists are nothing more than entrepreneurs-to-be
> As activists are jailed, maimed and killed around the world, this is grotesque

Adding fuel to the fire at the peak of the crisis was the critique of the show by one of its celebrity judges, who released a social media statement acknowledging that the idea "totally missed and disrespected the many activists who have been killed, assault, and faced various abuses fighting for their causes" (Hough in Wong, 2021). In containing the crisis, CBS released a statement saying that it had decided to re-develop the show into a documentary special and would be removing the competitive element; all of the involved activists would receive cash grants for the organizations of their choice. It also acknowledged the backlash that had engulfed the show, saying that

> *The Activist* was designed to show a wide audience the passion, long hours, and ingenuity that activists put into changing the world, hopefully inspiring others to do the same. However, it has become apparent the format of the show as announced distracts from the vital work these incredible activists do in their communities every day. The push for global change is not a competition and requires a global effort [CBS in Rindner, 2021].

The network, in its statement, also repeated its earlier hope that the (transformed) program would inspire others around the world to undertake their own activist work.

A statement released by Global Citizen also signaled that the learning phase of the crisis had been entered. In reflecting on the backlash, the advocacy organization stated:

> Global activism centers on collaboration and cooperation, not competition. We apologize to the activists, hosts, and the larger activist community—we got it wrong. It is our responsibility to use this platform in the most effective way to realize change and elevate the incredible activists dedicating their lives to progress all around the world [Iqbal, 2021].

The use of the apology—a rebuild strategy, as noted in the previous section (Coombs, 2007)—indicates that the organization had already realized, to some degree, where it had failed in co-developing the show. Needless to say, media analysis and commentary, pouring over the backlash, continued in this stage of the crisis.

The details of the content creators' actions in the resolution or recovery stage are opaque, as the publicly available documentation does not describe the steps that were taken by CBS, Global Citizen and Deviant Media in the months following the crisis. It is unlikely that other methods, such as interviewing, would shine a light on these steps, as professional communicators and organizations are often reluctant to reveal details about closely guarded internal activities following crises. This situation is echoed by the comments of one of the celebrity judges, Priyanka Chopra, who described the furor in a 2022 interview as "tragic," but also stated that she had "no idea" what was happening with the show (Chopra in Jeffrey, 2022). It remains to be seen whether CBS will air the documentary special.

Implications of Crises and Television Productions

The crisis that engulfed *The Activist*—resulting not only in its swift cancellation, but also in embarrassment for the professionals connected to it—highlights the implications of such crises on reputations. That is, as active (and, in particular, extreme) publics become increasingly comfortable with using the Internet to criticize content creators, individuals and organizations will increasingly have their reputations tarnished, especially following crises. In that respect, any crisis poses a severe threat to an organization's reputation, especially if the response to that crisis is perceived to be inappropriate (Coombs, 2007). As a result, the damaged reputation may negatively affect interactions between an organization and its publics, such as diminishing consumer loyalty and positive word-of-mouth behaviors (Walsh et al., 2009; Ma & Zhan, 2016). While societal-level, international crises such as Covid-19 have been found to stimulate news consumption, that effect was mainly seen "among those who already have a higher level of trust in legacy media and among people that were more concerned about the impact of the pandemic" (Van Aelst et al., 2021, p. 1208).

The responses of individuals and groups to crises of natural origin are very different to their responses to crises of human, and especially organizational, origin. Garcia-Avilés (2012) notes that "[b]oth public and commercial broadcasters are developing cross-media processes that enhance audience participation in a variety of ways" (para. 1). In a crisis, online audiences will not hesitate to express their opinions using these vehicles. Negativity bias (Rozin & Royzman, 2001) may produce a predominance of negative views, with flow-on effects to organizational reputation and audience willingness to pay for live or streaming performances. For example, Dai et al. (2018) showed that, in e-commerce, higher reputation scores of sellers elicited more purchase from buyers.

The Activist's crisis provides a representative illustration of the ways in which crises can play out for other television shows. Drawing on the details of the case, as well as Howell's (2012) framework, it is possible to suggest that television content creators will reach a stage in each crisis during which they will (1) defend their show and decisions, without changing the show, or (2) make changes to the show based on the comments made by audience members, or (3) cancel the show. These options are visually captured in the framework in Figure 1. The creators' responses will depend

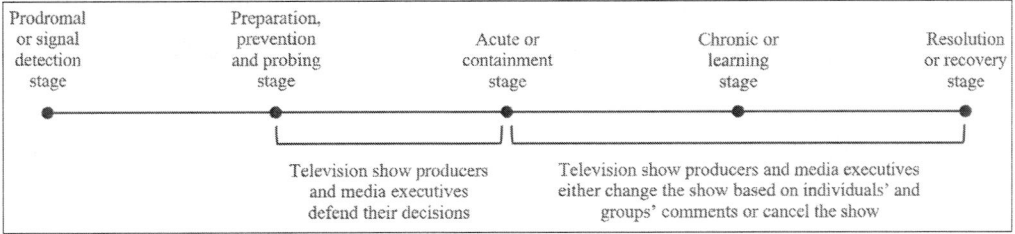

Figure 1. An illustration of television show creators' options, in response to online criticisms, at the different stages of a crisis.

on the nature and intensity of the comments being made by the public. Most likely, though, television content creators and executives are likely to accommodate audience members' wishes, in order to minimize reputational and financial damage. As the case study of *The Activist* shows, allowing an intense crisis to roll forward without an ending can be extremely detrimental for many different social actors (individuals and organizations) connected to the shows.

Activism and Media Corporations

The crisis that engulfed *The Activist* also highlights the tensions that arise when media corporations try to engage themselves in supporting the work of activists. The corporate pursuit of generating revenue can clash, as the case study has shown, with the activist pursuit of resolving social problems. In this respect, certain television formats—such as contents and competitions, especially ones involving audience voting—can be antithetical to the supportive, relational, community-focused approaches that activists use to undertake their work. Even though many organizations, including media outlets, increasing try to look after the triple bottom line—that is, not just profit, but also people and the planet (Elkington, 1994)—many corporate social responsibility initiatives, including the idea underpinning *The Activist*, still amount to little more than "window dressing" (Schleimer & Rice, 2016).

In particular, as the case study highlights, difficulties arise in any attempted corporate co-option of activism. While the co-option can sometimes be very public, swift and direct, it can be much more subtle and slow at other times. At best, King and Busa (2017) have shown, corporations can simply take over ideas and practices initiated by social change advocates; at worst, the corporations can come to dominate fields initiated by social movements, resulting in the "corporatization" of particular forms of activism. Jaffee and Howard (2009) have also highlighted the fact that corporations sometimes try to counter the reforms of activists by defusing threats to the status quo and, in particular, to profit margins. The online responses of individual and groups to *The Activist* show that cooption is not a fait accompli; in other words, cooption can be resisted.

More broadly, the case study highlights the significant obstacles facing individuals and groups in their struggle for social justice and, in particular, in their struggle to gain effective support from organizations. Activists must not only respond to the problems created by corporations—such as the media-related issues (ranging from unsanctioned deepfakes to flawed algorithms) stemming from the work of "Big Tech giants" like Microsoft and Google—but also try to counter these well-resourced corporations (Swiatek et al., 2023). In this respect, activists find themselves battling against an array of corporate staff, ranging from lawyers to lobbyists. Corporations, including media outlets, often do not just ignore activist voices; they also take punitive, retaliatory actions against employees who side with activists (Swiatek et al., 2023), thus creating even greater challenges for modern activists to gain support for their work.

Conclusion

As increasing numbers of individuals take to social media to share their views about television shows, and as those individuals feel less and less communicatively inhibited online, crises about shows will only grow in number and size in the coming years. This essay has argued that crises lead television content creators and executives to accommodate audience members' wishes, in order to ease tensions and minimize reputational damage, as well as to mitigate financial damage. The case study of *The Activist* has demonstrated the significant negative impacts that crises can have on the professionals connected with the production of the shows.

This essay opens a number of avenues for further research. Only the one case study was examined here; in future, further cases—of other crises that engulfed television shows—could be examined. Comparing the dynamics of these different crises would be useful in developing an even richer understanding of these extremely intense phenomena and their impacts on multiple social actors. Also, a different method could be used in the future to understand, in a more detailed way, the comments made by extreme publics online; for instance, intensive, large-scale data-mining and analysis of social media posts could be taken (with the help of specialist software) to understand the construction of the communications (such as tweets) of active publics. Such future research would not only provide even more valuable insights into the crises that affect television shows and the personnel connected with them, but also help to safeguard the wellbeing of those individuals during those crises.

REFERENCES

Anders, C.J. (2014, October 14). Has a new producer ruined your favorite TV show? That's nothing new. *Gizmodo*. https://gizmodo.com/has-a-new-producer-ruined-your-favorite-tv-show-thats-1646275078.

Asare, J.G. (2021, September 10). Performance activism personified: Why CBS's new show 'The Activist' is extremely problematic. *Forbes*. https://www.forbes.com/sites/janicegassam/2021/09/10/performance-activism-personified-why-cbss-new-show-the-activist-is-extremely-problematic/.

Austin, L., & Jin, Y. (Eds.). *Social media and crisis communication*. Routledge.

Brunner, B.R. (Ed.). (2019). *Public relations theory: Application and understanding*. John Wiley & Sons.

Brunner, B.R., & Hickerson, C.A. (Eds.). (2019). *Cases in public relations: Translating ethics into action*. Oxford University Press.

Bukar, U.A., Jabar, M.A., Sidi, F., Nor, R.B., Abdullah, S., & Ishak, I. (2022). How social media crisis response and social interaction is helping people recover from Covid-19: An empirical investigation. *Journal of Computational Science 5*, 781–809. https://doi.org/10.1007/s42001-021-00151-7.

Chewning, L.V. (2015). Multiple voices and multiple media: Co-construction BP's crisis response. *Public Relations Review, 41*, 72–79. https://doi.org/10.1016/j.pubrev.2014.10.012.

Coombs, W.T. (2007). Protecting organization reputations during a crisis: The development and application of situational crisis communication theory. *Corporate Reputation Review*, 10, 163–176. https://doi.org/10.1057/palgrave.crr.1550049.

Coombs, W.T. (2012). Parameters for crisis communication. In W.T. Coombs & S.J. Holladay (Eds.), *The handbook of crisis communication* (pp. 17–53). Wiley-Blackwell. https://doi.org/10.1002/9781444314885.ch1.

Coombs, W.T. (2013). Crisis and crisis management. In R.L. Heath (Ed.), *Encyclopedia of public relations* (Volume 1, pp. 216–219). Sage.

Coombs, W.T. (2022). *Ongoing Crisis Communication: Planning, Managing, and Responding* (6th ed.). Sage.

Coombs, W.T., & Holladay, S.J. (2012). The paracrisis: The challenges created by publicly managing crisis prevention. *Public Relations Review, 38*(3), 408–415.

Coombs, W.T., & Holladay, S.J. (2014). How publics react to crisis communication efforts. Comparing crisis response reactions across sub-arenas. *Journal of Communication Management, 18*(1), 40–57.

Dai, Y., Vikemn, G., Joo, E. & Bente, G. (2018). Risk assessment in e-commerce: How sellers' photos, reputation scores, and the stake of a transaction influence buyers' purchase behavior and information processing. *Computers in Human Behavior, 84* (July), 342–351. https://doi.org/10.1016/j.chb.2018.02.038.

Davies, L. (2021). The Activist: 'Tone-deaf' new TV show has activists compete to lobby G20 leaders. *The Guardian*. https://www.theguardian.com/global-development/2021/sep/15/the-activist-tone-deaf-new-tv-show-has-activists-compete-to-lobby-g20-leaders.

Elkington, J. (1994). Towards the sustainable corporation: Win-win-win business strategies for sustainable development. *California Management Review, 36*(2), 90–100. https://doi.org/10.2307/41165746.

Foss, K.A. (2020). Death of the slow-cooker or# CROCK-POTISINNOCENT? This Is Us, parasocial grief, and the crock-pot crisis. *Journal of Communication Inquiry, 44*(1), 69–89. https://doi.org/10.1177/0196859919826534.

Garcia-Avilés, J.A. (2012). Roles of audience participation in multiplatform television: From fans and consumers, to collaborators and activists. *Participations Journal of Audience & Reception Studies, 9*(2), 429-447. https://www.participations.org/Volume%209/Issue%202/24%20Garcia-Aviles.pdf.

George, A.M., & Pratt, C.B. (Eds.). (2012). *Case studies in crisis communication: International perspectives on hits and misses*. Routledge.

Guerrero-Pico, M. (2017). # Fringe, audiences and fan labor: Twitter activism to save a TV show from cancellation. *International Journal of Communication, 11*, 2071-2092. https://ijoc.org/index.php/ijoc/article/view/4020.

Harrison, K. (2011). *Strategic public relations: A practical guide to success*. Palgrave Macmillan.

Heath, R.L. (Ed.). (2013). *Encyclopedia of public relations* (second edition). Sage.

Hutchins, A., & Tindall, N. (2016). Introduction. In A. Hutchins & N. Tindall (Eds.), *Public relations and participatory culture: Fandom, social media and community engagement* (pp. 3–7). Routledge. https://doi.org/10.4324/9781315766201.

Jaffee, D., & Howard, P.H. (2010). Corporate cooptation of organic and fair trade standards. *Agriculture and Human Values, 27*, 387-399. https://doi.org/10.1007/s10460-009-9231-8.

Jenkins, H. (2006). *Convergence culture: Where old and new media collide*. NYU Press.

Kelty, C.M. (2013). From participation to power. In A. Delwiche & J.J. Henderson (Eds.), *The participatory cultures handbook* (pp. 22–32). Routledge.

King, L., & Busa, J. (2017). When corporate actors take over the game: The corporatization of organic, recycling and breast cancer activism. *Social Movement Studies, 16*(5), 549–563. https://doi.org/10.1080/14742837.2017.1345304.

Krishna, A. & Kim, S. (2016). Encouraging the rise of fan publics: Bridging strategy to understand fan publics' positive communicative actions. In A. Hutchins & N. Tindall (Eds.), *Public relations and participatory culture: Fandom, social media and community engagement* (pp. 21–32). Routledge. https://doi.org/10.4324/9781315766201-6.

Lee, H., Oshita, T., Oh, H.J., & Hove, T. (2014). When do people speak out? Integrating the spiral of silence and the situational theory of problem solving. *Journal of Public Relations Research, 26*(3), 185–199. https://doi.org/10.1080/1062726X.2013.864243.

Legaspi, A. (2021, September 16). 'The Activist' TV show is 'changing the format' following rampant criticism. *Rolling Stone*. https://www.rollingstone.com/tv/tv-news/the-activist-changing-format-cbs-1227538/.

Ma, L. & Zhan, M. (2016). Effects of attributed responsibility and response strategies on organizational reputation: A meta-analysis of situational crisis communication theory research. *Journal of Public Relations Research, 28*(2), 102–119. https://doi.org/10.1080/1062726X.2016.1166367.

Mitroff, I.I. & Pearson, C.M. (1993). *Crisis management*. Jossey-Bass.

Newsom, D., Turk, J.V. & Kruckeberg, D. (2013). *This is PR: The realities of public relations*. Wadsworth, Cengage Learning.

Ng, E. (2020). No grand pronouncements here…: Reflections on cancel culture and digital media participation. *Television & New Media, 21*(6), 621–627. https://doi.org/10.1177/1527476420918828.

Pauchant, T.C., & Mitroff, I. (1992). *Transforming the crisis-prone organization: Preventing individual, organizational, and environmental tragedies*. Jossey-Bass.

Phillips, W., & Milner, R.M. (2021). *You are here. A filed guide for navigating polarized speech, conspiracy theories, and our polluted media landscape*. MIT Press.

Pitman, R. (2022, August 29). *Netflix's Resident Evil cancellation was inevitable*. Screen Rant. https://screenrant.com/netflix-resident-evil-canceled-problems-explained/.

Quandt, T. (2018). Dark participation. *Media and Communication*, 6(4), 36–48. https://doi.org/10.17645/mac.v6i4.1519.

Rozin, P., & Royzman, E.B. (2001). Negativity bias, negativity dominance, and contagion. *Personality and Social Psychology Review*, 5(4), 296–320. http://dx.doi.org/10.1207/S15327957PSPR0504_2.

Schleimer, S., & Rice, J. (2016, October 4). Australian corporate social responsibility reports are little better than window dressing. *The Conversation*. https://theconversation.com/australian-corporate-social-responsibility-reports-are-little-better-than-window-dressing-66037.

Schwarz, A., Seeger, M.W., & Auer, C. (2016). *The handbook of international crisis communication research*. John Wiley & Sons.

Sheppard, B.H. (2020). *Ten years to midnight. Four urgent global crises and their strategic solutions*. Berrett-Koehler.

Swiatek, L., Vujnovic, M., Galloway, C., & Kruckeberg, D. (2023). *Artificial intelligence, strategic communicators and activism*. Routledge. https://doi.org/10.4324/9781003324027.

Trottier, D., Gabdulhakov, R., & Huang, Q. (2020). Introducing vigilant audiences. In D. Trottier, R. Gabdulhakov, & Q. Huang (Eds.), *Introducing vigilant audiences* (pp. 1–24). Open Book. https://doi.org/10.11647/OBP.0200.01.

Valentini, C., & Kruckeberg, D. (2015). The future role of social media in international crisis communication. In A. Schwarz, M. Seeger and C. Auer (Eds.), *The handbook of international crisis communication research*. Wiley-Blackwell.

Valentini, C., Romenti, S., & Kruckeberg, D. (2018). Handling crises in social media—From stakeholder crisis awareness and sense-making to organizational crisis preparedness. In Y. Jin & L. Austin (Eds.), *Social media and crisis communication*. Routledge. https://doi.org/10.4324/9781315749068-5.

Venable, N. (2022, June 16). *As fans rally to save Magnum P.I., star shares inspirational story (involving Tom Hanks) about save-the-show billboard being full-circle career moment*. Cinema Blend. https://www.cinemablend.com/television/as-fans-rally-to-save-magnum-pi-star-shares-inspirational-story-involving-tom-hanks-about-save-the-show-billboard-being-full-circle-career-moment.

Walsh, G., Mitchell, V.W., Jackson, P.R., & Beatty, S.E. (2009). Examining the antecedents and consequences of corporate reputation: A customer perspective. *British Journal of Management*, 20, 187–203. https://doi.org/10.1111/j.1467-8551.2007.00557.x.

Part 2

Network and Cable Television

Tug of War

Social Media, Cancel Culture, and Diversity for Girls *and* The 100[1]

JONINA ANDERSON-LOPEZ, R.J. LAMBERT,
and ALLISON CHRISTINA BUDAJ

After the last half of Season 8 streamed on HBO, 1.7 million *Game of Thrones* (2011–2019) fans signed a petition demanding new writers and an alternate ending (McCluskey, 2019, para. 2). HBO representatives responded, sharing how they had no intention of making changes. Instead of closing the chapter on *Game of Thrones*, the fans and critics continued to backlash. *Saturday Night Live* mocked the now infamous series finale. Former *Game of Thrones* co-star Jason Momoa publicized his disappointment with the last episode via an Instagram video that was viewed over 136,000 times (Baily, 2019). Showrunners D.B. Weiss and David Benioff were "extremely quiet, even going so far as to cancel their scheduled appearance at Comic Con" (Placido, 2019, para. 1). The pair had been signed to direct and write the next series of *Star Wars* projects. However, after the backlash, they signed with Netflix and bowed out of the *Star Wars* deal. Laura Bradley of *Vanity Fair* describes how Weiss and Benioff may have decided against joining the *Star Wars*-verse. After watching "Star Wars fans bully actors and directors [...] they began to have doubts about whether they should dip their toes in as well" because "who wants to go through that again?" (Bradley, 2019, para. 2).

Then, in the Fall of 2022, came the debut of HBO's *House of the Dragon* (2022–present), a prequel set some 200 years before the *Game of Thrones* storyline. Reviewers such as those at IGN noted that despite the show's ability to "sometimes [feel] too faithful to its predecessor," *House of the Dragon* "forged its own identity and established itself as a worthy prequel" (O'Hara, 2022, Verdict). Surveying the comments left by readers of this review, fans seemed to agree that *House of the Dragon* satiated their desire for an answer to the travesty that was the ending to *Game of Thrones*. One commenter even noted how, "I know this is beating a dead horse but the opposite can be said for *Rings of Powers*.... I was excited for *Ring of Powers* but I couldn't any finish the first season" (luke333Professor, 2022). Not too long after the debut of HBO's *House of the Dragon* came another highly anticipated series premier, *The Lord of the Rings: The Rings of Power* (2022–present) on Amazon Prime Video. Set in the "fabled Second

Age of Middle-earth's history," roughly 1,000 years before the events taking place in *The Hobbit* and *The Lord of the Rings* trilogy, *The Lord of the Rings: The Rings of Power* garnered a 83 percent on Rotten Tomatoes, but a dismal a 38 percent audience average (compared to the 82 percent rating audiences gave *House of the Dragon*) (House of the Dragon, n.d.; The Lord of the Rings: The Rings of Power, n.d.).

Of the "complaints" *The Lord of the Rings: The Rings of Power* received, one commentator griped about the series having too much focus on "social problems and excessive tolerance … we unfortunately received low-grade social banality" (Dolly P., 2023). Another comment praised the increased diversity of the characters when compared to the films by Peter Jackson (Conrad C., 2023). Unfortunately, it seems the praise received by this one fan was one of the few as other viewers openly lamented about the depiction of Black elves in the series. *House of the Dragon* did not escape this lament unphased with the casting of Steve Toussaint as Lord Corlys Velaryon (Holland, 2022). Such open backlash prompted *The View* host Whoopi Goldberg to call our fans for "accepting otherworldly creatures … but not accepting Black actors" (Sharf, 2022). Specifically, the host opined, "'There are no dragons. There are no hobbits. Are you telling me Black people can't be fake people too?'" (Goldberg, 2022, as cited in Sharf, 2022). *The View* co-host Sunny Hostin added to the fury by commenting on the acceptance of otherworldly creatures such as dragons but casting Black actors in fantasy narratives as taking the story too far (Sharf, 2022).

Game of Thrones, House of the Dragon, and *The Lord of the Rings: The Rings of Power* are but some examples of television audience participation and how the gears of reception and fandom push back against corporations, networks, and production companies. Though not necessarily a new constraint, audiences increasingly make demands of creators and studios to influence content and shape productions. The novelty, and sometimes effectiveness of such demands, is in part the result of social media platforms that allow for opinions to quickly spread and to then be picked up by news outlets and critics. This symbiotic relationship between creators, audiences, and critics can help boost or sink shows and films. While to some degree creators and commercial distributors have always considered audience needs and wants, the persistence of contemporary audience expectations has come to influence entertainment production. In particular, Wolfgang Iser's (2006) reception theory calls for text, context and text, and the reader (p. 58). In the case of this essay, the "reader" becomes the "audience," and "context and text" become "interpretation of critical reception." Audiences react to several types of fictional entertainment, but this essay investigates online audience reception of recent television shows. In conjunction with various reception theories, primary research was assessed from individual social media posts via X (formerly Twitter). Although other sites like Reddit and Tumblr encourage users to discuss media, X is easily accessible (for users and researchers) and was once quite popular (particularly when the two shows in question were televised). As the title of the essay suggests, the very act of watching may engender a feeling of possession for the audience, a feeling nurtured by online spaces. While at times considered toxic and labeled as cancel culture, this amplification of sentiment can also evolve into positive calls for change, such as calls for diversity. To further explore the phenomenon of audience sway over artistic ownership, this essay examines two television series, *Girls* and *The 100*, using such frameworks as audience reception, cancel culture, and diversity initiatives across media.

Background: Girls *and* The 100

First, an outline of rationale in choosing *Girls* and *The 100* as examples for this essay will establish greater context. In decades past, audiences have rallied to influence networks to stave off show cancellations, using letters, phone calls, and word-of-mouth campaigns with *Star Trek* and *Twin Peaks* (Guerrero-Pico, 2017, p. 2072). Additionally, there are several recent shows that could have been evaluated for audience reception; *Friends*, *Sleepy Hollow*, *Roseanne*, and the aforementioned *Game of Thrones* weathered controversies that reflect the influence of audience opinion. However, the focus of this essay is to explore what, if any, tangible production changes (i.e., new or revised characters) result in response to audience reception in which "television fans now make strategic use of social media" (Guerrero-Pico 2017, p. 2072). Thus, *Girls* and *The 100* are two shows that altered production in reaction to online controversy, rather than simply canceling, renewing, or re-naming a show through other means. In assessing these phenomena, it helps that *Girls* has concluded and *The 100* is ongoing as the authors of this essay originally wrote and submitted it for publication with *KOME—An International Journal of Pure Communication Inquiry*. After seven seasons, *The 100* ended with its final episode airing on September 30, 2020. In our original article, one show ended three years ago (*Girls*), the other (*The 100*) was still beholden to fans and critics. Furthermore, Twitter (now X) and other social media became more influential from 2012 onward, lending audience opinion and increased presence and influence. The focus on *Girls* and *The 100* also reviews the impact of audience reception in two distinct corners of television: *Girls* originates from a premium cable channel, HBO, whereas *The 100* represents a basic cable network, The CW. Even as their fan demographics may be similar in gender and age, their viewership is different enough to support the theory that audiences of all types can express expectations that influence production. However, as this essay will outline, the impetus and application of fan criticism varies and produces divergent results.

A brief overview of *Girls* (2012–2017) and *The 100* (2014–2020) will provide background on the impact of their audience reception, along with critical reception of the time. This is to ensure less of a nostalgic view as sometimes adopted by present-day critics that may not consider critical reception and categorization of television shows at the time of their release. Such a dualistic approach, critical plus audience reception, may help "readers to grasp a reality that was never their own" (Iser, 2006, p. 63). Starting chronologically, *Girls* premiered on HBO on April 15, 2012, amid rave reviews for "its voice and colorful storylines," even being compared to the network's other NYC dramedy, *Sex and the City* ("Lena Dunham," 2012, para. 1–2). The show follows a group of four post-college White women as they deal with life in New York City, specifically focusing on Hannah (Lena Dunham) and her career as a writer. Dunham, the show's co-creator, head writer, and lead actress, had written award winning independent films, and was labeled a "wunderkind" by several news outlets, such as *The New York*

Times and *Los Angeles Times*. Still, within hours of the premiere, viewers and critics criticized the show's penchant for an all–White cast lamenting upper-class privileged issues ("Lena Dunham," 2012, para. 3). That same year on NPR's *Fresh Air*, Dunham professed "sensitivity" to the diversity issues, but insisted she wrote the characters to "avoid rendering an experience I can't speak to accurately" ("Lena Dunham," 2012, para. 6). Yet, seemingly in acknowledgment of the diversity criticism, *Girls* began filming new episodes in May of 2012, with star Dunham spotted by outlets like *TMZ* with supposed cast addition, Donald Glover. In another interview, Dunham expressed excitement for adding "new characters into the world of the show. Some of them are great actors of color" (as cited in Storey, 2012, para. 5). Eventually, Glover's role was revealed as a guest star. His character is a soft-spoken law-student and Republican who only remains for two episodes. Though never as predominant as it had been in 2012–13, critique about diversity continued for the duration of the show.

In 2014, The CW released *The 100*, a sci-fi show based on the eponymous Kass Morgan book series. The plot centers around Clarke Griffin (Eliza Taylor), an incarcerated teen aboard a space station after a worldwide nuclear strike 100 years in the future. Clarke and 99 incarcerated (therefore disposable) teens are sent to Earth to see if it can be safely re-colonized. The first season was described as a futuristic *Lord of the Flies* by outlets like *The San Antonio Times* and *IGN* due to its proclivity for killing off main characters. Deviating from Morgan's novels, the television writers even killed off show favorites, like the character Wells Jaha (Eli Goree). This trend continued into Season 3, when Commander Lexa (Alycia Debnam-Carey) was killed by a stray bullet. In a show where so many characters die, Lexa's death could have been explained as par for the course. However, fans felt differently, pointing out on social media platforms how she was killed right after a sexual encounter with another female character, the protagonist Clarke. Thus, to viewers, Lexa's death paralleled trends in which LGBTQ characters were more dispensable than straight characters (Framke, 2016, para. 14). In online articles for *TVInsider* and face-to-face forums like the Writer's Guild Panel in 2016, showrunners of *The 100* openly discussed their snafu, and how it might be remedied. A staff writer for the Lexa-death episode, Javier Grillo-Marxuach, conceded, "I think it was a failure to recognize the cultural impact that this would have outside the context of the show" (as cited in Wagmeister, 2016, para. 4). Ultimately, showrunners did not revert Clarke (Lexa's lover) to a heteronormative relationship upon Lexa's death, as many viewers assumed would be the case. Queer and gender critiques of *The 100* persist to this day. Part of why *Girls* and *The 100* were chosen for analysis over series with similar issues is because of the presence of social media in response to controversies (or as an influence for what fans perceived as controversial). The fan voices were amplified due to the prevalence and easy use of social media, drawing attention to racial and queer issues of diversity.

Audience and Critical Reception

This essay will primarily rely on audience reception as the lens for interpretation. A rift between traditional criticism and popular receptions of media "raises a key issue regarding the use of film criticism in reception studies: to what extent can the critics' views be taken as representative?" (Chapman et al., 2007, p. 195). In an age of new "media citizenship" and "the ethics of performativity" (Elsaesser, 2004, p. 76), this question may be extended to revise (and re-envision) the very function of the critic, getting to the heart of contemporary reception studies. To what extent does the viewing public come to *perform* the role of film critic through new media participation, and what is the impact of such criticisms on televised content? Analyzing audience reception of *Girls* and *The 100* may illustrate how subsequent creative choices were informed, with little or lasting impact. As mentioned above, audiences for both shows expressed their displeasure for the perceived status quo of the narratives. Emily Keightly (2008) suggests that in research, memory is a useful method for cultural studies, as different voices come together to analyze one story (p. 181). Given that the diversity issues for the shows took place over ten years ago for *Girls*, and over six years ago for *The 100*, the audience critiques amount to a socially constructed memory of what occurred. Studying this in tandem with critical responses may reveal complexities in the showrunner's creative decisions.

Though memes and posts were widely shared on Facebook and other social media, Twitter produced the brunt of audience conversation. From its inception in 2006, Twitter was designed for mobile users and thus held greater appeal to younger users (the target audience for *Girls* and *The 100*) than the desktop site for Facebook (Jackson, 2012, para. 3). Twitter is a platform that empowers users to share, and then reshare, their opinions, particularly with showrunners. Mar Guerrero-Pico (2017) explores how following the internet's inception in 1989: "There has been an empowerment of consumers, who, thanks to the expansion of social media in recent years, now have more tools at their disposal to become more visible and ensure their comments, opinions, and requests reach the interested parties without intermediaries" (p. 2071).

Other series, like *Scandal*, also utilized Twitter in 2012 to their marketable advantage: "*Scandal* is also an important mark in the historical development of #TGIT (or Thank God It's Thursday) programming because it demonstrated the possible success of social television from an industrial perspective. Indeed, *Scandal* has come to be referred to as the industry standard for 'must-tweet television'" (McNamara, 2013).

With X, fans learned how to create an entire force, ready to mobilize and then capture the attention of critical news outlets. From Nagy and Midha (2015) in "The Value of Earned Audiences: How Social Interactions Amplify TV Impact": "As Tweet exposure drives actions across platforms including searching, engagement, and purchase, marketers should learn to integrate Tweet messages, #hashtags, and calls to action with campaigns on other media" (p. 453). The following section balances modern and past critical perspectives, while also allowing room for individual interpretation. As Halbwachs (1980) believes, memories are the products of something larger, or an "intersection of collective influences" (p. 44). Due to the ready availability of online spaces, audiences are now able to share their influence in an easier and quicker fashion, in opposition to the letter writing and phone calls of the past. Thus, truth and story are shaped by what is communicated, and in the context of others.

Analyzing audience reception through a relatively newer type of media, like X, may archive, analyze, and legitimize the vast array of popular responses to television across new media. Elsaesser (2004) notes how "theories of cinematic spectatorship, initially elaborated around class and (immigrant) ethnicity, have been extended to gender, race and other forms of cultural identity" (p. 76). Audience criticism for *Girls* involved complaints about a lack of diversity among the cast and charges of nepotism. The online discussions included fans and critics. Even before the premiere, critics like Judy Berman had early access, and posted articles decrying the series for covering "first-world problems" from a "White lens." As Berman (2012) suggests in an April 13 article (before the premiere), several popular shows of the time were guilty of promoting White "problems" without diverse voices entering in—*Two Broke Girls*, *How I Met Your Mother*—and yet, the need to examine *Girls*, and then examine it again, was oddly acute (para. 5). On the date of the premiere, April 15, 2012, viewer angst and independent think-pieces on the lack of diversity, like the *Intellichick* post "These Aren't My 'Girls,'" were widely shared on Twitter. Before such posts, there seemed to be an unspoken agreement from formal critics that the show "spoke" to young women's issues in big-city life. Not every Twitter user was unhappy with *Girls*, as @LCoan_'s tweet gives Dunham "props" for avoiding what she deems "forced and faked" diversity: "@lenadunham props for not trying to appease the critics with forced and faked 'diversity' #girls #HBO."

From April 12 to 17, there were only two tweets discussing race or diversity, increasing to nine tweets from April 18 to 22. On April 18, journalist Dave Weigel (2012) acknowledged the critique of *Girls* as a new "national pastime": "RT @radiomaru: white house declares 'talking shit about GIRLS' the new national pastime. thanks a lot obama #hbo #girls." Some tweets even mentioned "nepotism," since the four main co-stars all hail from famous and (or) wealthy families. Then, on April 23, there were seven tweets about race, almost the same amount there had been on a five-day run. April 23, a week after the first episode, was also the day CNN aired a panel critiquing *Girls* and representations of race on the show. The CNN panel was critical of a show that takes place in the diverse city of New York, and is yet full of so many White characters and themes (Crugnale, 2012, para. 2). On air, host Soledad O'Brien showed *Girls* staff writer Lesley Arfin's (2012) post in response to diversity criticism: "What really bothered me most about Precious was that there was no representation of ME."

Though not participating in the CNN panel, Arfin later deleted the post and apologized for her comment. Even as she tried to argue that narratives often focus on particular characters and their trials and tribulations, her tweet came off as dismissive and racially charged among some critics and fans.

Diversity and nepotism were not the only controversies to haunt the show in audience and critical circles, though they were two of the most prominent and persistent. Other controversies include depictions of nudity and sex acts. The web magazine *Vulture* chronicles all the controversies on their website, from 2012 to 2017 (Moylan, 2017). Interest in the show from critics and audiences was high. Notably, "The *New York Times* ran seven articles per week during the show's first three months" (Watson, 2015, p. 145). Dunham, as the main character Hannah, even reflects satirically on her role as "the voice of my generation" versus "a voice of a generation" (S1x1, "Pilot"). This could be because, months before the show aired, critics were already lauding *Girls* as "important" and a modern instantiation of feminism, which was assumed to be global feminism. Instead of including intersections on gender, race, and class in a way that was supposed to be "highly current, and thoroughly modern" and "unlike what was on TV" (Stewart, 2012, para. 7), the show released promotional posters featuring a cast of four White young women. The White feminist narrative seemed reminiscent of what viewers had seen from *Sex and the City* fourteen years earlier, and so the progressive expectations for the show did not meet with the show's creative reality.

In *The New Film History: Sources, Methods, Approaches*, Justin Smith (2007) describes the method of "web ethnography," identifying new media participation as constructing "the politics and rituals of cult film fandom" (p. 229). Approaches such as Smith's help illustrate the constraints of traditional critical reception studies, which prioritize critical discourse at the exclusion or marginalization of popular reception, and conversely suggests the benefits of more democratic approaches to media reception. Berman (2012) scratches at another plausible reason why *Girls* received so much critical attention: "It's almost as if we're holding Lena Dunham accountable in a way that these earlier Voices of a Generation didn't have to be because she's already somewhat outside the mainstream—a young woman whose body isn't magazine-perfect" (para. 6). The very title of the show, *Girls*, implies it appeals on a universal-feminist scale, though the main characters and their social and class concerns seem to refute the "everygirl" implication. Still, Ta-Nehisi Coates (2012) believes Dunham and Arfin should avoid adding in minorities simply because of audience and critical push-back. Instead, he calls for greater scrutiny for the platforms producing content like *Girls*: "There has been a lot of talk this week about Lena Dunham's responsibility, but significantly less about the people who sign her checks" (Coates, 2012, para. 12). In 2012, out of a few dozen offerings of original fictional content, HBO only had one show with a minority listed as the first lead character, with only another two featuring minorities as co-stars. However, their 2020 lineup and beyond has been building upon past diverse shows, to be explored later in this essay.

Through a comparative case study approach, this essay illustrates how such theories of popular reception are particularly insightful when analyzing the reception of contemporary television series like *Girls* and *The 100*. Ultimately, as shown below, sensitivity to actual audience reception may be understood as central to the success and creative trajectory of contemporary television series. Alternatively, The CW's *The 100* enjoyed almost no criticism for its casting, which was more diverse than *Girls*. It was not until Season 3 that creator Jason Rothenberg heard from upset viewers across various social media. By that time, *The 100* was notorious for killing off central characters, and did so with Commander Lexa in the episode "Thirteen" (S3x7). After this episode aired on March 3, 2016, viewers vented their disappointment on X, as the following posts and Figure 1 demonstrate:

> everyone mad about the 100, a cw show
> The 100 stans are becoming spn-stan-level-of better yes let's all come together and trash talk the cw for what they've done to us.
> Fuck the CW, Fuck the 100, Fuck JRoth, Fuck it all.

Rather than purport anger at the cast, the above tweets are emblematic of the anger fans expressed against those in power they deemed most responsible: showrunner Jason Rothenberg and the parent network, The CW. A total of seven negative tweets emerged on March 3 about Lexa's death, with another seven on March 4. For perspective, March 2 had only one promotional tweet, and March 1 had eight positive

Figure 1. Meme attached to tweet. 2020.

tweets and two negative tweets concerning the quality of the show. The discontent evolved into fan-led online petitions and a viral trend of the Bury Your Gays trope, that acknowledges how media will often portray an LGBTQ character, only to kill them off, usually after engaging in a sexual act. Originally a literary trope to "rid" storylines of characters unapproved by society, Haley Hulan (2017) notes how Bury Your Gays bled into other media forms (p. 17). Despite a growing empathy for differences in society, narratives still employ the trope. Often, if a character engages with someone of the same sex, it's merely a blip in the narrative, as they quickly return to heteronormative relationships. The violent deaths of *The 100*'s female LGBTQ characters brought #BuryYourGays to the forefront of online fan concerns, as noted by formal critics.

For instance, Dhaenens et al. (2008) have argued "that queer-sensitive audiences cannot be ignored in research on queer representations and reception in media studies" (p. 336). This essay will use as a starting point their description of a *queer reading* of film reception, "a multidisciplinary approach that includes queer theory frameworks and insights from audience" (Dhaenens et al., 2008, p. 336)—one which resists the strict categories of gender, sexuality, genre, and even the distinct categorization of "critic" and "popular audience." It is here that intersections of youth, queer-sensitive audience identification, and critical performativity allow us to better understand not only the reception of such films across a range of popular and critical responses, but indeed the very processes of film reception and criticism in a new media age.

Part of the audience dissatisfaction for *The 100* stemmed from expectations versus execution. At times, writers employ what fans call "queerbaiting," or writing in queer characters to attract queer audiences, only to then "ditch the characters so they can focus on developing heterosexual plots" (Guerrero-Pico et al., 2017, p. 3). With the development of Clarke and Lexa's relationship, and subsequent death of Lexa, the charge of queerbaiting on the part of *The 100* writers seemed valid to fans. Dorothy Snaker (2012) of *The Hollywood Reporter* notes how the Clarke and Lexa dynamic trended on social media during Seasons 2 and 3, "encouraged and engaged by series creator Jason Rothenberg and his staff" (para. 5). With tweets such as "You guys know I don't ship. But I gotta admit, #Clexa is seaworthy. #justsaying #The100 @miselizajan @debnam-carey," the showrunner cemented the potential for the Clexa dynamic to happen in the minds of fans almost a year before Lexa's death in the series (Rothenberg, 2015). Following the character build-up, the swift end did not meet fans' hopes for strong, feminist storylines, particularly for the LGBTQ community. Snarker (2016) states how "in retrospect, many now feel the show misled them into hoping" for those storylines (para. 5). The CW focused on Clarke and Lexa's relationship in the twenty-one second promo video by having a character chide Lexa: "Your feelings for Clarke put both of you in danger" (TV Promos, 2016, 0:10). In the context of Lexa's death, that particular line seems to further underscore the Bury Your Gays trope. In an online post, Rothenberg admits that the "aggressive promotion" of the episode and of Clarke and Lexa's relationship (also known as "Clexa"), "only fueled a feeling of betrayal" (as cited in Roth, 2012, para. 4). Initially, Rothenberg attributed Lexa's death to creative freedom, while apologizing for not understanding how hurtful the decision might seem to LGBTQ audiences.

When asked about re-writing Lexa's ending during a March 21 *TVInsider* interview, Rothenberg said he would have kept everything the same (as cited in Holbrook, 2012, para. 7). Though he expressed regret for unwittingly playing into the Bury Your Gays trope, Rothenberg was perceived as unconcerned with the audience impact. *Girls* and *The 100* had differences and similarities concerning audience and critical reception. The height of audience and critical reception occurred at different times; for *Girls* it was before and after the premiere, and for *The 100* it peaked during Season 3. Though both shows were analyzed for issues of diversity, the points of diversity were not the same. For instance, *Girls* was scrutinized for an all–White and upper-class cast, whereas *The 100* came under fire for upholding an anti-lesbian trope, Bury You Gays. It seemed that the formal media criticism for *Girls* increased the audience reception on Twitter, while the opposite was true for *The 100*. The perceptions of either show cannot be distilled through formal critical and audience reception alone, because "the first meaning of history—what has happened—posits a base reality whose totality can never be fully reconstituted" (Friedman, 1997, p. 233). Thus, the opinions of the audience and critics will be assessed through subsequent sections of this essay and will be treated as separate pieces of the puzzle. Audiences and critics can rally behind different points concerning fictional narratives. Generally, the increase in online discussion (whether audience-led or in the form of media criticism) elevated both shows and fostered more analysis of diversity issues. Once these initiatives gain momentum, for good or ill, they sometimes spiral into cancel culture.

Cancel Culture

Recently, audience reception has influenced decisions concerning creative control, which may be linked to cancel culture. There are several perceptions of cancel culture. Colloquially, the term is linked in the media with a public shaming, and a media snub of the guilty party in question (most often a celebrity or stakeholder in power). Jeannie Parker Beard (2020) codifies cancel culture as a hindrance to civic discourse, in the way that it "cultivates the mob mentality" and demands a "100% consensus" (para. 4–5). Another perception of cancel culture can be linked to what is perverse or taboo in a society. However, cancel culture goes further than recognizing supposed taboo words and actions because it also places pressure to withdraw the taboo words or actions. On X, users may "encounter an affective flow of outrage, as well as fun and enjoyment, at the expense of an evil other who must be 'canceled,' and the pleasures of moral posturing" (Bouvier, 2020, p. 10). In online spaces, cancel culture hashtags (or calls to publicly snub an individual) can go viral, resulting in online petitions or movements calling for the entertainment industry to make drastic changes. In the end, entertainment industries are also businesses and strive to keep fans (aka customers) happy. While this can be conflated with cancel culture, firings and other consequences may be indicative of a business decision and customer demand.

Online platforms could be changing society's response to taboo behaviors. X, Instagram, Facebook and more are making it easier to quickly share information, and then to quickly respond with individual opinion. Gwen Bouvier (2020) writes how Twitter drives users to share short, snappy comebacks that encapsulate "high levels of affect and emotion" and then "bind affective communities" (p. 2). This level of emotion is what can also ramp up the number of "likes" for a tweet (aka commentary), or hashtag (aka trending topic). The desire for increased exposure can lead to a cycle of provoking emotional response from other users (Bouvier, 2020, p. 2). Some incidents and opinions are widely disseminated, becoming "viral," and it becomes contingent upon users to either disagree or agree. Beard (2020) outlines how "what seems to be an escalation in the culture war and the demise of civic discourse could, in part, be a symptom of big tech's dominance over the modes of communication and dissemination of information" (para. 1). Before the internet, consumers and audiences complained mostly via newspapers, consumer groups, and letters to companies. The turn-around time on a substantive response was comparably slower than the swift responses as seen with the online campaigns against *Girls* and *The 100*. While the messages against the shows were amplified due to online delivery, the messages were perhaps shared because of the anonymity perpetuated by virtual spaces. Partha Kar (2019) recalls how at in-person healthcare conferences, one speaker referenced a joke about "choking a female partner but was not interrupted or challenged" and it was only afterward that "some people did protest on social media" (para. 2). There is an elusive element to sharing sentiments online. Bouvier talks about how tweeting takes place while doing other things, is done quickly, and so users may not think through their words before hitting "submit." This lack of reflection, "bolstered by a compelling sense of affective community, [ensures] there is a corresponding distance from the victim, and no real fear that there will be any consequences" (Bouvier, 2020, p. 3). The easy access of social media coupled with the distance provided by technology allows for a disconnect and sense of freedom that may be absent from in-person interactions. Therefore, live audiences may be less likely to call attention to taboo words or actions without the shelter of social media.

The motivation for canceling certain media depictions and actions could be construed as an attempt to challenge offensive behavior. In society, "if something is considered to be inappropriate or offensive, there must be some set of common cultural standards that tells us what is appropriate or what is not" (Jay, 2017, p. xiii). In the case of *Girls*, X users deemed the lack of diversity as inappropriate in a discriminatory context. For *The 100*, the death of Lexa was a resurgence and confirmation of the Bury Your Gays trope surrounding queer characters. Like Timothy B. Jay (2017) examined in *We Did What? Offensive and Inappropriate Behavior in American History*, "it is important to recognize that what is appropriate or not depends heavily on context, the 'who, what, where, and when' as something questionable happens" (p. xvi). In both cases, outraged users assessed the behaviors, deemed them taboo, and demanded change. In fact, what is coined as "cancel culture" can sometimes become synonymous with "outrage-culture," or an expectation to never be offended.

What often goes unrecognized is the hidden allure of taboos. As Jay (2017) further noted, "the force of taboos insulates us from danger (we abstain from the taboo behavior) but at the same time brings us nearer to them (our curiosity is aroused)" (p. xiv). The push and pull of the taboo may be what feeds into the outrage. As comedian Tom Segura shared in his Netflix special *Tom Segura: Ball Hog*, "I believe you [the audience] have the right to be offended and share these grievances publicly. I also believe you shouldn't expect anything to be done about it" (Hachachi, 2020, 38:01). Segura's point hinges on the belief that offensive things are going to be said and done, particularly with comedians, and that audiences can simply avoid being offended by never watching or listening, as is their choice. However, avoiding a taboo, as Jay describes, is hard because the very codification of an action or word as taboo builds a hidden attraction. Still, when an opinion is shared, and deemed by social media users (or other stakeholders) to be "unpopular" or taboo, this sort of outrage is construed as a cancellation, or even a threat to freedom of speech. For instance, the "Letter on Justice and Open Debate," released online by *Harper's Bazaar* in June 2020, chronicles the supposed threat of cancel culture. The letter was a collaborative effort, penned by public figures like Gloria Steinem, Margaret Atwood, David Brooks, Noam Chomsky, J.K. Rowling, and others, who felt

> the free exchange of information and ideas, the lifeblood of a liberal society, is daily becoming more constricted. While we have come to expect this on the radical right, censoriousness is also spreading more widely in our culture: an intolerance of opposing views, a vogue for public shaming and ostracism, and the tendency to dissolve complex policy issues in a blinding moral certainty [Ackerman et al., 2020, para. 1].

The collective authors are right to some degree: those "canceled" in Hollywood, such as actor Roseanne Barr and director James Gunn, faced swift consequences as a result of publishing their views online. While their firings could be considered a public shaming, it could also be considered a business decision on the part of Disney. Creative endeavors have been, and likely will remain, beholden to audience interest. Instead of equating cancel culture with first-amendment suppression, it can perhaps be viewed as another expression of free speech. Considered this way, writers of *Girls* and *The 100* were not *censored* in sharing their storylines. Once shared, social media users exercised their first amendment rights and responded, and showrunners made a business decision.

Rather than suppression, cancel culture can be a fervent exchange of ideas, and is the sort of dialogue spoken of by authors of the *Harper's Bazaar* letter. Segura may agree that just because opinions (or creative decisions as seen on *Girls* and *The 100*) are shared, don't expect anyone to *like* said opinions, as an expression of dislike does not necessarily translate to suppression. Social media users have become adept at hosting online campaigns to champion causes, and though this may seem like suppression, it is not that different from buying power (boycotting a product/opting out) that the public has been used to seeing and using for decades. Social media does not pose a threat to the creative nature of narrative storytelling; quite the contrary. What social media has done is made it easier to voice discontent when fans of a series feel compelled to bring wrongs to light. Social media is a platform for viewers to be heard, to let showrunners know they are watching, and offers a call to action when violations occur. There will always be delays and cancellations due to outside events and pressure. However, for shows like *Girls* and *The 100*, audience reception resulted in more than a cancellation. To call upon Iser (2006), the mishaps or misrepresentations in these narratives or "[n]egation and blanks" enable the process of determining, which is the role of the reader (or viewer) to implement (p. 69). Once viewers took to social media to vocalize their dissent and dissatisfaction, the foundations of these narratives shifted. Thus, it permeated the creative decisions of showrunners, which changed the course of each show and their characters.

After the critique of Season 1, casting decisions for Season 2 of *Girls* had changed. Laura Bennett (2013) of *The New Republic* writes how the "casting notices [were] seeking 'hipster types' of 'all ethnicities'" (para. 1). Eventually, the Season 2 cast role went to Donald Glover, a young Black actor. As Bennett (2013) mentions, television shows had added to their casts for similar "complaints of whiteness," like *Friends* adding Black guest stars Gabrielle Union and Aisha Tyler with "nearly identical storylines [… that …] felt like a cheap kind of appeasement" (para. 5). For some, Glover wasn't so much an addition as he was ill-used. In a piece from the *Huffington Post*, Kareem Abdul-Jabbar (2013) echoes other critics on how *Girls*' "world is mostly white," and emphasizes how "that white ghetto was breaching by a black character who is introduced as some jungle fever lover, with just enough time to have sex and mutter a couple of lines about wanting more of a relationship. A black dildo would have sufficed and cost less" (para. 4). From the perspective of online fans, adding Glover looked as "forced" as Abdul-Jabbar claims.

Though it's hard to say if Dunham did in fact cast Glover due to outside pressure, she at least used the on-screen relationship of Hannah and Sandy (Dunham and Glover) to enact brief but uncomfortable arguments rooted in racial difference. One of the arguments begins because Sandy dislikes Hannah's essay, admitting that "it wasn't for me," and her insisting, "It's for everyone" (Konner & Dunham, 2013, 09:48). Bennett (2013) observed how even this small slice of their conversation is a nod to the larger controversy surrounding *Girls*: "whether 'Girls' is about all girls or about four girls' very particular bubble" (para. 4). The types of viewers interested in the show do not support the "every-girl" theory. Per a report from *Vulture*, 56 percent of the audience for *Girls* are male, with 22 percent of them being "white dudes over 50" (Adalian, 2012, para. 2). Despite the audience metrics, Glover's casting and the meta-conversation appeared indicative of the validity of cancel culture. Dunham may have also yielded to the "whitewashing" claims because of the scrutiny surrounding *Girls*, even before the premiere. To sustain positive perceptions of the supposedly critically acclaimed show, tackling the lack of diversity (even in a short-lived manner) was necessary to keep in line with market demands from viewers.

As stated earlier, *The 100* fans created online petitions, calling for greater empathy and recognition for LGBTQ characters. Part of this was the trending #BuryYourGays and also #LGBTQDeservesBetter hashtags on X. Aside from the abstract demands, fans created a fundraiser for the Trevor Project, which is dedicated to LBGTQ issues. From the beginning of March 2016 until Rothenberg's *TVInsider* interview, the petition had raised over 80,000 dollars for the Trevor Project. On March 24, Rothenberg apologized again, and shared that he would have "handled Lexa's death differently" (as cited in Roth, 2012, para. 6). Originally, he most likely deemed fans were upset over the loss of a favorite character, much in the way fans denounced previous character deaths on *The 100* in a similar fashion. However, the mixture of fan backlash and fundraiser may have illustrated for Rothenberg the seriousness of the LGBTQ issue of character representation, which was separate and distinct from past instances of fan backlash over character deaths. Seeing as how writers could not "reverse" Lexa's death, they did write in a continued lesbian story arc. In Season 3, Clarke starts a relationship with Niylah, sustaining their bond through Season 4. Entering into Season 7, Clarke has yet to enter into a romance with a man. Through viewers' online demands, the showrunners of *The 100* changed the creative outcomes to align with what was deemed appropriate and fair.

Realistically, like with *Girls*, a combination of business and fan-fueled issues may have convinced Rothenberg to change course. For instance, the Trevor Project initiative grabbed the attention of advertisers like Maybelline, who promised to no longer air ads during *The 100* via X posts to fans. According to journalist Brian Steinberg (2016), this did not mean that the company was pulling ad revenue from The CW, but it was still a substantive threat in terms of "energizing a fan base" (para. 7). Even before the March 3 airing of episode "Thirteen," the sci-fi drama was rumored for cancellation. It's possible that the #BuryYourGays controversy simultaneously forced Rothenberg to yield some creative positioning to save face with The CW executives deciding the future of his show, while also giving Rothenberg reason to demonstrate how canceling his show would be counterproductive, given the boost in popularity. Both shows apparently capitulated to the online critique period. *Girls* was accused of White-washing and sought to counter this perception. *The 100* was accused of perpetuating anti–LGBTQ tropes and was likewise determined to "correct" the perception. However, *The 100* made a lasting change that the character trajectory for Clarke has followed for five seasons, whereas *Girls* made surface changes with a two-episode guest star, Glover. As identified by Watson (2015), in *Girls*, "non-white characters are often transient men and women—disposable figures quickly dismissed, or at the very least, marginalized by her group" (p. 147). The shorter and less-sustained response could be because of the nature of diversity issues on *Girls* that originated from a more ambiguous systemic trope (an all–White cast), compared to the violent and more "in-your-face" offing of an LGBTQ character under circumstances that reinforced another trope. It is worth noting that even as *Girls* remained transient in its inclusion of diverse characters, the critical and audience reception may have influenced HBO to cast increasingly diverse characters in subsequent show offerings (which will be explored later in this essay). While both tropes are hurtful to different groups, one for racial diversity and one for gender and sexuality reasons, lasting character changes may have occurred because of the substantive initiative taken by *The 100* fans. Instead of just writing or sharing memes, the fans decided to act, such as raising funds for The Trevor Project. The fandom also shifted from antagonistic rhetoric to instead "establish channels of collaboration for a common cause" (Guerrero-Pico, 2017, p. 2). The fandom tried to refocus the online discussion away from hate of the show and on to social recognition of a damaging trope. The newly adopted tone and efforts in campaigning for queer rights gained the notice of The CW network. Rallying as an online community and creating a tangible output (more than $80,000 raised) generated intense pressure for the showrunners. Fans of *The 100* built a smaller community-based following, and so they may have felt they had more buy-in, or even a type of ownership over the show.

Artistic and Creative Ownership

When audiences identify with a character (as they had trouble with *Girls* or found troubling when a queer character was killed off with *The 100*) they may feel a type of possession over that character. As Michel Foucault (1992) argues in "What Is an Author?" a writer's name and ownership may be "regulated" by a culture (p. 305). Foucault explains, "Partially at the expense of themes and concepts that an author places in his work, the 'author function' could also reveal the manner in which discourse is articulated on the basis of social relationships" (p. 313). By extension, "suspicions arise concerning the absolute nature and creative role of the subject" (Foucault, 1992, p. 314), which could mean that audiences also hold power over stories and increasingly express interest in influencing these outcomes. Thus begins a battle for control between the artist and the audience, who create and influence characters, respectively. The idea of artistic ownership and authorship is hard to pinpoint in an art form, like a play, film, or television show. These forms are penned by one or many people and require producers, editors, and other collaborators to bring the story to fruition. Michael J. Meyer (2004) suggests of the 1987 novel *Misery*: "[Stephen] King poses the ambiguous question faced by all writers: whether their concern for the symbiotic relationship with their reading public is great enough to overcome their fear of catering to inferior quality in order to attain a more measurable goal: reader acceptance and financial success" (p. 97).

Indeed, as displayed in the face-to-face power play between *Misery*'s characters Annie Wilkes and Paul Sheldon, artists must decide to concede or not concede, in varying degrees, with varying results. However, in making these changes, artists may believe the writing and characterization will be lessened, and the result will be not as envisioned. In a technical sense, this interplay between artists and audience may now also include the influence of online fandoms, whether it results in renewal, casting decisions, or new character arcs. With *The 100* in particular (and to a more limited degree with *Girls*), audiences were not so much "authors" as they functioned as what

Foucault (1992) might call "initiators." As he describes, "the distinctive contribution of these [sorts of] authors is that they produced not only their own work, but the possibility and the rules of formation of other texts" (Foucault, 1992, p. 310). Foucault uses "initiators" to describe authors like Homer, Freud, and Marx, and obviously online discussion is not an identical comparison. Yet, the moves made by *The 100* fandom are like the initiator in that it shifted discourse to focus on import larger than the original work in reference. In highlighting the social injustice of Bury Your Gays, *The 100* fandom may represent a more modern initiator, establishing a larger conversation of how the trope had permeated into other shows and films. This sort of action differs from the simplicity of "cancel culture," and may instead be cited as a diversity initiative. Instead of expecting creative changes based on want, like with *Misery*, the criticism of *Girls* and *The 100* was an expectation of change based on what was considered to misalign with reality. To see normative characters fixed in a setting that ignores, or at least doesn't showcase, a diverse reality is largely behind the diversity criticism for *Girls* and *The 100*. Essentially, as opposed to calling for creative change based on expectations of what is correct or appropriate, the diversity criticism aimed at *Girls* and *The 100* was more of a critique of social injustice, rather than an instance of cancel culture. Despite the negativity of the blanket term "cancel culture," this is not a reason to "disengage from Twitter and Facebook, as some commentators advocate, nor to give up on social media's potential for progressive action" (Ng, 2020, p. 622). As explored above, though audience pushback sometimes results in snap decisions, it can also inspire positive initiatives for diversity.

Diversity Initiatives Across Visual Media

Audience demands help sway the market and have opened diversity initiatives in various forms of media. A diversity initiative can be described as an attempt to acknowledge diversity gaps, while also promoting greater diversity. In the wake of the murder of George Floyd in 2020, protests across the U.S. have reignited conversations about race and representation (Burnett, 2022). Television executives have taken notice and have launched diversity initiatives. To start, in June 2020, Hackman Capital promised to invest two million dollars in diverse communities and media training for minorities. The funds will enable "work with local schools, production studios, and content creators to offer Black students and other underrepresented communities the resources to obtain mentorship, internships, scholarships, and the necessary education and onsite training to secure jobs in Los Angeles' largest industry" (Low, 2020, para. 5). Similarly, CBS has set a goal to hire more minority writers. The network hopes to expand to 40 percent diverse writers by the 2021–22 broadcast season, widening to 50 percent by the 2022–23 season (D'Zurilla, 2020, paras. 1–2). Even actors are making strides to develop opportunities for underrepresented writers. Working with the organization Color of Change, Michael B. Jordan started the #ChangeHollywood initiative in July 2020, which "outlines a road map with concrete ways to invest in anti-racist content and authentic Black stories, invest in Black talent and reinvest police funds to support Black communities" (Ali, 2020, para. 4). Even as the drive for greater diversity in visual media expands and is quantified, the current gaps in representation are still acute. Social media plays a role in how knowledge of representation is changing, because "as the communications landscape gets denser, more complex, and more participatory, the networked population is gaining greater access to information, more opportunities to engage in public speech, and an enhanced ability to undertake collective action" (Shirky, 2011, p. 29). The combination of communication and dissemination of sentiment can drive change, like a diversity initiative. As Meadow Jones (2014) tells it, "Artists and authors commonly strive to bring the viewer or reader into a world made through description or expression" (p. 49). So, it makes sense that those same audiences would voice their opinions to reach the authors in pursuit of new artistic development. Ultimately, collective action allowed *The 100* to sustain a longer lasting initiative, whereas the collective action for *Girls* was less focused and produced different results.

Though Dunham initially reacted to the lack of diversity by basically saying she "couldn't relate" and therefore "couldn't write to the experience," she nevertheless added a prominent Black guest star at the start of Season 2. Given that filming took place only one month after the premiere, the audience and critical reception may have swayed whom *Girls* ultimately chose to cast. Either way, Dunham's decision to publicize this choice was certainly in part a response to the critique. Similar to *The 100*'s Clexa promos, which built up a diverse and strong character, the promos for Glover's addition hinted that he would be a series regular. After the Season 2 premiere, rumors hit that he was only a guest star. Glover's departure after two episodes initiates when the main character, Hannah, confronts him for critiquing an essay she's written, a conversation that devolves into racial awkwardness with Glover's character shooting back, "Oh, I'm a white girl and I moved to New York and I'm having a great time and I got a fixed gear bike and I'm gonna date a Black guy and we're gonna go to a dangerous part of town" (Konner & Dunham, 2013, 14:06). His critique of Hannah's White privilege reflects self-awareness on the part of *Girls*. Importantly, Jones (2014) talks about how "empathy may be best understood through a narrative context" (p. 54). With the storyline including Glover's minority character, both the audience and artist may have experienced empathetic moments for diverse characters and situations. However, in a 2018 interview with *The New Yorker*, Dunham revealed that Glover ad-libbed the lines. His interpretation of Hannah's White privilege was "one hundred percent him. I emailed him later to say, 'I hope you feel the part on *Girls* didn't tokenize you,' and his response […]: 'Let's not think back on mistakes we made in the past, let's just focus on what lies in front of us'" (as cited in Friend, 2018, para. 70). As time passed from the 2012 premiere, Dunham seemed more comfortable expressing self-awareness for the diversity issues pointed out by fans and critics. During an interview with *Nylon*, Dunham professes, "I wouldn't do another show that starred four white girls" (as cited in Wappler, 2017, para. 8). In reflecting on other *Girls* controversies, the aforementioned claim of nepotism was perhaps linked to the lack of diversity.

Nepotism is a bias based on familial or friendly connections. There is an adage among writers to "write what you know," and Dunham acknowledges she "wrote" from what she knew. Jones (2014) believes that to truly write "what you know," greater reflection is necessary, because "the ability to synthesize information directly relates to one's ability to combine the given experiences and create new knowledge through appropriation and reconfiguration" (p. 50). If normative White showrunners continue to influence television, then falling back on "what you know" becomes a trap of bias couched in the myth of artistic freedom, lacking reflection or synthesis of self and of others. Thus, until more diverse showrunners are included at all levels of television, writing from beyond what is familiar (i.e., casting diverse leads) is a healthy start in combating a lack of diversity. Such steps should be taken with consideration, so as to avoid tokenism or misappropriation, but in moving from "what is known," or rather, "what is comfortable," new perspectives and stronger stories may flourish.

As outlined in the first section, staff writers of *The 100* ultimately decided for Clarke's character to remain bisexual rather than play out the potential heteronormative relationship with the protagonist Bellamy. Many factors could have influenced this decision, but the audience and critical response may have played a part. Likewise, before the Clexa debacle, audiences were previously on edge from another LGBTQ character death on *Jane the Virgin* in February 2016. In March 2016 came Lexa's death on *The 100*, Kira's death on SyFy's *The Magicians*, and Denise's death on AMC's *The Walking Dead*. The culmination of queer character deaths via various television shows accentuated the Bury Your Gays trope in a very short time span.

Fictional characters are killed off in any genre, regardless of demographics or social standing. However, fans of *The 100* believed queer characters have been repeatedly discarded in film and television. As the Bury Your Gays trope outlines, this is in part because such characters are cast so infrequently (or commonly as antagonists), so their deaths are all the more noticeable and give rise to the notion that these characters are expendable. Autostraddle published a list of 212 lesbian and bisexual characters that are killed off from 1976 through 2020 (Riese, 2016, online chart). Of all modern queer characters and relationships on television, not many end up surviving. Snarker (2016) reports that television has in large part allowed "happy endings" for "only around 18 couples, on some 16 TV shows" (para. 8). Like other fans, queer fans hope to see themselves represented in fictional characters. Erin B. Waggoner (2018) explains that

> for LGBTQ fans, this is especially important in their own meaning-making as representation becomes an important aspect of this process. Essentially, there needs to be good representation to help people understand who they are and the challenges they can expect to face with regard to this particular identity [p. 1880].

Audiences understandably want characters to identify with, to see themselves in, and to recognize. This representation is hard to come by for queer audiences, so instead of just being upset over the loss of a beloved character, fans were perhaps upset over the loss of a role-model. The limited or poor representations of queer characters in February and March 2016 led to an amplified response from fans. Such a response contributes meaningfully to participatory culture.

As noted above, certain hashtags trended on X to call more attention to the diversity criticism, like #BuryYourGays. *The 100* showrunner Rothenberg's X account lost 15,000 followers after the March 3, 2016, episode aired. Moreover, "fans got the hashtag #LGBTFansDeserveBetter to trend for hours worldwide on Twitter the week after Lexa's death to coincide with the airing of *The 100*" (Snarker, 2016, para. 15). Viewers also created two websites to express thoughts and discontent with queer representation on media (lgbtfansdeservebetter.com and wedeservedbetter.com), and raised over $100,000 to donate to the Trevor Project. The combination of social media blitzes and other forms of outreach effectively conveyed how powerful the audience's discontent could be. As Snarker (2016) observes, "The intricate pas de deux that shows and fans play with each other is the new social capital that drives ratings" (para. 20). Showrunners that ignore critics and fanbases are ignoring the potential for media exposure, which in turn could impact the number of viewers.

Diversifying Show Catalogs: The CW and HBO

Perhaps intent on investing the "new social capital" for creative and economic gain, The CW and HBO have diversified representation of writers and characters for their

Figure 2. CW 2020 promotional posters. 2020 (The CW).

Figure 3. CW 2021 promotional posters. 2021 (The CW).

media content. This brief analysis of CW and HBO content offerings ranged from 2020 to 2022, and accounted for characters outside the White, heteronormative paradigm.

The analysis of CW includes promotional posters for a visual progression of content offerings. In 2020, The CW featured six shows (see Figure 2) with minorities billed as lead and six shows with minorities as co-stars (out of twenty-four offerings of original content). Two shows star White women as the lead but are diverse in their characterizations: *In the Dark* is about a blind woman, while *Batwoman* features a queer lead as Batwoman (and the actress also identifies as lesbian). For the second season, Batwoman re-cast the lead with a Black actor (Javisia Leslie).

With HBO, an analysis of the network's content offerings is considered. Like CW, in 2020, HBO featured more than nine shows with minorities billed as the lead (out of

Figure 4. CW 2022 promotional posters. 2022 (The CW).

over thirty-six offerings of original content), with minority writers. As diverse successors to *Girls*, shows like *Insecure* (2016–2021), *Euphoria* (2019–), and *Betty* (2020–2021) reflect—respectively—on issues like relationships for women and teens working and dating in the city, overcoming drug use, and resisting sexism. Merely having diverse content does not mean networks like HBO or The CW are effectively finished with diversity. Still, the number of diverse offerings has increased, particularly since the 2012 release of *Girls*.

From the chronological depiction of promotional images for CW, there is a slight increase in diverse character representation. In 2020, The CW featured 6 diverse lead shows, while in 2022, the number increased to 12 (see Figure 3 and 4). A similar pattern is indicated by HBO from their numerous content offerings for 2022, even as the network has again shifted, becoming Max. Miller (2022) writes how "as many as 13 people of color who were previously in charge of developing [HBO] shows with diversity have been let go [...] and there are barely any non-white people left in the upper ranks of content" (para. 13). Though HBO's outlook on diverse opportunities may not be as promising as it once was, currently, they do offer more diverse content than they have in previous years. From a cancel-culture perspective, diversity of characterization could be cynically framed as a phasing out of White character leads. However, it is better understood as a diversity initiative, which the following section evaluates and distinguishes while considering both terms in relation to television.

Cancel Culture or Diversity Initiative?

As previously suggested, cancel culture can be perceived as a group mentality by which the actions or words shared in a public forum are deemed taboo, and therefore should be amended. Sometimes, the desire to "amend" goes too far (in which the push and the allure hit an apex), and online forums demand similar taboo action or content be deleted or "canceled." For *Girls* and *The 100*, the writers of this essay believe that the audience and critical receptions cut across cancel culture *and* the larger diversity initiative influencing Hollywood and other media spaces. Cancel culture can have negative connotations; however, in the cases of *Girls* and *The 100*, what was being identified as taboo coincided with diversity initiatives and could be deemed positive, instead of being classified with the more toxic elements of cancel culture, which sometimes lead to the dismantling of a cause without reflection. Instead of intending to "silence" what was considered taboo, the criticism surrounding *Girls* and *The 100* aimed to *remedy* problematic character representations. With these remedies, there is an intent to "end" or "cancel" the predominant representation of White and heteronormative characters. In that way, social media calls for change complicate negative connotations of cancel culture. Even as cancel culture and diversity initiatives may overlap, they are not the same. Cancel culture is a consensus to end taboos, whereas diversity initiatives constitute an attempt to add new perspectives to an otherwise homogeneous creative landscape. Even still, there are online fans who believe that diversity initiatives are a type of canceling, or destruction, of creativity. For example, X user Patrick stated:

> If Friends had aired with a "diverse cast" it would have very few fans and would have lasted 2 years tops

Don't apologize for a great show that was loved by 10's of millions ... the truth of the matter is diversity has destroyed far too many countries and cultures.

Patrick's tweets, shared back-to-back in the same month, received 218 likes and then 316 likes. His sentiment suggested the diversity criticism of *Friends* may have contributed to fewer viewers. This view also leads to the perception of diversity initiatives as "forced creativity" and therefore diminishing their quality, much in the way *Misery*'s Sheldon was concerned about forced revisions from fan Wilkes as a weakening of the storyline. Yet, diverse casting in shows like *Scandal* and *Evil* have drawn large audiences. Clearly, a series can be both diverse and profitable, as noted by Weinstein (2014): "*Scandal*'s success as both a form of social TV and Black female-centered programming encouraged ABC to sign Rhimes to a lucrative four-year contract and schedule their entire Thursday-night prime-time programming around a block of Rhimes-produced programs" (para. 5). There is also the line of reasoning to just let characters and storylines appeal to viewers without needing to infuse diversity. Lisa Kudrow explains how in *Friends* "there was a guy whose wife discovered she was gay and pregnant, and they raised the child together? We had surrogacy too. It was, at the time, progressive" (as cited in Donnelly, 2020, para. 11). Let's also not forget the captivating performance by Kathleen Taylor as a transgender woman named Helena Handbasket (dead name Charles Bing), often referred to as the "father" of Chandler Bing (Matthew Perry) in the series (McNiece and Jones, 2023). What this points to is that series like *Friends*, *Girls*, or *The 100* are not irredeemable for their audience-perceived issues of diversity. Rather, audiences have shifted their expectations of what character portrayals can mean on a personal level since *Friends* premiered in 1994, just as *Girls* and *The 100* manifest more recent societal trends. It's important to reassess where television content stands in the hopes of looking forward. Even if audiences admire television shows, they may still hope for new narratives that incorporate societal changes in a meaningful way.

Diversity initiatives may also be perceived as unnecessary because all–Black casts in similar shows promote a "separate but equal" ideal. As with the post below, X-user Jabber asks why minority-centric shows are not questioned for their lack of diversity: "Why don't they have this conversation about Sanford and son? Or good times?" Jabber's post was liked 511 times, and such analogy betrays a deceptively false equivalence, as minority-centric shows are so rare compared with the proliferation of White, heteronormative spaces. White showrunners may be given preference (for nepotism or other privilege), which excludes minorities from participation, even if all–Black cast members are promoted in shows like *Sanford and Sons*, *Good Times*, or more recently *black-ish*. Overall, though cancel culture and diversity initiatives share similarities, diversity more aligns with market sway (audience interest and trends) that many writers and distributors already account for and respond to.

Conclusion

Overall, our premise was to detail audience receptions for *Girls* and *The 100* and analyze how they affected each show's production. The writers of this essay believe that participatory culture reflects established online practices and may be used to sustain media projects, end them, or to invite revision and the production of new media content. While some use pejorative terms like "cancel culture," the term "diversity initiative" might be more appropriate and aptly describes viewer critiques of *Girls* and *The 100*. Creativity and authorship are *always* about reception and pleasing the audience; in a networked media age, the audience simply has more immediate and wide-reaching means to make their perspectives heard. The two cases of *Girls* and *The 100* diversified production in response to viewer criticisms. Considered separately, the more substantive change occurred with *The 100*, perhaps because writers weighed the pushback from fans in tandem with market concerns, since cancellation is of greater concern for basic cable networks like The CW. Even so, this confluence does not negate the strength of audience reception. Instead, it perhaps underscores how network series are at the mercy of the market, unlike series on premium channels like HBO that can respond in relatively minor ways (such as with tokenism). This essay also explored how diversity in television has a role to play in those very market concerns, and that writing from "what you know" can contribute to a lack of diversity if showrunners and writers are not representatively diverse. While tradition, or the familiar, is comforting, it can also perpetuate harmful practice. *Girls* is a high-profile example demonstrating how the temporary addition of "diverse" characters may not be the ultimate answer to television's lack of diversity, especially for guest-starring roles, which seems to diminish the cultures and criticisms (as a means of placating rather than consideration), whereas the sustained plot response from *The 100* showrunners with Clexa impactfully addresses a harmful trope. In the end, both series exemplify how diversifying characterization may prove to be a temporary fix so long as diverse writers and producers are not given more opportunities to co-create media.

Note

1. An earlier version of this essay appeared in *KOME—An International Journal of Pure Communication Inquiry*, Volume 9, Issue 1, Summer 2021, pp. 64–84. DOI: 10.17646/KOME.75672.59.

References

Abdul-Jabbar, K. (2013, January 31). Girls just wants to have (white) fun. *Huffington Post*. https://www.huffpost.com/entry/girls-review_b_2593756.
Ackerman, E., Ambar, S., Amis, M. et al. (2020, July 7). A letter on justice and open debate. *Harper's Bazaar*. https://harpers.org/a-letter-on-justice-and-open-debate/.
Adalian, J. (2012, June 14). More boys watch 'Girls' than girls. *Vulture*. https://www.vulture.com/2012/06/more-boys-watch-girls-than-girls.html.
Ali, R. (2020). Michael B. Jordan, Color of Change launch #changehollywood diversity campaign to change 'rules of the game.' *USA Today*. https://www.usatoday.com/story/entertainment/celebrities/2020/07/23/michael-bjordan-changehollywood-drive-aims-hollywood-diversity/5494068002/.
Bailey, A. (2019). Jason Momoa had the most Khal Drogo response to Daenerys' fate in Game of Thrones finale. Elle. https://www.elle.com/culture/celebrities/a27554717/jason-momoa-emilia-clarke-game-of-thrones-finale-instagram-comments/.
Beard, J. (2020). Click bait, cancel culture, and the rhetoric of civil discourse. *Georgia International Conference on Information Literacy*. https://digitalcommons.georgiasouthern.edu/gaintlit/2020/202.
Bennet, L. (2013, January 9). Lena Dunham caved to her critics on race, and it made 'Girls' a better show. *The New Republic*. https://newrepublic.com/article/111732/why-lenadunhams-response-her-critics-has-made-the-show-better-ever.

Berman, J. (2012, April 13). Why are we taking Lena Dunham's 'Girls' so personally? *Flavorwire*. https://www.flavorwire.com/279527/why-are-we-taking-lena-dunhamsgirls-so-personally.

Bouvier, G. (2020). Racist call-outs and cancel culture on Twitter: The limitations of the platform's ability to define issues of social justice. *Discourse, Context & Media, 38*, 100431. CrossRef.

Bradley, L. (2019, October 31). Benioff and Weiss reportedly left *Star Wars*, at least in part, due to "toxic fandom." *Vanity Fair*. https://www.vanityfair.com/hollywood/2019/10/game-of-thrones-benioff-and-weissstar-wars-netflix-lucasfilm.

Burnett, S. (2022). For world, Floyd's death was about race. Why not the trials? *AP News*. https://apnews.com/article/death-of-george-floyd-ahmaud-arbery-george-floyd-race-and-ethnicity-04ad7633c49f94475d5c9f5c5a381c24.

Chapman, J., Glancy, M., & Harper, S. (2007). *The new film history: Sources, methods, approaches*. Palgrave Macmillan.

Coates, T.-N. (2012, April 20). "Girls" through the veil. *The Atlantic*. https://www.theatlantic.com/entertainment/archive/2012/04/girls-through-theveil/256154/.

Conrad C. (2023, November 21). As a huge fan of the LOTR and The Hobbit movies (and a casual fan of the books) I don't [Comment on the webpage "The Lord of the Rings: The Rings of Power: Season 1"]. Rotten Tomatoes. https://www.rottentomatoes.com/tv/the_lord_of_the_rings_the_rings_of_power/s01.

Crugnale, J. (2012, April 23). CNN panel slams HBO's *Girls* for lack of diversity: "Odd," "out of step." *Media Ite*. https://www.mediaite.com/tv/cnn-panel-slams-hbos-girls-for-lackof-diversity-odd-out-of-step/.

Dhaenens, F., Van Bauwel, S., & Biltereyst, D. (2008). Slashing the fiction of queer theory: Slash fiction, queer reading, and transgressing the boundaries of screen studies, representations, and audiences. *Journal of Communication Inquiry, 32*(4), 335–347. CrossRef.

Dolly P. (2023, November 21). *Firstly, I would like to note that the actors' performances are not the most interesting; there are very long, protracted* [Comment on the webpage "The Lord of the Rings: The Rings of Power: Season 1"]. Rotten Tomatoes. https://www.rottentomatoes.com/tv/the_lord_of_the_rings_the_rings_of_power/s01.

Donnelly, E. (2020). Lisa Kudrow says *Friends* would be "completely different" now: "It would not be an all-white cast" [online]. *Yahoo! Entertainment*. https://www.yahoo.com/lifestyle/lisa-kudrow-friends-all-white-cast-progressive181508824.html.

D'Zurilla, C. (2020, July 13). CBS announces diversity overhaul of writers rooms and scriptdevelopment program. *The Los Angeles Times*. https://www.latimes.com/entertainment-arts/tv/story/2020-07-13/cbs-racial-diversityeffort-writers-development-bipoc.

Elsaesser, T. (2004). The new film history as media archaeology. *Cinémas: revue d'études cinématographiques / Cinémas: Journal of Film Studies, 4*(2–3), 75–117.

Foucault, M. (1992). What is an author? In J. Marsh, J.D. Caputo, & M. Westphal (Eds.), *Modernity and its discontents* (pp. 299–314). Fordham University Press. (Original work published 1969).

Framke, C. (2016, March 25). Queer women have been killed on television for decades. Now *The 100*'s fans are fighting back. *Vox*. https://www.vox.com/platform/amp/2016/3/25/11302564/lesbiandeaths-televisiontrope.

Friedman, S.S. (1997). Making history: Reflections on feminism, narrative, and desire. *The Postmodern history reader*. Routledge.

Friend, T. (2018, February 26). Donald Glover can't save you. *The New Yorker*. https://www.newyorker.com/magazine/2018/03/05/donald-glover-cant-save-you.

Guerrero-Pico, M. (2017). #Fringe, audiences, and fan labor: Twitter activism to save a TV show from cancellation. *International Journal of Communication, 11*, 2071–2092. CrossRef.

Guerrero-Pico, M., Establés, M.-J., & Ventura, R. (2017). Dead lesbian syndrome: LGBTQ fandom's self-regulation mechanisms in fan-producer controversies around "The 100." *Analisi: Quaderns de Comunicació i Cultura, 57*, 29–46. CrossRef.

Hachachi, R. (Director). (2020). *Tom Segura: Ball hog*. [Movie]. http://www.netflix.com.

Halbwachs, M. (1980). *The collective memory*. Harper & Row Colophon.

Holbrook, D. (2012, March 21). *The 100*'s executive producer breaks his silence about Lexa's death. *TVInsider*. https://www.tvinsider.com/81017/the-100-jason-rothenberg-onlexas-death/.

Holland, J.J. (2022, September 7). Some 'Rings of Power' and 'House of Dragon' fans are letting their racism roar. MSNBC. https://www.msnbc.com/opinion/msnbc-opinion/some-rings-power-house-dragon-fans-are-letting-their-racism-n1298720.

House of the dragon. (n.d.). Rotten Tomatoes. https://www.rottentomatoes.com/tv/house_of_the_dragon.

Hulan, H. (2017). Bury your gays: History, usage, and context. *McNair Scholars Journal, 21*(1), Article 6. https://scholarworks.gvsu.edu/mcnair/vol21/iss1/6.

Iser, W. (2006). *How to do theory*. Blackwell.

Jackson, E. (2012, September 26). Facebook's MySpace moment: Why Twitter is already bigger than Facebook. *Forbes*. https://www.forbes.com/sites/ericjackson/2012/09/26/facebooks-myspace-momentwhy-twitter-is-already-bigger-than-facebook/#cbc19e5e5a69.

Jay, T.B. (2017). *We did what?! Offensive and inappropriate behavior in American history*. Greenwood.

Jones, M. (2014). To write what you know: Embodiment, authorship, and empathy. *Sensoria: A Journal of Mind, Brain & Culture, 10*(1), 49.

Kar, P. (2019). Partha Kar: We must stand up and challenge offensive behaviour. *BMJ, 367,* l6749. CrossRef.

Keightly, E. (2008). Engaging with memory. In M. Pickering (Ed.), *Research methods for cultural studies* (pp. 175–192). Edinburgh University Press.

Konner, J. (Writer), & Dunham, L. (Director). (2013, January 20). I get ideas (Season 2, Episode 2) [TV series episode]. In J. Apatow, L. Dunham, B.E. Kaplan, J. Konner, & I.S. Landress (Executive Producers), Girls. Apatow Productions; I Am Jenni Konner Productions; HBO Entertainment.

Lena Dunham addresses criticism aimed at "Girls" (2012, May 7). *FreshAir.* https://www.npr.org/2012/05/07/152183865/lena-dunham-addresses-criticism-aimedat-girls.

The lord of the rings: Rings of power. (n.d.). Rotten Tomatoes. https://www.rottentomatoes.com/tv/the_lord_of_the_rings_the_rings_of_power/.

Low, E. (2020). Television city pledges $2 million to community, diversity initiatives in wake of LAPD presence at protests. *Variety.* https://variety.com/2020/biz/news/televisioncity-pledges-2-million-to-community-diversity-initiatives-in-wake-of-lapd-presenceat-protests-1234630574/.

luke333Professor. (2022, October 26). After season 8 of Game of Thrones. I thought I was done with series and didn't any plan on watching [Comment on the webpage "House of the Dragon—Season 1"]. IGN. https://www.ign.com/articles/house-of-the-dragon-season-1-review.

McCluskey, M. (2019, July 24). HBO rejects petition to remake *Game of Thrones* Season 8 once and for all. *Time Magazine.* https://time.com/5634309/hbo-rejects-game-ofthrones-season-8-petition/.

McNamara, M. (2013, May 11). "Scandal" has become must-tweet TV. *Los Angeles Times.* https://www.latimes.com/entertainment/tv/la-xpm-2013-may-11-la-et-st-scandal-abcsocial-media-20130511-story.html.

McNiece, M., & Jones, A. (2023, October 20). Kathleen Turner remembers TV son Matthew Perry's 'good eense of humor' and 'good heart' (Exclusive). People. https://people.com/kathleen-turner-remembers-matthew-perry-good-sense-of-humor-good-heart-exclusive-8384228.

Meyer, M.J. (2004). Stephen King's writers: The critical politics of literary quality in *Misery* and *The Dark Half. Literature and the writer* (pp. 97–117). Brill Rodopi. CrossRef.

Miller, A. (2022). Warner Bros. discovery's agenda is clear … and it's not pretty. *No Film School.* https://nofilmschool.com/lack-of-diversity-at-hbo.

Moylan, B. (2017). A complete timeline of all controversies *Girls* started. *Vulture.* https://www.vulture.com/2017/02/hbos-girls-a-complete-controversy-timeline.html.

Nagy, J., & Midha, A. (2015). The value of earned audiences: How social interactions amplify TV impact: What programmers and advertisers can gain from earned social impressions. *Journal of Advertising Research, 54*(4), 448. CrossRef.

Ng, E. (2020). No grand pronouncements here…: Reflections on cancel culture and digital media participation. *Television & New Media, 21*(6), Online First Publication. CrossRef.

O'Hara, H. (2022, October 28). House of the dragon—Season 1 review. IGN. https://www.ign.com/articles/house-of-the-dragon-season-1-review.

Parker Beard, J.C. (2020). Click bait, cancel culture, and the rhetoric of civic discourse. *Georgia International Conference on Information Literacy.* https://digitalcommons.georgiasouthern.edu/gaintlit/2020/2020/19.

Placido, D.D. (2019, October 28). "Game Of Thrones" showrunners David Benioff and D.B. Weiss confirmed the worst suspicions of the fanbase. *Forbes.* https://www.forbes.com/sites/danidiplacido/2019/10/28/game-of-thronesshowrunners-david-benioff-and-db-weiss-confirmed-the-worst-suspicions-ofthefanbase/#12736642f37c.

Riese. (2016, March 11). All 212 dead lesbian and bisexual characters on TV, and how they died. *Autostraddle.* https://www.autostraddle.com/all-65-dead-lesbian-and-bisexualcharacters-on-tv-and-how-they-died-312315/.

Roth, D. (2012, March 27). Why Jason Rothenberg's apology fell flat with *The 100*'s fans and the real lessons to learn. *SyFy Wire.* https://www.syfy.com/syfywire/why-jasonrothenbergs-apology-fell-flat-100s-fans-and-real-lessons-learn.

Rothenberg, J. [@JRothenbergTV]. (2015, January 28). You guys know I don't ship. But I gotta admit, #Clexa is seaworthy. #justsaying #The100 @miselizajane @debnamcarey [Post]. X. https://twitter.com/jrothenbergtv/status/560632588571009025.

Sharf, Z. (2022, September 7). Whoopi Goldberg rails against racist 'Rings of Power' and 'House of the Dragon' fans: 'What is wrong with y'all?' Variety. https://variety.com/2022/tv/news/whoopi-goldberg-racist-rings-of-power-house-of-the-dragon-fans-1235361828/.

Shirky, C. (2011). The political power of social media: Technology, the public sphere, and political change. *Foreign Affairs, 90*(1), 28–41. https://www.foreignaffairs.com/articles/2010-12-20/political-power-social-media.

Smith, J. (2007). *The Wicker Man* (1973) email digest: A case study in web ethnography. In J. Chapman, M. Glancy, & S. Harper (Eds.), *The New Film History, Sources, Methods, Approaches* (pp. 229–244). Palgrave Macmillan.

Snarker, D. (2016, March 21). Bury your gays: Why "The 100," "Walking Dead" deaths are problematic (guest column). *The Hollywood Reporter*. https://www.hollywoodreporter.com/live-feed/bury-your-gays-why-100-877176.

Steinberg, B. (2016, April 1). Maybelline downplays protest against CW's "The 100." *Variety*. https://variety.com/2016/tv/news/the-100-maybelline-cw-lexa-1201743857/.

Stewart, D. (2012, April 19). Why we need to keep talking about the white girls on "Girls." *Jezebel*. https://jezebel.com/why-we-need-to-keep-talking-about-the-white-girls-on-gi5903382.

Storey, K. (2012, May 18). "Girls" quick fix. *New York Post*. https://nypost.com/2012/05/18/girls-quick-fix/.

TV Promos. (2016, February 25). *The 100 3x07 promo "Thirteen" (HD)*. [Video file]. YouTube. https://www.youtube.com/watch?v=5bnPQe2ac_0.

Waggoner, B.E. (2018). Bury your gays and social media fan response: Television, LGBTQ representation, and communitarian ethics. *Journal of Homosexuality*, 65(13), 1877–1891. CrossRef.

Wagmeister, E. (2016, June 11). "The 100" producer applauds social impact of Lexa's death: "I am grateful for the tidal wave that came down on me." *Variety*. https://www.variety.com/2016/tv/news/the-100-lexa-dead-clarke-javier-grillomarxuach-reaction-lesbian-trope-1201793568/amp.

Wappler, M. (2017, January 11). Lena Dunham is our February cover star. *Nylon*. https://www.nylon.com/articles/lena-dunham-nylon-february-cover.

Watson, E. (2015). Lena Dunham: The awkward/ambiguous politics of white millennial feminism. In E. Watson, J. Mitchell, & M.E. Shaw (Eds.), *HBO's Girls and the awkward politics of gender, race, and privilege* (pp. 145–166). Lexington.

Weinstein, S. (2014, September 22). How "Scandal" paved the way for ABC's Twitter-based "#TGIT" marketing strategy. *Variety*. http://variety.com/2014/tv/news/scandaltwitter-shonda-rhimes-tgit-abc-shondaland-1201311282/.

Black Dude Dies First

Portrayals and Casting Choices in Fear the Walking Dead

Juanita "Tico" Tenorio

"T-Dogging" in The Walking Dead

Five seasons into the popular zombie apocalypse show *The Walking Dead* (2010–2022), Black viewers created a number of different names for what they perceived as cliche, like:

> the black guy swap, (Satryghen),
> the Black Highlander Theory, (kingkoons),
> 1 black man rule of *The Walking Dead* (UltraMegaMegaMan),
> the Law of Conservation of Color (Justin, Nerds of Color),
> the "Ongoing Black Man Problem" [attorneytracey, Nerds of Color]

or more simply, *The Walking Dead*'s "Black Man Problem" (Jenn, 2014). Horror aficionados have long been familiar with this trope by another name, "Black Dude Dies First" (Black Dude Dies First, n.d.). Especially in big-budget films where an effort is often made to include a "Token Minority" (another trope) so that filmmakers can boast of the diversity of their projects, the Token Minority was often the first to die. Taking into account the longevity of a television series such as *The Walking Dead* (or *TWD*), especially in comparison to a two-hour movie, Black viewers acknowledged that while the series appeared committed to including Black characters, as soon as a new Black man was introduced the previous one had to die. As a result, the "Black Dude Dies First" trope morphs into "the black guy swap" or "1 black man rule of *The Walking Dead*." Nerds of Color commentator Justin (2015) explained how "the Law of Conservation of Color" is analogous to the law of thermodynamics:

> I actually mentioned to a friend the fact that at the beginning of season 5 there were a reasonable number of central black characters, and his response was "Oh shit, you know their gonna clean house soon cuz the Law of Conservation of Color can't be violated." And sure enough, the house got cleaned! Bob, Tyreese, Noah in quick succession.

After acknowledging that "*The Walking Dead* has quietly assembled one of the most ethnically diverse casts on a top-rated TV show," critic Eric Deggans (2014) pointed out that the series' commitment to diversity does not extend to development of those characters. The series' first Black character, T-Dog (portrayed by Irone

Singleton) is "given little backstory and few lines. He even complained about his situation, but only when he was delirious from an infection" (Deggans, 2014). In an uncharacteristic meta-referential moment, T-Dog says:

> I'm the one black guy ... you realize how precarious that makes my situation? I'm talking about two good ol' boy cowboy sheriffs and a redneck whose brother cut off his own hand because I dropped a key. Who in that scenario do you think is going to be the first to get lynched? [Mazzara & Dickerson, 2011, 10:02]

Even within the world of the show, T-Dog's character is aware that his status as a token minority puts him at risk. Jason Johnson dubbed this phenomenon of only achieving some substance just before their death "T-Dogging" in his honor:

> T-Dog never had a storyline, his background was never really explored, and he didn't have a love interest, major kill or anything of substance throughout his run on the show.... Somewhere in the backs of the writers' minds, they must have been aware of this, so T-Dog was given depth, substance and even a shining moment on the show—just before he dies [as cited in Moyer, 2021].

Just prior to *The Walking Dead*'s Fall 2015 season six premiere, showrunner Scott Gimple continued to defend the series' treatment of Black men and insist that race was irrelevant during the casting process (Fitzpatrick, 2015). Yet, season six reintroduced the series' most well-developed and beloved Black male character, Morgan Jones (portrayed by Lennie James).

Take Two: Fear the Walking Dead's *Commitment to Diversity*

In addition to adding fan favorite, Morgan James to *The Walking Dead* in 2015, a prequel of sorts called *Fear the Walking Dead* (*FtWD*) also aired. Whereas the original *TWD* begins with the lead character, Rick Grimes (portrayed by Andrew Lincoln), waking from a coma after the zombie apocalypse has already transformed civilization, this *FtWD* would explore what happened during the initial outbreak. This prequel would take place in Los Angeles and would feature an entirely new cast, one that would of necessity reflect the diversity of Los Angeles. Sarah E. Turner and Sarah Nilsen (2014) explained that a desire to populate television shows with diverse casts is inextricably linked to the increasing popularity of color-blind casting: "Over the past few decades, television producers have employed a variety of colorblind strategies in order to counter charges of racism and racial insensitivity. One of the most dominant and persistent trends is diversity casting" (p. 5). Indeed, the producers of this *TWD* prequel publicly announced the series would not only reflect the ethnic and racial make-up of Los Angeles, but as Gimple had previously emphasized, a commitment to "casting the right actors came before any considerations of race, or intentions for the character" (as cited in Fitzpatrick, 2015). While defending the deaths of Black men in *The Walking Dead*, producer Gale Anne Hurd emphasized that it was the series' commitment to color-blind casting that led to these deaths:

> We've killed a lot more white characters than African-American characters. And not only that, I think it's important to point out that we did cast two African-American actors in roles

that were not African-American. In the comic books, Bob was white. And the character of Noah was not an African American. We just cast the best actor [as cited in Dos Santos, 2015].

Producers of *FtWD* appeared to continue a commitment to both color-blind casting and diversity, with the actors' enthusiastic support. The script's lead male character, Travis Manawa, was originally meant to be Latino but during the casting process, producers decided on actor Cliff Curtis, a New Zealander of Māori descent, and rewrote the script to reflect his ethnicity. In the original script, Manawa's ex-wife was meant to be White, but producers cast Latina actress Elizabeth Rodriquez (Hass, 2015). The son, presumably, is meant to be half Māori and half Latino. At the center of the drama is Manawa's relationship with a White high-school guidance counselor and her two children. The looming zombie apocalypse throws the blended families together in a household in El Sereno, California, one of Los Angeles' oldest and overwhelmingly Latino neighborhoods. Another family, an El Salvadoran immigrant, his wife, and adult daughter, end up in the same household.

Curtis, who has portrayed characters ranging from Latin American to Arab, was understandably excited by the opportunity to play a character closer to his roots:

> I mean they actually changed my character name to Manawa, which is a Māori name, which is the first time that that's ever happened. And I really felt that they were genuine and sort of saying, look, we are looking for the right actor for the role, you know. The color of my skin or my background was irrelevant to how I related to the character and the blend of this family. I really feel like sometimes they spin you a line about the casting of a family but I really felt like it was really important—this relationship was about getting the right actors in the role that approach their process and the characters from the heart ["'Fear the Walking Dead' Cast Talk Diversity and Shooting in Los Angeles"].

Other actors in the show have openly praised its color-blind casting and its effort to represent the diversity of Los Angeles. Elizabeth Rodriquez who plays Travis' ex-wife auditioned for the role even though it was written for a White female:

> I'm sitting where there was another role that was NOT written Latina and he [the producer] ultimately made a decision that he wanted to work with me and it didn't matter, and that he decided that why couldn't Travis once he hired Cliff [Curtis] just be American of Māori descent and it is the most eclectic, most incredible group of people that are playing just Americans, and people—and for me, I'm ultimately human first and a woman and it [ethnicity] doesn't have to play a role [Hass, 2015].

Ruben Blades, a renowned Panamanian singer, songwriter, actor, and activist, plays Daniel Salazar, the El Salvadoran immigrant, and has praised the show's producers for its depiction of Los Angeles' diversity: "The producers did the right thing, which is depict Los Angeles' diversity, and Latins are part of that. That diversity is impossible to ignore but is somehow ignored every day by casting directors" (Cobo, 2015). In addition to casting actors of color in lead roles, the show includes at least four interracial relationships: Travis and his White girlfriend, Madison (Kim Dickens); Manawa and his Latina ex-wife; Madison's teenage daughter and her African American boyfriend; and Ofelia (Mercedes Mason), the El Salvadoran daughter, and a White National Guard boyfriend (see Figure 1). Travis and Madison's El Sereno neighbors actually appear to reflect the Latino and Asian character of the actual community.

Unfortunately, despite its efforts at color-blind casting, casting Latinos, and even

Figure 1. *Fear the Walking Dead* Season 1 promotional full cast photograph. From left: Alicia (Alycia Debnam-Carey), Nick (Frank Dillane), Madison (Kim Dickens), Travis (Cliff Curtis), Liza (Elizabeth Rodriguez), Chris (Lorenzo Henrie), Daniel (Rubén Blades), Griselda (Patricia Reyes Spíndola), and Ofelia (Mercedes Mason) (AMC, 2015).

a Pacific Islander, many critics believe the show adheres to the propensity of television and movies in general, but the horror genre in particular, to treat Black men as dispensable. In the first episode of the six-episode season we're introduced to three Black characters. The first is a professional man, the high school principal where Travis and Madison both work. The second is Matt, the high-school boyfriend of Madison's daughter, Alicia (played by Alycia Debnam-Carey). The third, Calvin (played by Keith Powers), is a close friend of Madison's son, Nick (played by Frank Dillane). In all of these cases, critics of its predecessor, *TWD*, might feel hopeful that the stereotypical portrayals of Black men might not haunt this "diverse" prequel. For one thing, this is not the post-apocalyptic brutal world of *TWD*, where anarchy prevails, where southern rednecks freely express their racism. The general populace is unaware of any threat, and life, for the most part, goes on as normal. The high school principal appears to be a kind, but authoritative figure seen doing his job. Alicia's boyfriend, Matt (played by Maestro Harrell), an artist, makes his appearance working on a mural for the high school. Later, he comforts Alicia whose family life is complicated when her drug addict brother, Nick, is arrested and hospitalized. These scenes depict a certain normalcy before the storm, a quiet interlude between a young couple. After Nick escapes from the hospital, Madison and Travis look for him at his friend's house. Calvin, another young, clean-cut Black man, is cleaning the family car in a suburban neighborhood. But before any of these characters can be developed in any depth, the show succumbs to blatant stereotypes. That nice young friend of Nick's turns out to be his drug dealer—the person who supplies him with the heroine that landed him in the hospital. And he also ends up being the first casualty of our cast. He lures his friend, Nick, whom he now sees as a threat, to an out of the way place to kill him—yes, to *kill* him, because apparently when you sell drugs to your best friend and he starts "hallucinating" that his 100-pound girlfriend was feeding on a bloodied corpse, the obvious solution is to kill him. Despite his weakened and drug-addled condition, Nick is able to anticipate the attack, and in the ensuing struggle, turns the gun on Calvin. This scene illustrates an uncanny resemblance to a criticism pointed out by viewers of *TWD*:

> The fact that all the strong Black men in the show are still expressly depicted as physically inferior to our White male protagonist—in two separate scenes in two separate episodes, Rick subdues a hysterical Morgan and a hysterical Tyreese with his fists—results in the show remaining little more than a regressive and problematic reinforcement of existing White male power fantasies over Black masculinity [Jenn, 2014, para. 15].

Tananarive Due (1970), an award-winning author, self-described horror lover, and co-writer and co-producer of a short zombie film, was understandably outraged by Calvin's death:

> The first character killed off was black. Not just black—but a black drug dealer. And a *weak* black drug dealer who is fought off by his jonesing white client. So, yes, from the very start, the show has introduced an ineffectual black thug as the first zombie to die. A thug's black body laid out on the street. [As a culture, that's how we like men's black bodies: laid out dead on the street.]

Though our characters apparently live in a world where only the nerdy kid at school is familiar with zombie lore, viewers who are familiar with zombie conventions know that once a person dies, they come back to life as a flesh-hungry, mindless zombie—or *walker*, as they're called in *TWD* universe. And so after Travis and Madison show up, and Calvin has been resurrected, the weak White addict, Nick, has the wherewithal to run him over twice, leaving his body laid out on a street for the second time.

The second episode opens with a shot of Principal Costa (Scott Lawrence) patrolling the empty hallways of the high school. Though details are still sketchy, kids have been sent home in response to the civil unrest after reports of police shooting unarmed people. A day after being stood up by her boyfriend, Matt, Alicia finds evidence of a struggle in his home and him burning up with a fever. Again, wary viewers were forewarned when he did not show up for their date and our expectations are fulfilled when Madison and Travis, who are beginning to wise up, locate Alicia and discover bite marks on Matt. One writer found this looming death "the most irksome of these dismissals.... Although he goes out on an altruistic note, telling Alicia she has to leave him behind because he loves her, Matt's ending offers the viewers no closure—and, more importantly, denies Matt and real humanity" (Sprankels, 2015). While some are frustrated with the lack of character development and closure for Black characters, Due's (1970) criticism focuses on the toxicity of the racial imagery: "Then came Episode 2, which doubled down on the imagery. Because, boo-hoo, the white teenage girl's black boyfriend is INFECTED. [I could almost hear the collective sigh of relief as she was forced to leave him suffering in bed before he could bite anyone—or turn into a more serious relationship]." And indeed, while conducting research online, I unwittingly ended up on some forums where hatred for the young interracial relationship was expressed in language I won't repeat. One might praise the show for presenting these relationships. One might even argue that viewers can't have it both ways. If the show is going to work hard at providing diversity and at depicting interracial relationships in a dangerous world, then anyone can be killed. In fact, after enumerating the number of deaths in *The Walking Dead* universe according to race, some fans have argued, like Hurd, that far more White people are killed than Black people. Technically, seven deaths occur in *FtWD* before Calvin's, but in this case, two of the three Black male characters are killed in quick succession ("List of Deaths [Fear]").

A little later in the episode, when Madison and a student are scavenging for supplies at the high school, they are attacked by Principal Costa who has become a zombie. Madison realizes the danger and dispatches her former principal with a fire extinguisher. Sadly, just as some viewers were happy to see the biracial couple split up, there might be some viewers who cheered for the White woman who was able to put down her Black supervisor. Instead of redeeming *TWD*'s uneven track record dealing with Black men, the producers of *FtWD* have been widely criticized for killing all three Black men in the space of two episodes. Though the original show generally has adhered to the "One Black Man at a Time" rule, at least characters like T-Dog lasted three seasons, whereas in *Fear the Walking Dead*, Black men do not last beyond two episodes.

Producers for both shows are mindful of the criticism of its treatment of Black men and have repeatedly defended their plot and casting choices. After the first two episodes of *Fear the Walking Dead* had aired, its showrunner Dave Erickson was grilled about their deaths. When asked about decisions about their fate, he replied: "Ultimately, it came down to when we were casting those parts, we didn't know who was going to live, who would die or how those stories would arc out or *not* arc out. For us, it was about casting that felt reflective of the community and getting the best actor and that was the final determining factor" (as cited in Goldberg, 2015). His words echo those of *TWD* producer Hurd who doubled down on her commitment to color-blind casting at the end of its fifth season:

> We have to go with the story. It's really important to cast the best actors. Two of those characters were white in the comics. They could've been any ethnicity. Our casting calls are completely open and we always go with the best actor. Would African American actors want to be told, "We're not casting you, because in the storyline we're going to kill you off?" That's how we have to look at it. We want the best actor and then we have to stick to the storyline that was crafted months before we even cast the roles [as cited in Berkshire, 2015].

When characters live in a dangerous world in an era when no one on a television show is safe, even its primary characters, anyone can die. So when Erickson was asked if they considered tweaking the story when it became evident that the first three deaths would all be Black men, he replied:

> Once the story was set, it was the story. Once the story is playing out in a specific way, that's the line that you want to follow. It wasn't as though we were writing those characters and then casting those characters with an intention of, "*This* is going to be the death scene for this episode." For that episode, it was about how it would reflect on the characters themselves and how things would play out over the course of the season. I realize it's clearly become an issue and it's something we are mindful of.... When you're dealing with a show where you have a cast that is as diverse as ours is, it's inevitable that characters of color are going to get bit and are going to turn or die. If you look at the larger scope of this season, what people will see is

that there is parity. We want to tell the story in the best way we can and want the best actors to play those parts. It would have been a mistake to go with Anglo actors for those particular roles because I don't think that's honest to the world of the show [as cited in Goldberg, 2015].

Still, it's hard not to see a pattern, intentional or not. The pattern, however, is not necessarily due to a disregard for Black lives in particular so much as an unfortunate but inevitable result of color-blind casting.

The Perils of Color-Blind Casting

Despite the good intentions of its adherents, Turner and Nilson (2014) argued that color-blind casting ultimately functions as a form of racism perpetuated by the media, particularly television:

> Television, as the primary discursive medium today, plays a central role in the articulation, construction, and contestation of racialized identities in the United States.... While negative racial stereotypes do continue to circulate within the media, the dominant mode of televisual racialization has shifted to a colorblind ideology that foregrounds racial differences in order to celebrate multicultural assimilation while simultaneously denying the significant social, economic and political realities and inequalities that continue to define race relations today [p. 4].

While the producers of *FtWD* can brag about their commitment to diversity, ultimately their color-blind worldview simultaneously erases those characteristics that make people unique while undermining the struggles still faced by many Black and ethnic Americans.

Curtis may have been excited to see a Māori character in a major television series, but ultimately, his heritage plays no role in his character's development or lack thereof. White actors could just as easily have been cast in the roles of Calvin, Matt, and Costa as Black men for nothing actually distinguishes their characters as Black men. Ashley ("Woody") Doane (2014) explained how color-blind casting is predicated leads to the results in race to just another characteristic:

> The point of colorblindness is how we see color/race: in a "colorblind" world, race is most often (but not always) defined as a characteristic of *individuals* in a world where racism is no longer a major factor and race plays no meaningful role in the distribution of resources. In essence, race is reduced—in theory but not in practice—to another descriptor along the lines of "tall" or "left-handed" [p. 16].

What color-blind casting overlooks is that the lives of Black men in America *are* different from their White counterparts. When Black viewers see a clean-cut suburban Black youth turn out to secretly be a drug dealer, they see a stereotype. When they see that same clean-cut, healthy, and strong Black man beaten by a weak drug-addled White man, they see a "regressive and problematic reinforcement of existing White male power fantasies over Black masculinity" (Jenn, 2014, para. 15). And when that same young Black man lies dead in the street, not once, but twice, they fear a subconscious desire to see all Black men dead. Colorblind casting assumes that racism is a thing of the past, but most Black Americans will readily contest the veracity of its demise. In contrast, one should not be surprised to learn that a majority of White

Americans espouse some form of a color-blind racial worldview (Turner & Nilsen, 2014, p. 4). Perhaps many television executives can afford to only see the "best actor" when casting a role, but Black viewers in America do not usually have that luxury.

Conclusion: Diversity in the Writers' Room

Eric Deggans, who was an early critic of *TWD*'s handling of diversity, points out the difficulty of achieving true diversity in television:

> One thing I've noticed regarding diversity and television is that it's easier to cast a person of color who is essentially written as a white person—nothing distinctive about their ethnicity or racial background makes it into the show.... One has to wonder, is that really diversity? ... But most people of color nowadays live in a world where sometimes their race and culture is a big part of their life and sometimes it isn't. I think TV shows still struggle to portray that [qtd. in Hornik].

TWD and *FtWD* are hardly the first or only series to face this dilemma, and yet if you ask viewers of color how to solve the problem, the answer is simple: hire more people of color behind the scenes, particularly in the writers' room. Race in the Writer's Room: How Hollywood Whitewashes the Stories that Shape America (2017), published by Color of Change (COC) Hollywood, reports that 65.4 percent of all Hollywood writers' rooms do not have a single Black writer on staff. Out of 234 television series, only 4.8 percent of writers are Black with another 8.9 percent being other people of color. The statistic for showrunners is even more dismal; again, out of 234 television series, only 5.1 percent have a Black showrunner and 3.9 percent have other people of color (Hunt, 2017, p. 12). *FtWD*'s commitment to hiring the best writers regardless of race does not appear to match its charge to hire the best actors. The series aired its 101st episode on June 5, 2022. Out of 101 episodes, only two were written by a Black man, Justin Boyd. Black women actually fare better in the writers' room (and many viewers will argue on the screen); Calaya Michelle Stallworth is responsible for sixteen episodes during the recent seventh season of *FtWD* (IMDb.com, n.d.). Stallworth's inclusion raises *FtWD*'s percentage of Black writers to 18 percent, but it is worth noting that she was not hired until 2021 and that Black men are responsible for writing less than 2 percent of all the series' episodes. In fact, the COC report identifies AMC, the network that airs *TWD* and *FtWD*, as one of the "worst at including women and people of color" for having "100% of shows with not Black writers or just one" (Hunt, 2017, p. 16). AMC also has a terrible record when it comes to showrunners; as of 2017 they did not employ any women, people of color, or Black showrunners at all (until the promotion of Angela Kang ahead of the ninth season of *TWD*). The Black Filmmakers Academy argues that a lack of Black writers leads to fewer Black characters and "stereotypical or superficial depictions of Black characters" (as cited in toneka, 2015). The COC report includes anonymous excerpts from the experiences of Black writers that illustrate the difficulties of creating authentic Black characters when Black writers: "[Black characters] were like magical Negroes ... there's no life except for ... what I can do for my white friend" and "There is not an honest conversation in the room or with the creator. So I feel like [Black characters] turn to sort of plastic, cardboard characters."

In addition to improving characterizations of Black characters, involvement in the writers' room can lead to more freedom and inclusion for Black writers in the creative process (toneka, 2015). However, perhaps most importantly, "Liberated" writers' rooms (comprised of a Black showrunner and five or more Black writers) were described as "'democratic' spaces where race 'always came up,'" and where Black writers felt "at home" to freely explore the complexities of race with respect to characters and storylines … these spaces also tended to produce more nuanced representations of "Blackness" (Hunt, 2017, p. 20). In other words, in addition to striving for honest representations of Black America, Black writers working with other Black writers and showrunners would recognize immediately the folly of color-blind casting, especially when it results in three Black men being killed in succession within the space of two episodes. One cannot necessarily fault the well-meaning producers, showrunners, and writers who aim to cast the best actors, regardless of race, when they fail to anticipate the fallout among Black audiences of their color-blind casting. However, one can argue that Black representation in the writers' room would have probably recognized the potential negative optics of slaying its sole Black men. Whether it was intended or not, images of dead Black men, especially at the hands of White men and women, are offensive to Black viewers.

FtWD was only two episodes into its six-episode first season when it alienated many viewers by dispatching its only significant Black characters. If those viewers had made it to the fifth episode, they would've been introduced to a Black male character who actually doesn't die. I wonder what those viewers would make of Victor Strand (played by Coleman Domingo). A wealthy Black man, with a mysterious past and mysterious motives, he befriends Nick when they're both detained in a cell at a military-run hospital. Unapologetically self-serving, he bribes a guard to keep Nick from being removed to the hospital. The two of them escape the cell but make no effort to free anyone else. After Nick's family rescue them from the hospital compound, Strand takes the whole group to his luxurious ocean front home, packs some suits, and through a telescope shows Nick their destination, his yacht anchored offshore. The season ends with the survivors holed up in Strand's house, presumably preparing to get to the yacht. Strand, the sole surviving Black man, remains a question mark. Is he friend or foe? And in a franchise that hasn't been particularly adept at portraying realistic Black men, are there any other possibilities?

Devoted viewers of the franchise would have been rewarded for their loyalty in Season 4, 2018, when fan-favorite Morgan Jones made the transition from *TWD* to *FtWD*. One can't help but suspect that criticism of *FtWD* led the producers to poach the most fully formed Black male character in the franchise from its parent show. Moving forward, especially in light of AMC's disappointing track record, viewers can only hope that creators and producers of *TWD* and *FtWD* spinoffs make as much effort to diversify their writers' room and production staff as they do their cast.

References

Berkshire, G. (2015, March 27). Walking Dead finale preview: Gale Anne Hurd teases Glenn's fate, rEturn of the Ricktatorship. *Variety.* https://variety.com/2015/tv/news/walking-dead-finale-preview-gale-anne-hurd-rick-shane-glenn-deanna-1201461054/.

Black dude dies first. (n.d.). *TV Tropes*. https://tvtropes.org/pmwiki/pmwiki.php/Main/BlackDudeDiesFirst.

Cobo, L. (2015, August 21). Ruben Blades dishes on playing a zombie killer in AMC's 'Fear the walking dead' and his armageddon anthem. *Billboard*. https://www.billboard.com/music/latin/ruben-blades-the-walking-dead-interview-6671106/.

Deggans, E. (2014, November 28). Diversity on 'The Walking Dead' wasn't always handled well. *NPR*. https://www.npr.org/2014/11/28/366655295/diversity-on-the-walking-dead-wasnt-always-handled-well.

Doane, A. (2014). Shades of colorblindness rethinking racial ideology in the United States. In S.E. Turner & S. Nilsen (eds.), *The colorblind screen: Television in post-racial America* (pp. 255–279). NYU Press.

Dos Santos, K. (2015, February 10). *The Walking Dead producer explains why the latest shocking death had to happen, and more.* E! Online. https://www.eonline.com/news/623851/the-walking-dead-producer-we-ve-killed-a-lot-more-white-characters-than-african-american-characters.

Due, T. (1970, January 1). The toxic racial imagery in fear the walking dead—and why black lives matter on TV too. *Blogspot*. http://tananarivedue.blogspot.com/2015/09/the-toxic-racial-imagery-in-fear.html.

Erickson, D., & Kirkman, R. (2015, August 23). Fear the Walking Dead. whole, *AMC*.

Fitzpatrick, K. (2015, September 22). *'Walking Dead' boss on killing African-American characters*. ScreenCrush. https://screencrush.com/walking-dead-scott-gimple-african-american-characters/.

Haas, L.R. (2015, August 20). *'Fear the Walking Dead' cast talk diversity & shooting in Los Angeles*. CineMovie. https://cinemovie.tv/Television/fear-the-walking-dead-cast-talk-diversity-shooting-in-los-angeles.

Goldberg, L. (2015, August 31). *'Fear the Walking Dead' boss defends polarizing character deaths*. The Hollywood Reporter. https://www.hollywoodreporter.com/tv/tv-news/fear-walking-dead-boss-defends-818622/.

Hunt, D. (2017). (rep.). *Race in the writer's room: How Hollywood Whitewashes the stories that shape America*. Color of Change Hollywood. https://hollywood.colorofchange.org/wp-content/uploads/2019/03/COC_Hollywood_Race_Report.pdf.

Jenn. (2014, June 18). *The Walking Dead's ongoing black man problem*. The Nerds of Color. https://thenerdsofcolor.org/2013/10/29/the-walking-deads-ongoing-black-man-problem/.

Johnson, J. (2017, January 12). T-Dogging' through The Walking Dead season 5 finale. The Root. https://www.theroot.com/t-dogging-through-the-walking-dead-season-5-finale-1790859300 https://walkingdead.fandom.com/wiki/List_of_Deaths_(Fear).

IMDb.com. (n.d.). *Fear the Walking Dead: Full cast & crew*. IMDb. https://www.imdb.com/title/tt3743822/fullcredits/?ref_=tt_cl_sm.

Mazzara, G. (Writer), & Dickerson, E. (Director). (2011, October 13). Bloodletting (Season 2, Episode 2) [TV series episode]. In D. Alpert, F. Darabont, G.A. Hurd, R. Kirkman, & T. Luse (Executive Producers), *The Walking Dead*. AMC.

Moyer, J.W. (2021, October 25). 'The Walking Dead' finale recap: Black man survives. *The Washington Post*. https://www.washingtonpost.com/news/morning-mix/wp/2015/03/30/walking-dead-lets-black-man-live-despite-history-of-killing-african-american-males/.

Sprankles, J. (2015, August 30). Here's why some fans are saying *Fear the Walking Dead* is targeting African American characters. *SheKnows*.

toneka. (2019, July 15). *Black representation in writers rooms*. Black Filmmakers Academy. https://blackfilmmakersacademy.com/black-representation-in-writers-rooms/.

Turner, S.E. & Nilsen, S. (2014). Introduction. *Shades of colorblindness rethinking racial ideology in the United States* (pp. 1–11). NYU Press.

Some Kind of Wonderful

An Analysis of Audience Reaction for The Wonder Years *2021 Reboot*

Erin E. Gilles *and* Saleema Mustafa Campbell

"One thing about being 12 that hasn't changed over the decades is that it's around 12 where you figure out what your place is in the world. But being in my family made that hard. I'd never be as popular as my sister or as athletic as my brother, as smart as my mom or as bad as my dad. That's the problem with being the youngest. By the time you're born, all the good parts have been handed out," as narrated by the adult Dean, the protagonist of The Wonder Years *reboot, while reflecting on his childhood* ["Pilot," 2021].

How often have you discovered that your favorite television program has been canceled? This is a growing trend in today's television landscape, due to the immediacy of social media and blogging. Viewers can offer media writers and producers real-time feedback about writing, plot, casting, and other editorial choices. In an environment of amplified audience fragmentation and competition for viewer attention, audience influence on television content is increasingly impactful. *The Wonder Years* (2021–2023), with its audaciously subversive reimagining of the suburban American middle-class family, sets the stage for a range of critical engagement. From claims of cultural misappropriation rooted in cultural essentialism to characterizations of tokenism and shortsighted perspectives on the relationship between ethnicity and cultural experience, audience and critic speculation ran the gamut in 2021 when *The Wonder Years* (*TWY*) was announced. In general, the program won over audiences upon release. Running for a total of two seasons (before cancellation), the show cultivated a balance between wholesome, heart-warming storytelling and didactic portrayals that challenge restrictive cultural norms and antiqued dominant narratives. Owing to a diverse writing team and inclusive content, *TWY* found resonance with a multicultural audience. Moreover, this essay will explore the strategies employed by the show's creators, marketers, and production teams to maintain its on-air presence in an increasingly competitive media landscape.

Background on The Wonder Years

The first iteration of *The Wonder Years* (*TWY*) premiered on ABC in early 1988 directly after the Super Bowl, with the first season running only six episodes. Set in the turbulent 1960s America, *TWY* (1988) focused on the day-to-day lives of ordinary, middle-class White adolescents. Figure 1 shows the family from the original *TWY* (1988).

While the major news stories of the day were present, such as the Civil Rights Act, the Vietnam War, the Moon landing, the hippie counterculture movement, they were the backdrop against which the struggles of youth were foregrounded. However, Neal Marlens and Carol Black, the showrunners, endeavored to make the program more about the common coming-of-age experiences than the events of the era. According to Marlens, "When the show becomes more about a period than about people growing up, then there's a problem with the way we're writing the show" (as cited in Haithman, 1988, para. 18). *TWY*, ranking 63 on *Rolling Stone*'s top 100 TV shows of all-time list (Sheffield, 2016), has achieved a deep fan appreciation. Although it went off the air in 1993, the fan culture surrounding *TWY* still sustains active forums across the Internet. Fans discuss episodes, imagine potential plotlines, and chat about what cast members are up to.

Figure 1. *The Wonder Years* cast poses for publicity photographs in 1988. From left: Winnie (Danica McKellar), Wayne (Jason Hervey), Karen (Olivia d'Abo), Kevin (Fred Savage), Jack (Dan Lauria), Norma (Alley Mills), and Paul (Josh Saviano) (© 2021 ABC; IMDb.com).

In this current era, TV audiences have shifted, and the demand for better on-screen representation has grown. For example, the three TV genres in which Black Americans have the most representation are: action/adventure, music, and drama (Nielsen, 2021). The same report indicates that Black viewers are twice as likely to seek out media content in which they are represented. For instance, *Atlanta* (2016–2022) and *Empire* (2015–2020), with their nearly all–Black casts, had a Black viewership of 57 percent and 61 percent, whereas *Black-ish* (2014–2022) and *This Is Us*'s (2016–2022) more mixed casts drew a Black audience share of 28 percent and 10 percent, respectively (Lawler, 2018). Flach (2021) argues the reboot of *TWY* is part of ABC's practice of "racial inversion," a practice which dates back to the 1970s. Racial inversion, or simply inverting the race of the cast of a television program, was implemented to ease the racial tensions of the time, garner new viewers, and pacify the demands for more integrated content from the Federal Communications Commission and Black activists. However, criticism of this practice was abundant because the voices of writers of color were infrequently included to add authenticity to these inversions. Representation in the writer's room can set the tone of the programming. Nielsen (2021) reported that the television dramas with the most Black on-screen representation had program writing credits that had an average of 15 percent Black female writer contribution, and these programs demonstrate "themes like justice, power and glamour compared to how Black women are most often represented with themes such as competition and rivalry" (p. 8). An examination of the credited writers on *TWY*'s (2021) IMDb page appears to show some ethnic diversity, a gender balance, and writers of various ages.

Riding the wave of '80s nostalgia, such as *Stranger Things* (2016–) and other reboots of classic shows like *Roseanne* (1988–1997, 2018), *Full House* (1987–1995), and *Magnum, P.I.* (1980–1988), *TWY* (Black & Marlens, 1988–93) was rebooted in 2021 with a new family, a Black one. Set in Montgomery, Alabama, and focusing on the lives of this Black family, *TWY* was back with new stories to deliver. Even the promotional materials for the new *TWY* evokes an aesthetic comparable to the original series, including a similar logo. The new *TWY* (Daniels et al., 2021–2023) includes a diverse writing staff with a commitment to more realistic portrayals. Led by veteran producers Saladin K. Patterson and Lee Daniels, this reboot relied heavily on writing by Patterson based on his own experiences growing up in Montgomery (Andreeva, 2020). Fred Savage, who played the main character in the original series, was a director and executive producer on the new show. However, he was terminated in the first season due to inappropriate conduct (Hughes, 2022).

Figure 2. *The Wonder Years* family. From left: Laura Kariuki, Elisha Williams, Saycon Sengbloh, and Dulé Hill (© 2021 ABC; IMDb.com).

TWY (2021–2023) focuses on the Williams family, headed by Bill (Dulé Hill) and Lillian (Saycon Sengbloh). Similar to the original series, the story of the youngest child, Dean Williams (Elisha Williams), is the nucleus of the new *TWY*. The older children are Kim (Laura Kariuki) and Bruce (Spence Moore II), who was away serving his country in Vietnam in the show's earlier episodes. The show is similar to the original in that it is narrated by the main protagonist's older self (narrated by Don Cheadle). Figure 2 above shows the new cast for the reboot, minus the oldest brother who was not cast until midseason. The first season of both programs was set in 1968. Some critics wondered if the gap between when the show is set, and the current time was too great to evoke the same sense of nostalgia that the original series did when it was set in the near past. Patterson (Maglio, 2021) indicated that while there was certainly an option to set the show in a different time period, he and Daniels opted for the 1960s because "[w]hen you think of this time period in Black America, you don't really think of middle-class Black people, you think impoverished" (para. 6). Daniels wanted to showcase the Black middle-class stories that were missing from that narrative.

TWY was renewed for a second season, and according to IMDb, it was most favorably rated by females, males under 18, and U.S. viewers (see Table 1).

Table 1. IMDb Ratings by Demographics for *The Wonder Years* (2021–), Gathered from IMDb's Website in July of 2022

Variables	N	Rating (All Ages)	Rating (<18)	Rating (18–29)	Rating (30–44)	Rating (45+)
All	3,390	5.8	8.0	6.4	5.6	5.7
Males	1,451	5.0	10.0	6.2	4.9	4.9
Females	729	7.7	7.0	7.3	7.6	7.6
U.S. Users	1,155	6.2				
Non-U.S. Users	421	4.5				

Stuart Hall's Encoding and Decoding Models in Audience Reception Theory

Stuart Hall's encoding and decoding models in audience reception theory may be helpful in understanding the way viewers perceive the latest incarnation of *TWY*. Television programs have many variables to face beyond a ratings-based meritocracy in order to achieve resilience on the airwaves. Audiences are undeniably selective in how they consume, internalize, and interpret their media content. Often, there are disconnects between the intended appeal or meaning of certain content (for the purposes of this research television content is at focus) and how consumers translate that meaning. Primarily, viewers filter content through their own socio-cultural contextual awareness, and this can result in varied inconsistencies in how content is received by audiences. Stuart Hall, a sociologist and cultural theorist, has made significant contributions to understanding this conceptual paradigm. Best known for his ideological criticism in British Cultural studies, Hall's encoding/decoding models analyze the cognition process during the events of meaning reception (Ott & Mack, 2020). His research explores the various ways that active members of an audience can rework meaning. In *Encoding and Decoding in the Television Discourse,* Hall (1973) argued that "in societies like ours, communication between the production elites in broadcasting and their audiences is necessarily a form of 'systematically distorted communication'" (p. 1). Furthermore, Hall asserts that there are "various kinds of 'competencies' (at the production and receiving end) in the use of language" (Hall, 1973, p. 1). Television is unique in that its product or content is communicated in a symbolic form. Network production teams create a television program or product that is imbued with meaning and signification agency, but this meaning is coded in their language and knowledge systems. Hall suggested that these systems are not closed. The production teams are informed and influenced by their own knowledge frameworks and assumptions about the audiences' knowledge frameworks as well. Hall (1973) explained that "production and reception of the television message are, not, therefore, identical, but they are related: they are differentiated moments within the totality formed by the communicative process as a whole" (p. 3).

These moments of interpretation are informed by the audience member's own code system or certain ways of seeing the world, which function separately from the producer's code system. Hall (1973) suggests that interpretation engages related moments between creating and deciphering. *Encoding* is the process of creating a meaningful message according to a particular code, while *decoding* is the process of using a code to decipher a message and formulate meaning (Ott & Mack, 2020). Hall (1973) asserted that

> the codes of encoding and decoding may not be perfectly symmetrical. The degrees of symmetry—that is, the degrees of "understanding" and "misunderstanding" in the communicative exchange depend both on the degrees of symmetry/a-symmetry between the position of encoder-producer and that of the decoder-receiver: and also on the degrees of identity/non-identity between the codes which perfectly or imperfectly transmit, interrupt, or systematically distort what has been transmitted. The lack of "fit" between the codes has a great deal to do with the structural differences between broadcasters and audiences, but it also has something to do with the a-symmetry between source and receiver at the moment of transformation into and out of the "message-form" [p. 4].

Hall (1973) suggested that "misunderstanding" or "distortions" result from the differences in the "two sides of the communication exchange" (p. 4). Audiences combine a negotiated interpretation of media texts that utilizes some aspects of the production code, which may include the preferred reading of the text, with their own personalized codes to produce meaning (Ott & Mack, 2020). These negotiated readings demonstrate that no television or media program is neutral, and thus consumers will decode a program inconsistently at best.

Most importantly, storytelling involves a good deal of assumption making related to a particular audience. It is commonplace for producers of media content to appeal to a perceived dominant perspective, which delves into notions (hegemonic influence is often engaged at this juncture in the process) of conventional or traditional standards. Increasingly, consumers have become more effective, nuanced decoders and can demand television production content that is encoded with more diverse socio-cultural contextual considerations. With appeals to a dominant audience and/or traditional conforming narratives that are expected to be interpreted in a singular direction, producers should anticipate a greater diversity of reaction and a wider range of feedback for their content, especially with the feasibility of social media. There are social standards that are frequently used in television production, but not all viewers will receive content messages within the preferred code of expectation, especially those viewers who are mindful of rejecting recycled productions of hegemonic themes. For as Hall (2011) reminds us, hegemony is not fixed. Rather, it is a process, and it must be continuously reinforced and maintained.

Decoding Hegemony in Black Television Programs and Characters

The complicated history of racial representation in television and film in the U.S. is a central factor in how the audience decodes media content. *TWY* (2021–2023) is a television show about a Black family living in Montgomery, Alabama, and their depiction of the Black experience in the U.S. during the Civil Rights era is on display. In "New Ethnicities," Stuart Hall (1996) outlined an important transformation in the politics of representation and how black culture, in particular, is depicted. As Hall (1996) explained, this transformation endeavored to recognize

> the extraordinary diversity of subjective positions, social experiences, and cultural identities which compose the category "black"; that is, the recognition that "black" is essentially a politically and culturally *constructed* category, which cannot be grounded in a set of fixed trans-cultural or transcendental racial categories and which therefore has no guarantees in nature [p. 443].

Undoubtedly, depictions of Black characters and their cultural experiences are complicated by the social construction of race, which has been used historically as a tool of control and oppression. In viewing and depicting Black identity, a range of codes can be activated for popular reception. More specifically, Hall (1996) argued that there is a huge diversity and differentiation in the cultural and historical experiences of Black subjects. Of note for this research, there is also a huge diversity and differentiation in the interpretation of the Black experience by the audience at large.

Stereotypes of Black identity can be essentializing, causing damage to Black culture with their enduring negative portrayals. Hall (1996) alleged that the lack of acknowledgment around this issue results in a variety of fictional assumptions about Black identity such as "all black people are good or all black people are *the same*" (p. 444). This also explains why racial inversions in television programming can frequently occur in the absence of Black writer inclusion; fictional assumptions about black people have been a popular practice. When Black archetypes, caricatures, and stereotypical characters, etc., are removed from content, this loss of the "essential Black subject" can result in "a recognition that the central issues of race always appear historically in articulation, in a formation, with other categories and divisions and are constantly crossed and recrossed by the categories of class, of gender and ethnicity" (p. 444). Additionally, as a consequence of this recognition in Black politics, Hall (1996) asserted that "a renewed contestation over the meaning of the term 'ethnicity' itself" (p. 446) will occur. Hall suggests that "the new politics of representation therefore set into motion an ideological contestation around the term 'ethnicity.' But in order to pursue that movement further, we will have to re-theorize the concept of *difference*" (p. 446). This retheorization of difference, as Hall explains, does, in fact, involve a greater understanding of the concept of ethnicity (Hall, 1996). Hall (1996) argues that the work in this movement means separating the term "ethnicity" as it functions in dominant discourse from "its equivalence with nationalism, imperialism, racism, and the state" (p. 447). Therein lies an additional concern for producers of television programs that feature members of ethnic communities; for some viewers these shows are held responsible for cultivating a narrative that confronts hegemony in addition to celebrating diversity. For Hall (1996), this type of storytelling is possible and necessary, for it involves a "recognition that we all speak from a particular place, out of a particular history, out of a particular experience, a particular culture, without being contained by that position" (p. 447).

Often this recognition can feel more theoretical than practical because audiences have expectations that are not as respectful or aware of these difficult negotiations in the storytelling process with regard to ethnic characterizations. They also have an unlimited opportunity through social media platforms to elevate themselves to the position of invested stakeholders. Whether or not the showrunners acknowledge this online discourse is another matter. Ultimately, audiences can be expected to apply an even wider array of dominant and oppositional strategies to programs featuring ethnic characters on the complex continuum that represents their negotiated readings of content (Ott & Mack, 2020). The new *TWY* and other television programs that feature diverse characters may become contested sites where artistic interpretation is negotiated through various political agendas. In this climate of heightened social media engagement, the media landscape is a quickly changing frontier with new, complex challenges for those involved in media production.

Methods

Due to the robust discussion of media programming in online communities, active sites like IMDb, Reddit, Twitter, and The A.V. Club comments were chosen as the primary texts for analysis in this essay. These sites were chosen due to the high level of user participation and the accessibility of the comments by the general public. These online forums allow users to have real-time conversations and create robust communities of fans, which make them excellent platforms for studying audience reception (Lyles et al., 2013). This essay also uses articles written by professional and lay media critics on popular websites or news outlets. The critical articles were used to compare whether viewer sentiment was aligned with critics' views.

Each online space features different ways for users to interact and post their sentiments about *TWY*. The A.V. Club features a blend of both, as users can post comments at the end of the articles written by the site's writers. According to their website, The A.V. Club does moderate their comment section to remove trolling, bullying, and hate speech (*The A.V. Club*, 2022). The A.V. Club had just three articles about *The Wonder Years* (2021) but had active comments sections. Twitter's verified @WonderYearsABC account had 5,476 followers and 920 tweets. We used the official account as a way to collect tweets from viewers following *TWY* (2021–2023). IMDb had 188 reviews of *TWY* (2021–2023). Although there were fewer A.V. Club and IMDb comments, these were included because these sites are commonly used by engaged fans and the lack of post length allows users to create more in-depth responses. For IMDb especially, the volume of site data allows users to learn and confirm facts about the program (cast, directors, plots), which may enhance the quality and accuracy of their posts. For Reddit, three subreddits were evaluated for threads and replies (r/WonderYears, r/TheWonderYears, and r/TheWonderYearsABC) for a total of 78 threads and 536 comments. Some of these subreddits included threads about the original series, which were excluded from review and are not included in the numbers above. In addition, searching on these sites for comments related to *TWY* often yielded comments about the band of the same name, comments about the original series, and comments using the phrase without reference to the series. These comments were excluded from the analysis.

Comment collection from each online space varied in number, and thematic analysis was conducted after the data was collected. Comments were collected from Twitter (n=4,679), Reddit (n=536), IMDb (n=188) and The A.V. Club (n=180), for a total of 5,583 posts. All viewer comments were included verbatim, and were not edited to correct errors, remove emoji, or change inflammatory speech. This was done to ensure that the original language of the viewers was used in each excerpt (Noble & Smith, 2015). Data were sorted and coded using NVivo 12 using thematic analysis (Braun & Clarke, 2022). The creation of major themes began after reading through the viewer comments and critic articles. Specifically, major themes were developed after some familiarity was achieved with the data. The authors created a codebook related to key aspects related to the audience reception of the show's content and messages. The next section will begin with a brief analysis of some of the major themes of the show, and then analyze audience and critic comments which refer to these themes.

Results

Combating Themes of Tokenism and Stereotyping in *TWY* (2021)

TV programming with diverse casts risks the pitfalls of tokenizing or stereotyping them, whereas predominantly White casts are generally received as universal in terms of their appeal. Although the 2020 Census results revealed that America is more diverse than ever before, the "White population remained the largest race or ethnicity group in the United States, with 204.3 million people identifying as White alone" (Jones et al., 2021, para. 9). For television shows like *The Wonder Years* (2021–2023) with Black or ethnic casts, it can be daunting to avoid the designation as niche programming intended for a specific audience while simultaneously maintaining some broad appeal. Since *TWY* was renewed for a second season in May of 2022, it appears to have managed this difficult balance. Based on the renewal and audience reception, the show succeeds on several fronts. Namely, it delivers a diversity of themes that may have helped it garner a sizable viewership.

As a comedy, the show may invoke feelings of good humor and laughter. Twelve-year-old Dean Williams is often the show's focus, but he also learns many tough, moral lessons as the story's main comic foil. Throughout the 22-episode first season, the viewing audience is provided a first-hand, comedic exploration of his youthful discoveries, to include: envy, bragging, obedience, judgment, selfishness, overconfidence, loss, and jealousy. To many viewers, these may present as appealing, universal circumstances. Comedy is the primary tool the writers of *TWY* (2021–2023) employ to increase the accessibility and relatability of its cast. In addition, comedy is also the vehicle by which the writers confront prevalent social issues, such as discrimination and prejudice. It includes the traditional subjects associated with a coming-of-age story but also explores conflicts with antagonists both within and outside of the Black community. Dean experiences some very universal coming-of-age trials such as heartbreak, his first kiss, school dances, bullies, and sibling/best friend conflicts while he and narrator Don Cheadle (the actor who voices his internal monologue) also engage in and detail the tumultuous societal conflicts that occurred in the American South during the late 1960s. However, these reflections are filtered through the innocence and naivety of the show's sheltered and poorly-discerning protagonist, which makes these difficult subjects remarkably digestible.

In Episode 9, "Home for Christmas," Dean's older brother, Bruce, returns home after serving two years in the Vietnam war (Daily, 2021). Assimilation into civilian life proves to be a battle, and the job search process is emotionally defeating because Bruce is unable to activate privileges that he had hoped to have as a patriot and veteran. He discovers that the few offers of assistance that he earns in exchange for his service are still limited to janitorial or custodial work because of his race. Bruce says, "they only offer the good jobs to the White veterans" ("Home for Christmas," 2021). This particular telling of a Black veteran's return from the Vietnam War is analogous to well-documented struggles of other Black veterans returning to the U.S. from various wars before and during the Civil Rights Era. As a conscientious objector to the war in Vietnam, Muhammad Ali famously asserted:

> My conscience won't let me go shoot my brother, or some darker people, or some poor hungry people in the mud for big powerful America ... shoot them for what? They never called me nigger, they never lynched me, they didn't put no dogs on me, they didn't rob me of my nationality, rape and kill my mother and father. ... Shoot them for what? [as cited in Wolfson, 2018, para. 20].

Unlike Muhammad Ali, Bruce chooses to reenlist for another tour in the war at the end of the episode.

Bruce claims to miss the brotherhood that he had developed among the members of his troop. Bruce reveals "when I am here people just see me as just a janitor. Over there, my men respect me" ("Home for Christmas," 2021). He wants to make a career in the military and return to help his "brothers" make it home safely. Bruce's story is not about the cruelty and futility of war, which is often a common discussion when Black perspectives of war are highlighted on the small or large screen (see *Dead Presidents* [1995]), but Bruce's story highlights universal and more agreeable, mainstream themes of brotherhood and loyalty, observed through the lens of the Black experience. Meanwhile, Dean exercises some additional comic relief from this weighted subject when he allows his friends to convince him to pay close attention to his brother's post-war behavior. They sway him into believing that war can have devastating consequences, such as converting Bruce into a scary movie type monster; PTSD is apparently not in their realm of awareness. Notwithstanding, Dean makes it his episode-long mission to investigate his brother for signs of a vampire-like transformation. Dean also stages a very ineffective sit-in at the army recruitment office; he is offered a candy cane by one of the recruiters and encouraged to keep up his fight. In the end, Bruce joins Dean's sit-in briefly so that he can share his true feelings about the war. He tells his little brother that he wants to end the war too, but he "wants to make sure that [his] buddies get to spend next Christmas with their little brothers." Dean realizes that the war had changed his brother, but "not in the ways that he feared" (Daily, 2021). This episode strives to negate the notion of war as a negative influence on the lives of young people.

Dean's mother, Lillian, is an additional character on the program whom the writers frequently use to explore a range of societal themes and universal emotions. In episode 3, "The Club," Dean discovers his mother's stash of soft-pornographic magazines. Dean shows his classmates some of the magazines that he found in the basement. Later, the hall monitor catches Dean in the bathroom sharing the magazines, and takes Dean to the principal's office. He assumes they belong to his father, but his mother affirms her sexual liberation and informs her son that the magazines are actually hers. She also educates him about his sexual feelings, and she calls them "normal and healthy for both men and women." Her stated goal in this conversation is to ensure that Dean is a caring and tender man in adulthood. After some initial awkwardness and trouble at school surrounding his temporary custody of these magazines, Dean exclaims that he is proud that his mother is the "first woman to own a cardboard box full of porn" (Searle, 2021). He also celebrates her for being the first woman from her community to drive a car and graduate from college.

In episode 4 ("The Workplace," 2021), Dean shadows Lillian at her place of work. She is a Black woman with a master's degree in accounting (the only employee in her office who possesses an advanced degree) and works for the state treasury department. In this episode, the viewers are given a glimpse of what life was like for a Black mother working in the 1960s, who also happened to enjoy a leadership position at her place of business. Lillian navigates all kinds of workplace microaggressions and other frustrations. Her male co-workers treat her like a secretary, and the White female secretaries appear to alienate her because of her status as an executive. Dean observes that his mother spent her lunch breaks alone because in her position "she didn't have a place at anyone's table."

Through Lillian, the female viewership is given the opportunity to escape the normative practice of seeing women in the 1960s maintaining passive sexual roles, which were often assigned to them by cultural expectations. Lillian rejects restrictions being placed on her female agency and enjoys a progressive experience of equal partnership in marriage. Patriarchal structures do not censor her voice or quelch her ambition. She is fully aware of the power systems that exist in her world, but she represents an awakening of feminism, specifically the second wave of feminism, the movement of her era, which often involved women rejecting traditional roles and expectations (Valk, 2008).

140 Part 2: Network and Cable Television

In episode 10, "Lads and Ladies and Us," she discloses an essential life mantra that she frequently communicates to her children: "Be who [you] are and hope for the best" (Cofer, 2022). As a television character, Lillian may have global, multi-generational appeal, for her idealism and courage could appeal to a variety of viewers.

Viewer and Critic Reception

Relatability and Reboot

With some exceptions, audience reception of *TWY* (2021–2023) was generally positive. Many viewers enjoyed the reboot and found the stories to be compelling. Many online comments uttered sentiments along the lines of the following: "This is how to properly reboot a classic. Totally fresh take, great casting, loved the beginning narration showing that 50 years later, everything is pretty much the same" (Marymcfarland-01866, 2021). As is a common goal of a reboot, there is hope that previous fans will tune into the new series. The similarity of the format (such as the focus on the youngest child, the use of the older narrator, being set in the same year, and the identical family structure) was likely designed to make the program mimic the original and give viewers a sense of nostalgia. User comments indicate that some viewers watched the original series and miss the former cast: "Wonder years has been great so far. I really hope they have Daniel Stern or Fred Savage make a guest appearance at some point. I know Fred Produces and directs episodes" (u/Space2345, 2021). Comments frequently compared characters in the reboot to their counterparts in the original series, and speculated about how former characters could appear in the new series.

One viewer reminded us that sometimes nostalgia may leave us with overly fond memories:

> Despite the nostalgia, the original Wonder Years wasn't a very good show either. The plots are forgettable, the characters are okay but not endearing or particularly likable, and the forced humor is quite forced. The nostalgia for the original series is based on a handful of memorable moments, not the overall quality of the show [bitbucketchip, 2021].

But that type of post was firmly in the minority. In most cases the nostalgia for the original *TWY* seems to have set the bar quite high for some audiences. For instance, "they had big shoes to fill with the love of fans for the original ... they could have made this something that fans of the old one really could have liked with just a little bit more nuance and clever writing" (kuhlakunde, 2021). The amount of fan love for the original series permeated posts, and it was not uncommon to see a complaint about the new series combined with a praise of the original, like this one: "I went into the show so excited (i loved the original) and all the new show did was preach and has no redeeming value. This show destroyed a brilliant legacy and frankly, everyone involved should be ashamed" (ebgrkhf, 2022).

Some critics encouraged audiences to try the program, even if those audiences were wary of getting a dose of political consciousness mixed into their entertainment: "If you want an escape from racial politics, this is not the show for you. On second thought, it is exactly the show for you, because it just might make you reconsider the need for such racially themed shows in the first place as our nation finally reckons with its messy past" (Fraley, 2021, para. 19). Undeniably, there are honest and raw moments in the program. Watching an adolescent experience racism can be difficult for some viewers. As one critic summarizes the beginning of the rebooted series, "by the start of the school year, most of the students at Dean's school have adjusted to integration, but moments of microaggression and outright racism persist, from white students' refusal to use the water fountain to a teacher's insensitive remarks" (Tinubu, 2021, para. 10). But, despite these deep topics, the program was generally perceived by critics to be gentle and upbeat. Slaton (2021) describes it as "warm, lovely, and as suffused with gentle nostalgia as the original, this remake of the iconic late-'80s series recaptures the same sentimentality yet adroitly slips in modern cultural commentary" (para. 3).

Race and the Reboot

Pleasing audiences that are ever more fractured along demographic lines is increasingly difficult. A plenitude of content means that viewers can be quick to pan those programs that disappoint. The inclusion of a Black family excited some viewers, but also prompted them to question why others were upset by the newly diverse reboot: "So, if I can grow up watching White TV series but still relate to the characters—why is it that White people can't seem to accept watching Black-centered shows like The **Wonder Years** reboot? The answer is simple—White privilege" (@gimli0413, 2021). The race inversion described earlier in this essay seemed to instantly invoke some viewers' ire: "When we say we want diverse storytelling, that's what we mean. Diverse. Diverse casts, diverse storylines. This whole trend of 'your favorite show from forty years ago bUt bLaCk' is so pandering and played out" ([u/DoneDidThisGirl, 2021). However, other viewers appreciated the representation and enjoyed *TWY* characters: "So I just started the **Wonder Years** on Hulu and omg I love it! The main family is beautiful and darkskin and everybody is so undeniably **Black**. I love it so so so much" (@babypink410, 2021). This comment, along with others like it, expressed joy in rejecting the colorism that can be present in some ethnic communities.

The purpose of the race inversion was seemingly more aimed at calming racial strife among White audiences than providing Black audiences with the authentic stories they craved. Flach (2021) shared how

> the fact that television producers continue to employ the same method a half century later to provoke empathy and interest from White audiences in shows with Black casts speaks volumes about how White Americans still don't fully understand or accept the perspectives of people of color. Which is why the message about diversity in historical perspective is just as important as how that message is presented [para. 17].

The argument can be made that race inversions can provide empowerment because it does introduce characters into a previously barred universe. Deggans (2021) noted: "One big reason changing the races of characters in a series reboot can make sense is because the adjustment can reclaim a bit of cultural space—allowing people of color to tell their own stories in a fictional world where they had previously been rendered invisible" (para. 14). The success of this approach seems to be largely dependent upon a diverse writing staff to create realism in the experiences, rather than just swap Black actors for White actors in the same stories. But the writers can only drive the development so far—they still need executive-level support to support scripts, casting, and projects.

For some viewers, *TWY* (2021–2023) seemed too light-hearted and rosy to be an accurate depiction of life in the South for a Black family. In a post titled,"Another race swapping cash-cow remake," one viewer writes: "I'm also unsure how accurate the show is because African Americans unfortunately were not treated that well where the show takes place" (DonDiggity, 2022). Another poster had a similar question. "I wonder how the show will handle racial slurs. Not having them around will feel artificial, as will bleeping them out" (u/RefreshNinja, 2021). In other cases, some audience members found the program to be too focused on race to be enjoyable: "Where the original dealt from time to time with political issues this one has to fill every moment with it. Everything is literally black and white and nothing more" (kuhlakunde, 2021). The need to balance realism with stories that air for family audiences during primetime on a network owned by ABC (whose parent company is Disney) brings up important questions about the nature of family programming, profits, and palatability. However, it may be the ability of *TWY* (2021–2023) to integrate familiar storylines with moments that evoke normal Black life. Robinson (2021) argues that it may be classism that dampens the racism experienced by the Williams family. *TWY* (2021–2023) "promotes the *Cosby*-esque myth that a comfortable middle-class existence provides a refuge from racism. Middle class white people are presumably kinder and more tolerant than their lower income brethren, which is both classist and fundamentally untrue" (Robinson, 2021, para. 6). In this way, such programs are able to neatly sidestep dealing with the structural barriers and institutionalized racism that can perpetuate poverty.

As other viewers point out, racism in the South is more pervasive than other areas of the United States. Some viewers indicated that after watching the pilot, after having only seen the trailer, they erroneously assumed the show was set in Northern states. Another agreed, writing: "I think the problem is that in the time and place where the show is set, he wouldn't *need* to be preoccupied with racial issues, they'd crash into him many, many times a day" (Skipskatte, 2021). Still, the subtlety of the storytelling may more effectively help White audiences to navigate the race inversion than more overt storylines. As Deggans (2021) writes:

> What I love most about this new Wonder Years is how it balances coming-of-age moments which are universal for middle class Americans—bullies at school, wanting your crush to notice you, struggling not to embarrass yourself at a Little League game—with stuff that was specific to Black families like mine [para. 8].

Other viewers have similar hope for a representation of a middle-class Black family, but within the same universe as the original story: "We are now on the other side of the city with a Black family and this changes everything. I love what they've done so far and I can't wait for them to really dig into this decade from our perspective" (and_shove_it_up_your_butt, 2021).

Deggans might agree that it is the retelling of these moments in history from a non–White point of view that may help audiences understand the multifaceted nature of history. In particular, "and, just maybe, the rest of America might learn a little more about its history by seeing those pivotal moments from a perspective different than their own" (Deggans, 2021, para. 16). However, how accurate that history is remains to be seen. One viewer argues that in the notoriously racist South in the 1960s a Black family could not have such insulation from racism, as one viewer points out:

> Of all places to set a show like this, presenting *Montgomery, Alabama,* as a locale where the white people were pretty cool about integration and spoke in hushed tones about MLK's death displays a willful lack of historical knowledge. Check out the book *Bending Toward Justice* (Doug Jones' memoir on prosecuting the men responsible for the Birmingham bombing) if you want your eyes opened wide to how rampant the KKK was running in that part of the country in the late 1960s [Chavalina, 2021].

Indeed, Robinson's (2021) review of the pilot for The A.V. Club indicates that it will be a lost opportunity if *TWY* (2021–2023) fails to highlight the impact on the family of the major historical events of the Civil Rights Movement that unfolded in the state in which the show is set. Yet, some critics question the ability of the reboot to offer educational value for audiences. "No one should expect any sort of Black political or social education from *The Wonder Years* but the metanarrative around the update does imply a level of progressive politics that the show seeks to tap into" (Love, 2021, para. 3). In fact, Love argues that these quasi-progressive Black recasts allow studios to tout their efforts at diversity, but ultimately occupy airtime which could be devoted to original content from creators who are queer, nonbinary, and/or persons of color.

Discussion

The variety of reactions to *TWY* (2021–2023) certainly supports Hall's (1973) premise that encoding and decoding are processes within which a great deal of latitude can exist between the messages encoded into a media text and the messages decoded by the audiences. This was evident in the reaction to the discourse around race on the program. Interestingly, the divide was not always strictly between lay viewers and critics, for there was still a lack of consensus within these groups. However, while lay audiences often criticized the amount of racial discourse on the program, critics were more often critical of how race was handled. Many critic reviews indicated that the world in which *TWY* (2021–2023) was rebooted seemed softer for a Black family than what history has dictated. Yet, the warmth of the nuclear family provided a great deal of insulation in the new *TWY* and became a place of respite for audiences when the outside world became too cruel—a rejuvenating form of escapism.

Although this was sometimes not included in the above results section due to space limitations, in many cases users and even critics referred to their own ethnicity in subtle or not so subtle ways to support their stances. From plainly stating their race, to describing *TWY* (2021–2023) as a show that "reflect us" or one that "includes families like mine," these writers were able to offer their own authority about the authenticity of the program. This tactic also allowed these posters to offer critiques from a place of power. Hall (1973) also reminds us that the encoding and decoding processes are asymmetrical, meaning that the amount of understanding and misunderstanding may vary.

TV content is created in a high-pressure environment. Constraints of time, money, studio control, the medium itself, and the pressure to attract and retain audiences combine to influence the final product. The messages that the writers may intend to convey may be distorted along any of the channels of production. Within Hall's encoding process, a television text has natural generic expectations. These production codes combine with an audience's negotiated interpretations to produce meaning (Ott & Mack, 2020). For instance, a primetime, episodic broadcast TV drama aimed at families has constraints on its production by its nature. These shows may address some important topics, but they are generally protective of great harm or distress befalling their characters or addressing topics that parental audiences would have disliked their children to view. Whereas a program that airs after primetime or on a cable or streaming channel would be allowed greater latitude. *TWY* (2021–2023) did address some darker, more genre-bending topics. For instance, Episode 3's uncovering of Lillian's stash of pornographic magazines was a provocative and progressive storyline for this type of program.

As Hall (1973) reminds, no text is neutral. Especially in a program set in a real historical context, important decisions must be made about which historical events to acknowledge and which to ignore, let alone how to filter these events through the characters' narratives. As Robinson's (2021) review suggests, a program about a Black family in Alabama in the 1960s has the opportunity to tell stories about important moments in U.S. history that have seldom been captured elsewhere. However, this is only effective if the audiences are willing to expend the energy to decode these messages. While segments of the audience seem involved and ready for small screen representation and new stories, others reject these narratives as either superficial pandering or just offering more tiresome rhetoric about political correctness.

Limitations and Directions for Future Research

This study was undertaken to assess audience reception of the reboot of a classic TV program using online viewer commentary to assess audience responses. Critic reviews were also incorporated into the analysis, as savvy audiences often read critical reviews. One major limitation is that not all viewers post about the TV programs they view. Thus, this essay does not capture the reactions of all viewers. In addition, this analysis only examined viewer comments in specific online forums. The tenor of the commentary may be different on other online forums.

Another limitation is that some of the sites from which comments were taken are moderated. This means that in certain cases some commentary may have been deleted, which changes the conversation. Race is at the forefront of the conversation about *The Wonder Years* (2021–2023), and conversations around race can be particularly incendiary. Especially online, it would be surprising to only find civil discourse about the reboot.

One of the difficulties in studying a rebooted program is that audiences are naturally prone to comparing the new program to the original. This can obscure nuanced or unbiased discussions about casting, plot lines, music choices, acting, wardrobe, and other aspects of the program. However, it is also possible that audiences may have only been drawn to *TWY* (2021–2023) program because of the nostalgia that they felt for the original program. As discussed earlier in the essay, there are arguments among viewers *and* critics about how far in the past one can project nostalgia.

Conclusion

Comments posted on various media and social media outlets (Twitter, Reddit, and The A.V. Club) about *TWY* (2021–2023) support Hall's assertion that a "systematically distorted communication" exists between television production staff and their intended audience; this is chiefly a result of "various kinds of 'competencies' in the use of language" that are activated in the process of decoding television content (Hall, 1973, p. 1). Some viewers were beholden to the original *TWY*'s source material, characters, and storylines and proved to be unwilling to release any measure of sentimental attachment to the old model. This reluctance could be attributed to many factors. Some viewers may have found it difficult to accept a Black family as a fair equivalent to the original White one, and others may have been reluctant to receive any form of a racial education from an American television program. There were other commenters who would suggest that *TWY* (2021–2023) failed to showcase the Black experience or to project racism in the American South during the late 1960s through a more fitting historical lens. Others indicated a reluctance to accept social politics mixed with their entertainment. These lay critics called the show's efforts at ethnic storytelling docile and asserted that *TWY* (2021–2023) was an act of "race-swapping."

Mostly, the show's reception was positive. Viewers appreciated its themes, storytelling, relatability, humor, and originality. Although *The Wonder Years* (2021–2023) was obviously a reboot, they received it as a new story told from the perspectives of those living across the railroad tracks from the Arnolds in the original program. Viewer reaction seemed to indicate that they recognized the show's effort to highlight and include traditionally underrepresented cultural groups as genuine. This high praise is indicative of a modern audience in search of more depth, inclusion, and complexity in their television viewing options. Although they differed on how the Black experience should be depicted (which speaks to a need for a larger societal conversation about race, ethnicity, and representation), they seemed to value the opportunity to merely observe this particular rendition of Black culture on screen.

Notably, this appreciation seems to be directly correlated to diverse representation in *TWY*'s writing room. Problematic content appears easier to avoid when characters are written by those who have some knowledge of the characters' cultural experience, especially when the objective is to achieve some extent of historical accuracy in the content. *TWY*'s success speaks to a need for greater diversity across all spheres of television, film, and media production. A report from the Think Tank for Inclusion & Equity (2021) revealed that within the TV industry, there is a great deal of difficulty for underrepresented writers to achieve career advancement. The report also noted that most TV executives were White males: "Among broadcast and digitally scripted shows, white show creators outnumbered BIPOC show creators 8 to 1 and 6 to 1 in cable scripted television. Marginalized communities also remain underrepresented amongst directors, writers, and those who receive awards and recognition" (p. 6). Despite being canceled after two seasons, *The Wonder Years* (2021–2023) is an example of the tangible rewards of genuine investment in diversity, equity, and inclusion initiatives. Audiences have become increasingly discerning and critical of efforts that seem hollow or performative; they demand better alternatives.

References

Andreeva, N. (2020, July 8). 'The Wonder Years' reboot with Black family in works at ABC From Saladin K. Patterson, Lee Daniels & Fred Savage. *Deadline*. https://deadline.com/2020/07/the-wonder-years-reboot-abc-black-family-lee-daniels-saladin-k-patterson-fred-savage-1202979955/.

The A.V. Club. (2022). About. https://www.avclub.com/about.

Black, C., & Marlens, N. (Executive Producers). (1988–1993). [TV series] *The Wonder Years*. ABC.

Braun, V., & Clarke, V. (2022). Conceptual and design thinking for thematic analysis. *Qualitative Psychology*, 9(1), 3–26. https://doi.org/10.1037/qup0000196.

Cofer, J.E. (Writer), & Whittingham, K. (Director). (2022, January 5). Lads and ladies and us (Season 1, Episode 10) [TV series episode]. In L. Daniels, S.K. Patterson, F. Savage, M. Velez (Executive Producers), *The Wonder Years*. 20th Television; Disney Television Studios.

Daily, B. (Writer), & Savage, F. (Director). (2021, December 1). Home for Christmas (Season 1, Episode 9) [TV series episode]. In L. Daniels, S.K. Patterson, F. Savage, M. Velez (Executive Producers), *The Wonder Years*. 20th Television; Disney Television Studios.

Daniels, L., Patterson, S.K., & Savage, F. (Executive Producers). (2021–2022). [TV series] *The Wonder Years*. ABC.

Dawson, M. (Writer), Cole, K. (Writer), & Appleby, S. (Director). (2021, October 13). The workplace (Season 1, Episode 4) [TV series episode]. In L. Daniels, S.K. Patterson, F. Savage, M. Velez (Executive Producers), *The Wonder Years*. 20th Television; Disney Television Studios.

Deggans, E. (2021, September 24). ABC's new "Wonder Years" succeeds by centering a Black family in history. *NPR*, 3.

Flach, K.L. (2021, October 1). The "Wonder Years" remake resurrects a 1970 tactic to diversify TV viewing. *The Washington Post*. https://www.washingtonpost.com/outlook/2021/10/01/wonder-years-remake-resurrects-1970-tactic-diversify-tv-viewing/.

Fraley, J. (2021, September 22). Review: Black revival of "The Wonder Years" shows the other side of American history. *WTOP News*.

Haithman, D. (1988, April 8). 'Wonder Years' pays its respects to '60s suburbia. *Los Angeles Times*, 4.

Hall, S. (1973). Encoding and decoding in the television discourse. *Training in The Critical Reading of Televisual Language*.

Hall, S. (1996). New ethnicities. In D. Morley & K.-H. Chen (Eds.), *Critical dialogues in cultural studies* (pp. 441–449). Routledge.

Hall, S. (2011). The neo-liberal revolution. *Cultural Studies*, 25(6), 705–728. https://doi.org/10.1080/09502386.2011.619886.

Hughes, W. (2022, May 7). Fred Savage fired from Wonder Years reboot after inappropriate conduct investigation. *The A.V. Club*. https://www.avclub.com/fred-savage-fired-wonder-years-abc-1848895658.

IMDb. (2022, July 22). The Wonder Years *(2021–)* user ratings. https://www.imdb.com/title/tt12682076/ratings/?ref_=tt_ov_rt.

Jones, N., Marks, R., Ramirez, R., & Rios-Vargas, M. (2021, August 12). *2020 Census illuminates racial and ethnic composition of the country*. United States Census Bureau. https://www.census.gov/library/stories/2021/08/improved-race-ethnicity-measures-reveal-united-states-population-much-more-multiracial.html#:~:text=The%202020%20Census%20shows%20.

Lawler, K. (2018, June 28). Study: How diverse are the audiences for "This Is Us," "Empire," "Westworld"? *USA Today*, 1.

Love, T. (2021, September 23). The Wonder Years and the emptiness of the Black Hollywood recast. *The Daily Beast*. https://www.thedailybeast.com/the-wonder-years-and-the-emptiness-of-the-black-hollywood-recast.

Lyles, C.R., López, A., Pasick, R., & Sarkar, U. (2013). "5 mins of uncomfyness is better than dealing with cancer 4 a lifetime": An exploratory qualitative analysis of cervical and breast cancer screening dialogue on twitter. *Journal of Cancer Education*, 28(1), 127–133. https://doi.org/10.1007/s13187-012-0432-2.

Maglio, T. (2021, August 26). Why 'The Wonder Years' reboot is still set in the 1960s—and not a more recent decade. The Wrap. https://www.thewrap.com/the-wonder-years-reboot-why-no-decade-change-60s-90s-abc-lee-daniels-fred-savage/.

Nielsen, V.L. (2021). *Being seen on screen: The importance of quantity and quality representation on TV* (Diverse Intelligence Series). https://www.nielsen.com/insights/2021/being-seen-on-screen/.

Noble, H., & Smith, J. (2015). Issues of validity and reliability in qualitative research. *Evidence Based Nursing, 18*(2), 34–35. https://doi.org/10.1136/eb-2015-102054.

Ott, B.L., & Mack, R.L. (2020). *Critical media studies: An introduction.* John Wiley & Sons.

Robinson, S. (2021, September 22). ABC's *The Wonder Years* remake fails to capture the magic of the 1980s original. *The A.V. Club*, 6.

Searle, M. (Writer), & Savage, F. (Director). (2021, October 6). The Club (Season 1, Episode 3) [TV series episode]. In L. Daniels, S.K. Patterson, F. Savage, M. Velez (Executive Producers), *The Wonder Years*. 20th Television; Disney Television Studios.

Sheffield, R. (2016, September 21). *100 greatest TV shows of all time.* Rolling Stone. https://www.rollingstone.com/tv-movies/tv-movie-lists/100-greatest-tv-shows-of-all-time-105998/eastbound-and-down-106484/.

Slaton, J. (2021). *The Wonder Years (2021) TV review.* Common Sense Media. https://www.commonsensemedia.org/tv-reviews/the-wonder-years-2021.

Tinubu, A.A. (2021, September 22). ABCs reboot of "The Wonder Years" recaptures the dramedy's magic and adds its own. *NBC News*. https://www.nbcnews.com/think/opinion/abc-s-reboot-wonder-years-recaptures-dramedy-s-magic-adds-ncna1279844.

TTIE. (2021). *Behind the scenes: The state of inclusion and equity in TV writing.* Think Tank for Inclusion & Equity. https://seejane.org/wp-content/uploads/ttie-behind-the-scenes-2021-report.pdf.

Valk, A.M. (2008). *Radical sisters: Second-wave feminism and Black liberation in Washington, D.C.* University of Illinois Press.

Wolfson, A. (2018, February 19). Muhammad Ali lost everything in opposing the Vietnam War. But in 1968, he triumphed. *USA Today*. https://www.usatoday.com/story/news/2018/02/19/1968-project-muhammad-ali-vietnam-war/334759002/.

#TheySilencedThem

The Strange Case of Supernatural's *Queerbaiting*

Anna Caterino

On March 22, 2019, The CW announced that *Supernatural* (2005–2020), one of the "longest-running United States first-run syndicated television series" (Macklem & Grace, 2020, p. 1), would come to an end with its fifteenth season. The news was delivered through a video message, posted on Jared Padalecki's Twitter (now X) account, in which the actor, together with Jensen Ackles and Misha Collins, said that the final season would be a "big, grand finale of an institution" (Padalecki, 2019, 0:41). The announcement was received with mixed feelings and, even though the show's ratings had dropped significantly between 2005 and 2020, fans who were still watching *Supernatural* weekly and posting about it on social media, were looking forward to seeing their predictions come true and their requests satisfied. That summer at San Diego Comic-Con, showrunner Andrew Dabb discussed the upcoming season and the show's finale and described it as "scary and exciting" (Whedonopolis, 2019, 23:17), claiming that "about 30% of people will be happy" (32:21). His co-workers, particularly Rob Benedict, proceeded to compare it to *Game of Thrones* (2011–2019), a remark that fans found particularly baffling. After all, not only had the HBO Max (now Max) show ended with an episode that "prioritized shock value over cogent character development and attention to political detail" (Beauchamp, 2019, para. 6), but the network had also received such backlash that it was petitioned by fans asking for a rewrite (McCluskey, 2019).

In hindsight, the comment foreshadowed not only the content of *Supernatural*'s final episode "Carry On" (S15x20) but also its reception. At the time, however, Andrew Dabb's remarks were taken as a hint that the show would end with the explicit canonization of Destiel (that is the fan term for the supposed pairing of Dean Winchester and Castiel) after twelve years of presumed queerbaiting. Despite the little to no screen time that the two characters share in the last couple of seasons, fans allowed themselves to believe in a queer happy ending as both textual and paratextual elements seemed to steer towards this possibility long before The CW released the promotional material for the last three episodes. Notwithstanding twelve years of build-up, in "Raising Hell" (S15x02), Castiel (played by Misha Collins) tells Dean (played by Jensen Ackles), "You asked, what about all of this is real? We are" (Buckner et al., 2019, 17:30). Later, in "Unity" (S15x17), Chuck/God (played by Rob Benedict) remarks, "You know what every other version of you did after raising him from perdition? They did what they were told. But not you. Not the one off the line with a crack in his chassis" (Glynn & McKenzie, 2020, 40:33). These two moments in particular were seen by fans as an attempt on the writers' part to finally acknowledge the substantial homoerotic subtext and strike a balance at last.

At a convention in Washington, D.C., that same year, Jensen Ackles was asked about the upcoming finale and whether or not he was pleased with it. Ackles answered the question, saying, "I heard the pitch and I was like, okay. At first I was kind of.... At first I didn't.... It just didn't sit well with me" (Gayled_it, 2019, 26.17). Unlike his colleagues, he had not received the pitch positively and stated, "I wasn't big on it" (Gayled_it, 2019, 26:44) and "had a problem digesting it" (Gayled_it, 2019, 27:22). Ackles' dislike also led him to contact Eric Kripke, the creator of the show, in order to get the opinion of someone who "built this world" (Gayled_it, 2019, 27:16) and created the characters. Kripke suggested looking at it "from an audience perspective, from a fan perspective" (Gayled_it, 2019, 27:48) and keeping in mind both the characters and their development throughout the course of the show. All these remarks were taken as further confirmation that fans, especially Destiel shippers, would be rewarded. Although the comments referred to Dean Winchester's death in "Carry On," they were perceived by the fandom as homophobic and proof that "maybe Destiel will become canon" (les-beast, 2020).

Jensen Ackles' remarks were also seen as confirmation that the writers had ignored the actor's previous reluctance to discuss the topic of Destiel, thus dismissing his sensitivities in favor of the fandom's wishes. However, despite Ackles' potential prejudice, his words on his ideal finale also started to circulate again: after all, he had previously claimed that "when Sam Winchester dies for good, it's going to be good television. But when Dean Winchester lives on, it's going to be great television" (Highfill, 2017, para. 6). This was taken as reassurance that, at least when it came to the characters' survival, fans and showrunners were all on the same page.

Even though fans' hopes were grounded in textual and paratextual elements, their approach exposes a sense of entitlement which stems from their role of "loyal consumers" (Hills, 2002, p. 36). *Supernatural* fans, particularly Destiel shippers, have built their identities around the consumption of the show and, in doing so, ascribe their own perspective and lived experience on the characters. They hereby continue the tradition of fans who "construct their cultural and social identity through borrowing and inflecting mass culture images" (Jenkins, 1992, p. 23) while displaying an over-reliance on the product itself. Because of this, the dismissal of the show's main slash pairing has seemingly become an invalidation of fans' sexual identities by proxy. This letdown has since turned into a divided fandom, even more so in the aftermath of *Supernatural*'s prequel *The Winchesters* (2022). At the prospect of more content, some claim "we aren't going to get canon Destiel you dumb sluts" (themanwhowouldbefruit, 2022) and others simply admit that they "want to be pandered to" (angelinthefire, 2023).

The common ground found by these two groups (now as much as in 2020) is the use of social media as a tool used to fulfill personal and social needs (Freede-Blanar & Glazer, 2017). Given any television show's imperfections, unless they are created with the purpose of providing a safe haven to all and include "all the letters of the rainbow alphabet" (Tevin, 2023, para. 27), online platforms facilitate the sharing of alternate realities that include more diversity and strive to include it in shows themselves. Fans thus find themselves working toward common goals: better and more inclusive representation which keeps up the pleasurable nature of their activities and absolves them from consuming content that may be perceived as problematic. The sense of commonality that emerges from these activities also grants people the chance to be heard, feeding their illusion of power over the powers that be and the possibility to bring on change through cancel culture. Following this, the essay will analyze the audience reception for *Supernatural*, particularly concerning queerbaiting, CW advertising, Eric Kripke's bricolage, and the audience's perception of the show. It will particularly focus on the way fans, due to misunderstanding of the show's referentiality, rely on paratextual elements to validate their queer readings and how the lack of paratextual answers has since led them to rely on nit-picking and cancel culture.

Audience Expectations and Supernatural

Given that in the era of social media it is not uncommon for fans to influence the final product of a TV show or film, to the point of creating a "symbiotic relationship" (Anderson-Lopez et al., 2021, p. 2), it would not have been a long stretch to assume now that *Supernatural* was coming to an end, showrunners were no longer at risk of alienating part of their audience and therefore free to do something with the show's queer subtext. Long before season fifteen, the show had already been encouraging "feminist and/or queer readings" (Nicol, 2014, p. 165) despite being tied to the cultural landscape that emerged after the attack on the World Trade Center on September 11, 2001. Episodes such as "Skin" (S1x6), "Faith" (S1x12), "Point of No Return" (S5x18), and "Live Free or Twihard" (S6x5), for example, feature instances in which hegemonic masculinity is subverted through the re-introduction of non-masculine and non-heterosexual qualities. Even *Supernatural*'s longest running gag, namely Dean Winchester's love for pie and his inability to obtain it, ongoingly undermines the show's presumed heterosexuality. Ever since "Scarecrow" (S1x11), the screenwriters drew an association between the food item and the "domestic Americana and the American apple-pie life" (Wilhelm, 2020, p. 109) thus signaling Dean Winchester's inability to have access to a heterosexual lifestyle that is later presented as a ruse in "Exile on Main Street" (S6x1).

Furthermore, the relationship between fans and writers had been conflicting yet stable enough to give them false hopes that their requests would be fulfilled. The fandom had grown considerably throughout the years to the point of creating a global phenomenon that came to include both cast and writers (Wilkinson, 2014), and was labeled the "Supernatural family" (#SPNFamily). This solidified the idea that fans were part of the collaborative process that is serialized TV: they were allowed to play the role of agent in what Henry Jenkins (2006)defines as convergence culture and consequently believed they had the ability to shape the final product. It would not have been the first occurrence in which the audience altered the course of the show: in 2007, for example, the character Bela Talbot (played by Lauren Cohan) was killed off towards the end of the third season because some fans disliked her to the point of shutting off their television whenever she appeared on screen (Zubernis & Larsen, 2012). Also, during season seven, the departure of Castiel had caused ratings to plummet and the character was brought back in the episode "The Born-Again Identity" (S7x17). Instances such as these highlight the role played by fans in the creation of the final product as well the existence of a reciprocal relationship, as limited as it may be, enabled by social media.

Audiences' reactions generally lead to push back and occasionally change because they also allow for the inclusion of minorities and a greater sensitivity on certain topics. The debate on topics such as homophobia, misogyny, and racism ongoingly shape the course of a show (Zubernis & Larsen, 2012) even though the creators may feel some frustration. Even *Supernatural*, known for its problematic content and lack of representation, faced criticism after "Jus in Bello" (S3x12). The writers were accused of racism because of the death of FBI agent Victor Hernriksen (played by Charles Malik Whitfield), which Zubernis and Larsen (2012) found had a positive impact on the writers who were "uniquely open to listening" (p. 195). However, this may not be entirely true as the racism persisted throughout the course of the show. The accusations of homophobia after episodes such as "Bedtime Stories" (S3x5), "Ghostfacers" (S3x13), "Clap Your Hands if You Believe" (S6x9) and "Dark Dynasty" (S10x21), and the ongoing accusations of queerbaiting, did not lead the show to push for a change either. Rather, *Supernatural* featured a blink-and-you'll-miss-it "homosexual declaration of love" (Hasnaa, 2020, 0:41) in its antepenult episode "Despair" (S15x18) only to immediately fall back on the Bury Your Gays trope. The trope punishes LGBTQ characters "by erasing them from the narrative entirely if the depiction goes beyond subtext to include acknowledged queer identity" (Bridges, 2018, p. 116) and, indeed, Castiel was killed off immediately after his confession. Furthermore, the character did not appear again, and his queerness and sacrifice remained unmentioned in the final two episodes of the show.

These changes or lack thereof expose the tensions that underlie television production, highlighting the ephemeral nature of a supposedly democratic process. Even though fans are being heard, they partake in the production with no power or control. Within a late-capitalist landscape, such intervention takes on the semblance of yet another facet of the consumer strategy behind contemporary fandoms (Stevens, 2010). After all, online spaces allow fans to "become more visible" (Guerrero-Pico, 2017, p. 2071) and reinforces their "consumption-based belonging" (Wei, 2019, para. 8). In spite of the imbalance, fans are encouraged to pursue a dialogue but nevertheless fail to reach any position of power. The newly formed "social relations" (Arrojo, 2015, p. 37) facilitate debates (Choi, 2017) but do not necessarily budge any of the discourses. For all the media outlets that pick up their legitimate complaints their involvement remains precarious as the powers that be, writers, and even actors are in no way obliged to indulge their audience.

These dynamics make *Supernatural*'s audience reception particularly interesting, even more so because of the strange case of the show's queerbaiting. Marketing strategies were indeed used to make the show palatable to an LGBTQ audience, but the show itself was also queer from the beginning and textually never tried to steer away from its coding. Shippers, as well as critics, focus mainly on the first aspect which dismisses authorial intent entirely: every instance of queerness is seen as an accident that appeared in the finished product by chance rather than being the consequence of active writing decisions. Furthermore, fans' queer readings of the show are seen as a byproduct of Castiel's words to Dean in the episode "Despair" and "I love you" (Berens & Speight, Jr., 2020, 38:13) is itself a byproduct of shippers' requests. Even so, fans are still seeking paratextual validation of their interpretation of the show at conventions, or through Twitter (X) and Cameo, rather than looking for it in Eric Kripke's bricolage and his use of intertextuality, itself enough to warrant a queer reading of the show and a consequent reassessment of it. The lack of paratextual confirmation about the nature of the relationship between Dean Winchester and Castiel, then, seems to provide the starting point from which to engage in cancel culture and dislike.

Homophobia appears to be people's main preoccupation despite *Supernatural*'s recurrent problems, thus highlighting the odd use of cancel culture within the fandom. Fans claim the moral high ground and yet occasionally engage in the same rhetoric they try to condemn. For example, all arguments made against showrunner Sera Gamble, who is incidentally held more accountable than any of her male colleagues, echo the same misogynistic rhetoric used by the cast (30 wyn, 2012). Nevertheless, fans voice their dissatisfaction surrounding the representation of specific social groups (Gray, 2021) while still engaging with the text itself. As actors are called out and their words twisted, social media seems to enhance the lack of nuance in approaching transgressions, partially aided by the rise of purity culture (Brooks, 2019). After all, social media platforms "can foster ideological rigidity and lack of nuance" (Ng, 2020, p. 620) and their "sociotechnological forms" also "facilitate vitriolic exchange" (Udupa et al., 2019, p. 3052), leading to an increased backlash against acts that are perceived as problematic. Because of this, certain lines are taken at face value without further inquiry about their nature or the cultural landscape at the time they were written, which results in the source material being actively misunderstood and ignored.

On the Road *and* Supernatural

While showrunner Eric Kripke pitched *Supernatural* as "*Star Wars* in truck stop America" (Kripke, 2015), the show owes more to Jack Kerouac's *On the Road* than it does to George Lucas' trilogy, and remains a strong adaptation of the novel. The show was conceived as a horror monster-of-the week narrative and is deeply influenced by classic gothic elements such as the haunted castle now depicted by the iconic 1967 Chevrolet Impala (Knowles, 2016). Therefore, while muscle cars are generally associated with control and the possibility to escape women as well as domestic spaces (Fine, 2000; Jain, 2005), within the show, the car is transformed into the physical representation of the broken household. Only later did the show come to include angels, God, apocalypses, and ultimately shifted to sci-fi themes under showrunner Andrew Dabb.

The story of *Supernatural* follows brothers Sam and Dean Winchester traveling across the United States to save innocents and hunt demonic creatures. While Sam is the protagonist of the mythic quest, Dean Winchester, much like his literary counterpart Dean Moriarty from *On the Road*, is not only the story's hero but also the object of study and the issues he faces are "as rich, if not richer, than psychic children and demonic plans" (Kripke, 2007, para. 9). *Supernatural*'s main preoccupation may be family, but it also deconstructs Dean Winchester's gender and sexuality (Wright, 2016), offering the audience an analysis of toxic masculinity, particularly in relation to the myth of the independent Marlboro Man, a recurrent theme in Eric Kripke's writing.

Much like *On the Road*, *Supernatural* entered popular culture as a queerbaiting show and is still regarded as such. Based on Allen Ginsberg (1972), *On the Road* mislead "thousands of schoolboys for decades" (p. 7) into believing that the narrative was not only a glorification of life on the road but also a heterosexual story in which the ongoing use of the word brother has no connotations beyond the most common one. In this way, *Supernatural* and *On the Road* share another commonality. On Tumblr in particular, there is a flourishing of jokes about Dean Winchester being Eric Kripke's male power fantasy: after all, he is a swaggering hero in a leather jacket, a modern-day cowboy, a man who listens to classic rock, eats fast food, drinks beer, and drives a muscle car. Bundibird (2021), for example, calls Dean Winchester Erick Kripke's "accidentally bi female-coded male-power-fantasy-wanna-be." Later, that same Tumblr user also claims that while Kripke "aims for dudebros he actually (totally accidentally!!) creates complex and dynamic men who are the polar opposite of the cardboard cutout mens-magazine-cover dudebros he was aiming for" (bundibird, 2021).

Fan posts like these imply a dismissal of authorial intent. Similarly, fans of the show also remark that "the hypermasculine cw show that you wrote, loved by us soldiers for its male power fantasy, has become a queer love story" (castiels-pussy, 2021). This post highlights the deconstruction of the archetypes Kripke is supposedly trying to uphold. Nevertheless, such views are contradicted by the show itself, particularly in episodes that aired while Eric Kripke was still working as showrunner. The interpretation of Dean Winchester as a "being of love" rather than an "archtype male [...] a string of violent impulses" (castiels-pussy, 2021) does not exclusively exist in fans' heads but is also uphold by the show from its very first episodes.

Dean Winchester's sexuality is also perceived as an accident rather than an issue that has been explored from the very beginning, particularly in episodes such as "Skin." Online fans sarcastically ask, "how does it feel. your american male power fantasy is gay in at least three different ways. how are you coping" (thirdpartied, 2021). Another points out how "it states directly in the text that the only act of free will in the universe is one man's love for another" (castiels-pussy, 2021).

These issues, however, have been explicitly brought forward in several episodes, most notably "Lucifer Rising" (S4x22), written by Eric Kripke himself, and "Point of No Return" (S5x18). Scholarly articles too hint at the fact that in *Supernatural* the homoerotic subtext emerged by accident and thus distances it from shows such as *Hannibal* (2013–2015), aligning it more with a show such as *Sherlock* (2010–2017). Yet within the *Supernatural* narrative, the main traits that characterize Dean Winchester are treated as a façade, a performance that is slowly revealed to be crumbling. From the very beginning of season one, episodes such as "Dead in the Water" (S1x3) and "Skin" highlight both Dean Winchester's desire to settle down and have a family as well as his ongoing attempts to kill all those parts of himself that society labels monstrous. In episode "Faith," Dean Winchester is electrocuted during a hunt and consequently suffers from permanent heart failure. When he is healed by a faith healer, he finds out that he was given the heart of another man which saved him but killed the unwilling donor. Notably, the donor was a gay gym teacher, a detail that is continually highlighted especially in the context of what Dean Winchester does or does not deserve. Soon after Dean Winchester is healed, Sue Anne, the faith healer's wife, tells Sam, "The Lord chose me to reward the just and punish the wicked. And your brother is wicked, and he deserves to die just as Layla deserves to live. It is God's will" (Gamble et al., 2005, 36:02). Furthermore, all of this is contrasted by the heterosexual apple-pie life, often represented by the pie that the character always tries to eat but is denied. This apple-pie life, perhaps subtext for a "normal" American life, is something that Dean is not allowed to obtain and in which he will eventually discover he does not fit in.

Dean Winchester, a character commonly read as "aggressively straight explicitly queerphobic" (deancritblog, 2021), embodies the second homosexual archetype, which was born in post-war America and modeled after Marlon Brando and James Dean. It is a "more potent and compelling" (Corn, 2009) depiction than the previous one which heavily relied on the aesthetic of Oscar Wilde: old men and their young wards, both depicted as effeminate, involved in relationships that featured intellectualism and sexuality. During the 1950s and 1960s, however, the United States witnessed the first changes in the depiction of homosexual men. They were now adults of approximately the same age, men in denim clad in "blue jeans, boots, and denim or leather jackets" (Corn, 2009, p. 43). They belong to the working class and spill profanities and no longer speak in General American English, thus revealing their regional and socioeconomic background. *Supernatural* reprised this cultural landscape, providing working-class narratives that highlight the Dean Winchester's position as outsider (Wright, 2016) and distinctively mark his performativity.

While Dean Winchester is perceived as the main character of "a show fetishizing toxic masculinity" (omegaphobe, 2022), *Supernatural* presents him as a character who tries to uphold hegemonic masculinity in order to appease his absent father and ultimately failing to do so. Rather than being depicted as a real man, and therefore not displaying traits such as "toughness, power, control, independence, differentiation from womanhood, restricted emotions, physical and sexual competence, assertiveness, and aggressiveness" (Canham, 2009, p. 2), Dean Winchester is depicted as the fragile child of an abusive alcoholic Vietnam veteran. He travels across post–9/11 America, although Kripke recasts the unknown enemy as the father, thus "taking the supernatural out of the castle and into the average, ordinary homes" (Edmundson, 2016, p.1). *Supernatural*, therefore, focuses on the "failing fatherhood" (Hamad, 2011, p. 249) explored by post–9/11 American media and presents John Winchester (played by Jeffrey Dean Morgan) in an immediate unromantic light. He is a deadbeat and abusive father who neglects his children and imposes on them hegemonic masculinity, inserting them into a "crisis of longing" (hooks, 2004, p. 49) which takes a toll on his sons.

Dean Winchester shapes himself after his hypermasculine and violent father but fails to successfully occupy that space. This is explicated in episodes such as "Dream a Little Dream of Me" (S3x10), where Dean Winchester faces a nightmare version of himself, who taunts him about his lack of self-knowledge and interiority. The nightmare version says to Dean, "I mean, your car? That's Dad's. Your favorite leather jacket? Dad's. Your music? Dad's. Do you even have an original thought?" (Gamble et al., 2008, 33:49). These lines may reveal to the audience that Dean was nothing but his fathers' "blunt little instrument" (34:37), treated not only as a soldier, but also with indifference and dislike. In such an environment, characterized by a grim and violent aesthetic similar to the one in Richard Siken's *Crush* as the two are "products of a cultural moment" (Carlson, 2015, para. 9), there is no space for out-and-out representation of queerness. Furthermore, episodes like "Skin" or "Blood Brother" (S8x5) reprise the overlap of representational codes in horror movies and media coverage of the AIDS crisis (Benshoff, 1997), reprising "the same semantic charges" (Benshoff, 1997, p. 3). Because of its depiction of dysfunctional families and abuse, the show heavily relies on queer-coding, accessible to the audience because of the use of intertextuality. Such an approach, however, seems incapable of fulfilling "contemporary expectations" (McDermott, 2020, p. 849) or provide what fans consider positive LGBTQ representation. Consequently, *Supernatural*'s ongoing referentiality is mistaken by fans for queerbaiting and any hint at a queer subtext seems to be considered the direct product of their own desire to see themselves represented on screen.

Queerbaiting and Supernatural

Throughout the years, particularly from 2014 onwards, *Supernatural* has been repeatedly accused of queerbaiting its audience both by media outlets and fans themselves. After the airing of "Fan Fiction" (S10x5), the show's 200th episode, the audience accused the show and screenwriter Robbie Thompson of missing the point namely that "the subtext isn't based in S-E-X" (Gennis, 2014, para. 6) as the episode claimed, but "based in T-E-X-T" (Gennis, 2014, para. 6) which lead fans to urge "that the producers make good on the same-sex subtext" (Cruz, 2013, para. 13). As early as 2012, the relationship between Dean and Castiel was deemed significant and fairly important (Ryan, 2012) and showrunner Jeremy Carver even advised Misha Collins to play Castiel as a jilted lover in season nine (Prudom, 2013). Nevertheless, fans' queer interpretations were repeatedly dismissed by screenwriters, producers, and the actors. Their ongoing paratextual denial about the nature of Destiel matched with "several scenes that would seem out of place to occur between two heterosexual men who were 'just friends'" (Cruz, 2013, para. 14) resulted in fans accusing the show of queerbaiting them for fifteen years.

Queerbaiting is commonly defined as a business strategy which involves the creation of content that may be perceived as queer in order to appease an LGBTQ audience, only to "then emphatically denying and laughing off the possibility" (Fathallah, 2014, p. 491). Later, the same characters are usually revealed to be straight and end up in heterosexual relationships (Guerrero-Pico et al., 2017), with the homoerotic elements featured in the homosocial bond being completely dismissed. While it may be "a truth universally acknowledged that whenever there are two hot men in a TV show they must be slashed" (Wilkinson, 2013, p. 309), the case of *Supernatural* is more complicated. The homoerotic elements did not surface because of a "standard way of using camera angles or shot-reverse-shots or the requirements of physically staging a scene" (Click & Scott, 2015, p. 375), they were explicitly present within the show's canon.

Supernatural did rely on promotional material and jokes that highlighted the show's awareness of fans' queer readings, particularly while Jeremy Carver and Andrew Dabb worked as showrunners. The most notable example, perhaps, is the introduction to the episode "Destiny's Child" (S15x13) which reprised a scene from "Caged Heat" (S6x10) in which Castiel kisses the demon Meg (played by Rachel Miner). When asked "What was that?" (Matthews et al, 2010, 25:28), Castiel replies, "I learned that from the pizza man" (25:33), referencing a porn movie, featuring a babysitter and a pizza man, that he watched earlier in the episode. The scene implied that Castiel learned everything about sex from a porn movie, hereby identified with the character of the pizza man. However, in the introduction to "Destiny's Child," Castiel's lines from "Caged Heat" are followed by a series of shots of Dean Winchester eating pizza throughout the course of the show (Supernatural4Ever, 2020, 0:15), thus implying that the character learned everything about sex from Dean Winchester rather than a porno.

Unlike other TV shows accused of the same thing, many jokes in *Supernatural*, albeit perceived as homophobic or as bait, serve their purpose within the narrative by highlighting Dean Winchester's ongoing performance, notwithstanding the infamous behind the scenes content. For example, in "Bedtime Stories," Dean Winchester tells his brother, "Dude, could you be more gay?" (Humphris & Rhol, 2007, 17:34), a line that fits the character but nevertheless received backlash despite it being "a reflection of our culture" (Zubernis & Larsen, 2012, p. 180). Even lines that out-and-out point out instances of posing, as the ones featured in "Playthings" (S2x11), are put into question by fans. And yet, lines such as "The most troubling question is why do these people assume we're gay?" (Witten & Beeson, 2007, 9:30) and "Well, you're kinda butch. Probably think you're overcompensating" (9:34) speak for themselves. Exchanges such as these, coupled with the acting from Jensen Ackles, illustrate Dean Winchester's attitude towards his sexuality as they highlight instances of shame, self-deprecation, and barred contact.

Dean, however, is not the only character who is depicted as queer regardless of the show's main slash pairing. The angel Castiel too is a male character from *Supernatural* with undertones of queerness written into the subtext of his character. His first introduction in "Lazarus Rising" (S4x1) is seen by some online fans as Eric Kripke "accidentally writing thee most romantically/sexually charged meeting between two male characters" (sailorsally, 2021).

Despite the strict interconnection between violence and desire depicted in the scene where Dean Winchester plants a knife (*Supernatural*'s phallic symbol par excellence) in Castiel's heart as Castiel smirks and looks at Dean knowingly, it is understood not to have any meaning. His queerness, like Dean's, is neither depicted exclusively through jokes and innuendos nor a result of "so misogynistic u end up gay" (swallowflyingsolo, 2022) as fans seem to believe. His first arc, namely his fall from grace, happens in season four because of Dean while God is cast out of the picture and replaced. Castiel rebels to follow the righteous man, as explicated in episodes such as "On the Head of a Pin" (S4x16) and "Lucifer Rising" (S4x22), and like Angelo in William Shakespeare's *Measure for Measure*, he sins in loving virtue as he too "in desire" knows "the beloved / Good / God" (Fernie, 2013, para. 33). Subsequently, the persistent references to sin are not discarded: in season eight, Castiel is lobotomized by the angel Naomi in scenes that have clear connotations of conversion therapy. The same motif is reprised in "Lily Sunder Has Some Regrets" (S12x10), when Castiel is said to possess a weakness (Dean) from which he has to be cured by cutting it out.

Additionally, while the characters of Castiel and Dean on their own can be read as queer, the episodes that follow "Lazarus Rising" recreate the love story at the heart of Jack Kerouac's novel without shying away from the most iconic moments. For example, in season four, screenwriter Sera Gamble incorporates the symbolic wedding of Sal Paradise and Dean Moriarty in part three of the novel, a part that opens with mock nuptials (Weir, 2005). The scene is now translated to the twenty-first century while an apocalypse looms on the horizon and in "When the Levee Breaks" (S4x21) Dean Winchester promises that he will "give myself wholly to serve God and you guys" (Gamble & Singer, 2009, 16:02) and that he will "follow his will and his word as swiftly and obediently as you did your own father's" (16:10). The conversation sounds like an exchange of wedding vows, and the two men keep looking at each other long after words stop being spoken. More explicit references to Dean and Castiel's sexuality are also present such as the alley scene in "Point of No Return," in which Castiel beats Dean Winchester up while yelling, "I gave up everything for you. And this is what you give to me?" (Carver & Sgriccia, 2010, 25:32). As Castiel yells and hurts Dean, his character is unifying once more violence, panic, and desire to establish an interpretation beyond the literal meaning of his words. In "Point of No Return," screenwriter Jeremy Carver relies on the "spectacular violence" (Britnall, 2004, p. 71) used for "interrogating and deconstructing prevailing gender norms and imaging different ways of organizing bodies, desire, and erotic attachment" (Britnall, 2004, p. 71) typical of male genres. The fourth from last episode of season five, then, conflates violence with fulfilled desire and its potential ultimately highlighting the show's queer subtext.

Incidentally, the ending of *Supernatural*'s fifth season is the only occurrence in which one of the characters of the slash pairing of Dean and Castiel ends up in a heterosexual relationship. Dean is shown in a relationship with a single mother Lisa (played by Cindy Sampson), even playing house as a stepfather to her young son. However, even in this case, the choice as well as the life depicted on screen are nothing but a performance from Dean. Even Dean Winchester's decision to go live with Lisa Braeden is a request put forward by his brother Sam who, in "Swan Song" (S5x22) tells him, "You go find Lisa. You pray to God she's dumb enough to take you in. You have barbecues and go to football games. You go live some normal, apple pie life, Dean. Promise me" (Kripke et al., 2010, 8:21). While Dean Winchester went to live with Lisa, the apple-pie life was presented as a ruse and far from perfect. The episodes of season six, however, were received by fans as an attempt on showrunner Sera Gamble's part to do "everything to undermine Dean" (2badsosad21, 2021) and be petty rather than a continuation of his journey. The stress on Dean's queerness remains marked and the show exposes his inability to enter a happy heterosexual relationship as his performativity is repeatedly shown, even in bed. After his season six hetero relationship with Lisa dissolves, the appearances of women become sporadic and their role as Dean Winchester's love interests diminishes to the point that one can find an entire reddit thread titled *What Happened to All the Pussy in Supernatural* (u/deleted, 2015).

How Queerness Is Perceived by the Supernatural Audience

Within *Supernatural*, the "queer is uncanny and the uncanny is queer" (Royle, 2003, p. 43) and yet the preoccupation with queerness appears to be mostly by proxy rather than being the focus of the story. Happiness, an indicator of good representation (McDermott, 2020), could not be achieved by the characters of the show unless the show changed its distinct formula based on the two brothers' codependent relationship. In an era of heightened sensitivity, with increasingly diverse television shows, *Supernatural*'s reluctance to deviate from a White and, above all, heteronormative point of view may appear outdated. Online fans themselves argue that while *Supernatural* references classic horror stories with queer subtext, the show itself pushes "a heteronormative narrative and themes thus directly opposing their influences in the process creating an internal sense of cognitive dissonance" (hells-plaid-angel, 2022). Furthermore, its fandom was, and still is, made for the majority by LGBTQ people (Zubernis & Larsen, 2012) who are eager for meaningful representation and "the full dignity and presence that heteronormative media disallows" (Boulware, 2017, p. 112). However, the regulation of queer experiences within a narrative, regardless of the larger cultural frame in which they take place, poses new limits, and demonstrates the preference of some feelings over others even within the same community to the point of privileging one single experience and iteration of queerness over multiple and more diverse ones.

Backlash from fans almost inevitably leaves one wondering how, with the ghost of the Winchester father still present and the ongoing daily violence, there should be any space for outness within the play world of *Supernatural*. The average Destiel shipper also seems to believe that the show's actual gay subtext is nothing but a byproduct of their own wishful thinking unless the lines are out-and-out explicit. Castiel's love confession in "Despair," therefore, is said to have made "a fringe/controversial fan theory […] retroactively true" (lenore-tumbles, 2020). YouTube user lampstiel, for example, uploaded a series of videos titled *spn scenes that hit differently now that destiel is canon* (n.d.): these videos feature a series of exchanges between Dean Winchester, Castiel, and secondary characters that, in light of "Despair" can be considered romantic as "Cas's confession affects the story since season 4, when no-one on the writing team ever thought about Destiel" (lenore-tumbles, 2020). Similarly, an anonymous asker remarks, "was it season 4 or 5 that they made cas tell dean he was 'getting too close to humans, you' and they did nothing about it for 10 years" (sosaysdean, 2022). This comment could have misread how the show ongoingly analyzed these kinds of moments.

Most exchanges between Dean Winchester and Castiel can be read as declarations of love, reaffirmed by other characters' remarks about their relationship, yet the

Supernatural fandom strives for unmistakable queer lines that would not leave any scenes up for interpretation. Lines such as "The very touch of you corrupts. When Castiel first laid a hand on you in Hell, he was lost!" (Edlund, 2012, 37:07) and "I know. You're hoping Castiel will return to you. I admire your loyalty. I only wish he felt the same way" (Buckner et al., 2013, 22:50) are apparently void of meaning and dismissed because of the cut "I love you" in the episode "Goodbye Stranger" (S8x17) as several Tumblr posts seem to suggest. This attitude of retroactive canonization in light of *Supernatural*'s antepenult episode "Despair" and Castiel's love confession in the final season demonstrate the failings of the audience in playing the role of critic: on the one hand, as argued by Smith (2007), they detach themselves from previous forms of criticism that do not take into consideration inclusivity; on the other, such an attitude praises performative activism that favors sanitized cultural performances over well-rounded stories.

Including explicit wording about queerness in *Supernatural* may not have brought an ultimate resolution for the audience's confusion, particularly in the aftermath of The CW airing "Despair." In this episode of season, Castiel's love confession remains vague enough to leave the characters' sexuality up for interpretation. Other than the mere understanding on shippers' part that the declaration from Castiel ("I love you") was intended to be romantic rather than platonic, there is nothing in the scene itself or subsequent episodes to further enlighten the audience or provide clarification when it comes to reciprocated feelings between Castiel and Dean. Because of this, the discourse surrounding the scene does not differentiate the moment from any other scene that some of the fans have labeled as "gaslighting" and "literal psychological abuse" (deanwasalwaysbi, 2021). As a matter of fact, the scene achieves explicit queer representation which, immediately afterwards, collapses on itself due to the use of the Bury Your Gays trope. Since November 2020, the approach that *Supernatural* fans on Tumblr have to the confession has changed significantly: no longer mocking it, the scene is described as "one of the best things supernatural ever did" (virginwhoredichotomy, 2020). The now infamous "Despair" scene is strong enough for some fans that it changes every other interaction between Dean and Castiel to now be understood as outwardly queer.

More Impacts from "Despair"

Even though some fans may positively interpret the "Despair" scene, this specific *Supernatural* episode may only reinforce the show's heteronormativity. Despite its explicit content, the scene presents itself not only as a reaffirmation of the idea that "queer people don't deserve happy endings" (McDermott, 2020, para. 6), but also as a narrative that relies on a queer character coming out and then having to commit suicide. Regardless of whether or not queer amalgamation within heteronormative institutions work as a reinforcement of preexisting hegemonic structures (McDermott, 2020; Love, 2009), it has been one of the most frequent criteria of assessment used by fans when evaluating representation (Ng, 2008). And, indeed, fans across Twitter and Tumblr post daily about the characters being happy, together, and alive namely because the show itself, from the very beginning, featured a preoccupation with family (not by blood but chosen) and life as characters ongoingly opt for the "messy, sloppy, confused, selfish, bewildering imperfection of being human" (Kripke, 2009, 28:24). Yet, there has been a significant shift in audience reception as opposed to November 2020 (after the premiere of "Despair"), leading on the one hand to the reevaluation of the scene itself as well as the glorification of screenwriter Robert Berens. On the other hand, it has led to an insurgence in cancel culture and nit-picking behavior perpetrated whenever any member of the show fails to mention the love confession. For instance, former cast member Jim Beaver (who played Bobby Singer) faced backlash after he was asked about the love confession in "Despair" back in May 2022. Fan reports of the Purgatory Convention on May 28, 2022, report that Beaver "didn't think a lot about it but thinks Cas as an angel has a more cosmically spiritual view" and that "Cas was talking more about a transcendent love, Dean possibly didn't even understand the level of love of which Cas was speaking" (Vera, 2022). Fans linked Beaver's words to Jared Padalecki's who had also claimed the confession to be platonic and criticized Jim Beaver's acting as well as questioning Beaver's status of ally. The same observations about the vagueness of Castiel's confession, however, had been made by the fandom itself back when "Despair" first aired.

Back on November 5, 2020, when the CW aired "Despair," no one was expecting *Supernatural* to follow through and provide any kind of resolution to the relationship of Dean Winchester and Castiel or even acknowledge their subtextual queerness. Tumblr fans had predicted a confession scene, or something similar, because of the promo of the last three episodes, as it ended up happening. The scene, however, shows an unrequited love as Castiel's "I love you" is met by Dean Winchester's vague reply "Don't do this, Cass..." (Berens & Speight, Jr., 2020, 38:20) and heavily relies on mediatic stereotypes that, while making "visible the invisible" (Dyer, 2002, p. 16) also enhance its homophobia. Despite being written by an openly gay man, the scene was condemned for being homophobic, perpetrating harmful practices that are no longer counterbalanced by the mere presence of LGBTQ characters. Not only does Castiel die, he also claims that "happiness isn't in the having, it's in just being. It's in just saying it" (Berens & Speight, Jr., 2020, 36:14) thus obliterating a livable future of "positive affects" (McDermott, 2020, para. 20). The scene's quality and ambiguity did not impact fans' reactions and #Destiel and #Supernatural started trending on Twitter, ranking higher than the American presidential election for several hours. Longtime fans, casual watchers, and mere by-standers all engaged in the creation and circulation of memes that celebrated and, above all, mocked the moment. According to fans, Jensen Ackles' acting made the scene look as if Dean Winchester was trying to hold back a slur, a straight guy not reciprocating his friend's feelings, or holding back his vomit. *Supernatural* ultimately granted resolution to some of its fans but in an all but satisfactory manner.

Of course, death in the show means little as its protagonists come back to life again and again, leaving enough hope that Castiel would come back. In season fourteen, the episode "Game Night" (S14x17) also spent a considerable time explaining that angels and demons could be rescued from the Empty, the place where they ended up after being killed, and providing the audience information on how such rescues could be achieved. Furthermore, a tweet from the official account of cwphilly (2020) in which a picture of Misha Collins was posted to promote the show's final two episodes was also taken as reassurance that Castiel's death would be reversed. However, not only did "Inherit the Earth" (S15x19) and "Carry On" not star Misha Collins, it also did not acknowledge Castiel, his sexuality or his love confession: the only remarks, closure to a twelve-year long character arc, being an acknowledgment of his absence as well as his role in rebuilding Heaven. Additionally, Dean Winchester was also killed within the first twenty minutes of "Carry On" by being impaled on a phallic rebar which, given the queer-coding embedded in the show, made his death another instance of Bury Your Gays.

Supernatural *Fans Respond*

To counterbalance the show's homophobia, fans immediately organized a fundraising called *The Castiel Project*, the proceeds of which would go to the Trevor Project, dedicated to LGBTQ issues. The goal was to raise $1,500 but the sum was easily surpassed, and within a matter of days, the total amount had reached $55,000. On that occasion, Supernatural fans showed their willingness to defy stereotypes of passivity by taking change into their hands. In the brief description on the dedicated page, the organizers mention that "the ending left more than something to be desired" and that the reaction to *Supernatural*'s final episode "was unanimous—we weren't crazy" (The Trevor Project, 2020, para. 2). The reference to fans' delusion refers both to Misha Collins' tweet "You're not crazy" (Collins, 2013), tweeted years earlier in response to fans' outrage over the episode "I'm No Angel" (S9x3) in which Castiel has sex with a woman named April, and the general vagueness and elusiveness of cast, writers, and executives. Interestingly, the description goes on reading "Castiel had been pushed off screen for daring to be openly queer" while Dean was killed so that "there was no risk of him being coded as a queer character" (The Trevor Project, 2020, para. 7). The fundraising demonstrates that LGBTQ audiences' matter—that they are important, loved, and deserving of the same happy endings generally reserved to heterosexual couples—thus establishing "channels of collaboration for a common cause" (Guerrero-Pico, 2017, p. 2). However, it anticipates the interesting patterns for which Robert Berens and Misha Collins are considered to be beyond criticism. The two of them "fought to establish Castiel as a queer character" (The Trevor Project, 2020, para. 11) with Misha Collins admitting in an interview that he was on board as soon as "the writer proposed this ending" (Harbett, 2022, para. 49) and that it made him feel that his time on the show was "more meaningful and valuable" (para. 50) despite also having said that the scene itself was an instance of Bury Your Gays (Hasnaa, 2020).

However, while Robert Berens is occasionally called out for his racism, he is hardly ever condemned for his homophobia. Unlike other screenwriters, he is generally considered to be "not just another straight guy potentially just catering to fans" (castiellesbian, 2020). However, Castiel's confession in "Despair" is indicative of performative behavior on *Supernatural*'s part rather as it does not subvert the general idea that the show is "a very kind of macho hetero show" (Seriously, 2022, 0:28). While the episode acknowledges Castiel's feelings for Dean, it does not allow the subtextual relationship to reach its true fulfillment. Other episodes by the same screenwriter are not explicit either, always leaving the status of a character's queerness up for interpretation. Episodes such as "The Trap" (S15x9), for example, are praised by fans for their queer content and considered "the gayest episode of Supernatural" (deanwasalwaysbi, 2022, para. 10) even though the LGBTQ content remains implicit. "The Trap" relies on the parallel between queer couples and heterosexual ones, something *Supernatural* had already done in season eight with the introduction of Benny Lafitte (played by Ty Olsson). Just like Dean and Castiel were compared to Sam Winchester and Eileen Leahy (played by Shoshannah Stern), Dean and Benny were compared to Sam and Amelia Richardson (played by Liane Balaban). In season eight, however, the relationship between Dean Winchester and Benny Lafitte had unmistakably queer undertones and was developed even after the end of the so-called Purgatory arc. Episodes such as "Blood Brother" and "Citizen Fang" (S8x9) not only highlight *Supernatural*'s use of the vampire as a metaphor for sexual deviance, but also allow Sam Winchester, visibly repulsed, to speak and react in clear homophobic terms. Additionally, in episodes such as "LARP and the Real Girl" (S8x11), both the heterosexual and the homosexual separation are discussed in terms of a romantic break-up, equally affecting both brothers.

Up until November 23, 2020, despite being upset about the show's finale and the fact that "it spat in the face of its own themes" (Deidre T., 2020, para. 10), *Supernatural* fans did not particularly engage in "outrage-culture" for the sake of "moral posturing" (Bouvier, 2020, p. 10). Neither were they using social media and hashtags to go viral, and launch cancel campaigns towards The CW or, on a smaller scale, the actors by relying on the safeness and anonymity provided by online spaces (Kar, 2019). Things changed when the Latin American television channel Warner TV aired episode eighteen, which was now titled "La Verdad." Here, Castiel's love confession was answered with an unequivocal reciprocation rather than a line that may or may not refer to Castiel's imminent sacrifice. Despite still being the quickest U-turn in television history, both Castiel and Dean Winchester were now undeniably queer: Castiel because he used "amo" rather than "quiero," and Dean because of his own confession "y yo a ti" (Eliza Quinn, n.d., 0:26). This change led the fandom to accuse The CW of both homophobia and censorship rather than acknowledging the possibility of a mistranslation, which was indeed the case. Fans called for a boycott, asking people to unfollow any official CW account as the hashtags #TheySilencedThem and #TheySilencedYou started trending number one on Twitter in the United States.

The *Supernatural* fandom, that had asked for explanation and accountability in the past, aimed to engage with the powers that be in order for them to acknowledge the harm perpetrated by homophobic storylines that are nowadays outdated and superfluous. With their voices now "amplified due to the prevalence and easy use of social media" (Anderson-Lopez et al., 2020, p. 3) and "with more tools at their disposal to become more visible and ensure their comments, opinions, and request reach the interested parties without intermediaries" (Guerrero-Pico, 2017, p. 2071), Twitter launched #SomethingToSay a couple of days later. Unlike other occurrences, such as the 2013 #AskSupernatural event, the hashtag was created by fans to criticize the network rather than being created by the network and then used to initiate a conversation on diversity. This was taken as an opportunity to expand the issue to include female and disabled characters who had been killed and forgotten not only in *Supernatural*, but in other shows also, with the aim to empower minorities. However, unlike in 2015, when Jeremy Carver was forced to address the brutal death of Charlie Bradbury, *Supernatural*'s only recurring explicit queer character, in the episode "Dark Dynasty," neither The CW nor showrunner Andrew Dabb addressed the matter.

Misha Collins, however, did verge in and posted a video on his Twitter account. Here, he explained the situation saying it involved no conspiracy but that it had been caused by a "rogue translator" (Collins, 2020a, 0:16). Steering away from his previous admission that the scene was in fact homophobic, he explained that "Castiel is not a character that plays into any insidious trope of exclusion in Hollywood" (0:44) and that he was "proud of the ending of *Supernatural*" (0:21). According to Misha Collins, the ending was "intentionally inclusive and a celebration of someone expressing their truth and having good things come out of it" (0:25) and fans' reactions to "La Verdad" left him feeling "a little irked" (1:26). People immediately engaged with Collins online, replying to his video with didactic tweets that aimed to explain why exactly the scene could be seen as an instance of Bury Your Gays and why the audience felt hurt by Castiel's erasure from the story. Collins then replied, tweeting, "I naively thought Cas in 15.18 was going to feel validating. But this isn't about me. I'm going to shut up and listen for a change. If it's not too much to ask, please tell me what we could have done better" (Collins, 2020b). Misha Collins also apologized by saying: "I see a lot of comments about how tone-deaf my video is. I agree and I feel sick. I want to delete it, but I think that will erase all of your important comments & I feel like I should own my ignorance. […] Sorry" (Collins, 2020c). Many replies agreed with Collins when it came to feeling vindicated by the out-and-out love confession, although "this scene doesn't cancel out what happened after that episode and it also doesn't cancel out the show's flaws" (Mel, 2020). Fans also reiterated that it lasted as long as it took for Castiel to die, and that the ending still left enough freedom for interpretation regarding the characters' sexualities. The lack of explicit textual confirmation was considered as still not enough to stop perpetrating the depiction of Destiel shippers as delusional and stupid.

Fans' attempt to seek further validation that will somehow contrast whatever offense and harm *Supernatural* may have caused to any member of its audience, arguably avoidable had they stopped watching the show and engaging with it (Hachachi, 2020, 38:01), has since led fans to seek answers in paratext. This translates into an attempt to reverse the narrative and construct, at last, "interpretative consensuses that delegitimize institutional authority over the heterodiegetic text" (Johnson, 2007, p. 291). In doing this, fans are aided not only by the awareness of the now unnecessary need to keep the viewer interested and engaged (Jenkins et al., 2013), but also by *Supernatural*'s transmedia approach and the regularly scheduled conventions.

Until 2021, the show's subtext could only be mentioned to Misha Collins because of his "strategic support for a delimited realm of fan creativity" (Murray, 2004, p. 11) and Jensen Ackles' knee-jerk reactions when faced with transgressive behavior (Jenkins et al., 2013), namely slash shippers (people in a fandom who want to see a set of characters in a same-sex romantic or sexual relationship) and their questions. Now, however, the topic is no longer a taboo and, along with the awareness that everyone on set knew about it despite never discussing it (unknown, 2013), actors may be held accountable for past behavior and whatever hurt they may have caused. For example, Tumblr user seraphcastiel attended the *Supernatural* convention in Concord, North Carolina, back in November 2021. Her intention was to ask Jensen Ackles about Castiel's confession and the reasons that led him to agree on doing the scene, "because if i'm being honest, the way you have talked about the scene lately makes it seem like you regret agreeing to it, which is so disheartening for your lgbt fans" (seraphcastiel, 2021a, para. 2). While *Supernatural* conventions were, in the past, used as means by which to raise the show's profile and receive a new influx of engagement (Collier, 2015), they now reinforce parasocial behavior and celebrity culture while also allowing people who seek good representation that may reflect their own experiences and consequently provide a model for self-exploration (Waggoner, 2018) to obtain answers.

Fans try to dismantle and recreate power structures by insisting and resisting because of the text's lack of ambiguity. However, because such a reversal is increasingly resisted, thus perpetuating the idea that people working on the show do not understand the characters (Zubernis & Larsen, 2012), fandom "cultivates mob mentality" that operates on a "100% consensus" (Parker Beard, 2020, paras. 4–5) leading to performative and didactic behavior. *Supernatural* conventions, however, despite the show having ended in 2020, are still the sight of queerbaiting intended as "the outcome of increased paratextual discourse about LGBTQ content at a specific moment of queer contextuality" (Ng, 2017, para. 2.8) because it still reinforces the presence of diverging opinions and expectations, notwithstanding fans' attempt to "assert their authority over the text" (Collier, 2015, p. 119).

Actors are still hard pressed about not discussing the queer-coding present within the show, "Despair" and Castiel's sexuality, leaving LGBTQ fans to feel unvalidated and disheartened even more so because of revoked support. In short, homophobia at *Supernatural* conventions seems to be perpetrated with the same strength as in 2013 (Micarelli, 2021) contrasted with people's attempt to not only want better from their favorite show, but also push back against offensive behavior. This, however, seems to emerge exclusively in relation to the actors' reluctance or inability to provide answers in line with fans' own interpretations leading to a witch-hunt and nit-picking of past and present projects. Back in October 2021, for example, fans were outraged after Jensen Ackles said that he "never played that" (Gayled_it, 2021, 30:21) and Jared Padalecki's platonic interpretation of the love confession (Gayled_it, 2021). This led to fans calling out past instances of racism, misogyny, and homophobia or the involvement in projects that may contain instances of copaganda such as Padalecki's CW show *Walker* (2021–) or Jensen Ackles' involvement in *Big Sky* (2020–2023). There are entire Tumblr posts and YouTube videos dedicated to the matter and with the sole purpose of informing people of the actors' misgivings (capy, 2021) with detailed descriptions on why such behavior is both inappropriate and problematic. And, in the case of Jensen Ackles, even a Twitter page titled *Jensen Ackles' Receipts* dedicated to "dedicated to exposing Jensen Ackles' mild homophobia and biphobia, and will serve as an archive for past and future receipts on this subject" (Jensen Ackles' Receipts, 2021).

These instances that fans label problematic, however, are not necessarily accurate reports because of the features of social media such as "textual brevity of any individual post, the speed with which posts are disseminated, and the rapidity of online exchanges" (Ng, 2020, p. 623). Particularly Padalecki's words were, on more than one occasion, blown out of proportion due to the actors' lack of care in phrasing the sentence. At a convention in Denver, his stance that "I love you" could also be used platonically and among blood relatives (Gayled_it, 2021) was understood to be a comparison between gay love and pedophilia, "an incredibly problematic and dangerous thing to imply" (seraphcastiel, 2021, para. 2) and a statement that none of his colleagues condemned or apologized for. Jared Padalecki's words, then, made him "the evil other who must be 'cancelled'" (Bouvier, 2020, p. 10) and Jensen Ackles being "just as culpable" (thenightwemetnatural, 2021). Despite instances such as these, which inevitably go viral amidst fandom spaces, even in more recent conventions, LGBTQ fans continue to attend these events thus allowing the cycle of outrage to be repeated. Enhanced by the "affective communities" (Bouvier, 2020, p. 2) that these interactions establish, they may be seen as a way to change the show or any of the actors' attitude but ultimately are hardly effective: *Supernatural* stopped airing at the end of 2020 and conventions themselves are no longer means by which to attract an audience and better the show's ratings.

Conclusion

This essay set out the audience reception of *Supernatural* in light of fans' feeble democratic involvement, the accusations of queerbaiting, the show's referentiality, and fandom's approach and reception of the actual queer subtext. Kripke's adaptation of *On the Road* has long entered popular culture as a pillar of queerbaiting and an example of writers stouthearted refusing to embrace more diverse representation. The White, masculine, and heteronormative point of view was never discarded in favor of more contemporary models and diversity and, in spite of the ongoing exchanges on social media platforms like Tumblr and Twitter, the show remained centered around the Winchester brothers without ever featuring any real attempts to explicitly subvert the status quo.

The lack of positive results provided by any of these efforts highlights the illusive nature of the democratic power of television production, subverting the expectations derived from social media. Online platforms may facilitate exchanges and visibility but they do not necessarily bear any results. Or, at least, results that the more adamant audience can consider satisfactory. After all, reactions to individual characters like Bela Talbot and Victor Henriksen did shape the course of the show by changing its plot or raising more sensibility on topics such as racism and homophobia. The fascinating nature of *Supernatural*'s audience reception is therefore two folded insofar that the attempts at bettering the show not only stem from a misunderstanding of its narrative, but also highlight the lack of power that fans have.

Within the show, queerness and masculinity are inextricable: partly, because the characters move in a world that is deeply affected by the socio-political landscape of post–9/11 America; partly, because the story reprises the depiction of homosexual men in American culture of the 1950s and 1960s. Fans seem to condemn any instance of queerness either as homophobic or as a result of the construction of their own identity through mediatic consumption. Because of the letdown derived from the latter, any refusal to acknowledge its subtext is seen as an attack on fans themselves rather than the story's prerequisites. This, in turn, has led fans to look for answers in paratext and take advantage of the show's transmedia approach. The hints at a collaborative and reciprocal relationship between equals, however, are merely hints. The audience does not hold the same power as those actively working on the show, something that is particularly visible in *Supernatural*'s final episodes.

In theory, "Despair" caters to Destiel shippers because it features a homosexual love confession. In practice, it unsatisfyingly introduces explicit diversity that verges on being tokenistic, undermining the consistent subtext through the use of insidious and homophobic tropes. The episode does not satisfactorily answer any of the show's questions of gender and sexuality nor does it extinguish fans' feelings of indignation. Even though fans praise and deify Robert Berens and Misha Collins, they continue to challenge those in charge and seek validation. These activities reinforce the sense of unity based not only on the belonging of minoritarian groups but also the sharing of a common goal, they reinforce capitalist dynamics.

Fans continue to be consumers to be catered to and strung along only this time the object of consumption is paratextual in nature. Nevertheless, the strive for validation remains the same and, as in the case of *Supernatural*, the lack of confirmation grants a sense of control and leads to the recurrent reliance on cancel culture and nit-picking. Problematic behavior is called out and words are twisted, often to the point of exaggeration. The network, however, is never affected and neither are any of the actors or the show itself. As money continues to circulate, in forms of conventions' exorbitant fees, the only thing exposed is the fallacy at the heart of parasocial and reciprocal relationships. Capitalism may sell the idea of control but the traditional power structures with actors and showrunners on top are left intact. In the meanwhile, as consumption continues to feed into economic circulation, fans continue to pursue justice with scarce results. If not that of upholding tokenistic and exploitable diversity all because of the adherence to models and discourses that they consider to be more contemporary, diverse, and in line with their own perspectives of the world today.

References

angelinthefire. (2023, December 4). *I just wanna see them togetherrrrrrrrr agaaaaaaaaaaaain* [Tumblr post]. Tumblr. https://angelinthefire.tumblr.com/post/735737576751841280.

Arrojo, M. (2015). Social television as new relationship between conventional tv and the audience: an analysis of its aims, processes, and results. *International Journal of Social Science Studies*, 3(4), 37–49. http://dx.doi.org/10.11114/ijsss.v3i4.854.

Beauchamp, Z. (2019, May 20). *Game of Thrones* finale betrays shows' core themes. *Vox*. https://www.vox.com/game-of-thrones/2019/5/20/18632343/game-of-thrones-finale-season-8-bran-tyrion-iron-throne.

Berens, R. (Writer), & Speight, R., Jr. (Director). (2020, November 5). Despair (Season 15, Episode 18) [TV series episode]. In Berens, R., Buckner, B., A. Dabb, Ross-Leming, E., & Singer, R. (Executive Producers), *Supernatural*, The CW.

Boulware, T. (2017). *Fascination/Frustration: Slash fandom, genre, and queer uptake*. [Doctoral dissertation]. ProQuest Dissertation Publishing.

Bouvier, G. (2020). Racist call-outs and cancel culture on Twitter: The limitations of the platform's ability to define issues of social injustice. *Discourse, Context & Media, 28,* 1–11. https://doi.org/10.1016/j.dcm.2020.100431.

Bridges, E. (2018). A genealogy of queerbaiting: Legal codes, production codes, "Bury Your Gays" and "The 100 mess." *The Journal of Fandom Studies, 6*(2), 115–132. doi:10.1386/jfs.6.2.115_1.

Britnall, K.L. (2004). Tarantino's incarnational theology: *Reservoir Dogs,* crucifixions and spectacular violence. *Current Currents, 54*(1), 66–75.

Brooks, D. (2019, January 14). The cruelty of call-out culture. *New York Times.* https://www.nytimes.com/2019/01/14/opinion/call-out-social-justice.html.

Buckner, B., & Ross-Leming, E. (Writers), Bee, G. (Director). (2013, April 3). Taxi driver (Season 8, Episode 19) [TV series episode]. In Carver, J., Glass, A., McG, Sgriccia, P., & Singer, R. (Executive Producers), *Supernatural,* The CW.

Buckner, B. & Ross-Leming, E. (Writers), Singer, R. (Director). (2019, October 17). Raising hell (Season 15, Episode 2) [TV series episode]. In Berens, R., Buckner, B., A. Dabb, Ross-Leming, E., & Singer, R. (Executive Producers), *Supernatural,* The CW.

bundibird. (2021, February 14). *SOMEONE GO WAKE ERIC UP, HE'S RUNNING LATE* [Tumblr post]. Tumblr. https://bundibird.tumblr.com/post/643134532923621376/someone-go-wake-eric-up-hes-running-late-hes.

Canham, S.L. (2009). The interaction of masculinity and control and its impact on the experience of suffering for an older man. *Journal of Aging Studies, 23*(2), 90–96. https://doi.org/10.1016/j.jaging.2008.12.003.

capy. (2021, October 17). *Worse 3 moments of the 16/10/2021 Spn Con.* [Video]. YouTube. https://www.youtube.com/watch?v=xpRn-4xn3j8&t=6s.

Carlson, A. (2015, June 19). The poet laureate of fanfiction. *The Awl.* https://www.theawl.com/2015/06/the-poet-laureate-of-fan-fiction/.

Carver, J. (Writer), & Sgriccia, P. (Director). (2010, April 10). Point of no return (Season 5, Episode 18). [TV series episode]. In Edlund, B., Gamble, S., Kripke, E., McG, Sgriccia, P., & Singer, R. (Executive Producers), *Supernatural,* The CW.

castiellesbian. (2020, December 1). *I feel like i need a glossary of terms or a contact list* [Tumblr post]. Tumblr. https://castiellesbian.tumblr.com/post/636325192563621888/i-feel-like-i-need-a-glossary-of-terms-or-a.

castiels-pussy. (2021, February 8). *KNOCK KNOCK KRIPKE ARE YOU THERE* [Tumblr post]. Tumblr. https://castiels-pussy.tumblr.com/post/642553082730954752/knock-knock-kripke-are-you-there-the.

Choi, Y.J. (2017). Emergence of the viewing public: Does social television viewing transform individual viewers into a viewing public? *Telematics and Informatics, 34*(7), 1059–1070. https://doi.org/10.1016/j.tele.2017.04.014.

Click, M.A., & Scott, S. (2018). *The Routledge companion to media fandom.* Routledge.

Collier, C.M. (2012). *The love that refuses to speak its name: Examining queerbaiting and fan-producer interactions in fan cultures.* [Masters dissertation]. Electronic Thesis and Dissertations. https://doi.org/10.18297/etd/2204.

Collins, M. [@mishacollins]. (2013, October 25). *You're not crazy.* [Tweet]. Twitter. https://twitter.com/mishacollins/status/393627512166567936.

Collins, M. [@mishacollins]. (2020a, November 26). *I'm seeing a lot of commentary on the ending of #SPN & the recent Spanish dub & am disheartened to* [Tweet]. Twitter. https://twitter.com/mishacollins/status/1331801645152288768?ref_src=twsrc%5Etfw.

Collins, M. [@mishacollins]. (2020b, November 26). *I'm sorry if I spoke defensively. I naively thought Cas in 15.18 was going to feel validating* [Tweet]. Twitter. https://twitter.com/mishacollins/status/1331825062060515329.

Collins, M. [@mishacollins]. (2020c, November 26). *I see lots of comments about how tone-deaf my video is. I agree and I feel sick* [Tweet]. Twitter. https://twitter.com/mishacollins/status/1332095770988691456.

Corn, A. (2009). Existentialism and hin Gunn's early poetry. In J. Weiner (Ed.), *At the barriers* (pp. 35–44). University of Chicago Press.

Cruz, E. (2014, July 17). Fans take *Supernatural* to task for 'queer baiting.' *Advocate.* https://www.advocate.com/bisexuality/2014/07/17/fans-take-supernatural-task-queer-baiting.

Cwphilly. [@cwphilly]. (2020, November 17). *#Supernatural is coming to an end on THURSDAY. Will you be tuning in to the series finale?* [Tweet]. Twitter. https://twitter.com/cwphilly/status/1328739260506247169.

deanwasalwaysbi. (2021, January 27). *They really were just gaslighting the fandom for a decade* [Tumblr post]. Tumblr. https://deanwasalwaysbi.tumblr.com/post/641484116212252672/they-really-were-just-gaslighting-the-fandom-for-a

deancritblog. (2021, November 11). *I will never understand how this fandom took an aggressively straight* [Tumblr post]. Tumblr. https://deancritblog.tumblr.com/post/667585107135201280/i-will-never-understand-how-this-fandom-took-an.

deanwasalwaysbi. (2022, June 14). *I am once again going insane over the subtleties of The Trap* [Tumblr post]. Tumblr. https://deanwasalwaysbi.tumblr.com/post/686993959478788096/i-am-once-again-going-insane-over-the-subtleties.

Deidre, T. (2020, November 23). *Supernatural*'s legacy: The trauma of silence. *Buzzfeed*. https://www.buzzfeed.com/deidre-t/supernaturalas-legacy-the-trauma-of-silence-1b17yhc5ye.

Dyer, R. (2002). *The culture of queer*. Routledge.

Edlund, B. (Writer & Director). (2012, May 4). Reading is fundamental (Season 8, Episode 21). [TV series episode]. In Gamble, S., McG, Sgriccia, P., & Singer, R. (Executive Producers), *Supernatural*, The CW.

Edmundson, M. (2016). Introduction. In M. Edmundson (Ed.), *The Gothic tradition in* Supernatural: *Essays on the television series* (pp. 1–12). McFarland.

Eliza Quinn. (n.d). *Supernatural 15x18 Spanish dub confession scene* [Video]. YouTube. https://www.youtube.com/watch?v=0Jsb6S1IkJw.

Fathallah, J. (2014, July 17). Moriarty's ghost: Or the queer disruption of the BBC's *Sherlock*. *Television & New Media, 16*(5), 490–500. https://doi.org/10.1177/1527476414543528.

Fernie, E. (2013). 'To sin in loving virtue': Desire and possession in *Measure for Measure*. *Sillage Critiques, 15*. https://doi.org/10.4000/sillagescritiques.2608.

Fine, L.M. (2000). Rights of men, rites of passage: Hunting and masculinity at Reo Motors of Lansing, Michigan, 1945–1975. *Journal of Social History, 33*(4), 805–823.

Freede-Blanar, Z., & Glazer, A.M. (2017). *Superfandon: How our obsessions are changing what we buy and who we are*. W.W. Norton.

Gamble, S., & Humphris, C. (Writers), & Boyum, S. (Director). (2008, February 7). Dream a little dream of me (Season 3, Episode 10). [TV series episode]. In Kripke, E., Manners, K., McG, & Singer, R. (Executive Producers), *Supernatural*, The CW.

Gamble, S. (Writer), & Singer, R. (Director). (2009, May 7). When the levee breaks (Season 4, Episode 21). [TV series episode]. In Kripke, E., Manners, K., McG, & Singer, R. (Executive Producers), *Supernatural*, The CW.

Gamble, S., & Tucker, R. (Writers), & Kroeker, A. (Director). (2006, January 17). Faith (Season 1, Episode 12). [TV series episode]. In Kripke, E., McG, & Singer, R. (Executive Producers), *Supernatural*, The CW.

Gayled_it (2019, November 3). *Supernatural DC 2019 Jensen Ackles Gold Panel* [Video]. YouTube. https://www.youtube.com/watch?v=NjGuuqOYod0.

Gayled_it (2021, October 23). *SPNDENVER 2021 Jared Padalecki and Jensen Ackles panel* [Video]. YouTube. https://www.youtube.com/watch?v=pFzXsFbPPAc.

Gennis, S. (2014, November 17). *Supernatural* has a queerbaiting problem that needs to stop. *TV Guide*. https://www.tvguide.com/news/supernatural-queerbaiting-destiel-1089286/.

Ginsberg, A. (1972). The visions of the great remembered. In J. Kerouac, *Visions of Cody* (pp. 1–10). Penguin.

Glynn, M. (Writer), & McKenzie, C. (Director). (2020, October 29). Unity (Season 15, Episode 17) [TV series episode]. In Berens, R., Buckner, B., A. Dabb, Ross-Leming, E., & Singer, R. (Executive Producers), *Supernatural*, The CW.

Gray, J. (2021). *Dislike-minded: Media, audiences, and the dynamics of taste*. New York University Press.

Guerrero-Pico, M. (2017). #Fringe, audiences, and fan labor: Twitter activism to save a TV show from cancellation. *International Journal of Communication, 11*, 2071–2092.

Guerrero-Pico, M., Establés, M.. & Ventura R. (2017). Dead lesbian syndrome: LGBTQ fandom's self-regulation mechanisms in fan-producer controversies around *The 100*. *Analisi: Quaderns de Comunicació i Cultura, 57*, 2071–2092. http://doi.org/10.5565/rev/analisi.3110.

Hachachi, R. (Director). (2020). *Tom Segura: Ball hog*. [Movie].

Hamad, H. (2011). Extreme parenting: recuperating fatherhood in Steven Spielberg's *War of the Worlds* (2005). In Radner, H., & Stringer, R. (Eds.), *Feminism at the Movies: Understanding gender in contemporary popular cinema* (pp. 241–253). Routledge.

Harbett, X. (2022, February 9) What Misha Collins learned on *Roadfood*, eating on *Supernatural*, and GISH. *Mashed*. https://www.mashed.com/762327/what-misha-collins-learned-on-roadfood-eating-on-supernatural-and-gish-exclusive-interview/.

Hasnaa. (2020, December 5). *Misha and the cast of Supernatural talk about Destiel going Canon* [Video]. YouTube. https://www.youtube.com/watch?v=xdPzG1yqjEU.

hells-plaid-angel. (2022, June 17). *For better or for worse, LGBT+ themes and characters have* [Tumblr post]. Tumblr. https://hells-plaid-angel.tumblr.com/post/687266657281998848/for-better-or-for-worse-lgbt-themes-and.

Highfill, S. (2017, September 29). The stars of *Supernatural* break down the moments that changed the show. *Entertainment Weekly*. https://ew.com/tv/2017/09/29/supernatural-cast-breaks-down-the-moments-that-changed-show/.

Hills, M. (2002). *Fan cultures*. Routledge.

hooks, b. (2004). *The will to change: Men, masculinity, and love*. Atria Books.

Humphris, C. (Writer), & Rohl, M. (Director). (2007, November 1). Bedtime stories (Season 3, Episode 5). [TV series episode]. In Kripke, E., Manners, K., McG, & Singer, R. (Executive Producers), *Supernatural*, The CW.

Jain, S. (2005). Violent submission: Gendered automobility. *Cultural Critique, 61*, 186–214.

Jenkins, H. (1992). *Textual poachers: Television fans and participatory culture*. Routledge.

Jenkins, H. (2006). *Convergence culture*. New York University Press.

Jenkins, H., Ford, S., & Green, J. (2013). *Spreadable media: Creating value and meaning in a networked culture.* New York University Press.

Jensen Ackles Receipts [@jensenreceipts] *This page is dedicated to exposing Jensen Ackles' mild homophobia and biphobia.* [Twitter profile]. https://mobile.twitter.com/jensenreceipts.

Johnson, D. (2007). Fan-Tagonisms: Factions, institutions, and constitutive hegemonies of fandom. In J. Gray, C.L. Harrington, C. Sandvoss (Eds.), *Fandom: Identity and communities in a mediated world.* New York University Press.

Kar, P. (2019). Partha Kar: We must stand up and challenge offensive behavior. *BMJ, 367,* 16749. http://doi.org/10.1136/bmj.l6749.

Knowles, T. (2016). The automobile as moving castle. In M. Edmundson (Ed.), *The Gothic tradition in Supernatural* (pp. 25–36). McFarland.

Kripke, E. (2007, February 15). Eric Kripke fields your questions about *Supernatural. TV Guide.* https://www.tvguide.com/news/eric-kripke-fields-35627/.

Kripke, E. (Writer & Director). (2009, May 19). Lucifer rising (Season 4, Episode 22). In Kripke, E., Manners, K., McG, & Singer, R. (Executive Producers), *Supernatural,* The CW.

Kripke, E. (Writer), & Boyum, S. (Director). (2010, May 13). Swan song (Season 5, Episode 22). [TV series episode]. In Edlund, B., Gamble, S., Kripke, E., McG, Sgriccia, P., & Singer, R. (Executive Producers), *Supernatural,* The CW.

Kripke, E. [@therealkripke]. (2015, December 9). *#SPNArtifact. In honor of tonight, the first page from my #SPN pitch to the studio. Never before seen.* [Tweet]. Twitter. https://twitter.com/therealkripke/status/674659951747334144?lang=bg.

lampstiel. (n.d.). *Spn scenes that hit different now destiel is canon—part 1* [Video]. YouTube. https://www.youtube.com/watch?v=-u8SyBnli64.

lenore-tumbles. (2020, November 11). *We've been berend.* [Tumblr post]. Tumblr. https://lenore-tumbles.tumblr.com/post/634517774006370304/weve-been-berened.

les-beast [@spidervrese]. (2020, October 2). *Y'all maybe Destiel will become canon...* [Tweet]. Twitter. https://twitter.com/spidervrese/status/1311855180489474048.

Love, H. (2009). *Feeling backward: Loss and the politics of queer history.* Harvard University Press.

Macklem, L., & Grace D. (2020). Unpacking *Supernatural:* What's in the box? In L. Macklem, & D. Grace (Eds.), *Supernatural out of the Box* (pp. 1–11). McFarland.

Matthews, B. (Writer), & Singer, R. (Director). (2010, December 3). Caged heat (Season 6, Episode 10). [TV series episode]. In Edlund, B., Gamble, S., Kripke, E., McG, Sgriccia, P., & Singer, R. (Executive Producers), *Supernatural,* The CW.

McCluskey, M. (2019, July 24). HBO rejects petition to remake *Game of Thrones* Season 8 once and for all. *Time Magazine.* https://time.com/5634309/hbo-rejects-game-of-thrones-season-8-petition/.

McDermott, M. (2020, December 30). The (broken) promise of queerbaiting: Happiness and futurity in politics of queer representation. *International Journal of Cultural Studies, 24*(5), 844–859. https://doi.org/10.1177/1367877920984170.

Micarelli, N. (2021, November 8). Casual homophobia at *Supernatural* conventions just won't die. *The Mary Sue.* https://www.themarysue.com/casual-homophobia-at-supernatural-conventions-just-wont-die/.

Murray, S. (2004). 'Celebrating the story the way it is': Cultural studies, corporate media and the contested utility of fandom. *Continuum: Journal of Media & Cultural Studies, 18*(1), 7–25. https://doi.org/10.1080/1030431032000180978.

Ng, E. (2008). Reading the romance of fan cultural production: Music videos of a television lesbian couple. *Popular Communication, 6*(2), 103–121. https://doi.org/10.1080/15405700701746525.

Ng, E. (2017). Between text, paratext, and context: Queerbaiting and the contemporary media landscape. *Transformative Works and Culture, 24.* https://doi.org/10.3983/twc.2017.0917.

Ng, E. (2020). No grand pronouncements here…: Reflections on cancel culture and digital media participation. *Television and New Media, 21*(6), 621–627. doi: 10.1177/1527476420918828.

Nicol, R. (2014). "How is that not rape-y?": Dean as anti–Bella and feminism without women in *Supernatural.* In S.A. George & R.M. Hansen (Eds.), *Supernatural, humanity, and the soul. On the Highway to Hell and Back* (pp. 155–168). Palgrave Macmillan.

omegaphobe. (2022, March 12). *eric kripke 2005: i'm gonna make a show fetishizing toxic masculinity* [Tumblr post]. Tumblr. https://omegaphobe.tumblr.com/post/678560116859174912/eric-kripke-2005-im-gonna-make-a-show.

Padalecki, J. [@jarpad]. (2019, March 22). *Hey #SPNFamily here's a little message from @JensenAckles @mishacollins and me. I'm so grateful for the family that's been built* [Tweet]. Twitter. https://twitter.com/jarpad/status/1109190627634434049?ref_src=twsrc%5Etfw.

Parker Beard, J.C. (2020) Click bait, cancel culture, and the rhetoric of civic discourse. *Georgia International Conference on Information Literacy.* https://digitalcommons.georgiasouthern.edu/gaintlit/2020/2020/19/.

Prudom, M. (2012, July 31). *Supernatural* season 8: Misha Collins talks Castiel's big return and more. *The Huffington Post.* https://www.huffpost.com/entry/supernatural-season-8-misha-collins_n_1726114.

Royle, N. (2003). *The uncanny*. Manchester University Press.

Ryan, L. (2013, October 8). *Supernatural* premiere: Misha Collins talks Castiel's humanity, sexual prowess and season 9 journey. *The Huffington Post*. https://www.huffpost.com/entry/supernatural-premiere-season-9-misha-collins_n_4066250.

sailorsally. (2021, October 1). *eric kripke accidentally writing thee most romantically/sexually charged* [Tumblr post]. Tumblr. https://sailorsally.tumblr.com/post/663785713230348288/eric-kripke-accidentally-writing-thee-most.

seraphcastiel. (2020a, November 7). *This was the question i wanted to ask at the j2 panel btw idk in case anyone was wondering* [Tumblr post]. Tumblr. https://seraphcastiel.tumblr.com/post/667243430937788416/this-was-the-question-i-wanted-to-ask-at-the-j2.

seraphcastiel (2020b, November 7). *Okay. I need to type this out and get it down bc it really did affect me* [Tumblr post]. Tumblr. https://seraphcastiel.tumblr.com/post/667237336893014016/okay-i-need-to-type-this-out-and-get-it-down-bc.

Seriously. (2022). *Misha Collins révèle tout sur la relation Dean/Castiel* [Video]. YouTube. https://www.youtube.com/shorts/FEwSuGqAKg0.

Smith, J. (2007). *The Wicker man* (1973) email digest: A case study in web ethnography. In J. Chapman, M. Glancy, & S. Harper (Eds.), *The new film history, sources, methods, approaches* (pp. 229–244). Palgrave Macmillan.

sosaysdeans. (2022, August 15). *Was it season 4 or 5 that they made cas* [Tumblr post]. Tumblr. https://sosaysdean.tumblr.com/post/692655005859217408/was-it-season-4-or-5-that-they-made-cas-tell-dean.

Stevens, C.S. (2010). You are what you buy: Postmodern consumption and fandom of Japanese popular culture. *Japanese Studies, 30*(2), 199–214. https://dx.doi.org/10.1080/10371397.2010.497578.

Supernatural4Ever. (2020, March 24). *Supernatural 15x13 - the road so far!* [Video]. YouTube. https://www.youtube.com/watch?v=01a0cAghW7U.

swallowflyingsolo. (2022, August 15). *The fact that the other side of the fandom were* [Tumblr post]. Tumblr. https://swallowflyingsolo.tumblr.com/post/692658365512417280/the-fact-that-the-other-side-of-the-fandom-were-so.

Tevin, J.D. (2023, September 6). *The wholesome façade of Heartstopper*. Medium. https://medium.com/@jdtevin/the-wholesome-facade-of-heartstopper-8c7170931c98.

themanwhowouldbefruit. (2023, December 2). *we aren't going to get canon destiel you dumb sluts* [Tumblr post]. Tumblr. https://themanwhowouldbefruit.tumblr.com/post/735602801003085824/we-arent-going-to-get-canon-destiel-you-dumb-sluts.

thenightwemetnatural. (2022, May 28). *i'd like to take the time to remind everyone that jensen ackles is just as culpable* [Tumblr post]. Tumblr. https://thenightwemetnatural.tumblr.com/post/685519973861457920/id-like-to-take-the-time-to-remind-everyone-that.

thirdpartied. (2021, September 4). *watching jake, kim, and misha talk about midam, jodydonna, and destiel makes me wanna spy on kripke* [Tumblr post]. Tumblr. https://thirdpartied.tumblr.com/post/661437629325295616/watching-jake-kim-and-misha-talk-about-midam.

30wyn. (2012, May 5). *Jensen & Misha Abt the scene where Dean gave Cas his coat back.* [Video]. YouTube. https://www.youtube.com/watch?v=YQTq-9kHYxc.

The Trevor Project. (2020). *The Castiel project*. https://give.thetrevorproject.org/fundraiser/3037563

2badsosad21. (2021, September 25). *Star gambled was obsessed with Sam* [Tumblr comment]. Tumblr. https://carzinization.tumblr.com/post/663269484242616320/did-sera-gamble-have-girl-power-did-sera-gamble.

u/deleted. (2015). *What happened to all the pussy in Supernatural* [Online forum]. Reddit. https://www.reddit.com/r/Supernatural/comments/3pom21/what_happened_to_all_the_pussy_in_supernatural_no/.

Udupa, S., & Pohjonen, M. (2019). How social media took us from Tahir Square to Donald Trump. *International Journal of Communication, 13*, 3049–3067.

Unknown. (2013, September 20). *Supernatural - 9.07 - Dean and Castiel's reunion and queer-baiting*. SpoilerTV. https://www.spoilertv.com/2013/09/supernatural-907-dean-and-castiels.html.

Vera [@raths_kitten]. (2022, May 28). *Cas was talking more about a transcendent love* [Tweet]. Twitter. https://twitter.com/raths_kitten/status/1530497743336120320.

virginwhoredichotomy. (2020, December 11). *I really think castiels confession scene was one* [Tumblr Post]. Tumblr. https://virginwhoredichotomy.tumblr.com/post/637208405949480960/i-really-think-castiels-confession-scene-was-one.

Waggoner, B.E. (2018). Bury your gays and social media fan response: Television, LGBTW representation, and communication ethics. *Journal of Homosexuality, 65*(13), 1877–1891. https://doi.org/10.1080/00918369.2017.1391015.

Wei, S. (2019, October 25). *Fandom, the highest stage of capitalism?* Varsity. https://www.varsity.co.uk/features/18086.

Weir, J. (2005). Everybody knows, nobody cares, or: Neal Cassady's penis. *Triquarterly, 122*(122), 117–125.

Whedonopolis (2019, July 22). *SDCC 2019: Supernatural panel part 1* [Video]. YouTube. https://www.youtube.com/watch?v=fBxAlzTtBoo.

Wilhelm, K. (2020). "Where's the pie?" Nostalgic and apocalyptic foodways in *Supernatural*. In L. Macklem & D. Grace (Eds.), *Supernatural out of the box* (pp. 107–119). McFarland.

Wilkinson, J. (2013). The epic love story of *Supernatural* and fanfic. In A. Jamison (Ed.), *Fic: Why fanfic is taking over the world* (pp. 309–315). Smartpop.

Wilkinson, J. (2014). Post, reblog, follow, tweet: Supernatural fandom and social media. In L. Zubernis & K. Larsen (Eds.), *Fan phenomena: Supernatural* (pp. 46–55). Intellect Books.

Witten, M. (Writer), & Beeson, C. (Director). (2007, January 18). Playthings (Season 2, Episode 11). [TV series episode]. In Kripke, E., Manners, K., McG, Shiban, J., & Singer, R. (Executive Producers), *Supernatural*, The CW.

Wright, J.M. (2016). *Men with stakes. Masculinity and the Gothic in US television*. Manchester University Press.

Zubernis, L., & Larsen, K. (2012). *Fandom at the crossroads*. Cambridge Scholars.

Celebration and Mourning

Audience Reception of Queer Relationships in Schitt's Creek *and* The 100

CHANDRAMA BASU

Michael McConnell (2016) asserted how "marriage was our pledge to one another, the nucleus of our personal agenda. We knew our love was as meaningful, as beautiful, and as valid as the love of any two people on Earth, and we are determined to have our sacred bond recognized by the country in which we lived" (p. 65). McConnell is the legally married spouse of Jack Baker who pursued a law degree for the primary reason of getting married to the man he loved. McConnell and Baker were the first known gay couple to apply for a marriage license and became the first gay couple to acquire a marriage license in 1971, a period when same-sex relationships, as well as marriage, were still proscribed and subject to dominant social castigation, evident in the series of state bans on homosexual marriage. According to the report "The State of Marriage Equality in America" (2015), several American states like Maryland, Arizona, Colorado, Florida, and San Francisco opposed and censored same-sex marriage in the 1970s due to various religious, legal and social disputes. However, over the past decades, same-sex marriage laws have changed, and with it, the on-screen portrayals of homosexual couples have changed.

Although the legal approval of marriage Connell-Baker marriage was perceived as a stance against the perception of marriage as an exclusively heteronomative practice, and the portrayals of homosexuals have continued to increase substantially since the coming out of Ellen DeGeneres in *Ellen*, GLAAD's Where We Are on TV 2020–2021 Report (2022) manifests that about 9.1 percent of the regular characters to appear on primetime television are LGBTQ (p.10), which is one of the highest records recorded by the survey, following a highest of 10 percent inclusion of LGBTQ characters in 2020. With shows like *Euphoria, Pose, The 100, Adam, Portrait of a Lady on Fire, Schitt's Creek,* and *The Politician,* to name a few, the media representation of homosexual characters has undergone a drastic change since mainstream films and primetime television shows have conventionally been endued with heterosexual characters—their lives, their conflicts and their passions and often ended up straight washing queer characters.

Even if some of the shows incorporated LGBTQ characters, they were essentially stereotypical and topical, like the White, rich, handsome, overdramatic, flamboyant, or feminine gay men or masculine, sexually active, grave or overtly feminine lesbians, creating and fixating a static image of them in the social consciousness. Richard Dryer (2012) explains that one of the reasons why queer characters are often stereotyped is because the heterosexual society attempts to "define us for ourselves in terms that inevitably fall short of the 'ideal' of heterosexuality (that is, taken to be the norm of being human), and to pass this definition off as necessary and natural" (p. 357). David Halperin accords similarly that homosexuality is not regarded as a natural category but symbolically, as an antithesis to heterosexuality—it is defined in opposition to normality and therefore, in negation. As such, they were customarily portrayed within a set framework on TV and films either for evoking comic effects or as the trustworthy and astute companions of the straight protagonists of a show, who provided insight into their lives and romantic relationships, yet would inevitably remain the one bereft of an amatory experience. In *My Best Friend's Wedding* (1997), Jules's gay friend George pretends to be her fiancé to make Michael jealous, while imparting wisdom about her love life, and *Mean Girls* (2004) depicts Damian and Janis as the homosexual best friends of Cady, who remain the more sensible and commonsensical characters throughout the film.

One of the significant films marking an exception in this direction was *Sex and the City 2* (2010), where the marriage of Carrie Bradshaw's gay best friend (Stanford Blatch to Anthony Marentino) is depicted and celebrated elaborately with a picturesque setting and friends and family members who are delighted about the culmination of their marriage. The gay couple of *Modern Family* (2009–2020), Cam and Mitch, contribute to the exception not only through their marriage in the Season 5 finale but also through a representation of the travails of their romantic life and as homosexual parents. According to Jude Dry (2020), "Over 10 million viewers tuned in for the wedding, and the very same day a new Gallup poll announced that support for marriage equality had reached a new high" (para. 4). A similar celebratory reaction was also evident in the culmination of the relationship of the flamboyant and eccentric David Rose (Dan Levy) and the grounded and prudent Patrick Brewer (Noah Reid) into marriage in *Schitt's Creek*, on the development of a romance between Lexa and Clarke in *The 100* (2014–2020), Marianne and Héloïse's relationship in late-eighteenth-century France in *Portrait of a Lady on Fire* (2019), Quentin and Eliot's nuanced and complex relationship in *The Magicians* (2015–2020) and Santana and Brittany's marriage in *Glee* (2009–2015). Audiences may revel at these rare and special instances that validate gender variation and homosexual relationships in media. Additionally, these depictions corroborate the function of television and media as potent socio-cultural arbitrators, confronting, challenging and sustaining crucial gender issues transpiring in society. Following this, the present essay focuses on the audience's reception of the romantic relationship and the resolution attested to the queer couples in the television shows *Schitt's Creek* and *The 100* to discern the key issues and incidents that influenced the audience.

Context: Same-Sex Marriage

To provide an alternate perspective to McConnell and Baker, Marjorie Jones and Tracy Knight's appeal for a marriage license in 1970 was scoffed at and rejected by

James Hallahan, the Kentucky county clerk who presided over their appellation, on the ground that marriage only between a man and a woman was the bedrock of the procreation and social continuity. He further warned that if such appeals were taken seriously by the law and the government, it could prove dangerous for the foundation of the social structure leading to the breakdown of established covenants (Fosl, 2012, p. 45). Unlike McConnell and Baker, the first lesbian couple's request for a marriage license was rejected outright by the court. Homosexuality or homosexual relationship is generally seen as a disruptive force which destabilizes, what Judith Butler terms the "prediscursive" notions of gender and sexual identity, engenders confusion and chaos in the society, paves the way for attacking those who challenge the norm, finally explicating the stigma associated with homosexual relationships and the intense social pressure to conform to gender stereotypes. This fear of social harrying and persecution had naturally compelled numerous homosexual individuals throughout history to sustain a closeted life in repression of their natural yearnings, instincts, and propensities.

This is indicated by the revelation of the life of J. Edgar Hoover, the first director of the FBI and an ostensible patriarch, who had spent his life in stern rejection, condemnation, and persecution of homosexuals, as a closeted homosexual himself. He, allegedly, protected his propriety, heterosexual reputation, and threats of being exposed as gay, through his draconian actions against homosexuals (Summers, 2011). Although he has been condemned as a perpetrator of and encouraging crime against homosexuals, his abomination promulgates the intolerant and mistrustful climate of the period, as evidenced by Dr. Charles W. Socarides, an American psychiatrist, who derided homosexuality as a mental illness that could be cured through psychotherapy (Reilly, 2015). The late twentieth-century society, therefore, was rife with misgivings, negation and repression of homosexual identities, making it an oppressive social atmosphere for the expression of homosexual identities.

Amidst the prevailing atmosphere of dismissal of homosexual individuals, the society also witnessed burgeoning unrest and activism within the LGBTQ community, demanding the government, law and society to accept them and their orientation as just as natural as heterosexuals. They continue to fight against the homophobic temperament of the society, demand and acquire legal rights to perform their natural gender disposition and the liberty to engage in and culminate same-sex relationships to marriage if desired. The Stonewall Uprising is regarded to be one of the most cogent events to propel and bolster the cause, leading to the emergence of worldwide movements to materialize their demands. The eventual declaration of June as Pride Month by President Bill Clinton (1999–2000) in commemoration of the Stonewall Uprising and later pronouncement of the month by President Barack Obama as the Pride+ LGBTQ month are the consequences of the extensive Stonewall Movement (Tandon & Rao, 2021, pp. 210–211). The year 2019 marked the 50th anniversary of the Stonewall incident and the world witnessed thousands marching the streets in various countries on June 28 and 29th to celebrate queer lives, their campaign for equal rights in society and revise their vow to continue the operation.

While the Stonewall riot was by no means the originator of the movement for gay rights, it had undeniably influenced the legal transformations and social developments that happened since then, prompting the upliftment of federal exclusions on homosexuals, anti-sodomy laws and employment discrimination and presently, 27 countries allow for same-sex marriage. According to the Ipsos LGBT+ Pride Global survey (2021) comprising twenty-seven countries, most of the twenty-seven nations support "anti-discrimination laws and equal marriage and adoption rights for LGBT people," "corporate activism promoting equality," "LGBT people being open about their sexual orientation or gender identity with everyone," "LGBT people displaying affection in public and more LGBT characters on TV, in films and in advertising," and "for lesbian, gay and bisexual athletes in sports teams being open about their orientation" (para. 3). The Gallup's Annual Mood of the Nation (2022) survey also accords that a record high of 62 percent of the survey participants was satisfied with the acceptance of gays and lesbians (para. 14), compared to the 55 percent acceptance in 2021. These reports testify to an increasingly positive environment across the world where homosexual individuals are encouraged to act and behave more freely and self-assuredly in the wake of a more liberating attitude toward them, evincing greater visibility of homosexual individuals in society. One of the direct consequences of the evolving social atmosphere is reflected in the increasing representation of homosexual characters in films and television, particularly in *Schitt's Creek* and the aforementioned discussion of the social scene in which the evolution of same-sex marriage in the U.S. transpired serves to add context to the analysis of the same sex on-screen portrayals later in this essay.

Schitt's Creek: "*i deserve a happy ending*"

In *Schitt's Creek*, the character David (Dan Levy) portrays a gay man who is not ashamed of his identity, which in turn may encourage audience members to approve of the portrayal. A viewer of the show, for instance, applauds the representation of the character of David on Twitter which has helped him to recognize his own identity in life: "Thanks to #SchittsCreek, I am learning to embrace my inner David. Even after coming out, I have struggled with the #extra over-the-top parts of me. But I want to work at being more authentic ... so, Thanks #David" (Smith, 2021). David or any of the characters of the show can hardly be considered role models for emulation, as they are all (including Johnny and especially Alexis and Moira), to different degrees, patronizing and insensitive narcissists possessing a sense of entitlement and lacking any sense of the real world. Their attitudes are somewhat understandable, stemming from their lifelong residence in the ivory tower and their complete detachment from the mundane lives of common people, at least at the start of the series. Nonetheless, the character of David is considered to be a significant ideal by the viewer quoted above, because he can resonate with the demeanor and circumstances of David's life, more than any individual in his/her own life. More importantly, the viewer implies that he finds hope in the resolution of his life thanks to David's on-screen portrayal.

Since the beginning of Dan Levy and Eugene Levy's creation of *Schitt's Creek* in 2015, the show manifests the monetary struggles of David (and his entire family) and is mainly about their ability to emote to others and express themselves. For David (and Alexis), demonstrations of the most basic acts of love even to his parents are awkward and groundless. His romantic relationships, correspondingly, have been emotionally unsatisfactory and established as temporary, built on the common elements of fortune, luxury and social eminence. This changes when David encounters an entirely disparate individual with whom he evolves, Patrick (played by Noah Reid), reaching a point in his life where he manages to communicate himself and engage in a fulfilling relationship. According to the Ryff Scale of Psychological Well Being (1995), building and sustaining satisfying and positive relationships is significant because "people score high on well-being when they report having warm and satisfying relationships, trust others, care for other people's well-being, are capable of empathy, tenderness, emotional proximity and experience the reciprocity of human relations" (Mertika, Mitskidou & Stalikas, 2020, p. 116). Consequently, the positive resolution attributed to the relationship between David and Patrick may be stirring and motivating for the viewers, considering the rarity of its actualization both in real lives and in the representation of same-sex relationships on TV and in films.

An interesting aspect of *Schitt's Creek* resides in its illustration of the diametric positions occupied by David and Patrick in terms of their expression of their sexual relationship in their social circle. In the course of the show, David at no time expresses or suffers from an identity crisis because of his non-binary identity. In fact, David confidently asserts himself as pansexual, implying his preference for partners of any biological sex using the infamous wine analogy. For example, when Stevie (played by Emily Hampshire) thought that David was gay, the latter corrects her by exclaiming, "I do drink red wine. But I also drink white wine. And I've been known to sample the occasional rose. And a couple summers back I tried a merlot that used to be a chardonnay, which got a bit complicated…. I like the wine and not the label. Does that make sense?" (Levy & Levy, 2020, 09:53). Likewise, as denoted in the show, David has been exploring his relationships with people from various gender orientations throughout his life and in full knowledge of his family. None of his family members expresses shock or amazement at his sexual identity at any point in the show. They seem more concerned about the tenure and quality of his relationship with his erstwhile and present partners and his emotional wellbeing than the sex of his partners. When Moira and Johnny chances upon Jake, one of David's potential romantic interests, neither of them are astonished by his presence, may be momentarily staggered by the knowledge that David might be seeing someone. Moira, in fact, brazenly announces: "If you take half as much care of our son as you do your physique David should be in very good hands" (Levy & Levy, 2020, 01:56). Again when Patrick sings and dedicates "Simply the Best" to David in front of the entire town and his family, Moira, proud, appeased and elated at the success of her son's relationship says to the Schitts: "My boy right now is being serenaded by his butter-voiced beau" (Levy & Levy, 2020, 19:26). The portrayal of the positive attitude of the parents to David and his relationships is important because "parental acceptance and support plays [a significant role] in furthering the psychological well-being of gay, lesbian, and bisexual individuals … [and] in reducing the stigma of being gay, lesbian, or bisexual and in mainstreaming gay, lesbian, and bisexual issues" (Goldfried & Goldfield, 2001, p. 681). The show repetitively demonstrates on different occasions the relief and happiness Moira, Johnny, and Alexis may feel as they categorize the relationship with David and Patrick as "beautiful." He is shown to be unconventionally open about his sexual identity and relationships with his family, who treat his relationships with utter disgust, concern or support depending on his feeling of comfort or tribulation from a relationship.

While David's confidence and openness about his sexual identity represent the longed fantasia (the conviction of David and in terms of his sexual identity is a pleasant and desired state for many homosexuals who long to attain liberation from their closet) yet to happen in the real world, Patrick's experiences and complexities concerning his sexual orientation are the prevailing norms in society. Unlike David, Patrick has neither been engaged in relationships with same-sex partners nor has he explored his sexuality as openly and confidently as David. On the contrary, Patrick has barricaded his sexual identity from his parents and got engaged to a female in order to conform to and perform conventional gender expectations which are constructed by society. Amy M. Blackstone (2003) explained, "The social construction of gender is demonstrated by the fact that individuals, groups, and societies ascribe particular traits, statuses, or values to individuals purely because of their sex" (p. 335). According to such constructions, as a male, Patrick is supposed to build a relationship with a female, consequent to which he remains closeted for most of his life and shares how David is his first male kiss, which confounds David, given his long experience in the arena. In the episode called "Grad Night," Patrick confesses to David that he has never kissed a guy before, his fear of being shunned by him for this reason but David accepts his openness and vulnerability wholeheartedly and viewer touched with the intimacy of the scene exclaims: "So sweet. Pretty realistic too. That moment when David is worried, I can hear him thinking 'Where is he going with that?' when Patrick says 'I've never done that with a guy.' I totally get that moment of worry, but then he is reassured when Patrick further explains his though[t]s" (blackmakup, 2023).

Similarly, Patrick's fear that the knowledge of him being a homosexual might change his parents' perception of him may be extremely relatable for some, as one viewer comments on the scene on YouTube, "I cry while watching this literally everytime. I've never cried while watching a show until I watched *Schitt's Creek*. It hits too close to home" (RainbowPanic, 2021). Patrick's nervousness, anxiousness and agitation while coming out to his parents and his relief thereafter, when his parents accept him with all his true essence unquestionably relates to the whirlwind of emotions felt by the audiences of the show either through their personal experiences or of their friends and family members. Accordingly, one viewer confesses: "No joke I cried during this scene. Having homophobic parents is tough and I really related to Patrick in this episode" (Ultra Magnum, 2021). Another viewer discloses a similar experience she encountered:

> literally cried the first time I saw this. then my little brother came out to us. And my parents reaction was great. But Patrick's dad's reaction made me think of my dad's. Just very "okay soooooo anyone who seems interesting to you?" Just like when I started dating. Awkward weird but happy dad [Katie, 2022].

The construction of normative gender roles, its impact on the homosexual community and its dissolution and the variant identity of Patrick attune with the audience as they pronounce their disquiet with such circumstances in their own lives.

Despite the inherent tension depicted in the series through both Patrick and his parents, the scene of his coming out to his parents was met with great appreciation from many audience members, perhaps because of the positivity and support that he receives from his parents for himself as well as his relationship with David. Unlike the commonplace depiction of anxious parents who after acquiring the knowledge of their children's non-binary identity, either negate their feelings or take time for themselves to figure out the unconventional gender identity of their children, only to accept the truth eventually, thus increasing the anxiousness of the subject concerned, Patrick's parents are shown to be instantly supportive of Patrick, creating a similarly positive possibility for the viewers of the show. Darshana (2021), for example, raves at the prospect: "S5E11—Meet the parents is a beautiful episode, thank you for portraying #DavidPatrick relationship so beautifully and support of their parent's" (18:19). Likewise, Cindy Terhune (2021) effuses at the portraiture: "One scene that was left out of this montage, truly one of my favorites is in 'Meet the Parents' When David is sitting with Patrick discussing coming out to his parents. It shows Patrick's vulnerability and the depth of David's love and empathy. Brilliantly done! I am crushing on their relationship so bad." The interest of the audience in the reciprocation of the parents towards Patrick's admission suggests their own concern at the prospect as they are apprehensive about the outcome of their declaration to their own families, hoping just like Patrick for appreciation and support.

Viewers have also lauded a significant aspect of the relationship between David and Patrick: like their families, the eponymous town in which they reside manifests no perturbation at their sexual orientation or their relationship. Most of the new friends and neighbors of the Rose family at Schitt's Creek are as excited, curious, chatty or placid and sedate about David and Patrick as they are with Alexis's dalliances. Like the families, the macroscopic society does not pay special attention to the gay couple, not because they intended to disregard their relationship but because they treated them and their liaison as only a typical instance. This makes it easier for the couple to ameliorate their involvement without any misgivings about social acceptance because "although same-sex relationships are forged for many of the same reasons as cross-sex relationships, the influence of social acceptance is unique to them because of the marginalized status of same-sex couples" (McDonald, 2011, p. 2). According to David (2021), a follower of the show, *Schitt's Creek* is one of the best productions ever because of the stock reaction of the citizens to the diverse relationship between David and Patrick: "The point of making a gay relationship so common place among the entire small town in the middle of nowhere was genius. No shocked faces, no one tried to change them, no protesting. It wasn't about being gay—it was about love. Unfortunately that world just don't exist." The depiction of the small town, in fact, has not only been lauded for its accommodation of eccentric characters but also its unquestionable tolerance of individuals, occasions and relationships that are conventionally treated as extraordinary and outré by society. This is because social acceptance is especially crucial for such individuals who are stereotypically demeaned, degraded and stigmatized by the public on account of their diversity, which is most commonly treated not as a distinct quality but relegated as frailty or infirmity of their character.

As such, I maintain that the efficacious reaction of both David and Patrick's families to their relationships is comparatively related to the response of the society they inhabit considering, as many researchers have argued, "Stigma felt by parents about their family composition may in turn negatively affect their mental health as well as perceived competence in parenting through internalized homophobia" (Farr and Vázquez, 2020, p. 2). In other words, the reaction the parents receive from society is generally directly proportional to the reaction they have towards their LGBTQ children. In the show, the congenial, and more importantly, the very natural outlook held by the overall citizenry of *Schitt's Creek* created a more conducive environment wherein the parents could accept their children in their true selves without fear of their social stigmatization. As a substantive struggle of the LGBTQ community involves gaining social acceptance of their identities and relationships, the indulgent atmosphere of the town of Schitt's Creek possibly stimulated the audience at the prospect of a similarly buoyant ambience in the real world.

Further, unlike the representation of most on-screen gay relationships and like all heterosexual relationships, the romance between Patrick and David has not been specialized because of their gender identities. They undergo the same trials and errors of romantic affairs as experienced by straight couples and the complexities of emotions felt by them in the course of their relationship are similar to those experienced by all couples in love. This is asserted by Kenneth E. Carter and Dr. Colleen M. Seifert (2012) who maintained:

> While the challenges and cultural messages may be different for homosexuals, there are far more similarities than differences between homosexual and heterosexual relationships. Most gay men and lesbians form close, enduring relationships that are happy and functional and enjoy similar family and social support networks [p. 388].

The normalcy of the relationship between David and Patrick can be discerned in juxtaposition to the relationship between Alexis and Ted (played by Dustin Wallace Milligan). In the episode "Grad Night" both the siblings experience intense emotional moments in their relationships; while Ted joins Alexis in her graduation ceremony despite her former refusal of his marriage proposal, emphasizing the great esteem to which Ted holds her and implying the impending evolution of their relationship, Patrick presents David with the receipt of the first sale at their store, thereby paying respect and imparting significance to their joint association both in terms of business and the burgeoning relationship between them and the same episode is also appended by the first kiss shared by David and Patrick. The normalcy of their relationship is what attracts some viewers and makes the non-binary individuals dream of a similar romance:

> I love them so much, We never get a gay couple happy ending, they love to play out tragedies. but seeing them really made me believe i may actually deserve my happy ending and that'll forever be my favourite thing. this show let me know i deserve a happy ending and i will forever be grateful for it [Rios, 2021].

The nature of the relationship and the emotional upheavals experienced by the homosexual couples, therefore, are as natural and wholesome as their heterosexual counterparts and it is the recognition and representation of the inherent familiarity of their relationship by the showrunner of *Schitt's Creek* that engages the audience.

Additionally, the depictions of David and Alexis manifest symptoms of self-centeredness, and their respective partners (being aware of this trait), attempt to respectively redress their foibles through open and considerate communication to reform them for the betterment of their interpersonal relationships as well as the partner, himself or herself and accept them with all their idiosyncrasies. The intention of either Patrick or Ted in addressing the flaws of their partners is not to criticize or deride them but is considered an important strategy of positive relational maintenance that involves "communicating with emotional intelligence, offering acceptance, reciprocity and displaying a heightened awareness of their partner's needs" and ensures "interpersonal connectedness and moderate closeness with the other in a romantic relationship" (Nicholson, 2020, p. 19). In the course of their relationship, Patrick tries to make Alexis understand animals by gifting her a book titled *Opening Your Heart to Animals: A Guide to the Benefits of Caring for Something Other Than Yourself.* He also exclaims that presenting Alexis with a puppy would be punitive to the animal more than her, thereby directing a subtle jibe at his partner for her foible that is meant to reform her. David's self-obsession is also repeatedly observed and exposed by Patrick. One of the memorable instances of such an occasion is depicted in the episode "Asbestos Fest" where Patrick teases his partner for his fixation on being complimented for his fashion sense, in the garb of which local youth are stealing from their stores, generating remarks like these:

> The fact that Patrick is not immune to being annoyed by David's flaws but still loves him so much not despite them but because of them.... This couple means so much to me [Flores, 2021].
> Their foibles are human foibles, not gay men's foibles [CubsandCulture, 2021].

By juxtaposing the relationship of David and Alexis, the show successfully manages to demonstrate the often-overlooked fact that homosexual individuals and couples embody rudimentary humane characteristics. This includes their range of emotions, expressions, virtues or capabilities at committing foibles and that their actions and words are to be analyzed based on their individuality and not necessarily on their gender identities.

The dynamics and intricacies of the relationships of both Alexis and David, therefore, trudge along similar paths, underlying the verisimilitude of all romantic relationships and the emotions associated with them, irrespective of their sexual identities. The fact that *Schitt's Creek* manages to register and portray these innate nuances of the relationship of David and Patrick as well is what normalizes their relationship, motivating an admirer to exult at the rendition: "Most natural, relatively less dramatic gay love story I have ever seen!!! Love how they naturalized their relationship and the progress" (Fan, 2021). It is this standardized depiction of their relationship that may strike the queer viewers of the show who struggle to normalize their identity and relationships in society and garner hope of the same from the show. One commentator exclaims, "This is exactly the kind of thing I want in my life! And thank you to Dan for normalizing gay relationships and making it seem possible for any of us to get" (Walker, 2021). Another post drafts a heartfelt tribute to the show for its normalizing and inclusive portrayal of characters:

> Schitt's Creek has become so much more to me over the last couple seasons, the final season hit me so hard. The Patrick and David storyline and how the whole show treats the LGBT

part of the show is so refreshing and normal. I haven't seen a gay love story so organically produced not from struggle or heartache but from genuine love.... As a pansexual/gay man who has struggled for years to come to terms and accept myself for who I am, I am so grateful and honored to live in a world where content like this is created, and I haven't touched on the story and importance of Love that is also portrayed so beautifully in this... [Zediest, 2021].

The reaction of the audience to Patrick and David in *Schitt's Creek*, is evidently celebratory and positive, whereas, in other shows, same-sex couples are portrayed to include negative stereotypes, like with Lexa and Clarke in Jason Rothenberg's *The 100*.

The 100—"We're left to mourn what could have been"

The relationship between Lexa and Clarke, similarly, had received great appreciation and support from the viewers leading to an outpour of accolades from the viewers of *The 100*. Unlike the romantic comedy of *Schitt's Creek* that is set against the contemporary period, *The 100* is a science-fiction featuring war, horror and bloodshed. This setting features Lexa (Alycia Debnam-Carey) as the commander of the Grounder clans, and Clarke (Eliza Taylor) is one of the hundred residents of a space colony sent to the Earth to investigate its habitability. In the course of Clarke's visit to Earth, she encounters Lexa. Like David and Patrick's romance, some viewers may have been mesmerized by the strength of the individual characters, their initial conflict against each other, the course of their falling for each other, and the final consummation of their romance. As David has inspired many to embrace their true selves and express their true identities, the same quality has been attributed to Lexa: "thankyou lexa. thankyou for everything, teaching me to be okay with who I am today and who I'll be forever" (Reiswig, 2020). Another online viewer exclaims:

> There are lots of wonderful couples on TV these days and there will be many others in the future ... but no one EVER will be as special as Clarke and Lexa. Never ever as good. They were special, I can't imagine anyone who was their fan, ever forget them, regardless age sex race.... Clexa will be in our hearts forever [Naira G, 2020].

A similar emotion has been communicated by another viewer, who opines: "Lexa's character is so strong. The love Clarke and Lexa had was the most beautiful thing I've ever seen on TV" (kaja123, 2021). The audience reception of David-Patrick is conjoined with Lexa-Clarke, on their evocation of conviction and promise of a wholesome future for same-sex couples in the real world.

Nevertheless, in contrast to the positive resolution attested to David and Patrick, Lexa and Clarke suffer an untimely dissolution of their much-appreciated relationship when in the seventh episode of season 3 of *The 100*, Lexa is mistakenly and fatally wounded by the fire shot by Titus (played by Neil Sandilands), Lexa's Flamekeeper, who had actually intended to kill Clarke. This incident outraged some outspoken viewers, leading them to mourn and protest her shocking death. Lexa's death engendered one viewer to comment: "Lexa's death was the biggest mistake in world TV series history" (Gemi, 2021). Another enthusiast of the show exclaims, "When I found out that lexa was gonna die, I was so sad ... she was my absolute favorite character when it came to Clarke ... they belonged together and Clarke will never get over her truly. She loved Finn, but she loved lexa like no other" (Astral Sky, 2021). A similar emotion has been expressed by another audience on YouTube: "I can't accept that Lexa is never coming back, it just doesn't feel right, This the most solid love story I have ever watched and how it ended WAS VERY CRUEL it hurts so much I hope that Lexa can make a comeback back to the show even if it's in dreams" (R.T, 2020).

The vacancy and sense of desertion felt by the audience at the death of Lexa has is also evident in the opinion of the following audience: "I'm binge-watching The 100..i was already loving it, esp #Clexa … until they killed Lexa at 03x07..now i can't finish watching, i stopped watching after they killed Lexa's character … urhgggg!!i hate!" (madi, 2021). The pervasive outrage of the audience on social media platforms not only demonstrates the extent to which they related to the relationship of Lexa and Clarke and how the series impacted their lives but also grabbed the attention of the showrunners.

In the face of acute protestation from the viewers, the showrunners attempted to justify the death of Lexa in the series. Showrunners made several claims like her death was eventuated by "practical (Lexa planned on leaving the show), creative (it's a story about reincarnation) and thematic (it's a show about survival)" reasons (Rothenberg, 2016, para. 6). Showrunner Rothenberg (2016) also states, "And I am very sorry for not recognizing this as fully as I should have. Knowing everything I know now, Lexa's death would have played out differently" (para. 6). One of the recurring accusations some viewers launched against the makers of the show debates the necessity to destroy Lexa's character in terms of the storyline primarily because her death is portrayed as accidental. This is problematic because the death of same-sex couples after they confess their love to one another is a recurring theme in media. As observed by Dr. Elizabeth Aiossa (2018) in the case of *The Walking Dead* where after the consummation of their relationship, Denise "is callously murdered at Negan's (Jeffrey Dean Morgan) instruction … [was] never afforded the opportunity to tell Tara she loved her" and Tara is denied "very little if any on-screen time to process and grieve her immense loss" (p. 137). Another critic adds to the picture by noting the death of Tara in *Buffy the Vampire Slayer* (2002) and that both "died after a long awaited romantic (re)union, from being struck by a stray bullet meant for the lead character, thus instantiating a 'Bury Your Gays Trope'" (Ng, 2022, p. 23). One viewer criticizes this recurring approach by stating: "I don't understand why Lexa's death affected me soo much. For Finn, I was sad but I got over it pretty quick but there was something special about lexa and I just can't get over her death. It all happened so quickly and her death was easily avoidable" (Vanessa, 2021). Another viewer reiterates similar sentiment:

> She did give her life to save Clarke. She heard the gunshots and went rushing in to save her. Dying for the one you love is the most honorable death possible no matter how it plays out. However, the fact that she was killed off at all was completely unnecessary and tremendously hurt the story line and ratings [Duncan, 2020].

The death of Lexa had especially impacted the audience because the showrunners were actively engaged in online interaction with the supporters of the show and the relationship of Lexa and Clarke. The death of Lexa, despite the showrunners' awareness of the popularity of their relationship and the importance it held for the diverse community, was met with vehement protests and criticisms.

Rothenberg attempted to manage the situation by pointing out how accidents are an unfortunate, tangible part of human existence, the viewers of the show felt betrayed by such a resolution being attested to Lexa and by extension to her relationship with Clarke. Rothenberg (2016) defends the death of Lexa as part of the representation of the real world that comprises both negative and positive aspects, which further infuriates some viewers who took issue with the comparison to the on-screen same-sex couple of Clexa. Like David and Patrick, the relationship of Lexa and Clarke provided the viewers, especially the LGBTQ community, with an ideal instance that instilled optimism and certitude. The death of Lexa marked not only the dissolution of their same-sex relationship but also crushed the possible hopes of millions belonging to the LGTBQ community—it served to provide a precedent to them that negated their aspirations and dreams in life. When a viewer laments how "the trauma of watching Lexa die when i was just starting to discover my sexuality was truly horrific" (soph the wilds spolers, 2022). This post divulges the direct impact of the representation of LGBTQ characters on the viewers and attests to the extent to which it operates to encourage, or as evident in this case, thwart their sense of self.

More dismally, when a queer character is provided with a negative resolution, it threatens to and standardizes the cynical and detracting opinions conventionally attested to them by society, constraining them from expressing their true selves in the foreboding of being despised and belittled by the general public. As Sean Robinson and Bernice Alston (2014) observe, "Television depictions may spark homosexual youth's self-discovery, especially among those young individuals who are not as exposed to homosexuality, but the inauthenticity of the characters may do more harm than good" (p. 42). It functions to reaffirm the sense that they don't deserve happiness and love in their lives or that it is not possible for them to sustain a normal life filled with respect, appreciation and a family in the present conditioning of society. This is because, such elements though considered to be habitual parts of human lives, have perennially been associated with a specific gender condition that has refused homosexual individuals from forming a family and attaining the so-called "happy ending" customarily associated with heterosexual beings. Consequently, the death of Lexa was followed by a torrent of voices from the viewers of *The 100*, underlining that Clarke and Lexa have been denied the positive closure that they might deserve. A viewer states: "Their story was a great one, from the beginning to the end. They brought out so much in each other, I loved how Clarke told Lexa that her legacy would be peace. They deserved a happy ending" (Perey, 2021). A similar observation is made by another online viewer: "First gay couple tv show I ever shipped n it had me crying why did clexa have to end they were both truly in love with each other they deserved better" (Parada, 2020). These are some of the instances that demonstrate their perturbation not only for killing off the character of Lexa but denying them the social and domestic happiness that is fitting for them. An admirer of the show, for example, attests, "they could have lived, get married, settled in a domestic life and be parents to Aden and Madi cause that's what deserve. but meh they killed off my might Heda with a stray bullet" (ashara chae, 2021).This is similar to the sentiment of another enthusiast: "They loved each other so much. I wish we could've seen them getting married and raising Madi" (Singer, 2020).

The aspiration of the spectators to witness Lexa and Clarke sustaining a conventional life with a married partner and children echoes the longing of the entire

LGBTQ community who are still struggling in different parts of the world to get recognition for their sexual identities and obtain legal permission and social acceptance for their marriage. This sentiment is testified by one of the enthusiasts of the show who rages: "So they really killed them when they found happiness Sick bastards" (Alyciaisagod, 2022). Another viewer laments: "Sometimes crappy circumstances come in the way of something so beautiful and all we have left are a few moments of perfection and then we're left to mourn what could have been (btvscharmedgirl, 2022). The sudden, untimely, and (according to the viewers) avoidable dissolution of their relationship corroborated their fears and anxieties of the homosexual individuals aspiring to form families that it is a future not meant for them and that their happiness is short-lived.

The negative resolution attested to Lexa and Clarke and the representation of their thwarted desires and dreams, evinces but one of the singular instances of the stream of disappointing public reaction to the deaths of queer characters on TV and in films. The public was similarly disappointed and outraged at the death of Tara in *Buffy the Vampire Slayer*, Denise in *The Walking Dead*, Jule Neumann in *Hinter Gittern,* Rose in *Jane the Virgin*, Quentin from *The Magicians*, Lily Baker in *Supernatural*, Delphine from *Orphan Black*, Maya from *Pretty Little Liars*, Villanelle in *Killing Eve* to name only a handful of them. Below, viewers share different views on the sinking and death of Villanelle:

> this feels like the confirmation of my own internalized homophobia like they actually confirmed my fears. killing eve represented HOPE for me : to find love, to be understood and accepted. having that ripped out from me i feel so lost now. i wish i was straight rn [lena, 2022].
>
> This show was about two women who found each other and saved each other—the potential, in this highly complex, female-centric show, was off the charts. Instead, they did the same old #BuryYourGays in the name of some batshit crazy idea of art. Still so angry [SFGreek, 2022].
>
> #killingeve season 4 was incredible bad and the ending is the exact definition of the #BuryYourGays trope ! Don't be proud because the homophobic ending hurt so many people [StellaCherie228, 2022].

The death of Quentin was similarly condemned by the viewers as their indignation was poured down on social media platforms, like:

> YAY! Good job, #Queliot fans. I'll never get over the fact that when they finally became canon #BuryYourGays struck (yet again) [brieburnham, 2019].
>
> And on THIS day, the first day of #PrideMonth, it's also worth remembering that the death of Quentin Coldwater in #TheMagicians is currently the worst example of the Bury Your Gays trope on television, in any genre [DI_Doughnut, 2019].
>
> #themagicians if you really want to subvert a trope, listen to your fans and undo the shit you did (it's not to late to, you know, not kill Q, like you not-killed Alice). At least apologize. At least ACKNOWLEDGE this [myosotis_arvenc, 2019].
>
> #TheMagicians was my absolute favorite show, but I'm done. Can someone PLEASE point me in the direction of a tv show that embraces queer characters, doesn't #BuryYourGays, doesn't tell its queer audience that M/F romances are more worth their investment? I'm so over this [la_belle_laide, 2019].
>
> If you are trying to claim "we thought really hard about this" okay, then be transparent about what the conversation involving killing off a mentally ill and bisexual character entailed [LizzyLaurie, 2019].

It is important to consider these reactions and the fact that the trope has been reprised constantly, because, although death by natural cause, accident, suicide or disease is but a natural part of human lives and happens to every being and has been employed as a plot device by several shows, the matter is not uncomplicatedly simple for the homosexual audience who perceive these deaths as a deliberate attempt to distort and negate their representation and to retain the "Bury Your Gays" trope.

This literary trope gained currency in the twentieth century and continues to be applied to modern representations of homosexual relationships, according to which one of the lovers of a same-sex couple must die or be dematerialized by the end of the narrative, leading to the disintegration of their relationship. Although, as accorded by Haley Hulan (2017), the trope was devised and implemented historically to avoid legal complications and censure from the authorities for promoting homosexual relationships at a time when it was subject to far more social stigmatization, its application in recent times, when various activists and campaigns are working to develop gender consciousness and greater acceptability of homosexual individuals, invites widespread protestation and upheaval from the LGBTQ community. This is evidenced by a viewer's agonizing opinion on the matter:

> Still trying to cope with the death of lexa ... it's been so many years and till this day I continue crying whenever I see that scene. I really don't know WHY but clexa was something so special and I think I can speak for all of us lgbtq people when I say their love story should have ended way better! [Erkan, 2021].

The recurring deaths of LGBTQ characters on TV, moreover, are perceived by the community as a pattern that threatens to stereotype tokenism and complicate and subjugate their position in the real world as they relate with the characters and envision their lives and circumstances as a reflection of their own lives leading them to a trauma about their own possible predicament.

I contend that while the resolution of David and Patrick in *Schitt's Creek* evoked in them a hope for a better future, the death of Lexa and the termination of her budding relationship with Clarke left the audience to mourn for what could have been. The positive attitude of the audience towards the success and their negative reactions to the ruination of the aforementioned homosexual relationships reflect the thwarted desires and aspirations of the queer community. They apprehend such embodiments as either positive or negative reinforcement of their existence, behavior and relationships in the larger society and the question of social acceptance or rejection is of vital importance to them as it greatly impacts their psychological, intellectual and behavioral issues. This association again is intricately associated with prevalent the socio-cultural position of homosexuals in society, which although considerably reformed, their situation is still vulnerable and afflictive. The Sexual Harassment Survey (2020) conducted by the Government Equalities Office of the United Kingdom reported

> about two-thirds (64%) of LGB people had experienced at least one form of sexual harassment in the last 12 months and the vast majority (86%) had experienced it at some stage in their lifetime. This was a significantly higher incidence compared to heterosexual people who had a significantly lower (though still high) incidence of two-fifths (42%) having experienced sexual harassment in the last 12 months and just less than three-quarters (72%) reporting the same over their lifetime [p. 43].

Similar conclusions have also been derived from the survey conducted by Trades Union Congress, according to which, almost 68 percent of lesbian, gay, bisexual and trans (LGBT) people report being sexually harassed at work. According to another study conducted by David M. Huebner et al. (2004):

> Thirty-seven percent of men reported experiencing anti-gay verbal harassment in the previous 6 months; 11.2% reported discrimination, and 4.8% reported physical violence. Men were more likely to report these experiences if they were younger, were more open in disclosing their sexual orientation to others, and were HIV positive. Reports of mistreatment were associated with lower self-esteem and increased suicidal ideation. [p. 1200]

Despite the legal transformations concerning them, homosexual individuals face widespread harassment, denunciations and ostracism from society that continues to push them to the periphery of sustenance, affecting their mental health and social wellbeing. Amidst these circumstances, their predicament is markedly affected by their representation in media as it continues to exert a great impact on the public and popular consciousness including GLB individuals who identify with both GLB and non–GLB media personalities as their role models when represented positively. On the other hand, "the negative impact of the limited and stereotypical representation of GLB individuals in the media, which they reported made them feel excluded from society and limited their identity expression" (Gomillion & Giuliano, 2011). This drives home the significance of the responsible and sensitive representation of the conventionally marginalized LGBTQ community on television and the importance it holds for the audience.

According to cultivation theory, formulated by George Gerbner and Larry Gross, recurrent contact with a set of ideas influences people's perception and comprehension of reality and the media, especially films and TV plays a prominent role in forming, perpetuating, and disseminating messages to the society and "cultivating" a definite ideology in the audiences. The homophobic or accepting views of society, therefore, are markedly influenced by the representation of the homosexual community or same-sex relationships on screen. Calzo and Ward's (2009) survey on American college students employing cultivation theory, for instance, manifests that "increased media exposure may draw groups with disparate attitudes towards a more similar viewpoint on homosexuality" (p. 280), implying the ability of screen representation to form and disseminate social ideas about the concept. This also suggests that while consumption of positive representation may influence the viewers into greater acceptability of them, misrepresentation, underrepresentation or mere tokenism imperils their prospect of social acceptability.

Representing Responsibly

More importantly, the inclusion and propitious representation of LGBTQ relationships on TV act as a space of resistance against heteronormativity and validation for the community because the present socio-cultural climate although not as incommodious of homophile relationships as the previous century, is still in an ongoing phase. It can more appropriately be branded to be in its nascent years as far as social acceptability is concerned for although laws and regulations might permit their relationship in some countries and though their success so far is of vital consequence, their struggle to attain an equal space as their non-binary counterparts in the society, lingers. As such, a meaningful, nuanced, normalized and constructive representation of homosexual individuals and their relationships on television and in films, acts as an agency to create a room for themselves in society, otherwise abounding in conversations about the cares and conflicts of male and female. It would also help society to become more tolerant and sympathetic to them, promote positive reception of their relationships and experiences in the real world, instead of exterminating them from the narratives. It would be responsible of the showrunners to weigh the nuances of homosexual representation on media at least till the time when the larger populace becomes as tolerant (or grudging) of them as they are of heterosexuals, they have equal rights and opportunities in the society, none of the homosexual kids is shunned by their parents for being gay, provoking them to commit suicide, they can live as happily as drearily as they choose to be and their relationships are perceived by everyone to be just as normal and conventional as others This is because the essence of their endeavor is not to possess a special position in the social structure but to be accepted just like another, equally befitting element of the world.

REFERENCES

[@la_belle_laide]. *#TheMagicians was my absolute favorite show, but I'm done. Can someone PLEASE point me in the direction of a tv* [Tweet] Twitter. (2019, April 18). https://twitter.com/la_belle_laide/status/1118698750812274688.

A Rainbow in beige boots #killingeveseason5 [@StellaCherie228]. (2022, May 16). "#killingeve season 4 was incredible bad and the ending is the exact definition of the #BuryYourGays trope ! Don't be" [Tweet; image attached, reply to @BBCAMERICA]. Twitter. https://twitter.com/StellaCherie228/status/1525952789704232961.

Aiossa, E. (2018). *The subversive zombie*. McFarland.

Astral Sky. (2021). *When I found out that lexa was gonna die, I was so sad. she was my absolute favorite character* [Comment on video "Clarke & Lexa || Another Love (+7x16)"]. YouTube. https://www.youtube.com/watch?v=y2IcY4S1LSE&t=1s.

blackmakup. (2023). *So sweet. Pretty realistic too. That moment when David is worried, I can hear him thinking "Where is he going with that?"* [Comment made on video "Schitt's Creek (Season 3 Finale) - David & Patrick's First Kiss!"] YouTube. https://www.youtube.com/watch?v=1LnGunyEdnw.

Blackstone, A. (2003). Gender roles and society. In J.R. Miller, R.M. Lerner, & L.B. Schiamberg (Eds.), *Human ecology: An encyclopedia of children, families, communities, and environments* (pp. 335–338). ABC-CLIO.

Brie (in theory) [@brieburnham]. (2019, September 11). *YAY! Good job, #Queliot fans. I'll never get over the fact that when they finally became canon #BuryYourGays struck* [Tweet; gif embedded] Tweet. https://twitter.com/brieburnham/status/1171573820555223041.

btvscharmedgirl [@btvscharmedgirl]. (2022, May 21). *Sometimes crappy circumstances come in the way of something so beautiful and all we have left are a few moments* [Tweet; image attached]. Twitter. https://twitter.com/btvscharmedgirl/status/1527811038044987392.

Calzo, J.P., & and Ward, L.M. (2009). Media exposure and viewers' attitudes toward homosexuality: Evidence for mainstreaming or resonance? [Abstract] *Journal of Broadcasting & Electronic Media, 53*(2), 280–299. 10.1080/08838150902908049.

chae, a. (2021). *they could have lived, get married, settled in a domestic life and be parents to Aden and Madi cause that's* [Comment made on video "Clarke & Lexa | Full Story"] YouTube. https://www.youtube.com/watch?v=N7vPkInx_Z8.

Carter, K.E., & Seifert, C.M. (2012). *Learn psychology*. Jones & Bartlett Learning.

Clarus [@Alyciaisagod]. (2022, April 10). *So they really killed them when they found happiness* [smiling face with tear emoji] *Sick bastards #killingeve #VILLANELLE #villaneve #the100 #lexa #clexa* [Tweet; image attached]. Twitter. https://twitter.com/Alyciaisagod/status/1513128028687278085.

CubsandCulture. (2021, December 13). *There is a lot to love about this show but to me it is an all time great show* [Online forum post]. IMDb. https://www.imdb.com/review/rw7640975/?ref_=tt_urv.

Darshana [@DarshanaWadhwa]. (2021, February 22). *@SchittsCreek S5E11 - Meet the parents is a beautiful*

188   Part 2: Network and Cable Television

episode, thank you for portraying #DavidPatrick relationship so beautifully and support [Tweet]. Twitter. https://twitter.com/DarshanaWadhwa/status/1363871766783746053.

David D. (2021). *The point of making a gay relationship so common place among the entire small town in the middle of nowhere* [Comment on video "The Love Story of David and Patrick In Full" | Schitt's Creek]. YouTube. https://www.youtube.com/watch?v=_68rPYEX-A0&t=35s.

detective donut is a supervillain [@DI_Doughnut]. (2019, June 1). *And on THIS day, the first day of #PrideMonth, it's also worth remembering that the death of Quentin Coldwater in* [Tweet] Twitter. https://twitter.com/DI_Doughnut/status/1134707915087126528.

Dr J forever demanding justice [@SFGreekSFGreek]. (2022, May 23). *This show was about two women who found each other and saved each other—the potential, in this highly* [Tweet; Reply to @GaysGaze]. Twitter. https://twitter.com/SFGreek/status/1528652910212665345.

Dry, J. (2020). *Modern Family' finale: What Cam & Mitchell did for gay families on TV.* IndieWire. https://www.indiewire.com/2020/04/modern-family-finale-cam-mitchell-gay-families-1202224229/.

Dryer, R. (2012). Stereotyping. In D.M. Kellner & M.G. Durham (Eds.), *Media and cultural studies keyworks* (pp. 253–365). Blackwell Publishing.

Duncan, J. (2020). *she did give her life to save Clarke. She heard the gunshots and went rushing in to save her* [Comment on video "Clarke & Lexa | Full Story," reply to mauropedagogo]. YouTube. https://www.youtube.com/watch?v=N7vPkInx_Z8&t=468s.

Erkan, G. (2021). *Still trying to cope with the death of lexa… it's been so many years and till this day I continue* [Comment on video "Clarke & Lexa | Full Story"]. YouTube. https://www.youtube.com/watch?app=desktop&v=N7vPkInx_Z8&lc=Ugxgpn5D3j03XHHEDHN4AaABAg.

Fan, A. (2021). *Most natural, relatively less dramatic gay love story I have ever seen!!! Love how they naturalized their relationship* [Comment on video "David and Patrick's Love Story—Schitt's Creek"]. YouTube. https://www.youtube.com/watch?v=gLXT76m_880&t=934s.

Flores, P. (2021). *It's just…. The fact that Patrick is not immune to being annoyed by David's flaws but still loves him so* [Comment on the video "David and Patrick's Love Story—Schitt's Creek"]. YouTube. https://www.youtube.com/watch?v=gLXT76m_880&t=284s.

Fosl, C. (2012). It could be dangerous! Gay liberation and gay marriage in Louisville, Kentucky, 1970. *Ohio Valley History, 12*(1), 45–64. https://www.muse.jhu.edu/article/571585.

Gomillion, S.C., & Giuliano, T.A. (2011). The influence of media role models on gay, Lesbian, and Bisexual Identity. *Journal of Homosexuality, 58*(3), 330–354. 10.1080/00918369.2011.546729.

G, N. (2020). *There are lots of wonderful couples on TV these days and there will be many others in the future* [Comment on video "Clarke & Lexa" | Full Story] YouTube. https://www.youtube.com/watch?v=N7vPkInx_Z8&t=468s.

Gallup. (2021). *Annual mood of the nation.* https://news.gallup.com/poll/389309/americans-offer-gloomy-state-nation-report.aspx.

Gemi, S. (2021). *Lexa's death was the biggest mistake in world TV series history* [Comment on video "Clarke & Lexa | Full Story]. YouTube. https://www.youtube.com/watch?v=N7vPkInx_Z8&t=468s.

Glaad Media Institute. (2022). Where we are on TV report—2021–2022. *Glaad Media Institute*, 1–46. https://www.glaad.org/sites/default/files/GLAAD%20202122%20WWATV.pdf.

Goldfried, M.R., & Goldfried, A.P. (2001). The importance of parental support in the lives of gay, lesbian, and bisexual individuals. *Journal of Clinical Psychology, 57*(5), 681–693. https://doi.org/10.1002/jclp.1037.

Huebner, D.M., Rebchook G.M., & Kegeles, S.M. (2004). Experiences of harassment, discrimination, and physical violence among young gay and bisexual men. *American Journal of Public Health, 94*(7), 1200–1203. 10.2105/AJPH.94.7.1200.

Hulan, H. (2017). Bury your gays: History, usage, and context. *McNair Scholars Journal, 21*(1), 17–27. https://scholarworks.gvsu.edu/cgi/viewcontent.cgi?article=1579&context=mcnair.

Ipsos. (2021, June 9). *LGBT+ pride 2021 global survey.* https://www.ipsos.com/en/lgbt-pride-2021-global-survey-points-generation-gap-around-gender-identity-and-sexual-attraction.

kaja123. (2021). *Lexa's character is so strong. The love Clarke and Lexa had was the most beautiful thing I've ever seen on TV.* [red heart emoji] [Comment on video "Clarke & Lexa | Full Story"]. YouTube. https://www.youtube.com/watch?app=desktop&v=N7vPkInx_Z8&lc=Ugxgpn5D3j03XHHEDHN4AaABAg.

Katie. (2022). *literally cried the first time I saw this. then my little brother came out to us. And my parents reaction* [Comment on video "Schitt's Creek 5x11 - Patrick Came Out to His Parents"]. YouTube. https://www.youtube.com/watch?v=-nNEE1O7gm4&t=14s.

lena [@killinglena]. (2022, April 12). *this feels like the confirmation of my own internalized homophobia like they actually confirmed my fears. killing eve represented HOPE* [Tweet; image attached]. Twitter. https://twitter.com/killinglena/status/1513777708379037696.

Liz is unimpressed [@LizzyLaurie]. (2019. April 23). *If you are trying to claim "we thought really hard about this" okay, then be transparent about what the conversation* [Tweet]. Twitter.

madi. [@petit_heart09]. (2021, November 10). *I'm binge-watching The 100..i was already loving it, esp*

#Clexa..until they killed Lexa at 03x07..now i can't finish watching [Tweet]. Twitter. https://twitter.com/petit_heart09/status/1458291754671689730.

Maryland Office of the Attorney General. (2012). *The State of Marriage Equality in America. Maryland Attorney General*, 1–35. https://www.marylandattorneygeneral.gov/Reports/The%20State%20of%20Marriage%20Equality%20in%20America%202015.pdf.

McConell, M., & Baker, J. (2016). *The Wedding Heard 'Round The World America's First Gay Marriage*. University of Minnesota Press.

McDonald, P. (2011). The influence of social approval and support on the maintenance behaviors of same-sex and heterosexual relationships. [Master of Arts Thesis, Arizona State University]. Core.

Mertika, A., Mitskidou, P., & Stalikas, A. (2020). "Positive Relationships" and their impact on wellbeing: A review of current literature. *Psychology: The Journal of the Hellenic Psychological Society, 25*(1), 115–127. doi: https://doi.org/10.12681/psy_hps.25340.

Ng, Eve. (2022). *Cancel culture: A critical analysis*. Springer International.

Nicholsan, J. (2020). Positive communication in romantic relationships. [Conference Session]. UNLV Undergraduate Research Symposium, Fall 2019, University of Nevada Las Vegas (UNLV).

Parada, A. (2020). *First gay couple tv show I ever shipped n it had me crying why did clexa have to end they* [Comment on video "Clarke & Lexa | Full Story"] YouTube. https://www.youtube.com/watch?app=desktop&v=N7vPkInx_Z8&lc=Ugxgpn5D3j03XHHEDHN4AaABAg.

Perey, J. (2021). *Their story was a great one, from the beginning to the end. They brought out so much in each other* [Comment on video "Clarke & Lexa | Full Story"]. YouTube. https://www.youtube.com/watch?app=desktop&v=N7vPkInx_Z8&lc=Ugxgpn5D3j03XHHEDHN4AaABAg.

Rainbowpanic. (2021*). I cry while watching this literally everytime. I've never cried while watching a show until I watched Schitts Creek* [Comment on video "Schitt's Creek 5x11 - David & Patrick Part 1]. YouTube. https://www.youtube.com/watch?v=0vZJ-b4xNuM.

Reilly, R.R. (2015). *Making gay okay how rationalizing homosexual behavior is changing everything*. Ignatius Press.

Reiswig, A. (2020). *thankyou lexa. thankyou for everything, teaching me to be okay with who I am today and who I'll be forever.* [Comment on video "Clarke & Lexa | Full Story"]. YouTube. https://www.youtube.com/watch?v=N7vPkInx_Z8&t=468s.

Rios, K. (2021). *I love them so much, We never get a gay couple happy ending, they love to play out tragedies* [Comment on the video "David and Patrick's Love Story—Schitt's Creek]. YouTube. https://www.youtube.com/watch?v=gLXT76m_880&t=284s.

Robinson, S., & Alston, B. (2014). Lavender identity and representation in the media: The portrayal of gays and lesbians in popular television. In B. Kaklamanidou, & M. Tally (Eds.), *The millennials on film and television essays on the politics of popular culture* (pp. 31–45). McFarland.

Rothenberg, J. (2016, March 25). The life and death of Lexa. *Medium*. https://medium.com/@jrothenberg/the-life-and-death-of-lexa-e461224be1db.

R.T. (2020). *I can't accept that Lexa is never coming back, it just doesn't feel right* [Comment on video "Clarke & Lexa | Full Story]. YouTube. https://www.youtube.com/watch?v=N7vPkInx_Z8&t=468s.

The Sexual Harassment Survey. (2020). 2020 sexual harassment survey. *Government Equalities Office of the United Kingdom*, 1–189. https://assets.publishing.service.gov.uk/government/uploads/system/uploads/attachment_data/file/1002873/2021-07-12_Sexual_Harassment_Report_FINAL.pdf.

Singer, E. (2020). *They loved each other so much. I wish we could've seen them getting married and raising Madi* [Comment on video "Clarke & Lexa | Full Story"]. YouTube. https://www.youtube.com/watch?app=desktop&v=N7vPkInx_Z8&lc=Ugxgpn5D3j03XHHEDHN4AaABAg.

Smith, K. [@mushyboyKarl] (2021, March 5). *Thanks to #SchittsCreek, I am learning to embrace my inner David. Even after coming out, I have struggled* [Tweet; Image attached]. Twitter. https://twitter.com/mushyboyKarl/status/1367868973132382209.

soph the wilds spolers [@fullmoonyelena]. (2022, April 10). *the trauma of watching lexa die when i was just starting to discover my sexuality was truly horrific* [Tweet]. Twitter. https://twitter.com/fullmoonyelena/status/1514935067050758153.

Summers, A. (2011). *Official and confidential: The secret life of J. Edgar Hoover*. Ebury.

Suppe. [@myosotis_arvenc] (2019, April 21). *#themagiciansspoilers anyway #themagicians if you really want to subvert a trope, listen to your fans and undo the shit you* [Tweet; image embedded]. Twitter. https://twitter.com/myosotis_arvenc/status/1119633221623459843.

Tandon, A., & Rao, T.S.S. (2021). Pride parades. *Journal of Psychosexual Health, 3*(3), 209–211. https://doi.org/10.1177/26318318211038118.

Terhune, C. (2021). *One scene that was left out of this montage, truly one of my favorites is in "Meet the Parents"* [Comment on video "David and Patrick's Love Story—Schitt's Creek"]. YouTube. https://www.youtube.com/watch?v=gLXT76m_880&t=934s.

Ultra Magnum. (2021). *No joke I cried during this scene. Having homophobic parents is tough and I really related to Patrick* [Comment on video "Schitt's Creek 5x11 - Patrick Came Out to His Parents"]. YouTube. https://www.youtube.com/watch?v=-nNEE1O7gm4&t=14s.

Vanessa. (2021). *I don't understand why Lexa's death affected me soo much. For Finn, I was sad but I got over it* [Comment on video "Clarke & Lexa | Full Story"]. YouTube. https://www.youtube.com/watch?v=N7vPkInx_Z8&t=468s.

Walker, T. (2021). *This is exactly the kind of thing I want in my life! And thank you to Dan for normalizing gay* [Comment on video "Schitt's Creek (Season 3 Finale) - David & Patrick's First Kiss!"]. YouTube. https://www.youtube.com/watch?v=1LnGunyEdnw.

Zediest. (2021). *Schitt's Creek has become so much more to me over the last couple seasons, the final season hit me* [Comment on video "The Love Story of David and Patrick In Full | Schitt's Creek"]. YouTube. https://www.youtube.com/watch?v=_68rPYEX-A0&t=35s.

Part 3

Streaming Television

The Races and Genders of Jarl Haakon
Historical Fiction Caught Between Accuracy and Authenticity in Vikings: Valhalla

PAUL CSILLAG

Black female Vikings, an image unknown to spectators of twenty-first-century cinema, became reality in early 2022. To represent famous Viking warrior Jarl Haakon, the showrunners of *Vikings: Valhalla* (2022–present) have chosen the Swedish-Danish singer and actress Caroline Henderson. This decision, to give a role traditionally reserved for White males to a Black actress, led to a public outcry. In particular on the internet platform YouTube, fans began to show their indignation. Video titles like *Vikings: Valhalla: Diversity Goes off Track* (Echo Chamberlain, 2022), *Black Vikings? The Race-Swapped "Queen" who Never was* (Jayne Theory, 2022), and *Vikings: Valhalla Destroying our Heroes* (Viking Stories, 2022) were only some of many that displayed a critical view of the new show. The reason for the widespread disappointment on behalf of the fans lay in the change of the outer appearance of Jarl Haakon, an already established and beloved figure of historical fiction.

Changes of canon-lore have always been unpopular. When showrunners, graphic novelists, or authors decided to alter the tone of their story or to give one of their characters a new look, resentment in the circles of fans followed. Nevertheless, color and gender-blind casting remains a strong trend in mainstream media from the beginning of the twenty first century to the present day (Shaw, 2022). Fans of medievalized fantasy or historical drama are especially offended when their favored characters are depicted with a different hair or skin color. The YouTuber Dominic Noble (2020) complained that one of his favorite stories, the novel series *Earthsea*, was whitewashed in its movie adaptation. Famous pop culture-commentator Nostalgia Critic (2015) attacked the same tendency of "race-swapping" in his review of the film *The Last Airbender* (2010), whereas fans of the TV show *The Witcher* (2019–present) took umbrage at the changed skin and hair color of a leading character, Triss Merigold (xLetalis, 2019). Liberties taken by the showrunners concerning race usually ignite an uproar that intensifies when historical figures are concerned. For example, the 2021 show *Anne Boleyn*, with a Black Tudor-Queen, has caused a fury among fans, as the YouTuber JOJOBEE (2021) demonstrates. Yet why does historical fiction arouse more agitation than shows set in the modern day, which also change the gender or ethnicity of characters as they appear in their original form? Why did the showrunners' decision to reinterpret the identity of a historical character in *Vikings: Valhalla* conjure such an extreme negative echo, with fans already lambasting the show even before its release?

These are some of the questions this essay will analyze. Their answer is ultimately linked to the notion of historical accuracy, again and again mentioned by YouTubers when criticizing the show. It is in the interest of this essay to unveil the underlying political connotations of accuracy in YouTube's discourse. To comprehend the YouTubers' motivation behind their criticism of the Black, female version of Jarl Haakon, I will mainly analyze the contributions of three channels, namely HistorySpark, Metatron, and Echo Chamberlain. By evaluating their appraisals of the show, I attempt to demonstrate how accuracy as a term is used to underpin a certain worldview in popular discourse. Three subessays will illustrate how YouTubers (1) try to engender accuracy, (2) instrumentalize the concept to attack opinions different to their own, and (3) claim history for a personalized racial identity. Finally, the underlying political, present-oriented motivation behind the outcry resurfaces from the demonstrated fear for (historical) truth and faithfulness to the original story. Through an analysis of depictions on *Vikings: Valhalla*, this essay will illustrate that the idea of accuracy is linked to a nineteenth-century materialist positivism and should, therefore, be replaced with authenticity.

The Concept of Accuracy as an Indicator of a Nineteenth-Century Positivism

Ever since historical fiction entered literature and media, the depictions of Vikings became a leading trope in its repertoire of stories. Historical novels and plays of the nineteenth century told the tales of the brutal but heroic invaders. While their myth became especially popular in Scandinavian, Anglophone, and German fiction, the hype around Vikings constituted a global trend. In the twentieth century, movies based on the preceding novels enjoyed broad popularity, as for example Richard Fleischer's 1958 film *The Vikings* impressively demonstrated (Harty, 2011). At the end of the nineteenth century, however, the imagery of Vikings had been imbued with the political and scientific thinking of the time (Teulié, 2020, p. 1), shifting to a new perspective of their mythos. The discipline of history and other emerging academic fields occupied with the past, like linguistics or archeology, supported positivism, which gave material evidence increasing primacy when making historical claims (Dowling, 1985, p. 580). While linguists referred to notes in texts, archeology drew upon material objects like weapons, houses, or clothes (Arnold, 1992, pp. 32–33). The fin-de-siècle materialist, positivist trend understood accuracy as historical correctness, meaning objective knowledge on past events. A positivist urge for "real history" in opposition to formerly unscientific ambiguity in academia soon also inspired authors of historical novels (Wawn, 2002, p. 372). Instead of the arguably anachronistic approach of early-nineteenth-century Romantic novelists, the new propagators of historical fiction called for a Viking lore that was both captivating and educational.

At the same time, new academic disciplines like history, anthropology, or sociology tried to approach the description of diverse people of past and present in a more scientific manner. Intellectuals of the nineteenth century increasingly adhered to biologically determined racist ideas. With the statutes of Social Darwinism, which adopted the language of materialist positivism, racial taxonomies sounded more scientific (Treslow, 2014, p. 20). Famously, phrenologists and other body-focused disciplines began to feverishly collect data to verify humanity's compartmentalization into races. Judging from the coeval rise of both scientific movements, it can be stated that racial theory depended on materialist positivism as its base idea.

Race theory could then be used to describe historical societies, like the medieval kingdoms of Scandinavia, and to insert them into an evolutionist human genealogy. The imagined Vikings acquired, hence, the role of a biological predecessor to other ethnic groups in the nineteenth century. According to this positivist-materialist worldview, races were unchanging historical entities (Berghoff, 2001). As a logical consequence, all present human cultures appeared as the latest generation of their individual biological developments. This theoretical outset enabled race-theorists to rhetorically construct lines of kinship between their own culture and other historical societies who had putatively shared the same race. The Vikings became a favorite group among these historical cultures, to whom novelists, historians, and archeologists attempted to connect contemporary nation states. German (Kipper, 2002, p. 225), Scandinavian (Deeks, 2016, p. 58), and British (Sundmark, 2014, p. 205) intellectuals referred to the Vikings as their biological predecessors, thus asserting their right to call the history of the Nordic kingdoms their individual heritage. To underpin one's own claim to Viking heritage and undermine the one of others, nationalists wielded the notion of historical accuracy as a political weapon. Genes, skeletons, material objects, and erudite argumentation as indicators of objective science provided a racial historical worldview with the apparent authority of positivist, materialist accuracy (Kipper, 2002, p. 267). Thinking of the human species as a taxonomy of different races—each one equipped with its own biological characteristics, culture, and history—appeared to tie in with the findings of natural sciences. Human history could, therefore, be organized according to racially separate pasts. According to this narrative, only light-skinned Vikings seemed accurate since their history belonged to the White race (Young, 2021, p. 29). Because of the ties between positivist science and a racialized worldview, accuracy has become a favorite discursive tool among YouTubers who also identify with a certain ethnic group.

Accuracy affirms the idea of objective truth as perceivable to human beings. As a term, accuracy acquired the meaning of infallibility in discourse on YouTube and other digital platforms. What can be proven by referring to guarantees of accuracy, like academic articles or material evidence, is accepted by the fans. Conversely, non-proven parts of a story, like in this case the portrayal of Jarl Haakon, are strenuously debunked as inaccurate (Saxton, 2020, pp. 127–128). YouTubers instrumentalize the idea of an objective perception of reality to engender a dichotomy between their own correct version of history and the incorrect view of the opponent.

Authenticity, a term unavoidably linked to accuracy by partly overlapping with its definition and partly rejecting its premises of objectivity, describes felt reality. According to Jerome de Groot (2015), whereas accuracy bespeaks a rationally conceived picture of what has really happened, authenticity rather implies an affective function (p. 14). Laura Saxton (2020) states that authenticity is connected to the emotional connotations of historical fiction. As an idea, the term is more lenient in its connotations than accuracy because it describes how historical truth is generated not only by scientific research but also by personal experience. Saxton (2020) argues that historical truth is always characterized by authenticity as well as accuracy, since historical factuality is created by erroneous human senses limited in their capability to fathom reality (p. 141). An advantage of applying authenticity to historical fiction is that novels and series like *Vikings: Valhalla* conceded more liberty in their depiction of past events. Authenticity allows for an increased personal input into a story in opposition to the wrong-right dichotomy of the accuracy-concept. Another advantage is that authenticity invites self-reflection of one's worldview. While discourse-participants who believe in historical accuracy corroborate the existence of ultimate factuality, adherents to authentic thinking are more prone to question the constructed character of their knowledge (Saxton, 2020, p. 141). The term authenticity is steeped in multiple definitions and perspectives. For this reason, I will not rely on one definition of authenticity, but may refer back to several theorists, like de Groot and Saxton.

Finally, the positivist narrative of Viking lore grew historically and does not portray an eternal, self-evident common truth. Traditionalist, accuracy-using YouTubers have obtained their view on Norse culture through their reading, watching, and listening-habits, accumulating knowledge over a lifetime. Their image of Viking history has been built up through a permanent education (Houghton & Alvestad, 2021, p. 1). Early teachings have been entrenched over the course of childhood and adolescence and feel therefore to be additionally true. A viewer who has received the idea of Vikings being generally White at the age of ten will struggle more to adjust to a diversified narrative than a person who has first heard about the Vikings' existence a couple of minutes ago. Knowledge acquired during childhood and continually learned over the years appears to us as intrinsically true, although the sources proving this ostensible accuracy are not always at hand. Historical accuracy is, thus, learned or constructed and not evident to common sense.

However, YouTubers and fans at large use conceptual accuracy to cover the synthetic character of historical knowledge. This is especially the case when the viewer writes from the perspective of a positivist narrative with its strong affiliation to factual, rationalist rhetoric (Houghton & Alvestad, 2021, p. 4). To leave the ivory tower of academic discussion, it is vital to comprehend the YouTubers' understanding of accuracy. It is important to historical fiction studies to consider how accuracy is used as an illocutionary act and as a theoretical weapon in the discourse circling shows like *Vikings: Valhalla*. This consideration develops an enhanced critical potential when macrosocial political or cultural matters are discussed by referring to the series. *Vikings: Valhalla*, for example, has led to a discussion tackling virulent issues like race, ethnicity, gender, liberalism, and the nature of history.

To unravel the riddle surrounding the meaning of accuracy on YouTube, I have focused my analysis on three major YouTubers called HistorySpark, Metatron, and Echo Chamberlain, whose combined videos have managed to receive around seven hundred thousand views. Over the last two decades, the platform YouTube has become a portal for many reviewers and film critics with their specialized focus and own agenda. A big production like *Vikings: Valhalla* commonly spawns multiple reaction videos, which are then again watched by thousands if not millions of followers. These digital discussants offer fans an interlocutor with whom they can exchange their opinion on the show and its portrayal of history. YouTubers who concentrate on historical fiction and its accuracy fill, thus, an important gap in the consumption of fiction. Countless reviews would have been available for the envisaged analysis of this essay, but its limited frame will not allow for such an extensive endeavor. Comments beneath YouTube videos have been eschewed for similar reasons. The three selected YouTubers, however, provide a productive sample since each of them has a specialized argument with an individual political stance and focus.

Proofs of Accuracy

Although a rule not followed by all YouTube critics of historical fiction, many reviews refer to sources and secondary literature to approve or deny the accuracy of a show. Thus, the methods of YouTubers and academic historians do not differ as decisively as might have been expected (Beavers & Warnecke, 2021, p. 80). Some YouTube critics have even studied a related discipline, like history or archeology, underlining their expertise in the videos. The only contrast between YouTubers and historians lies in the chosen object of criticism. While historians tend to argue over assumptions concerning the past, the critics analyzed here grapple with the anachronisms of historical fiction.

Since the topic of the discussion is a historical show and not a matter of academic dispute, reviews of *Vikings: Valhalla* develop their own criteria to judge historical accuracy. Because the show, as television in general, has a predominantly visual appeal, critics focus on the visible, material aspects of *Vikings: Valhalla*, such as medieval costumes, buildings, and people. Instead of analyzing a historical text, these YouTubers concern themselves with film requisites. Various channels cater to reenactment audiences who are interested in how accurate costumes appear in the show (Bunnenberg & Steffen, 2019, p. 12). While for some archaeological focused commentators, like the Welsh Viking, *Vikings: Valhalla*'s armors and costumes are inaccurate to an extent that they also become unauthentic (2022), many more take issue with the infamous "race swap" of Jarl Haakon.

Race, then, turns into a visible, material indicator of accuracy among many others with, however, a more political connotation. Because of these connotations, which have more to do with ideology and identity than historical accuracy, more attention is paid to the correctness of human facial features than to other visual impressions. The portrayal of an imagined White historical male figure by a Black actress constitutes for some YouTubers a breach in accuracy that delegitimizes the whole series (for example, JosiahRises, 2022). Even before the show had been released and before it could have been watched, fans lambasted the casting-choice of Henderson. In doing so, they reduced the actresses' performance as Jarl Haakon to her skin color and hair color. As Helen Young (2021) has stated in her analysis of race in historical video games, diverging outer features of human faces are seen as an indicator of their biological race and of race in general (p. 29). In the discourse circling *Vikings: Valhalla*, Henderson's acting as Haakon had been equally reduced to her physical body. Through this reduction to a visible, material appearance of race, the casting of Henderson has become a matter of accuracy.

In the ensuing discussion concerning the accuracy of Black people being Vikings, YouTubers and showrunners enter a rhetorical confrontation. Both sides try to argue in favor of their historical narrative, hence pro and contra the image of a Black jarl, by drawing on academic secondary literature and medieval sources. Remarkable in this context is that discourse participants, either defending or rejecting Henderson's portrayal, use similar references to underpin their viewpoint. Although opinions on the matter of Black Vikings essentially differ, the methods discussed remain the same. Both the YouTubers and showrunners point to medieval sources, climate theory, DNA research, or pictorial evidence when they attempt to make a point. The discussion, however, becomes increasingly confused as participants are unclear about the nature of Henderson's Jarl Haakon. If the role in the show is fictional or historical is left in the open. YouTubers are somewhat baffled when it comes to categorizing the show as a fantastic tale, a historical series, or as something else. The usage of concepts such as authenticity, accuracy, or plausibility, turns increasingly volatile. Hence, although both parties introduce scientific proof into the discussion, it remains uncertain if the discussion in itself ought to be scientific. Because of this question being unanswered, the debate around *Vikings: Valhalla* is, firstly, essentially different to academic disputes, and secondly, frustrating for positivists. The critics who argue with accuracy, thus, are disheartened by the nature of the controversy, somewhere to be found between factuality and fictionality. One of these YouTubers who finds the statements of the producers and actors unsatisfyingly unclear in this regard is Metatron.

After a short advertisement for his sponsor, Metatron reads official statements and interviews of *Vikings: Valhalla* director Jeb Stuart and actress Henderson. The latter states in an interview: "My character, Jarl Haakon, is a completely fictional character. She was not a real-life historical person, but that being said, she's probably inspired [by one]" (Metatron, 2022, 11:53). The definition remains arguably ambiguous. A Black female Haakon appears at the same time "completely fictional" but also "probably inspired" by a historical figure of reality. This ambiguity leaves a lot of room for diverse interpretations on behalf of the fans, meaning to what degree they believe the show's depiction to be accurate, authentic, or fictional. A changed portrayal of the figure Jarl Haakon, according to critics like Metatron, caused an affront to many because of the name being connected to a person who has really existed. Repeatedly, YouTubers like Norse Magic and Beliefs (2022) assure their audience that they would have accepted Henderson in the story, if she had not assumed the role of such an important figure. In the videos, Haakon is staged as the representation of White masculinity, non-compliant with the portrayal by a Black actress. Although the show underlines that its version of Haakon is not (entirely) accurate and only inspired by the "real" Jarl, fans continue to defend their insulted hero. In this context, Metatron (2022) retorts: "Mrs. Henderson, yeah, no disrespect but that is not how you do history. Probably does not work like that [sic]. You need solid evidence to say that it was inspired by a real historical character." Quite paradoxically, because of the bifurcated nature of historical fiction, Metatron (2022) urges for "solid evidence" for a "completely fictional" but "probably inspired" figure (12:12).

Since *Vikings: Valhalla*'s plot and characters are fictional, but its setting is in a real historical place and time, a new term, plausibility, is introduced into the discussion. Plausibility functions in both the producers' but also YouTubers' accounts as an indication for something that cannot be proven but could have happened. Because *Vikings: Valhalla* depicts a period (the early Middle Ages) with very little historical information available, only plausibility can be achieved (Lake, 2009, p. 222). This blurriness of historical factuality allows shows more creativity but also invites more controversies because clear factual statements on the era are rare. Plausibility then assumes a similar role as authenticity, filling the gaps of historical narrative caused by a lack of sources. However, plausibility is more intertwined with accuracy, circumscribing the probability of a certain figure or scenario to be accurate.

Plausibility is used in a similar fashion as accuracy when the discussion touches upon "unknown facts." Although the facts are unknown, they are still checked for probability. As with accuracy, YouTubers and showrunners adduce references and theories to substantiate their version of Vikings. In this context, Henderson holds that Black Vikings are indeed plausible. Using migration theory to strengthen her position, the actress expounds that the Scandinavians had been in contact with people all over the globe. She explains that other ethnicities, such as Mediterranean people or even Native Americans, could have partaken in Viking ventures (as cited in Metatron, 2022, 10:53). As Metatron reads the interview in the video, he adopts a sarcastic demeanor. While a picture of a Viking warrior with the photo of a nineteenth-century native chieftain enters the frame (Figure 1), positioned as something ridiculous, the YouTuber states:

Figure 1. Metatron being perplexed by the idea of a Native American Viking (Metatron, 2022, 10:59) (YouTube, Raffaello Urbani).

[…], it seems to me that the approach here is the fact that if something such as an American native Jarl has any number, any statistical number that is higher than 0% then it is absolutely fine to show it as something that absolutely happened. […] but it would significantly surprise me if they were higher than two per cent [Metatron, 2022, 11:10].

The answer to the question if Black or simply non–White Vikings are plausible relies on the singular opinion of the discourse participant. YouTubers who reject this idea, like Metatron, think it to be implausible, whereas Henderson and the producers assert the possibility of a diverse medieval Scandinavian population. Plausibility as a concept evolves into an empty signifier to be instrumentalized by either side, being somewhat distant to any notion of accuracy in its traditional sense. Ironically, discourse participants accuse each other of misusing the concept of plausibility for their own needs.

Despite the arbitrariness of plausibility, YouTubers attempt to increase the believability of their point by invoking sources and material proof. To argue in favor or against the plausibility of Black Vikings, YouTubers and showrunners still draw on scientific references. To further underpin his position, Metatron, for example, narrates the story of Ljufvina, a woman of Mongolian descent with dark skin color who had apparently lived in medieval Scandinavia (Metatron, 2022). As the YouTuber extrapolates, Ljufvina had been the victim of rampant racism during her time. Metatron hereby endeavors to dismantle the image of cultural inclusivity conceived by Henderson. He argues that racial segregation was the norm during the early Middle Ages and not tolerance as depicted in the show. His tale stems from a medieval saga, a semi-fictional account itself, and thus a text with reduced trustworthiness (O'Donoghue, 2021, p. 1). In the discourse circling *Vikings: Valhalla*, nevertheless, the saga develops an affirmative function as it constitutes a medieval source. For Metatron, medieval documents possess more power to engender accuracy or plausibility than Henderson's mobility theory. The temporal and spatial proximity of the saga, although being probably fictional, functions as an ultimate reference. When popular discourse touches upon time periods with scarce source material, the few texts available increase in value. This aspect of discussions on YouTube circling historical fiction does not diverge decisively from academic practices but its tone when arguing with the sources is more assertive. Metatron (2022) clarifies: "And we have proof of that, as we read the sagas" (19:25).

As supplementary strategies to legitimize their historical worldview, YouTubers equally draw upon climate theory and genealogical references. Both arguments, in opposition to Henderson's migration theory, had been popular in a nineteenth-century positivism. Because climate theories and biology were considered natural sciences, they appealed to materialist historiography. Where the showrunners claim that "Viking society" was dynamically changing and multicultural because of migration, the traditionalist YouTubers prefer these more static premises. The idea of a constant climatic and genealogical development corroborated, according to their argumentation, the continuity of race (Livingstone, 2012, p. 565). Essentialist in nature, both theories intrigued YouTubers with a proclivity towards positivist rhetoric. Nevertheless, climate and genealogy are used by critics and showrunners to bolster their arguments. If the individual theories are deployed, depends on the manner how they fit the reasoning of the respective party.

Describing a connection between temperature and culture, YouTuber Echo

Chamberlain implies that Black Vikings are inaccurate because of the cold climate in Scandinavia. He says: "In contrast, having a Black woman featured not only as a believable character but as a noblewoman in a show set in the icy and wind-swept northern regions of Europe in the eleventh century is so glaringly out of place [...]" (Echo Chamberlain, 2022, 04:48). Being first conceived by Aristotle, the compartmentalization of human existence by climate was revitalized as a common trope in later centuries (Harvey, 2012, p. 126). Scientists and other intellectuals ascribed physical and non-physical qualities to certain races according to their natural environment. In this context, Vikings were thought to be especially strong and enduring since they lived in a hostile climate (Livingstone, 2012, p. 565). Eventually, a nineteenth-century biological Darwinism in combination with this climatic determinism induced the idea of human races being linked to the area they evolved in. The problem with this assumption, as research has demonstrated, is the exclusion of historical mobility (Schultz, 1998, p. 127). It seems unnecessary to point out that a person stemming from Africa could have simply traveled to northern Europe. Echo Chamberlain's misconception stands out bewilderingly as Vikings often serve as a symbol of mobility, traveling, and intracultural contact. One might wonder if the Nordic pirates would be popular at all if they had been imprisoned by climatic essentialism to the Scandinavian Peninsula (O'Donoghue, 2008, p. 129). Arguably, it was the tales of their voyages to America, the Mediterranean (including Africa), Constantinople, and Russia that have made the Vikings the myth of historical fiction they are today.

Next to academic articles, genealogy, medieval texts, and climate, discourse participants use images as accuracy-generating references. A technique most of the

Figure 2. A comparison between a nineteenth-century depiction of Jarl Haakon (left, drawing by Christian Krohg [1852–1925], Wikimedia Commons) and the actor Caroline Henderson (photograph by Krimidoedel, Dr. Jost Hindersmann, Wikimedia Commons) is deployed to prove a dissimilarity between ostensible "real history" and fiction.

negative YouTube reactions to Henderson's casting have in common is the comparison between a seemingly ancient depiction of Jarl Haakon and actress Caroline Henderson. In Figure 2, the supposedly original drawing of Haakon depicts him as a tall, muscular, White man with an elaborate beard, while a smiling Henderson opposes him as the Black female counterexample. This juxtaposition of two contrasting visuals ought to function as the final proof of the inaccuracy of Henderson's character for some YouTube critics. However, the putative unassailability of this argument suddenly crumbles when the image's origins are traced back to the late nineteenth century. Apparently fooling a general public even one hundred years later, Norwegian painter Christian Krohg had produced the drawing of Jarl Haakon in an historicized style in the 1890s (Nasjonalmuseet, 2022).

Most factual references used by popular discourse circling historical fiction are predicated on narrative traditions of the nineteenth century. Still, the amount of material assembled to support one's standpoint sometimes reaches an impressive scale. Some YouTubers like Metatron could equally partake in an academic discussion, considering the amount of effort and time they invest into proving something to be accurate or not. The way popular commentators reference sources and secondary literature intersects with the manner how historians, the present paper not excluded, would insert citations into their texts to sustain their credibility. However, differences persist. Firstly, in YouTube's discussions, references to sources and literature are often taken as unassailable proofs of accuracy, while a more scientific approach would additionally question their trustworthiness. Formulations that something is objectively true because of an article saying so are less read in academic papers than in comments on YouTube. Not the sources used by the YouTubers are positivist, often dovetailing with current scientific standards, but it is rather the claim to absolute truth that ought to be considered a heritage of nineteenth-century positivism.

Secondly, the argument swirling around the accuracy of *Vikings: Valhalla* circles a fictional tale and not historical research. Nevertheless, both parties (the YouTubers and the showrunners) use positivist strategies to prove their point of view. The discussants attempt to navigate the issue of the story being fictional and thus unprovable by using the term plausibility instead of accuracy. YouTubers and showrunners try to prove that their version of history could have happened. Yet, the story remains a nearly entirely fictional tale, hence the product of twenty-first-century imagination. Already because the fictional world of *Vikings: Valhalla* was made by modern producers for a modern audience, its nature is inaccurate and implausible. The decision to portray Haakon as a Black woman was equally inspired by present politics as were the critical responses on behalf of the YouTubers. The discourse participants projected the question of race as a whole into the past, using their own presentist concepts. It remains doubtful if the controversy would have mattered to the actual inhabitants of medieval Scandinavia. An answer to this question, however, ought to be found by consulting the sources and not by focusing on a show of historical fiction. Because of this, an argument over race considering *Vikings: Valhalla* can never be really accurate but constitutes an issue imported into history by current ideologies. Scientific theories and sources in discourse on YouTube are often at the mercy of polemical instrumentalization. Arguments based on climate, pictures, ancient texts, or genealogy are only spearheaded when they match the opinion of the discussant. Methodologically speaking, this disposition implies that political narratives, not the sources, dictate the verdict of the YouTubers and the producers. Because of the ambiguity concerning historical fiction, concepts are misunderstood and mixed at will. Eventually, discussants like Metatron and Henderson end up fighting over the historical accuracy of a (non-) plausible figure in a fictional story.

The "Woke Crowd" as the Enemy of Historical Truth

The perceived dichotomy between an accurate past and inaccurate identity politics is central to the discussion circling the casting of Henderson. For instance, Metatron argues: "The whole defense system I see here put forward towards this idea of a Black jarl or a Native American jarl does not really seem to come from a natural place of historical curiosity" (Metatron, 2022, 11:40). Metatron questions the real intentions of the showrunners behind the decision to change the outer appearance of Jarl Haakon. The YouTuber HistorySpark (2022) is equally skeptical, stating, "But, I feel like *Vikings: Valhalla* is going to be another TV show that will fall victim to the woke crowd and will be more focused on being politically correct rather than historically accurate" (00:36). Political correctness catering to the infamous "woke crowd" opposes, according to the YouTubers, historical accuracy. The accusation as such is that *Vikings: Valhalla* as a show rather targets a political narrative than what actually happened. YouTubers like HistorySpark experience diversified casting as a betrayal of historical curiosity in favor of a political agenda which would coercively impinge on the depicted plot. Not only would this hinder any chance to generate accuracy and hence authenticity but also exclude viewers who do not share the same historical or political opinion.

The past, according to the argumentation of these YouTubers, constitutes a defenseless entity which perseveres at the mercy of the present. To defend this semi-holy history, the YouTubers see it their duty to criticize the preaching of the "woke crowd." In this context, the "woke crowd" serves as an ambiguous, generalizing term that offers a symbolic enemy. It includes various political opinions, whose only common denominator is constituted by a shared dissatisfaction with the traditional way of portraying race in the media. According to YouTubers, the main incentive of the "woke crowd" is a diversified casting or an improved inclusivity. Although this demand for a more just representation of various ethnic groups is seen positively, some YouTubers think it misled in the context of historical fiction. Here, woke politics would be nonsensical and out of place. The "woke crowd" is then increasingly portrayed as a blind, irrational mass, following a directionless, iconoclast movement. JosiahRises (2022), for example, laments: "Nothing is sacred anymore. Just change everything," (02:13), deploring the "race swap" of Jarl Haakon. The ire of these accusations is targeted at two groups who are held accountable for the perceived historical inaccuracy: the "woke crowd" and the showrunners (JosiahRises, 2022).

Tackling the former of the two, YouTuber Echo Chamberlain made it his goal to pinpoint the absurdities of liberalism. According to his definition, the liberalist political movement has caused a mania over diversity and inclusivity (Echo Chamberlain, 2022). Even though he declares himself a liberal and intimates that liberalism has co-founded modernity, he differs between a positive and negative form of liberal ideology:

> The great failure of modern liberalism is the inability to make any distinction between dynamic, grounded, and relatable liberalism on the one hand, and the flaky, strident, and lecturing, and indulgent extremes of identity politics on the other [...] cultural progressivism that jarringly stamps its social agenda of diversity and inclusivity as it wishes, alienating and confounding huge numbers of people [Echo Chamberlain, 2022, 02:44].

According to the YouTuber, liberal interaction with historical fiction can be separated into two factions, creating a dichotomy between the "woke crowd" and his own moderate standpoint.

While moderate liberalism is portrayed as rational and laudable, Echo Chamberlain equates a woke casting of Black characters with irrational identity politics. The image of radicalism evoked in this description implies the idea of a nonsensical crowd who is rather led by fanatical politics than by the wish to experience true history. In his videos, the YouTuber Echo Chamberlain stages woke people as a generalized group with extreme ideas. By doing so, he positions himself in opposition as the moderate center. Echo Chamberlain wants the listener to believe that he is arguing from a position of scientific rationality, the moderate status quo, and an universally shared notion of common sense. However, as Hayden White (1973) suggests, the status quo is not fixed, and scientific rationality can be just as transient. Nevertheless, Echo Chamberlain defines "woke" idealists as a group of sheepish radicals who follow ideals they do not fully comprehend. In a popular fashion, Echo Chamberlain performs as the singular voice of sanity against the ephemeral waves of mass politics.

YouTubers who adapt this position as the individual criticizing the perception of the masses share a proclivity to self-victimization. In their narrative, they represent critical thinking. If these YouTubers encounter disagreement, they accuse the antagonist of muffling their right to free speech. Metatron (2022), for example, states: "My statements are based on evidence, and they are refuted on the basis that I am light-skinned" (23:49). The idea is that the dumbfounded woke crowd silences its opponents because of its political ideology, while the YouTuber himself argues with reason. Echo Chamberlain represents himself as only interested in accuracy, while he scolds diversified casting in historical fiction as a political movement without rational backup. In a moderate fashion, the YouTuber nevertheless tries to arbitrate:

> The notion to cast actors of color to expand and normalize diversity and inclusivity is in many ways an admirable one but lately this trend has expanded beyond context and even common sense, to place ahead diversity and inclusivity of historical accuracy, ahead of audience's suspension of disbelief, and ahead of any willingness to work within or accept limitations, creating a new weird relativism where we are now expected to accept that diverse actors are entitled to play completely incongruous characters, with an implication that if you are not accepting such choices than you are belatedly or openly biased and in the way of progress [Echo Chamberlain, 2022, 11:34].

Although Echo Chamberlain declares himself a liberal, who would greet diversity in the present, he rejects inclusivity in historical fiction as inaccurate political fanaticism, baptizing it the "new weird relativism."

While the liberalists evoked by Echo Chamberlain are mainly accused of blind radicalism, the second group of enemies, the production companies, are blamed for their greed. The argument goes that Netflix and others would instrumentalize the shortsighted ideas of the "woke crowd" and try to gain from it. If showrunners introduce a diversified cast into a historical society that Echo Chamberlain perceives as homogeneous, their mistake must lie in the willingness to forgo accuracy for money. HistorySpark and Metatron complement this proposition, stating that companies like Netflix try to produce income by pleasing the general political consensus. Metatron warns his listeners that the showrunners would discharge not only accuracy but also diversity if they drew profit from it. HistorySpark (2022) deplores that the makers of *Vikings: Valhalla* were only interested in "tick[ing] boxes" when choosing a Black actress as a Jarl. Real diversity in historical fiction would look differently (03:34).

By setting the motivation behind diversified casting in the present, being identity politics or money, YouTubers deny companies like Netflix any genuine interest in the past. Because of this, shows like *Vikings: Valhalla* would be more presentist than accurate, hence more motivated by current issues than by an urge for historical objectivity. That the YouTubers' own imagery of what is historically accurate was also conceived in the present is hidden through the notion of accuracy (Houghton & Alvestad, 2021, p. 4). Connected to the concepts of rationality and historical factuality, it tries to obscure the constructed and impure nature of the human perception of the past. By declaring their loyalty to accuracy, YouTubers attempt to cover their own dependency on narratives of the nineteenth and twentieth century.

Racial Accuracy and the Segregation of Historical Fiction

To fans of a traditional Viking lore, the infamous race-swap constitutes an especially unpardonable affront against historical accuracy. While the (racial) outer appearance of an actor does not matter to the viewer who has given up on accuracy, materialist positivists attempt to painstakingly recreate the look of a historical character. This strict method excludes any performer from starring as a Viking who does not dovetail with the visual picture imagined by the positivist. As such, accuracy is used to exclude certain races from performing as specific people in historical fiction. YouTubers argue that Henderson simply does not fit the description of Jarl Haakon because of her outer, material appearance. Similar to nineteenth-century positivism, the accuracy-concept reduces race to the physical features of a person, pursuing a biological determinism. Accuracy in itself as a category of historical fiction, therefore, becomes a racist idea.

YouTubers who adhere to such a nineteenth-century narrative compartmentalize human experience, both in past and present, according to racial categories. Races turn into eternal continuities linking, for example, Vikings to Scandinavian but not to African people. According to this logic, every ethnicity should remain in its own orbit, especially when it comes to historical fiction. HistorySpark (2022), for example, reasons:

> So, my first and primary reason why I feel that *Vikings: Valhalla* will be a letdown is due to the casting of Caroline Henderson as Jarl Haakon. [...] by casting a Black woman to play one of the most important Viking figures who historical figures have described as a large strong and fearsome White male is just offensive, rude, and in my opinion downright racist. We would not let Tom Cruise play the role of Martin Luther King or have Denzel Washington play the role of Mahatma Gandhi [...] [00:58].

For critics like HistorySpark, history is separated by race. Projecting racial thinking into the past, he ascribes various historical figures to certain ethnicities.

YouTubers like Echo Chamberlain and Metatron assure their viewers that they are in favor of diversity and equality in the present. However, assuming the existence of such an inclusivity in the Viking Age, they say, constitutes a bold anachronism because of medieval racism. One might insinuate that HistorySpark's, Chamberlain's, and Metatron's argument performs a reverse but comparable action, projecting present racial segregation into the past. It is in this instance that identity politics resurface in their ostensibly accuracy-focused line of reasoning. By proposing to perform a reversed "race-swap," for example casting the White American performer Tom Cruise as Martin Luther King, the HistorySpark believes to evoke a scenery that must sound abstruse also to "woke" and Black people. With this, YouTubers try to find a mutual understanding of how historical fiction should achieve a proper presentation of race. The solution critics such as Metatron and Echo Chamberlain usually arrive at is a compartmentalization of history according to continents. White actors then should be limited to European history, whereas Black performers could only personify African figures. The various continental or racial histories are, consequently, made a property that belongs to different races. In this theory, as long as no participant interferes with the heritage-property of the other race, all humans could enjoy their past-based identity. The argument goes as far as to portray history as something that can be owned by different races or individuals in the form of heritage, making past events a human property.

This topographic thinking can conversely also be instrumentalized by other "races" to engender their own historical and continental identity. Adherents of White Vikingness even welcome this response, stating that they would gladly watch a series focused on African history with African actors. Both essentialist identitarian groups could, so the hope of traditionalist Viking fans, support each other in their right to an exclusive ethnic identity. Their hope to succeed in this regard was not in vain, as many comments from people who identify as Black (or pretend to do so on YouTube) corroborate their assumption. These users agree that Vikings should remain White since that would be the only believable version (Young, 2021, p. 29). Because of their identity politics, both Black and White fans reject the so-called "weird [racial] relativism" of twenty-first-century cosmopolitans. Metatron (2022) summarizes the idea of an interracial alliance against the "woke crowd": "This is not a White versus Black. This is a Black and White versus people with specific political agendas that are ready to bend the truth" (24:15). According to the YouTubers, the cause of indignation over *Vikings: Valhalla* is not a racist confrontation but a conflict between the cosmopolitan diversifiers and fans believing in secluded, authentic cultures. In this narrative, the discussion appears as a dichotomy between greedy corporations such as Netflix allied with the arbitrary "woke crowd" and YouTubers who try to preserve a true, historical, and racial identity.

Some commentators maintain that making Jarl Haakon Black is an affront to Scandinavian people. It would be a disfigurement of Nordic cultural heritage to reimagine the legendary ruler as a Black woman. The YouTuber Norse Magic and Beliefs (2022) complains: "I have not seen the new series, but I already know how much historical inaccuracies are going to be in there [...] and unfortunately it is borderline slander on our ancestors" (00:27). By arguing against the race-swap and referring to heritage, the speakers develop an increasingly emotional tone. The equally present-focused intention of YouTubers partially unveils as positivist rhetoric is put aside to allow for an expression of personal identity.

Conclusions

This essay's analysis of popular discourse on YouTube circling *Vikings: Valhalla* has shown how YouTubers reappropriate a nineteenth-century notion of accuracy. In a creative manner, Metatron, Echo Chamberlain, and HistorySpark have engendered their own sense of accuracy to criticize the show's portrayal of race and to argue in favor of nineteenth-century positivism. The YouTubers try to portray their version of the past as the most accurate one by instrumentalizing various references, such as secondary literature, climate theories, or DNA. However, many of these sources come as the scientific heritage of nineteenth-century positivism. What is often perceived as objective proof actually serves to entrench the ideas of separate races into historical fiction, following ephemeral narratives instead of eternal factuality. YouTubers are prone to brandish these references as symbols of ultimate accuracy and omit their relative truthfulness.

Adherents to a traditionalist version of Viking lore present themselves as defenders of historical accuracy. Staged as a threat to this accuracy, the showrunners of *Vikings: Valhalla* or the so-called "woke crowd" are made enemies of true history. The YouTuber performs as the lone voice of rationality against the capitalist media and the emotionally blinded masses. As such, it is only him who could guarantee accuracy, while the production companies are exempted from this position by their more financial than scientific objectives. Netflix's decision to portray the Viking leader as a Black female is perceived as a politically motivated action. The reaction against it, however, similarly predicates on ideology. YouTubers assert that there are racially separated forms of heritage—White Vikings being distinct from Black Africans—to corroborate their own identity politics. At this point, it is pertinent to state that the mentioned YouTubers are not necessarily racists in the sense of White supremacists. Especially the three YouTubers mentioned in this paper did not call for any hatred towards people believed to be different. And yet, discussing race with accuracy when concerning historical fiction often develops an exclusive dynamic. Considering that discussions circling shows like *Vikings: Valhalla* predicate rather on opinions than sources, racial accuracy must be identified as an ideological and not historical idea. This racial accuracy can hardly be found in medieval sources but rather in popular discourse when pondering on historical fiction. As such, racial accuracy might as well be considered a fiction.

The cause of the outcry lies mostly in *Vikings: Valhalla*'s and the YouTubers' claim to historical accuracy. By reinterpreting a fictional (and even fantastic) story as a source of history, a pseudo-scientific objectivism is applied onto popular entertainment. YouTubers and showrunners seek to curtail each other's right to determine accuracy, as there could be only one objective truth. The re-establishment of authenticity as a concept in popular discourse proposes a solution to this conflict. Authenticity as an idea intimates the learned, experienced, and emotional nature of historical perception and acceptance thereof. Such newly gained tolerance towards non-factual history allows a plethora of opinions or truths to coexist simultaneously. Contrary to exclusive accuracy, authenticity facilitates diversity and inclusivity in discourse because it accepts multiple perspectives into its fold without falling prey to the infamous "weird relativism."

Finally, by admitting to the constructed character of one's view, one lays open the origins of the individual narrative. In the case of Viking lore defended by the here mentioned YouTubers, a thorough analysis reveals an influence of positivist racism. To excavate the origins of historical knowledge means to disclose how it was generated, transmitted, and influenced by former generations. Authenticity as a concept permits the discussants to acknowledge the relativeness of their views without losing face, inviting to a more critical self-reflection. It ought to be a task of historical fiction studies to highlight this option and thus, facilitate a more productive and inclusive discourse. Only by (partially) bidding farewell to the idea of objective accuracy, historical fiction and popular history can achieve what are said to be common values among all discourse participants: authenticity, diversity, and inclusivity.

References

Arnold, B. (1992). The past as propaganda. *Archaeology, 45*(4), 30–37.
Beavers, S., & Warnecke, S. (2021). Audience perceptions of historical authenticity in visual media. In K. Alvestad & R. Houghton (Eds.), *The Middle Ages in modern culture: History and authenticity in contemporary medievalism* (pp. 74–89). Bloomsbury Academic. http://dx.doi.org/10.5040/9781350167452.0013.
Berghoff, P. (2001). Das Phantasma der "kollektiven Identität" und die religiösen Dimensionen in den Vorstellungen von Volk und Nation. In Stefanie v. Schnurbein and Justus H. Ulbricht (Eds.), *Völkische Religion und Krisen der Moderne. Entwürfe „arteigener Glaubenssysteme seit der Jahrhundertwende* (pp. 56–74). Königshausen u. Neumann.
Bunnenberg, C., & Steffen, N. (2019). Broadcast yourself: history stories! Geschichte auf YouTube—eine Bestandsaufnahme. In C. Bunnenberg & N. Steffen (Eds.), *Geschichte auf YouTube. Neue Herausforderungen für Geschichtsvermittlung und historische Bildung* (pp. 3–26). De Gruyter. https://doi-org.eui.idm.oclc.org/10.1515/9783110599497.
Channel Awesome. (2015). *The Last Airbender—Nostalgia Critic* [Video]. YouTube. https://www.youtube.com/watch?v=6jvpOpDraZU.
De Groot, J. (2015). *Remaking history. The past in contemporary historical fictions*. Routledge.
Deeks, M.D. (2016). *National identity in Northern and Eastern European heavy metal* (uk.bl.ethos.701729) [Doctoral Dissertation, Leeds University]. White Rose eTheses Online.
Dominic Noble. (2020). *Earthsea—Lost in adaptation* [Video]. YouTube. https://www.youtube.com/watch?v=_mfnVK9RdZk.
Dowling, L. (1985). Roman decadence and Victorian historiography. *Victorian Studies, 28*(4), 579–607.
Echo Chamberlain. (2022, March 02). *Vikings Valhalla: Diversity goes off track* [Video]. YouTube. https://www.youtube.com/watch?v=9P5t4eR-9r4.
Harty, K.J. (Ed.). (2011). *The Vikings on film: Essays on depictions of the Nordic Middle Ages*. McFarland.

Harvey, D.A. (2012). *The French enlightenment and its Others. Palgrave Studies in cultural and intellectual history*. Palgrave Macmillan. https://doi.org/10.1057/9781137002549_6.
Houghton, R., & Alvestad, K.C. (2021). Introduction: Accuracy and authenticity—interactions in contemporary medievalism. In K. Alvestad & R. Houghton (Eds.), *The Middle Ages in modern culture: History and authenticity in contemporary medievalism* (pp. 1–11). Bloomsbury Academic. http://dx.doi.org/10.5040/9781350167452.0013.
Jayne Theory. (2022, March 08). *Black Vikings? The RACE-SWAPPED "Queen" who never was... | Netflix* [Video]. YouTube. https://www.youtube.com/watch?v=sThlLEznKfI.
JOJOBEE. (2021, February 17). *Jodie Turner-Smith to play Black Anne Bolyen/ Black Tudors, Black Royalty & Blackwashing/ JOJOBEE* [Video]. YouTube. https://www.youtube.com/watch?v=KOdd-rJNFqQ.
JosiahRises. (2022, February 26). *Vikings: Valhalla gets DESTROYED by fans for woke nonsense!* [Video]. YouTube. https://www.youtube.com/watch?v=S6uj8dvenm0&t=130s.
Kipper, R. (2002). *Der Germanenmythos im deutschen Kaiserreich: Formen und Funktionen historischer Selbstthematisierung*. Vandenhoeck & Ruprecht.
Lake, J.C. (2009). Truth, plausibility, and the virtues of narrative at the millennium. *Journal of Medieval History, 35*(3), 221–238.
Livingstone, D.N. (2012). Changing climate, human evolution, and the revival of environmental determinism. *Bulletin of the History of Medicine, 86*(4), 564–595.
Metatron. (2022, April 28). *Is the Black Jarl in Vikings Valhalla historical? The truth* [Video]. YouTube. https://www.youtube.com/watch?v=uB27ViMwrQY&t=717s.
Nasjonalmuseet (2022, May 26). *Håkon jarl*. https://www.nasjonalmuseet.no/en/collection/object/NG.K_H.B.03324.
Norse Magic and Beliefs. (2022, February 23). *Vikings Valhalla series real history* [Video]. YouTube. https://www.youtube.com/watch?v=_VvgmOl-8_w&t=65s.
O'Donoghue, H. (2008). *From Asgard to Valhalla. The remarkable history of the Norse myths*. Tauris Academic Studies.
O'Donoghue, H. (2021). *Narrative in the Icelandic family saga: Meanings of time in old Norse literature*. Bloomsbury Academic. http://dx.doi.org.eui.idm.oclc.org/10.5040/9781350167445.ch-00I.
Saxton, L. (2020). A true story: defining accuracy and authenticity in historical fiction. *Rethinking History, 24*(2), 127–144. 10.1080/13642529.2020.1727189.
Schultz, H.-D. (1998). Herder und Ratzel: Zwei Extreme, ein Paradigma? (Herder and Ratzel: Two Extremes, One Paradigm?). *Erdkunde, 52*(2), 127–143. http://www.jstor.org/stable/25647039.
Shaw, C. (2022, February 18–20). *It's pretty future-y: Retro futurism and historical anachronism in Loki* [Paper presentation]. Historical Fiction Research Conference 2022. Digital.
Stuart, J., et al. (Execute Producers). (2022). *Vikings Valhalla* [TV series]. Metropolitan Films International; History; MGM Television.
Sundmark, B. (2014). Wayward Warriors. The Viking motif in Swedish and English children's literature. *Children's Literature in Education, 45*(3), 197–210.
The Welsh Viking. (2022, January 22). *Archaeologist reviews Vikings Valhalla trailer* [Video]. YouTube. https://www.youtube.com/watch?v=pnXXHtAO5pA.
Teulié, G. (2020). Henry Rider Haggard's Nordicism? When Black Vikings fight alongside White Zulus in South Africa. *E-rea, 18*(1). DOI: https://doi.org/10.4000/erea.10251.
Viking Stories. (2022, February 02). *Vikings Valhalla destroying our heroes* [Video]. YouTube. https://www.youtube.com/watch?v=qwc9jUOUE8Q&t=271s.
Wawn, A. (2002). *The Vikings and the Victorians. Inventing the Old North in 19th century Britain*. D.S. Brewer.
White, H. (1973). *Metahistory: The historical imagination in Nineteenth-Century Europe*. Johns Hopkins University Press.
Willingham, C. (Writer), Wasserman, D. (Writer), & Fleischer, R. (Director). (1958) *The Vikings*. Brynaprod Curtleigh Productions.
xLetalis. (2019). *The Witcher's Netflix producer responds to fan criticism: Skin color, Witcher games & Slavic spirit* [Video]. YouTube. https://www.youtube.com/watch?v=JIoa26sJ8zU.
Young, Helen. (2021). Race and historical authenticity: Kingdom Come: Deliverance. In C. Bunnenberg & Steffen, N. (Eds.), *Geschichte auf YouTube. Neue Herausforderungen für Geschichtsvermittlung und historische Bildung* (pp. 28–39). De Gruyter. https://doi-org.eui.idm.oclc.org/10.1515/9783110599497.

The Marketing of Fictional Portrayals of Real-World Social Causes on Broadcast and Streaming Networks

Ronen Shay *and* Arien Rozelle

As civil unrest erupted across the U.S. in the summer of 2020 in response to the murder of George Floyd, many of those at home due to the pandemic were in front of their screens, watching in real time. In June of 2020, after seeing an increase in searches for the phrase "Black Lives Matter" over several weeks, Netflix launched a "Black Lives Matter" collection of movies, TV shows and documentaries, featuring 45 titles about racial injustice and the Black American experience (Spangler, 2020). This era's marked increase and interest in social movements creates the possibility for media firms like Netflix to not only curate content for viewers based on relevant and timely social issues and causes but creates the potential for social issues and social movements to be remediated into storylines of scripted video programming.

While the inclusion of real-life social issues and causes into television programming is not new, the emergence of contemporary social movements, as well as the overturning of *Roe vs. Wade,* has led to an increase in topics like racism, sexism and reproductive rights appearing in fictional storylines. In 2021, ANSIRH (Advancing New Standards in Reproductive Health) tracked 47 plotlines that involved abortion over 42 shows (ANSIRH, 2021). Abortion was included in dramas like Hulu's *The Handmaid's Tale* and NBC's *This Is Us,* in addition to comedies like *Hacks* on HBO Max (now Max) and *Workin' Moms* on Netflix. This is a marked increase, as just five years ago, there were only 13 plotlines involving abortion (ANSIRH, 2016). Despite the increased use of real-world social causes, issues, and movements in fictional storylines there is still a deficiency of literature regarding the way these portrayals are marketed.

For example, in season 5, episode 15 of the original *Fresh Prince of Bel-Air* (NBC, 1994) Will Smith's character is shot while trying to protect his cousin Carlton from a bank machine robbery gone wrong. The content of the episode calls for stricter gun legislation when Carlton begins carrying a gun for his protection after the incident. Despite this commentary on a social issue, the episode description reads, "*Carlton buys a gun after he and Will are robbed*" (HBO Max, 2022) making no mention of Will getting shot, or his successful emotional appeal to Carlton that carrying a gun likely increases the risk of violence occurring, after which Carlton decides owning a gun will not make him safer. This raises questions regarding whether excluding the content creator's commentary on gun violence from the episode descriptions was an oversight, implicit bias, or an intentional strategy to prevent alienating pro-gun viewers.

While the widespread adoption of the internet, ensuing audience fragmentation, and the proliferation of over-the-top (OTT) services from new entrants like Netflix, Amazon Prime, and HBO Max presents an opportunity for the degree of transparency in marketing materials to improve, there is a little evidence to suggest that this is the case. For example, *Grey's Anatomy* season 6 is available for viewing on Netflix. In season 6, episode 24 of *Grey's Anatomy* (2005–present, ABC) there is a fictional portrayal of a hospital shooting where 11 different people die. The episode description on Netflix reads, "*Cristina and Meredith's surgical skills are put to the ultimate test*" (Netflix, 2022). With this in mind, the purpose of this essay is to examine the ways that fictional portrayals of real-world social movements are marketed by contemporary broadcasters and streaming platforms.

Literature Review

Given the social movements of the '60s and '70s, it is unsurprising that the '70s saw an increase in television programming related to social issues. In 1972, American Broadcasting Company coined the term "after school special," for programs dealing with socially relevant issues that were broadcast in the late afternoon to appeal to teenagers coming home after school (Weiss, 2006). The *ABC Afterschool Special*, an anthology series, aired from October 4, 1972, to January 23, 1997. Most episodes, which aired in the late afternoons on weekdays after kids came home from school, featured dramatic and often controversial topics like divorce, domestic violence, child abuse, substance abuse, and teenage pregnancy.

Notably, the topics of abortion and violence against women have been covered in popular television for decades. Famously, in the first season of *Maude* (1972–1978), a spin-off of *All in the Family* (1971–1978), 47-year-old Maude Findlay, a liberal, independent woman and grandmother, finds out she's pregnant. In the second part of the two-part series called "Maude's Dilemma," she decides to terminate her pregnancy. Despite selecting to have an abortion, the episode description for part two of "Maude's Dilemma" reads:

> Maude's unexpected pregnancy wreaks havoc in the lives of Maude and Walter while they try to decide what to do about it, in the conclusion of a two-part story. Along with morning sickness and a sudden urge for pickles, Maude gets advice about her problem from Carol and Florida while Walter commiserates with Arthur in a nearby bar [Amazon, 2022].

Again, there is an omission of the social issue from the episode description despite being featured in the content in itself. Violence against women has also been written into plotlines, including in one of *All in the Family*'s most-well known episodes, "Edith's 50th Birthday" (season 8), in which Edith unknowingly lets a serial rapist into her home. The episode description for this reads: "Archie, Mike and Gloria plan a surprise party for Edith to celebrate her 50th birthday. But an unwelcome visitor to the Bunker's home—while Edith is home alone—has a much different surprise in mind for the Bunker matriarch" (Amazon, 2022). In this example the social issue is implied, but not directly mentioned.

Whereas fictional portrayals of real-world social causes in the 1970s predominantly followed the "after school special" model, the 1980s saw the birth of "A Very Special Episode," in which primetime sitcoms or dramas like *Family Ties* (1982–1989) or *Diff'rent Strokes* (1978–1986) tackled social issues ranging from racism to sexism to drugs, sexual abuse and HIV (Moss, 2015). Other shows like *The Golden Girls* (1985–1992) featured special episodes addressing LGBTQ+ topics, sexuality, and women's health. *Full House* (1987–1995) aired special episodes addressing eating disorders and child abuse. *Roseanne* (1988–1997) featured special episodes about physical abuse and bigotry. It seems "Very Special Episodes" peaked in popularity in the '80s, and faded away by the late 1990s (Moss, 2015; Weiss, 2006), with ABC's "After School Specials" ending in 1997.

As the HIV/AIDS crisis raged in the '80s and into the '90s, shows like CBS's *Designing Women* incorporated storylines about the epidemic into the show. In *Designing Women*'s (1986–1993) episode "Killing All the Right People" (October 5, 1987) a young gay man and friend of the designers is dying of AIDS and asks the women to design his funeral. They agree, and the episode goes on to educate viewers about how AIDS is and isn't transmitted. The episode description reads: "A wonderful young friend enlists the Sugarbaker firm's services for an unusual project—he is dying of AIDS and wants them to design his funeral, and Mary Jo becomes involved in a PTA debate over sexually active school students" (Hulu, 2022). This example directly mentions the social cause within the episode description, demonstrating significant variance from the previous two examples that either omitted the social movement, or just implied the social issue without directly stating it. It should be noted the aforementioned episode was nominated for two Emmy awards. Another example of marketing materials directly stating the social cause can be seen in the *Golden Girls* episode (1985–1992) "72 Hours" (February 17, 1990), the character Rose is concerned that a blood transfusion she had may have contained HIV-infected blood. The episode description for this transparently and directly states, "Rose discovers that she may be carrying the HIV virus" (Hulu, 2021).

From 1994 to 2009 NBC's long-running medical drama *ER* not only tackled a broad spectrum of social issues throughout its 15 seasons, it also featured a diverse cast. Issues ranged from poverty to gun violence to race, war, white privilege, addiction, suicide, AIDS, debt, and mental illness. Such topics are covered as the show follows the life of ER staff at a fictional hospital in Chicago. The show won 23 Primetime Emmy Awards and has grossed over $3 billion in revenue.

The late '90s and early 2000s saw shows like NBC's *The West Wing* (1999–2006) feature an array of social and political issues, even addressing abortion in the pilot episode. *The Wire*, HBO's crime drama series (2002–2008), covered a variety of social issues ranging from the illegal drug trade to education and schools to government corruption and the media. *The Wire* has been critically acclaimed for its accurate portrayals of society, politics and urban life, and is often cited as one of the greatest television series of all time. In 2019, Fernandez (2019) shares how the final season of *Orange Is the New Black* (2013–2019) quickly received high praise from critics and audiences for its portrayal of the hardships faced by immigrants under the previous U.S. administration. Nussbaum (2019) believes this proves that "TV shows, unlike novels, are never truly unaware of their audience: if they are, they don't get renewed. Even in the streaming era, television is still a call-and-response medium, absorbing and reflecting viewer reactions. That's both its strength and its limitation."

While contemporary social movements like #MeToo and Black Lives Matter (BLM) continue to be woven into the plots and storylines of fictional streaming content like *The Assistant* and *Seven Seconds*, it is worth noting that the inclusion of real-life social or political issues into scripted television has, however, not always been positively received. When *South Park* attempted to comment on the 2005 and 2007 controversies surrounding cartoon portrayals of Muhammad, the episodes were censored, and eventually cut from the series by HBO (Haring, 2020). While it would be interesting to see if the distributors omitted, implied, or directly mentioned the controversies within the marketing materials used for the initial airings, the episode descriptions for these censored episodes were not available at the time of this study.

Given the paradoxical relationship between the existence of social movements in contemporary entertainment media, and the frequency to which those same movements are omitted from the episode descriptions this study seeks to identify the degree to which social causes like #MeToo and BLM appear in the marketing materials (i.e., episode descriptions) of contemporary entertainment media. It will also attempt to identify the media platforms most likely to transparently communicate about the presence of social causes in their fictional content. Examining the aforementioned constructs will allow for the establishment of best practices for marketing the portrayal of social causes in fictional content in a fashion that can be empowering to both audiences and media firms. Accordingly, the following research questions are posited:

RQ1: *To what degree do social causes, issues, or movements appear in the episode descriptions of contemporary fictional video series?*

RQ2: *Which video platforms are most likely to include a social cause, issue, or movement in the episode descriptions of contemporary video series?*

Method

Content Analysis and Sampling Procedures

This study was conducted using a content analysis that produced an original set of data that includes observations from 408-episode descriptions, from 27 different video series, across 9 different video platforms. The video platforms that were included for analysis include broadcasters: ABC, FOX, NBC, CBS, and The CW, as well as over-the-top (OTT) video streamers: Netflix, Amazon Prime Video, Hulu, Disney+, and HBO Max. The five national English language broadcasters available in the United States (U.S.) were included to ensure a cross-section of broadcasters and streamers, and the top five performing U.S. streamers were selected based on their subscriber numbers at the time the study was conducted.

Once the platforms to be included in the study were identified, the top three shows from each platform were selected for analysis based on their IMDb Pro MOVIEmeter performance. MOVIEmeter is designed to provide industry professionals with an indication of what is currently considered popular content in film and television (IMDb, 2022). While IMDbPro's algorithms are proprietary they do acknowledge that their primary measurement is how often a film or television series has their IMDb profile page viewed by visitors (IMDb, 2022). They also disclose that IMDb averages 160 million visitors each month (IMDb, 2022), and as result the MOVIEmeter metric is able to be based on a cumulative sum of more than 3 billion page views each month (IMDb, 2022). These claims are consistent with IMDb's traffic rankings, as at the time of this study, IMDb was the fifth most visited News and Media website globally after YouTube, Wikipedia, Twitter, and Instagram (Semrush, 2022). In June 2022 IMDb.com had 801,300,811 visits (Semrush, 2022).

When selecting the top three shows from each platform the parameters for inclusion were that the video content was episodic (i.e., not a feature film), and that the content was distributed by the platform in question during its original airing of its most recent season. For example, *The Office* (2005–2013) is an episodic sitcom originally distributed by NBC and had a top three MOVIEmeter score among NBC programs. Given that canceled programs like *The Office* (NBC) can rank higher on IMDb than newer series like *This Is Us* (2016–2022, NBC), and streaming video platforms allow for canceled programs to compete against new series for contemporary video audiences, canceled programs were not excluded from analysis.

To ensure study feasibility and data relevancy for multi-season shows (e.g., NCIS just concluded season 19), the most recent season of each program was included for analysis. This led to the exclusion of two shows, *Lucifer* (2016–2021) and *Brooklyn Nine-Nine* (2013–2021). While *Lucifer* did rank in the top three for FOX shows, the most recent season was distributed by Netflix, and therefore the analysis would be a reflection of Netflix's strategy, not FOX (*Lucifer* was not in the top three for Netflix). *Brooklyn Nine-Nine* did rank in the top three for FOX shows as well, but the most recent season was distributed by NBC, and it did not rank in the top three for NBC. Ultimately, the aforementioned sampling methodology led to a sample that is reflective of the current demand among U.S. video consumers as determined by IMDb pro and is a reflection of what audiences are consuming in 2022: a combination of streaming and broadcast, as well as a combination of new and canceled series.

Sample Characteristics

The series included for analysis include—ABC: *Grey's Anatomy* (S18), *Modern Family* (S11), *The Rookie* (S4); CBS: *NCIS* (S19), *Criminal Minds* (S15), *The Big Bang Theory* (S12); FOX: *The X-Files* (S11), *Family Guy* (S20), *House* (S8); NBC: *The Office* (S9), *This Is Us* (S6), *The Blacklist* (S9); The CW: *Supernatural* (S15), *All American* (S4), *The Flash* (S8); Netflix: *Stranger Things* (S4), *The Lincoln Lawyer* (S1), *Love, Death, & Robots* (S3); Amazon Prime Video: *The Boys* (S3), *Night Sky* (S1), *Bosch Legacy* (S1); Disney+: *Obi-Wan* (S1), *Ms. Marvel* (S1), *The Mandalorian* (S2); HBO Max: *The Staircase* (S1), *Game of Thrones* (S8), *Barry* (S3); and Hulu: *The Orville* (S3), *Candy* (S1), and *Shoresy* (S1).

Coding for Content Analysis

Once the video series relevant to this study were identified, a census of the episode descriptions for the most recent seasons was content analyzed for the presence of a social cause, issue, or movement. Each episode description was coded by two independent coders on a 3-point Likert scale, where 1 = social cause not implied, and not directly mentioned; 2 = social cause implied, but not directly mentioned; and 3 = social cause directly mentioned.

Data Analysis

Once the data collection was complete the data was analyzed using descriptive statistics, and single factor ANOVA. Descriptive statistics were used to report both the frequency to which an episode description either directly mentioned or implied the presence of a social cause, issue or movement, as well as to calculate the mean performance of each individual show on the aforementioned Likert scale, as well as the cumulative mean performance of a platform's three shows. Single factor ANOVA was used to determine if there was a statistically significant difference between the cumulative mean performance of each platform.

Findings

RQ1: *To what degree do social causes, issues, or movements appear in the episode descriptions of contemporary fictional video series?*

Social Causes, Issues, and Movements Present

NETFLIX (CUMULATIVE MEAN SCORE: 1.4)

Netflix is an OTT streaming video service available to consumers directly via a web-based subscription. In addition to content aggregation from existing distributors, Netflix's content offerings also include original series and films. Netflix's original content is sometimes made available for purchase by non-subscribers and existing consumers via home video offerings (e.g., *House of Cards* is available on DVD and Blu-ray). The Netflix shows included in the sample are *Stranger Things* (S4), *The Lincoln Lawyer* (S1), and *Love, Death, & Robots* (S3).

Eleven percent of *Stranger Things* episode descriptions (n = 1) directly mention a social cause/issue (i.e., bullying), 22 percent (n = 2) imply the presence of a social cause/issue without directly mentioning it (i.e., U.S.-Russia relations), and 67 percent (n = 6) do not imply or make mention of a social cause. 10 percent of *The Lincoln Lawyer* episode descriptions (n = 1) directly mention a social cause/issue (i.e., human trafficking), 10 percent (n = 1) imply the presence of a social cause/issue without directly mentioning it (i.e., police misconduct), and 80 percent (n = 8) do not imply or make mention of a social cause. None of the *Love, Death, & Robots* descriptions directly mention a social cause/issue, 44 percent (n = 4) imply the presence of a social cause/issue without directly mentioning it (i.e., human extinction; blasphemy; conspiracy theories; hearing loss), and 56 percent (n = 5) do not imply or make mention of a social cause.

On a 3-point Likert scale, where 1 = social cause not implied, and not directly mentioned; 2 = social cause implied, but not directly mentioned; and 3 = social cause directly mentioned, *Stranger Things* (S4) episode descriptions mean score (M) was 1.44, *The Lincoln Lawyer* (S1) M = 1.3, and *Love, Death, & Robots* (S3) M = 1.44. Netflix's cumulative average across all three shows was M = 1.4. Of the 28 Netflix episode descriptions analyzed across the three shows, 32 percent (n = 9) either implied or mentioned a social cause/issue, whereas 68 percent (n = 19) did not.

ABC (CUMULATIVE MEAN SCORE: 1.17)

ABC is a broadcast television network available to consumers directly over the air, as well as through cable and satellite companies that pay for carriage. ABC is also available to consumers via some OTT services that offer a live television add-on (e.g., Hulu). The ABC shows included in the sample are *Grey's Anatomy* (S18), *Modern Family* (S11), and *The Rookie* (S4).

Five percent of *Grey's Anatomy* episode descriptions (n = 1) directly mention a social cause/issue (i.e., hate crimes), 10 percent (n = 2) imply the presence of a social cause/issue without directly mentioning it (i.e., LGBTQ rights; legalization of marijuana), and 85 percent (n = 17) do not imply or make mention of a social cause. None of the *Modern Family* episode descriptions directly mention a social cause/issue or imply the presence of a social cause/issue without directly mentioning it, and therefore 100 percent (n = 18) of the episode descriptions do not imply or make mention of a social cause. 9 percent of *The Rookie* episodes (n = 2) directly mention a social cause/issue (i.e., active shooter; domestic terrorism), 14 percent (n = 3) imply the presence of a social cause/issue without directly mentioning it (i.e., election fraud; universal healthcare; domestic terrorism), and 77 percent (n = 17) do not imply or make mention of a social cause.

On a 3-point Likert scale, where 1 = social cause not implied, and not directly mentioned; 2 = social cause implied, but not directly mentioned; and 3 = social cause directly mentioned, *Grey's Anatomy* (S18) episode descriptions mean score (M) was 1.2, *Modern Family* (S11) M = 1, and *The Rookie* (S4) M = 1.32. ABC's cumulative average across all three shows was M = 1.17. Of the 60 ABC episode descriptions analyzed across the three shows, 13 percent (n = 8) either implied or mentioned a social cause/issue, whereas 87 percent (n = 52) did not.

FOX (CUMULATIVE MEAN SCORE: 1.17)

FOX is a broadcast television network available to consumers directly over the air, as well as through cable and satellite companies that pay for carriage. FOX is also available to consumers via some OTT services that offer a live television add-on (e.g., Hulu). The FOX shows included in the sample are *The X-Files* (S11), *Family Guy* (S20), and *House* (S8).

None of *The X-Files* episode descriptions directly mention a social cause/issue, 9 percent (n = 1) imply the presence of a social cause/issue without directly mentioning it (i.e., algorithmically-driven society), and 91 percent (n = 10) do not imply or make mention of a social cause. None of the *Family Guy* episode descriptions directly mention a social cause/issue, 10 percent (n = 2) imply the presence of a social cause/issue without directly mentioning it (i.e., blindness; opioid addiction), and 90 percent (n = 18) do not imply or make mention of a social cause. 13.5 percent of *House* episodes (n = 3) directly mention a social cause/issue (i.e., drug abuse; immigration), 4.5 percent (n = 1) imply the presence of a social cause/issue without directly mentioning it (i.e., gun control), and 82 percent (n = 18) do not imply or make mention of a social cause.

On a 3-point Likert scale, where 1 = social cause not implied, and not directly mentioned; 2 = social cause implied, but not directly mentioned; and 3 = social cause directly mentioned, *X-Files* (S11) episode descriptions mean score (M) was 1.1, *Family Guy* (S20) M = 1.1, and *House* (S8) M = 1.32. FOX's cumulative average across all three shows was M = 1.17. Of the 53 FOX episode descriptions analyzed across the three shows, 13 percent (n = 7) either implied or mentioned a social cause/issue, whereas 87 percent (n = 46) did not.

Amazon Prime Video (cumulative mean score: 1.125)

Amazon Prime Video is an OTT streaming video service available to consumers directly via a web-based subscription. In addition to content aggregation from existing distributors, Amazon's content offerings also include original series and films. Amazon's original content is sometimes made available for purchase by non-subscribers and existing consumers via home video offerings (e.g., *The Boys* is available on DVD and Blu-ray). The Amazon shows included in the sample are *The Boys* (S3), *Night Sky* (S1), and *Bosch Legacy* (S3).

Twelve and a half percent of *The Boys* episode descriptions (n = 1) directly mention a social cause/issue (i.e., human trafficking; January 6), 12.5 percent (n = 1) imply the presence of a social cause/issue without directly mentioning it (i.e., endangered species), and 75 percent (n = 6) do not imply or make mention of a social cause. None of the *Night Sky* episode descriptions directly mention a social cause/issue or imply the presence of a social cause/issue without directly mentioning it, and therefore 100 percent (n = 8) of the episode descriptions do not imply or make mention of a social cause. None of *Bosch Legacy* episode descriptions directly mention a social cause/issue or imply the presence of a social cause/issue without directly mentioning it, and therefore 100 percent (n = 10) of the episode descriptions do not imply or make mention of a social cause.

On a 3-point Likert scale, where 1 = social cause not implied, and not directly mentioned; 2 = social cause implied, but not directly mentioned; and 3 = social cause directly mentioned, *The Boys* (S3) episode descriptions mean score (M) was 1.375, *Night Sky* (S1) M = 1, and *Bosch Legacy* (S1) M = 1. Amazon's cumulative average across all three shows was M = 1.125. Of the 26 Amazon episode descriptions analyzed across the three shows, 8 percent (n = 2) either implied or mentioned a social cause/issue, whereas 92 percent (n = 24) did not.

The CW (cumulative mean score: 1.1)

The CW is a broadcast television network available to consumers directly over the air, as well as through cable and satellite companies that pay for carriage. The CW's content is also available to consumers via the network's vertically-integrated OTT service offerings which include ad-supported streaming video on their website and app. The CW shows included in the sample are, *Supernatural* (S15), *All American* (S4), and *The Flash* (S8).

None of the *Supernatural* episode descriptions directly mention a social cause/issue or imply the presence of a social cause/issue without directly mentioning it, and therefore 100 percent (n = 20) of the episode descriptions do not imply or make mention of a social cause. None of the *All American* episode descriptions directly mention a social cause/issue, 30 percent (n = 6) imply the presence of a social cause/issue without directly mentioning it (i.e., alcoholism; mental health; name, image, and likeness of student athletes), and 70 percent (n = 14) do not imply or make mention of a social cause. None of *The Flash* episode descriptions directly mention a social cause/issue or imply the presence of a social cause/issue without directly mentioning it, and therefore 100 percent (n = 20) of the episode descriptions do not imply or make mention of a social cause.

On a 3-point Likert scale, where 1 = social cause not implied, and not directly mentioned; 2 = social cause implied, but not directly mentioned; and 3 = social cause directly mentioned, *Supernatural* (S15) episode descriptions mean score (M) was 1, *All American* (S4) M = 1.3, and *The Flash* (S8) M = 1. The CW's cumulative average across all three shows was M = 1.1. Of the 60 CW episode descriptions analyzed across the three shows, 10 percent (n = 6) either implied or mentioned a social cause/issue, whereas 90 percent (n = 54) did not.

No Social Causes, Issues, and Movements Present

NBC (CUMULATIVE MEAN SCORE: 1)

NBC is a broadcast television network available to consumers directly over the air, as well as through cable and satellite companies that pay for carriage. NBC is also available to consumers via some OTT services that offer a live television add-on (e.g., Hulu). The NBC shows included in the sample are *The Office* (S9), *This Is Us* (S6), and *The Blacklist* (S9).

None of *The Office* (n = 25), *This Is Us* (n = 18), or *The Blacklist* (n = 22) episode descriptions directly mention a social cause/issue or imply the presence of a social cause/issue. On a 3-point Likert scale, where 1 = social cause not implied, and not directly mentioned; 2 = social cause implied, but not directly mentioned; and 3 = social cause directly mentioned, *The Office* (S9) episode descriptions mean score (M) was 1, *The Is Us* (S6) M = 1, and *The Blacklist* (S9) M = 1. NBC's cumulative average across all three shows was M = 1. Of the 65 NBC episode descriptions analyzed across the three shows, 100 percent (n = 65) did not imply or mention a social cause/issue.

CBS (CUMULATIVE MEAN SCORE: 1)

CBS is a broadcast television network available to consumers directly over the air, as well as through cable and satellite companies that pay for carriage. CBS is also available to consumers via some OTT services that offer a live television add-on (e.g., Hulu). The CBS shows included in the sample are *NCIS* (S19), *Criminal Minds* (S15), and *The Big Bang Theory* (S12).

None of the *NCIS* (n = 21), *Criminal Minds* (n = 10), or *The Big Bang Theory* (n =24) episode descriptions directly mention a social cause/issue or imply the presence of a social cause/issue. On a 3-point Likert scale, where 1 = social cause not implied, and not directly mentioned; 2 = social cause implied, but not directly mentioned; and 3 = social cause directly mentioned, *NCIS* (S19) episode descriptions mean score (M) was 1, *Criminal Minds* (S15) M = 1, and *The Big Bang Theory* (S12) M = 1. CBS's cumulative average across all three shows was M = 1. Of the 55 CBS episode descriptions analyzed across the three shows, 100 percent (n = 55) did not imply or mention a social cause/issue.

HBO Max (cumulative mean score: 1)

HBO Max is an OTT streaming video service available to consumers directly via a web-based subscription. In addition to content aggregation from existing distributors, HBO Max content offerings also include original series and films. HBO Max's original content is often made available for purchase by non-subscribers and existing consumers via home video offerings (e.g., *Game of Thrones* is available on DVD and Blu-ray). The HBO Max shows included in the sample are *The Staircase* (S1), *Game of Thrones* (S8), and *Barry* (S3).

None of *The Staircase* (n = 8), *Game of Thrones* (n = 6), or *Barry* (n = 8) episode descriptions directly mention a social cause/issue or imply the presence of a social cause/issue. On a 3-point Likert scale, where 1 = social cause not implied, and not directly mentioned; 2 = social cause implied, but not directly mentioned; and 3 = social cause directly mentioned, *The Staircase* (S1) episode descriptions mean score (M) was 1, *Game of Thrones* (S8) M = 1, and *Barry* (S3) M = 1. HBO Max's cumulative average across all three shows was M = 1. Of the 22 HBO Max episode descriptions analyzed across the three shows, 100 percent (n = 22) did not imply or mention a social cause/issue.

Hulu (cumulative mean score: 1)

Hulu is an OTT streaming video service available to consumers directly via a web-based subscription. In addition to content aggregation from existing distributors, Hulu content offerings also include original series and films. Hulu's original content is sometimes made available for purchase by non-subscribers and existing consumers via home video offerings (e.g., *The Handmaid's Tale* is available on DVD and Blu-ray). The Hulu shows included in the sample are *The Orville* (S3), *Candy* (S1), and *Shoresy* (S1).

None of *The Orville* (n = 8), *Candy* (n = 5), or *Shoresy* (n = 6) episode descriptions directly mention a social cause/issue or imply the presence of a social cause/issue. On a 3-point Likert scale, where 1 = social cause not implied, and not directly mentioned; 2 = social cause implied, but not directly mentioned; and 3 = social cause directly mentioned, *The Orville* (S3) episode descriptions mean score (M) was 1, *Candy* (S1) M = 1, and *Shoresy* (S1) M = 1. Hulu's cumulative average across all three shows was M = 1. Of the 19 Hulu episode descriptions analyzed across the three shows, 100 percent (n = 19) did not imply or mention a social cause/issue.

Disney+ (cumulative mean score: 1)

Disney+ is an OTT streaming video service available to consumers directly via a web-based subscription. In addition to content aggregation from existing distributors,

Disney+'s content offerings also include original series and films. Disney+'s original content is often made available for purchase by non-subscribers and existing consumers via home video offerings (e.g., *Soul* is available on DVD and Blu-ray). The Disney+ shows included in the sample are *Obi-Wan* (S1), *Ms. Marvel* (S1), and *The Mandalorian* (S2).

None of the *Obi-Wan* (n = 6), *Ms. Marvel* (n = 6), or *The Mandalorian* (n = 8) episode descriptions directly mention a social cause/issue or imply the presence of a social cause/issue. On a 3-point Likert scale, where 1 = social cause not implied, and not directly mentioned; 2 = social cause implied, but not directly mentioned; and 3 = social cause directly mentioned, *Obi-Wan* (S1) episode descriptions mean score (M) was 1, *Ms. Marvel* (S1) M = 1, and *The Mandalorian* (S2) M = 1. Disney+'s cumulative average across all three shows was M = 1. Of the 20 Disney+ episode descriptions analyzed across the three shows, 100 percent (n = 20) did not imply or mention a social cause/issue.

RQ2: *Which video platforms are most likely to include a social cause, issue, or movement in the episode descriptions of contemporary video series?*

ANOVA

A one-way ANOVA was performed to determine if there was a statistically significant difference between the average performance of each platform in regard to the number of episode descriptions that either implied or directly mentioned a social cause/issue. The ANOVA revealed that there was a statistically significant difference in the variance between groups (F [9, 398] = [4.483], p = <.001).

Tukey's HSD Test for multiple comparisons found that the average performance of Netflix (M = 1.4) was significantly different than that of The CW (M = 1.1; p = 0.012, 95% C.I. = [0.0352, 0.5505]), Disney+ (M = 1; p = 0.007, 95% C.I. = [0.0632, 0.7225]), NBC (M = 1; p = <.001, 95% C.I. = [0.1384, 0.6474]), CBS (M = 1; p = <.001, 95% C.I. = [0.1315, 0.6542]), HBO Max (M = 1; p = 0.004, 95% C.I. = [0.0721, 0.7136]), and Hulu (M = 1; p = 0.008, 95% C.I. = [0.582, 0.7275]).

Alternatively, there was no statistically significant difference between Netflix (M = 1.4) and ABC (M = 1.17; p = 0.227), FOX (M = 1.17; p = 0.288), and Amazon Prime Video (M = 1.125; p = 0.115).

Discussion / Conclusion

Holistically within the market the frequency of social causes, movements, issues appearing within the marketing materials for video series is low. Of the 408-episode descriptions analyzed, only 8 percent (n = 32) either implied or mentioned a social/cause issue. This is paradoxically different from the content itself, as shows like *Ms. Marvel* and *Modern Family* are known for regularly addressing the topics of Islamophobia and LGBTQ+ rights, despite no mention of either cause/issue within the episode descriptions. This conservative approach to composing marketing materials for video series is likely an attempt by content distributors to avoid alienating subsets of the overall audience based on religious, social, and cultural beliefs. Given that video content is an experience-based good, an audience member can only evaluate the quality of video programming after consumption. Therefore, should a viewer be dissatisfied with the inclusion or portrayal of a social cause/issue within the program, the effect of this dissatisfaction on audience metrics is mitigated because they still consumed the episode. This contradicts the overall messaging provided by companies like Disney, CBS, and The CW, who trumpet diversity, equity, and inclusion (DEI) as a key part of their content strategies, but then subsequently try to retain viewers who may not agree with a pro–DEI strategy.

A comparative-analysis of the variance across platforms does reveal some granular differences in regard to the inclusion of social causes/issues within the episode descriptions of video content. While HBO Max, Disney+, Hulu, CBS, and NBC made no mention of a social cause, movement, or issues within their episode descriptions, The CW, FOX, ABC, Amazon Prime Video, and Netflix did to varying degrees. Most notably the ANOVA revealed there was a statistically significant difference between the average performance of the top performing platform, Netflix (M = 1.4), relative to the bottom performing platforms The CW (M = 1.1), Disney+ (M = 1), NBC (M = 1), CBS (M = 1), HBO Max (M = 1), and Hulu (M = 1). It is worth noting that The CW did either imply or mention a social cause/issue in 10 percent (n = 6) of the episode descriptions analyzed, but despite this, their mean performance was still statistically significantly lower than that of Netflix. Alternatively, there was not a statistically significant difference between the top performing platform Netflix (M = 1.4), relative to ABC (M = 1.17), FOX (M = 1.17) and Amazon Prime Video (M = 1.125).

This suggests there are three tiers of performance within the market relative to the likely inclusion of a social cause/issue within the episode descriptions of video series content. Netflix (i.e., tier 1) appears to be the platform most likely to either imply or directly mention a social cause or issue within their episode descriptions, followed by ABC, FOX and Amazon (i.e., tier 2), who do so to a lesser degree that Netflix, but still more than HBO Max, Disney+ Hulu, CBS, and NBC (i.e., tier 3). Tier 3 platforms did not make mention of a social movement in their episode descriptions. It is important to note that no platform scored an average score of a 2 or 3 on a 3-point Likert scale, where 1 = social cause not implied, and not directly mentioned; 2 = social cause implied, but not directly mentioned; and 3 = social cause directly mentioned. This suggests that while Netflix's performance of M = 1.4 was the best of the platforms analyzed, there is still significant room for improvement. It is also worth noting that it does not appear that being a broadcaster versus an OTT service likely played a role in the results given that streaming services and broadcasters were both present in tier 2 and 3, although further research would be necessary to substantiate such a claim. Future research should attempt to identify the predictor variables that could contribute to the inclusion of social causes, issues, and movements within the episodic marketing of a series. These variables could potentially include the position of the parent brand on DEI topics and content genres. Future research should also attempt to assess whether the frequency of social causes being featured in episodic marketing changes over time based on the social, cultural, and political values of the era.

The current state of episodic descriptions for video series suggests a reluctance to include social causes and issues within the information being shared with the audience, despite the content itself regularly remediating real-world movements. While Netflix, ABC, FOX, and Amazon are showing some willingness to transparently share this information in advance of consumption, HBO Max, Disney+, Hulu, CBS, and NBC have not. While further research is necessary to substantiate whether this is an oversight, implicit bias, or intentional strategy to prevent alienating conservative viewers, ultimately it demonstrates there is large room for improvement in the transparent marketing of fictional portrayals of real-world social causes.

References

ANSIRH. (2016). *Abortion on Screen*. Retrieved from https://www.ansirh.org/sites/default/files/publications/files/abortion_onscreen_in_2016_0.pdf.

ANSIRH. (2021). *Abortion on Screen*. Retrieved from https://www.ansirh.org/sites/default/files/202112/Abortion%20Onscreen%202021.pdf.

Bernabo, L. (2019). Expanding Television's Cultural Forum in the Digital Era: Prime Time Television, Twitter, and Black Lives Matter. *Journal of Broadcasting & Electronic Media, 63*(1), 77–93. doi:10.1080/08838151.2019.1566862.

Bullets over Bel-Air. (2022). *HBO Max*. Retrieved from https://play.hbomax.com/page/urn:hbo:page:GXdXh7QJpA6XCPQEAABNb:type:episode.

Death and All His Friends. (2022). *Netflix*. Retrieved from https://www.netflix.com/search?q=grey%27s%20anatomy.

Designing Women. (2022). *Hulu*. Retrieved from https://www.hulu.com/series/designing-women-2786c4a6-d4fd-4ca6-bc38-a764c55257d1.

Edith's 50th Birthday. (2022). *Amazon*. Retrieved from https://www.amazon.com/Ediths-Crisis-Faith-Part-II/dp/B0999225Z9/ref=sr_1_7?keywords=all+in+the+family&qid=1658920055&s=instant-video&sprefix=all+in+t%2Cinstant-video%2C65&sr=1-7.

Fernandez, M.E. (2019). Why *Orange Is the New Black* Brought the Immigration Crisis to Litchfield. New York Media. Retrieved from https://www.vulture.com/2019/07/orange-is-the-new-black-immigration-storyline-bts.ht ml.

Fresh Prince of Bel-Air. (1994). *NBC*. Retrieved from https://play.hbomax.com/page/urn:hbo:page:GXdXh7QJpA6XCPQEAABNb:type:episode.

Golden Girls. (2022). *Hulu*. Retrieved from https://www.hulu.com/series/the-golden-girls-a6e5db1c-ab70-451d-8b8c-2fba9ea29248?&cmp=7958&utm_source=google&utm_medium=cpc&utm_campaign=BM+Search+TV+Shows&utm_term=where%20can%20i%20stream%20the%20golden%20girls&gclid=Cj0KCQjwof6WBhD4ARIsAOi65ajHRqMnYnEVp352wiYotgAbk573JF1C7174CAb0_llvjda7dbbyy2IaAqYLEALw_wcB&gclsrc=aw.ds.

Grey's Anatomy. (2010). *ABC*. Retrieved from https://www.netflix.com/search?q=grey%27s%20anatomy.

Haring, B. (2020). South Park Missing Five Episode From HBO Max Offerings Because of Prophet Muhammad Depictions. Deadline Hollywood. Retrieved from
https://deadline.com/2020/06/south-park-episodes-missing-hbo-max-prophet-muhammad -1202969280/.

Mattoni, A. (2017). A situated understanding of digital technologies in social movements. Media ecology and media practice approaches. *Social Movement Studies, 16*(4), 494–505. doi:10.1080/14742837.2017.1311250.

Maude's Dilemma. (2022). *Amazon*. Retrieved from https://www.amazon.com/Maudes-Problem/dp/B099FH5SQH/ref=sr_1_1?crid=P5S3ZYUFC4VV&keywords=maude&qid=1658920005&s=instant-video&sprefix=maude%2Cinstant-video%2C58&sr=1-1.

Moss, T. (2015). The Evolution of TV's Very Special Episode. The Atlantic. Retrieved from https://www.theatlantic.com/entertainment/archive/2015/07/very-special-episode/398432/.

Nussbaum, E. (2019). TV's Reckoning with #MeToo. *The New Yorker*. Retrieved from https://www.newyorker.com/magazine/2019/06/03/tvs-reckoning-with-metoo.

Spangler, T. (2020). Netflix launches "Black Lives Matter" collection of Movies, TV Shows and Documentaries. *Variety*. Retrieved from https://variety.com/2020/digital/news/netflix-black-lives-matter-collection-1234630160/.

Top Websites, News and Media. (2022). *Semrush*. Web. Retrieved from https://www.semrush.com/website/top/global/news-and-media/.

Weiss, J. (2006). The strange afterlife of the After School Special. *The Boston Globe*. Retrieved from http://archive.boston.com/ae/tv/articles/2006/01/01/the_strange_afterlife_of_the_after_sc hool_special/.

What are STARmeter, MOVIEmeter, & COMPANYmeter. (2022) *IMDb*. Web. Retrieved from http://www.imdb.com/help/show_leaf?prowhatisstarmeter.

"An absolute travesty"

Probing Parasocial Relationships and Audience Negativity in HBO's And Just Like That...

Erin E. Gilles

In 2021, when HBO's *And Just Like That...* (*AJLT*), the follow-up to the critically acclaimed series *Sex and the City* (*SATC*) which ran from 1998 to 2004, was announced, long-time fans were thrilled. The Internet was abuzz as fans speculated about *AJLT* plotlines and took to social media to share snapshots of characters they spotted during the filming. However, just a few episodes into the 10-episode run of *AJLT*, online reception among critics and audiences had soured. Dramatic shifts in character portrayals left many fans puzzled and upset. Specifically, they communicated displeasure with the show's handling of complex and emotionally charged topics like race, LGBTQIA+, gender identity, and aging/ableism. The show's fanbase and critics conveyed many of these frustrations on social media under the official Twitter handle #AndJustLikeThat, on Reddit, and in The A.V. Club's comment section.

This essay will apply parasocial relationship theory (J.A. Baldwin & Raney, 2021; Horton & Wohl, 1956; Wulf & Rieger, 2018) to explain how changes in television character storylines impact audiences. The success of *SATC* elevated the four main protagonists to new heights in terms of popularity; women around the world declared allegiance to these imaginary characters. Some did so by donning visible tokens and symbols of their fandom, such as the then-trendy t-shirts that read "I'm a Carrie" or "I'm a Miranda." The original *SATC* characters were fully developed, with vibrant backstories, careers, fashion styles, interests, and problems. They were both aspirational and relatable, for *SATC* encapsulated a moment in time for women and the metropolis of New York City. In the age of social media, audiences can swiftly express elation or disapproval to producers and networks. For this reason, this essay will examine a variety of social media posts to study how fans express their parasocial relationships online.

Background of Sex and the City *and* And Just Like That...

AJLT picks up where *SATC* left off, so it is important to understand the plot and cultural significance of the original series. *Sex and the City* (*SATC*) premiered on HBO in 1998, and went off of the air in 2004. The series followed four single, professional women in New York City as they navigated careers, dating, and friendship. The series finale launched a media maelstrom of tributes, editorials, and the imprint of a program whose fans felt the show deeply (Gerhard, 2005). Based on the bestselling book of the same name by Candace Bushnell, the program quickly became a fan favorite for its edgy content, progressive characters, and relatability. Garnering an impressive 90 percent on the Tomatometer from critics in the 6th season, Rotten Tomatoes widely praised the show. For example, "Despite problematic blindspots, *Sex and the City* secures its spot as a harbinger of authentic, women-centric ensemble television to come" (Rotten Tomatoes, 2022b, para. 1). Among the blindspots was the noticeable absence of racial and ethnic diversity in the cast. Nahman (2019) suggested, "This was the most egregious part of *SATC*, the only people of color are literally serving the main characters" (para. 58). Sexual fluidity was not normative on *SATC* either, although the topic was introduced in various episodes. Arthurs (2003) detailed the fluidity as mentioned in the show:

> These women are of a generation old enough to have been influenced by feminism (in their thirties and forties) but too old to participate in a newly fashionable queer culture, despite their appropriation of camp as a style. They are resolutely heterosexual, despite occasional short-lived encounters with gays, lesbians, and bisexuals that simply reconfirm it [p. 11].

Due to the popularity of the program, there was an enormous number of reviews, episode recaps, and editorials about the revival. Although there was some criticism of the program, *SATC* earned plenty of critical acclaim. Longeretta (2021) writes how the show compiled 54 Emmy and 24 Golden Globe nominations over its run, with seven and eight wins, respectively. After *SATC*, two films were made to continue the storyline, *Sex and the City* (2008) and *Sex and the City 2* (2010), although these were generally poorly received by critics (Freeman, 2010). A third movie was in development for 2016, but Kim Cattrall (who played Samantha Jones) declined to reprise her role, and the film was never made. However, in 2021 *And Just Like That…* aired, which was named after the phrase that the main character, Carrie Bradshaw (played by Sarah Jessica Parker), often uttered in *SATC* when summarizing plot points or moving the story forward. The new series went forward without Cattrall, who told reporters that she was not asked to join the cast: "Everything has to grow, or it dies. I felt that when the series ended, I thought that's smart. We're not repeating ourselves" (as cited in Sharf, 2022, para. 5). The absence of Cattrall's character was explained by her relocation to Europe.

Critical reception of the reboot fell short of the acclaim of the original series. Critics on Rotten Tomatoes (2022a) wrote how "*And Just Like That…* fails to recapture *Sex and the City*'s heady fizz, but like a fine wine, these characters have developed subtler depths with age" (para. 1). Even Bushnell indicated the characters did not resemble those she created so many years before. When asked about the characters in *AJLT* and how they seem out of touch with a diverse and progressive culture, Bushnell told *The New Yorker* that she found many of the reboot decisions startling, but that they were driven by Sarah Jessica Parker (the show's star) and Michael Patrick King (who has served as executive producer, writer, and director for both *SATC* and *AJLT*) (Tolentino, 2022).

Some critics and fans of *AJLT* accused the story of falsely weaving in themes of solidarity. There were allegations of *AJLT* following hollow models of performative allyship (Goss, 2021), or "a performance put on by an individual from a non-marginalized group to show solidarity with a marginalized group, but in a way that is not helpful" (Kalina, 2020, p. 478). An op-ed in *The L.A. Times* written by two long-term fans and TV critics lamented that various characters fell prey to committing racial microaggressions, perpetuated gender norms, seemed detached from modern technology and media, and spouted ageist rhetoric (Blake & McNamara, 2021). Yet, as Blake and McNamara (2021) affirm, "critics are not the audience; 'SATC' fans are the audience" (para. 1).

Parasocial Relationships and Interactions

Parasocial relationship theory can help to explain how viewers connect with media figures, such as actors, newscasters, musicians, and athletes. Midway through the 1950s, researchers observed that the characteristics of the era's popular media (television, radio, and films) created an immediacy with the audience that led to the perception of a relationship with the actors and newscasters. Horton and Wohl's (1956) pioneering work examines this phenomenon, and draws a distinction between what they termed para-social relationships (PSRs) and para-social interactions (PSIs). PSIs occur when some form of internal back-and-forth is elicited from the audience, through the nature of the medium (e.g., the speaker facing the camera) or the performance of the actor (e.g., speaking conversationally or using direct address).

PSRs are intimate, one-sided, non-reciprocal, and are wholly managed by the media figure, which Horton and Wohl (1956) call personae. A great deal of effort is expended by those involved in media production (such as directors, producers, actors, and others) in ensuring that the mediated behaviors of personae are as engaging as face-to-face interactions. Later research has expanded the repertoire of behaviors included in the conceptualization of parasocial interactions. Rubin et al. (1985) found "[t]hat involvement may take many forms including seeking guidance from a media persona, seeing media personalities as friends, imagining being part of a favorite program's social world, and desiring to meet media performers" (pp. 156–157). Our mediated interactions with others may be built around the same relational schemas that guide our interactions with others (Baldwin, 1992). These interactions, which include many processes too extensive to review in this essay, rely upon various types of knowledge. One of these is episodic knowledge, which includes background knowledge of events in people's past. It follows, therefore, that the more parasocial interactions that one has with personae, the more that the audience knows about these characters and the greater the likelihood for the formation of parasocial relationships. In fact, Bernhold and Metzger (2020) indicate that it takes frequent and enduring parasocial interactions to develop parasocial relationships. Gender seems to influence PSIs and PSRs. Women tend to form stronger parasocial bonds than men (Cohen, 2003), and PSRs are stronger with same gender characters (Hall, 2019).

Research on parasocial interactions and relationships has continued into the digital age. Although some scholars study these concepts as distinct constructs, a great deal of researchers across varying fields (such as communication, media psychology, film, and others) have conflated the two terms (Klimmt et al., 2006). However, PSIs are typically conceptualized as a short-term occurrence, typically happening when the media is being consumed, whereas PSRs are more enduring and extend beyond when the media is consumed (Dibble et al., 2016; Hartmann & Goldhoorn, 2011). Parasocial relationships have been studied across a wide variety of media applications. For instance, among the media studied are: audiobooks (Vinney & Vinney, 2017), broadcast news (Rubin et al., 1985), fictional TV series (Eyal & Cohen, 2006; Q. Tian & Hoffner, 2010), social media (Lacalle et al., 2021; Stever & Lawson, 2013), reality stars and influencers (Lueck, 2015; Y. Tian & Yoo, 2015), online gaming communities (Leith, 2021; Wulf et al., 2021), radio (Savage & Spence, 2014), podcasts (Zuraikat, 2020), movies (Hall, 2019), books (Schmid & Klimmt, 2011), streaming video (Ferchaud et al., 2018; Rasmussen, 2018), and professional sports (Bostwick & Lookadoo, 2017). This list is by no means exhaustive, rather this is just a sampling of the media forms to which this theory has been applied. The abundance of recent studies portends a thriving future in PSR studies as the media landscape continues to grow and evolve.

Audiences experience many benefits from their parasocial relationships. In some cases, PSI may alleviate loneliness. Wang et al. (2008) learned women are more likely to seek PSIs when they feel detached from their families and slightly more likely when they feel romantic loneliness, whereas this is not the case for men on either account. Men are more likely to seek PSIs when they feel chronic loneliness, however, this does not hold true for women. The degree of fondness one feels for a fictional character can increase the anthropomorphism of that character. That is, the more than one likes a character the more real that they seem (Gardner & Knowles, 2008). Identifying with a character can change for fans based on media attributes.

Parasocial Relationship and Media Attributes

Characteristics of the medium or the production strategies used in the media text can influence the parasocial bond felt by the audience. One common technique for increasing this parasocial affinity is through the use of direct address. When a media personality or character speaks directly to the audience, this can increase the sensation of intimacy. Some media do this routinely, such as in news broadcasts, many types of influencer videos, or some reality programming's confessional camera interviews (Lunt & Pantti, 2007). In programming in which the characters do address the audience, this technique is called "breaking the fourth wall" (Auter, 1992; Auter & Davis, 1991). This technique stems from live theater, but it translates well to media such as television or streaming video. Studies have demonstrated that parasocial affinity was higher for characters in programming in which the fourth wall was broken by a character (Auter, 1992; Cohen et al., 2019). A similar study supported the finding that parasocial interactions were stronger when the speaker in a video was facing the camera (direct address) versus facing slightly angled and looking off screen (Dibble et al., 2016). Auter and Davis (1991) discovered viewers enjoyed being addressed directly, perhaps because of the enhanced engagement of feeling like the characters were speaking to them directly. Auter and Davis (1991) related how, "That interactive relationship [of direct address] redefines the normally passive relationship with a given show and makes the viewers a part of the action" (p. 170). Semmler et al. (2015) established the use of narration in dramatic programming enhances audience perceptions of parasocial interaction and increased engagement with the narrating character.

Parasocial Relationships and Binge Watching and Second Screening

The effects of the PSRs and PSIs may be enhanced through engaging in binge watching and second screening. The more time that audiences spend with characters, especially when watching episodes back-to-back (binge watching) can lead to deeper, more emotional relationships with these characters (Tukachinsky & Eyal, 2018). Binge watching has been shown to increase one's immersion in the narrative; however, desensitization seems to occur as this effect does weaken with the more time that one spends binge watching (Warren, 2020). Frequently, audiences are using additional media forms while they watch television. This practice (variously called the second, dual, or companion screen), can increase audience engagement with the programming. While some second screening is using unrelated media (i.e., watching TV while shopping online), viewers can engage with other program viewers in real or near-real time to facilitate a social viewing. Wilson (2016) discussed, "Viewed in this way, the second screen, particularly when connected to social media, is holding opposing forces of connection and dispersal in tension and offering the means through which audiences (re)connect" (p. 176). The combination of social media with other forms of media may strengthen the PSI. A recent study discovered when viewers of a television program were able to befriend the show's protagonists on Facebook via fictional character accounts, those viewers who did reported stronger PSI effects (Kyewski et al., 2018).

Parasocial Breakups, Grief, and Forgiveness

What happens when good parasocial relationships go bad? The termination of PSRs are referred to as parasocial breakups (PSBs) (Cohen, 2003). This can happen for many reasons: a show getting canceled, the end of character arcs, actors being replaced or retiring, individuals deciding to stop viewing, or disinterest. In a study examining audience reactions to *Friends* (1994–2004) going off of the air, Eyal and Cohen (2006) found that the biggest factor predicting the PSB despair was the strength of the PSR, followed by how well one liked the program, how popular they considered their favorite character, and the level of loneliness of the audience member. This result was confirmed in a study of forced PSBs caused by the 2007–2008 writers' strike—those with stronger PSRs had greater distress when the TV programs went off of the air (Lather & Moyer-Guse, 2011). However, other research has not confirmed this relationship (Ferchaud et al., 2022). In other cases, PSRs end when a beloved fictional character dies. This parasocial grief may be publicly displayed in online communities, which allow members to share enactments of grief, including expressing emotions, reminiscing, creating memorials, and suggesting what should have happened in the storyline instead or future plotlines (DeGroot & Leith, 2018). Foss (2020) suggests that certain tactics, such as stretching a character's death over multiple episodes (i.e., ending one episode showing a house fire, but waiting until the next episode to reveal if any characters were casualties) may amplify the intensity of the parasocial grief.

Method

Data in this study were obtained via publicly available social media posts and comments on Twitter, Reddit, and The A.V. Club. Social media platforms are ideal for the study of audience reception due to the real-time aspect of user interactions and the ease with which users can discover posts of interest through wide user networks of followers (Lyles et al., 2013). Further, these media-rich posts can express a great deal of information through the use of emoji, photos, videos, links, and information from previous conversations. Emoji from the original posts were also included, to maintain the sentiments of the original posts, although these were primarily used on Twitter. The A.V. Club was chosen because the site has a robust comment section with a large variety of insightful fan comments. The site boasts many articles about *AJLT*, as well as episode-by-episode reviews. As they say on their site, "We strive to cover pop culture with intelligence and wit," (*The A.V. Club*, 2022, para. 4). The AV Club also moderates the comment section to remove trolling, bullying, and offensive comments. The subreddit r/Andjustlikethat had 811 individual posts, The A.V. Club had 30 *AJLT* individual stories with comment sections, and X's (formerly Twitter's) verified #Andjustlikethat account had 25,600 followers, 365 tweets, and 26,420 retweets. Comments were collected from Twitter (n=9,103), Reddit (n=51,927), and The A.V. Club (n=1,584), for a total of 62,614 posts. Comments stemming from each post were tallied by hand to arrive at the final total. To ensure that rich and thick descriptions of poster attitudes were documents, posts were not edited for spelling or grammar to maintain the language of the commenters (Noble & Smith, 2015).

Due to the volume of data, NVivo 12, a qualitative content analysis software program, was used to sort and code the data thematically. Data were coded using thematic analysis (Braun & Clarke, 2022), which relies on some initial familiarity with the data before codes are developed. In this thematic analysis, major themes were identified in the dataset to guide the analysis. Then, subthemes were identified and coded. The themes identified reinforce the presence of parasocial relationships with *AJLT* characters, and a codebook was developed to evaluate the data for additional themes related to the audience reception of the show content and messages. Additional themes included audience reactions to *AJLT*'s treatment of race, sexuality, gender, and aging.

As a note, although the introduction to this essay reviewed literature about parasocial interactions and parasocial relationships, the results section will refer solely to the concept of parasocial relationships. Further, this essay argues that the depth of emotion and the volume of posts on social media about *AJLT* support the premise that the audience has parasocial bonds with the characters on the show. In accordance with Bernhold & Metzger (2020), the episodic nature of the program means the relationship with the *SATC* and *AJLT* characters is ongoing and has continued for up to several decades (when factoring in the number of seasons, the two films, and the rebooted show). The evaluated posts frequently reference historical character behavior, indicating long-term viewership.

Results

(1) Fan Indications of Parasocial Relationships

PSRs are built from repeated exposure. Many posts discussed the longevity of the viewers' relationships with the characters. For some, these characters were influential in their youth: "This is where I learned so much! I was watching this show as a teenager. And I feel just as much like I grew up with these women" (u/bluehour17, Reddit, January 2022). In other cases, the relationships are discussed as persisting into the future: "I will watch the girls until the end of time because I will always love them no matter how crazy the writing gets lol" (Yuppersforreal, Reddit, February 2022). Even when users were discussing how bad they thought the show was, it seems likely that their PSR was too strong to stop watching it: "I'm just too attached to these characters to not watch every episode/movie ever made" (u/SurrrealThing, Reddit, February 2022). An oft-shared, humorous tweet read: "'And Just Like That' is the worst show on television. If they released a new episode every day I would watch it. It never should have been made. I want 17 more seasons. It deserves every Emmy" (@doioweyoumoney, Twitter, February 2022). This tweet exemplified the common sentiment that fans had a love/hate relationship with *AJLT*. This may have been due in part to the format change that occurred wherein the narration by Carrie, which was omnipresent in the original series, was removed. This did not go unnoticed by viewers: "I miss the voice-overs and the comedy vibe" (RingtailJackman, AVClub, January 2022). The loss of this insight into character behaviors may have seemed like a loss to some viewers, who would no longer be able to peek into the minds of their "friends."

The amount of criticism of the show led one Redditor to post a thread calling for *SATC* and *AJLT* fans to come together and call a "truce" and stop fighting about the show. They write: "I want us to come together as Carries or Charlottes or Samanthas or Mirandas (maybe past Miranda makes more sense—yo I get it, nobody wants to be rom com Miranda) or Anthonys or Stanfords" (u/linds360, Reddit, February 2022). This post harkens back to the *SATC* viewers' identities matching their favorite characters.

However, there are indications that viewers are upset by narrative arcs in *AJLT* that they feel are out of sync with the *SATC* characters. This seems to indicate how much they care about the characters and the story. This mismatch of expectations was often frustrating for the viewers, many of whom had been waiting for another installment in the series for a long time: "They're just pulling storylines out of their asses at this point. I want the old sex and the city where Carrie dates all kinds of dudes. Give me more of that and less of this garbage" (u/TheClaireShow, Reddit, December 2021). Still, some viewers were just so happy to be reunited with their characters that the content was of a lesser concern: "These familiar characters gave me such comfort, I could really care less if the plot holes were big enough to drive a semi through (and they were)!" (u/Dharmatron, Reddit, February 2022). These comments are indicative of long-established, pre–*AJLT* parasocial relationships.

Another indication of the development of PSRs with the characters is when viewers project themselves into the scenes and discuss how they would handle situations. After the *AJLT* main characters got into an argument during a picnic (Season 1, Episode 6), one viewer wrote: "If I were Miranda, I'd be like, yeah get over yourself Carrie, I'm pissed and I'm going to cool off and call Charlotte 1:1 to have an adult conversation with her without you triangulating and making annoyed side comments" (BarbaraDeDrew, The A.V. Club, January 2022). In another example, a user commented about the lack of boundaries between Carrie and her boss, Che, after Che continued to arrive unannounced to visit her in her home after surgery: "I would feel pissed off and humiliated if I were in Carrie's shoes. Back tf [the fuck] up and let me recover in peace around people who are actually family" (u/strike_match, Reddit, December 2021). Such examples demonstrate how viewers are enmeshed in the lives of these characters and feel entwined in the *SATC/AJLT* universe.

(2) Fan Indications of Parasocial Grief

Several events happened in *AJLT* that may have contributed to audience grief. To start, Kim Cattrall did not return to the series to reprise her role of Samantha Jones. Then in the first episode, Carrie's husband John (played by Christopher Noth), but most commonly referred to as Big in the series, died of a sudden heart attack while exercising. Lastly, actor Willie Garson, who played Carrie's gay best friend Stanford, died of pancreatic cancer (Melas, 2021). He was only able to film three episodes, and his character was written off of the show in episode four.

The absence of Samantha Jones' character (played by Kim Cattrall) from *SATC* was a frequent topic on social media. She was tweeted about, and gifs and photos of her were commonly posted on the official *AJLT* Twitter. She elected not to rejoin the cast and the character was written off of the show for *AJLT*.... One fan posted about the reboot: "Lovely! But can't you just cast a look-a-like for the role of Samantha? I like the show, but do miss the character very much. It would only be awkward for one episode and than you'll forget" (@Sneeckertje, March 2022). Clearly, the presence of Samantha is an important part of the overall narrative of this program. Fans even suggested replacement possibilities for this character: "[W]ho will replace Samantha in season 2, Sharon Stone? We need Samantha..(and less Che) I Hope season 2 focus more at you 3–4 girls, like SATC did, too many new characters/stories in AJLT" (@Tazimo22, March 2022). Such comments evidenced PSRs, because the loss of primary characters were felt deeply, and there was a hearty desire to engage more deeply with the *SATC* main four characters, with outside characters seeming to dilute the attention given to the original women.

In the first episode, the loss of Carrie's husband devastated many fans. In Figure 3, above, Carrie attends Big's funeral in episode 2 with her friends Anthony and Stanford. Due to the PSR that viewers had with Carrie and/or Big, who was admittedly a polarizing figure, there were frequent online expressions of grief: "I bawled my eyes out!!!! I was soo shocked and did not see that coming at all. Literaly, snot nose crying … he was such a central focus of the show and I honestly really liked him, flaws and all" (u/Beneficial-Cow-2544, Reddit, February 2022). This sentiment was not unique, as seen in the following post: "I honestly FELT Carrie's pain and grief at Big's funeral" (anewfaceinthecrowd, Reddit, February 2022). For some fans, there seemed to be an intertwined grief of the loss of a long-time character in the program *and* the sensation of empathy on behalf of a character who lost a loved one.

Stanford's character (Willie Garson) was written off of the show quickly as his illness prevented him from wrapping up his character's arc in a meaningful way. Showrunner Michael Patrick King told *E! News* that killing Blatch's character off right after they killed off Big would have put an emotional damper on the show (Contreras, 2022). *AJLT* had Stanford send a letter to Carrie explaining that he was moving to Tokyo to manage a TikToker and another to his husband, Anthony, requesting a divorce. King acknowledged that this was "threadbare" writing, which did not go unnoticed by fans: "Watched and Just Like That and while I appreciate how difficult it was to deal with the death of Willie Garson (on the heels of a major fictional character's death), the way they dispatched Stanford Blatch was pretty shabby" (@Geniusbastard, Twitter, December 2021). There were numerous posts lamenting his death and expressing feelings of loss: "I still can't believe he is gone 💔" (u/OhTinyOne, Reddit, December 2021). In some cases, users posted about real life, but used the character's name, not the actor's name: "I know the big spoiler in 'And Just Like That' is a shocker but losing Stanford in real life hurts so much more. 😢" (@gilbertvotion, Twitter, December 2021). At other times posters suggested possible different storylines for the character, such as moving to Japan with his husband, traveling abroad for an extended period, or moving to a sunny climate.

There was a lot of time spent discussing whether Stanford would get a funeral, and the general sentiment was that the *AJLT* owed him a decent farewell: "I'm sure his passing will be dealt with next season when they have time to give him a proper sendoff" (AndtsNMyEyes, The A.V. Club, December 2021). Others contemplated how difficult it must have been dealing with a storyline involving the death of a main character when Garson was aware that his pancreatic cancer was terminal: "I can't be the only person finding it hard to watch Stanford's reactions to Big's death only to know his own real life death was just around the corner. It's top tier #existentialism" (@eightywone, Twitter, January 2022). In some cases, the PSRs that fans had made the combination of all of the losses quite unbearable: "Watching and just like that, so sad to know Willie Garson aka Stanford is no longer on this earth is so sad. His character was one of my faves. And MR Big 😱 I'm shocked. I must admit I miss Samantha. Since loosing my mum I get so emotional" (@RachAlvarez007, Twitter, December 2021). This comment was consistent with other expressions of grief on social media about these deaths.

(3) Fan Reactions to the Treatment of Race on *AJLT*

The fan reactions to the treatment of race on *AJLT* varied. Many new characters were introduced in *AJLT*, which greatly increased the amount of ethnic diversity to the series. However, there were strong reactions from viewers because each main character got a person of color as a friend, or sidekick, in the program. Dr. Nya Wallace, a Black female professor (played by Karen Pittman), was introduced as Miranda's professor and later as her friend. Seema Patel, played by Sarita Choudhury, is Carrie's high-powered Indian realtor until after the business deal is done and a friendship develops. Charlotte's friend is Lisa Todd Wexley, played by Nicole Ari Parker. She's a stylish Black documentarian whose son takes piano lessons with Charlotte's daughter. These new and diverse characters mark a dramatic turn for the series, both because they represent recurring outside characters (which wasn't common in *SATC*), and because they add new perspectives to a heterogeneous cast.

Audience reactions to the new cast members were mixed. Some viewers lauded the writers and casting directors for moving in the right direction by posting online in defense of these choices to widen the diversity within the narrative. However, there was also a significant amount of online vitriol: "These repeated posts trashing the show's diversity read as super racist and transphobic.—Signed a black woman—with nb [non-binary], trans, and high achieving academics in my friendship circle—who is enjoying the show" (u/SunriseJazz, Reddit, January 2022). As some viewers remark, change must start with the writers: "Screenwriters need to be more aware of the power they have in 'defining' our realities. And we need more POC, transgender and neurodiverse screenwriters for heightened true representation" (u/Nonofyourdamnbiscuit, Reddit, January 2022). Shifts in culture and increased sensitivity to issues of social justice mean that viewers are increasingly more likely to call out writers and producers for poor representation, performative allyship, and other errors of judgment.

Some viewers pointed out that bringing in so many new diverse characters without developing these characters fully created new problems: "I'm a little tired of #andjustlikethat articles saying this show sparked 'lofty and trivial' convo's. This show has the audacity to not reflect on the tokenism, racism & diversity accessorizing they're doing w/ all the black & brown characters" (@moonchild991234, Twitter, January 2022). Another user agreed, adding: "I am glad though that Nya is getting plot lines outside of being Miranda's friend because it was bordering on tokenism" (u/default-user-login, Reddit, January 2022). Yet, some expressed a desire to have more development of these characters: "Nya and LTW were so under utilised. They both had great potential and could have been amazing characters. It's such a shame" (u/rockthrowing, Reddit, December 2021). Online posts indicate how audiences want more than tokenized casting; they want authentic and integrated characters.

A frequent criticism was that the show was trying too hard to be "woke," which may have seemed disingenuous and forced to some fans: "Lol they don't realize that in their virtue signaling about diversity, they ended up looking like they're pandering. Now everyone has a 'Black' friend lol 😂. Racism solved" (@KeonJsteele, Twitter, January 2022). In other cases, this latest effort is just another misstep in a franchise with a troubled track record: "Its like the tone deafness they [*The SATC 2 Movie*] had for the Arab world, they now bring to the woke generation. I enjoy it in a rubbernecking kind of way" (cjob3, The A.V. Club January 2022). Some viewers indicated that this felt off-brand for the characters: "#andjustlikethat went too far to the left. It's too much, and it's not even realistic. Women in their '50s are not going to be that damn #woke!" (@girl_judah, Twitter, December 2021).

The nearly two-decade gap between *SATC* and *AJLT* means some viewers felt that the characters did not evolve in sync with the audience. Figure 1 shows an early encounter between Miranda and Nya. Other viewers complained that the original characters seemed to awkwardly interact with these women of color. Complaints about Miranda and Charlotte were most common: "#AndJustLikeThat is so cringey around race, in a way that clearly we're supposed to be in on the joke about these aging rich white women being well-meaning and clueless, but the effect was that every time a character of color was on, I braced myself for racism" (@SandrasWatching, Twitter, December 2021). However, not all posters agreed. One perceived nuance and redeeming qualities in Miranda's interactions with Nya:

> [As] a poc in nyc, i think her behavior with race seems pretty realistic to me and is not antithetical to her being a progressive. i think the point is Miranda is progressive and woke enough to think that she needs to reflect on and become more aware of how she engages with poc [persons of color]. BUT she's reading a lot of theory and it's coming out weird, bc she is just beginning to apply it in practice [u/sardonicoperasinger, Reddit, January 2022].

The storyline with Miranda and Nya received a lot of criticism and praise. This storyline has more nuance than Lisa or Seema's narrative. However, this does not

Figure 1. Dr. Nya Wallace (Karen Pittman, left) and Miranda Hobbes (Cynthia Nixon) on the subway platform after Miranda helps Nya fend off a mugger (HBO).

mean that it flowed well with the rest of the *AJLT*: "I feel like Nya has had actually the most focus but ... she doesn't really have any connection to the other girls and It's making it feel like a completely separate show when they give Nya POV focus" (u/ShalidorsHusband, Reddit, January 2022). For one thing, as Miranda's professor, there were complaints about the power dynamic: "100% like Nya seems accomplished, professional, put together, not the type of Professor to get super friendly with her students, yet alone the student who is low-key dominating class time with her white fragility" (u/default-user-login, Reddit, January 2022). The show did not directly address the nuances of power dynamics involved in student and professor relationships, but this power disparity was not unnoticed by viewers.

In some cases, the intersectionality of race and class were discussed. One poster indicated that making Nya outrank Miranda was a good idea: "[T]hey were going for a dynamic where the Black character was of higher status. I think it could have worked well if Miranda wasn't so dithering and had her original wit and confidence" (esmeraldaknowsbest, Reddit, January 2022). Ultimately, though, this post seems to indicate that Miranda was unable to skillfully navigate the complexities of the relationship. Another viewer pointed out that working was not a mainstay of the White characters on *AJLT* (although Miranda, and at times Carrie, is an exception): "It's also telling that the POC [persons of color] characters (Che, Lisa, and Seema) all have very clear, believable and visible jobs that are central to their plotlines, while the OG women ... don't. Evolve these women! Let them struggle with ageism and sexism in the workplace at 55" (u/Chazzyphant, Reddit, January 2022). This level of engagement with the current and historical lives of the characters reinforces how PSRs inform character attachment.

(4) Fan Reactions to the Treatment of Gender and Sexuality on *AJLT*

One of the popular topics across social media sites was the show's handling of gender and sexuality. While *SATC* had always featured gay characters and same-sex couples, new characters on *AJLT* expanded the ways that gender and sexuality were depicted. One of the most polarizing characters on the show is Che Diaz, played by Mexican-American actress Sara Ramirez. Che is a non-binary comedian, Carrie's podcast co-host, and they later became romantically involved with Miranda. In Figure 2, Che and Miranda have their first romantic encounter. King insinuated that season 2 of *AJLT* would have much more of Che (Aurthur, 2022). Controversially, the same article questioned whether Che was disliked due to the character's strong personality, that they were the cause of Miranda's betrayal of Steve, or that fans weren't ready for a non-white, non-binary love interest.

One fan expressed pleasure in the inclusion of non-binary characters: "Love it great job. 👣👣👣 Sincerely, a trans nb [non-binary] loving CHANGE and character evolution 💚" (@SlySarkisova, Twitter, March 2022). Others were less enthusiastic: "Hopefully Miranda will get rid of bloody Ché ... please please please. Nothing likeable about that character ... nothing!!" (@KarenNI, Twitter, March 2022). Yet, for many fans the dislike for Che transcended sexual identity. In a response directly to King's

Figure 2. Che Diaz (Sara Ramirez, left) and Miranda Hobbes (Cynthia Nixon) get to know each other better after Che's stand-up comedy show (HBO).

assertion about Che's gender identity causing the negative reaction to the charter, one viewer wrote: "No. It had nothing to do with Che being non-binary. Che was not a likeable character. Example: They told Miranda they were moving across the country in song in front of all their family and friends" (lashesnlipstick, Reddit, June 2022). NoireN (Reddit, June 2022) agreed, writing: "If Che had been more fleshed out and not just the "magical Latinx" person for Miranda's awakening, they would probably have been better received. Instead he [King] wants to go claim people who don't like Che are transphobic." Indeed, the viewers' discussion of Che's character was largely respectful of identity and was careful to use correct pronouns, but many posters indicated feeling insulted by King's assertion that they were perhaps not ready for these progressive storylines.

The fact that there are few non-binary characters cast in mainstream programs was not lost on some viewers: "They finally hire a nonbinary actor to play a nonbinary character and they get THIS storyline and script. I'm honestly embarrassed for Sara Ramirez, who is SO much better than this material" (grasscut_, The A.V. Club, January 2022).

Many people also posted about Miranda's role in the relationship, and how her character was behaving unpredictably by suddenly ending her marriage for a new relationship: "I was also a little bothered by Miranda's erratic nature, as I had always considered myself a 'Miranda' in the past" (Cable, The A.V. Club, January 2022). Indeed, viewers frequently complained about the storyline and the stereotypical behavior: "I'll put it this way: Imagine if they wrote a black character who did nothing but eat fried chicken and watermelon in every scene. Che is that character to the queer community. And before you try to 'Charlotte' me again. I'm a member of the community. And I'm FAR from alone in my opinion" (Spaz, The A.V. Club, January 2022). Viewers who commented on the Che storyline often revealed their own status as nonbinary or Latina/o, which reinforced their opinions about their dissatisfaction with how Che represented these groups on *AJLT*.

Another storyline that received a lot of online attention was the same-sex relationship between Stanford and Anthony. One Redditor mentioned that the open relationship dynamic between this couple, the only recurring gay couple on the show, reinforces gay stereotypes: "I think the community would benefit from seeing a serious, non-straying gay couple on the air. I'm gay and I'm aware I sound pretentious saying this, but it is frustrating that the media typically portrays us as constantly single, hooking up, or reveling in excess. I love me some excess, but there is also very real, very raw emotional & romantic connections we have with each other—and that part just not seen very often in the media" (u/starlightsteward, Reddit, January 2022). Another poster, who self-identified as a gay man, commented that the depictions of gay men on the series was shallow and reductive: "I personally never liked how infantile they made Stanford out to be. It'd be nice to see gay men kinda just existing successfully not tagging along their best girlfriend quipping one liners all the time or next to shirtless men" (u/Cabinet-Exotic, Reddit, January, 2022). Viewers often wrote that gay males on *AJLT* seemed to fulfill a superficial role on the fringes of their straight female friends' lives.

(5) Fan Reactions to the Treatment of Aging on *AJLT*

After the long gap between *SATC* and *AJLT*, the characters and their children, partners, and relationships had obviously aged, leading some viewers to share their reactions. For some viewers, this was an opportunity to applaud the depictions of aging and changes in life stages. For others, the depictions failed to meet expectations or did not ring true. Specifically, several topics in the show attracted viewer attention and prompted online conversations. These were: the physical appearance of the women, Carrie's hip dysplasia, and Steve's hearing aids.

The most visible, and also superficial, topic was the appearance of the characters. One Redditor said that Carrie should wear her hair shoulder length, not long as it was in *AJLT*. Disagreement came swiftly to that post, and one user commented: "I don't agree with her hair having to be shorter due to her age. People have been so harsh on the leading ladies looks. I wish there was more support. We all age" (u/Chandlery, Reddit, December 2021). In other cases, plastic surgery or other aesthetics work was assumed or criticized. Charlotte (Kristin Davis) had multiple threads about her alleged use of fillers: "Oh Christ, Kristen Davis's face 😐. I'm sure she'd look a million times better with no fillers" (u/LakeLov3r, Reddit, January 2022). Others argued that it was overdone and disrupted her speech: "She looks botched, and I'm sure it's completely unnecessary. The fillers or whatever is happening are really distracting and make her lisp!" (u/sweetdee12, Reddit, January 2022). Some posters argued not that the work looked good or bad, but that it was unnecessary in the first place: "[L]et women look their age jfc [jesus fucking christ] this is just downright misogyny they dont have to look 'fuckable to be worthy'" (u/tracynad, Reddit, January 2022). In one episode, Carrie visits a plastic surgeon for a consultation about a face lift. However, one viewer projects herself into Carrie's perspective, and writes: "If I were Carrie, I wouldn't change a thing. Just goes to show you, no one sees themselves the way others do and we all pick ourselves apart" (u/wasitmethewholetime, Reddit, January 2022). There was an abundance of comments about aging naturally, and a lot of criticism of choosing surgical anti-aging beauty procedures.

Other common discussions about the series and aging focused on how the characters were portrayed. Some viewers felt that some in the *SATC* universe seemed older than their characters' chronological ages: "they made women in their 50's look like these little old, feeble ladies who can barely walk while one was trying to look younger than her age and it showed. I especially didn't like the fact that they put hearing aids on Steve. He definitely didn't deserve that lol" (KingJoy79, Reddit, April 2022). Another user responds that it made sense to incorporate hearing aids into Steve's character, and would add dimension to the program: "The actor wears hearing aids. A disability isn't a horrible thing to write in to a plot anyway" (ill-disposed, Reddit, April 2022). Another viewer had a different take on Steve's hearing aids: "The way they have portrayed Steve as some doddering, deaf and confused old man at 55 just to try and make Miranda cheating on him sympathetic is an absolute travesty" (@mikaltempo, Twitter, January 2022). Aging is an uneven process, and it affects people differently. The inclusion of an actor's real-world disability into their character is an admirable choice for supporting inclusivity and authentic representation.

The inclusion of characters' aging process could be important for accurate representations of diversity. There are far fewer shows focusing on the lives of older generations, which gives these viewers fewer opportunities to form PSRs with characters in their age cohort: "I realised while watching it that shows of older women just living their lives are few and far between so I really hope it doesn't go anywhere" (u/Gisschace, Reddit, February 2022). Similar sentiments were exhibited by others, too: "It has been so wonderful seeing a show about the issues that middle aged women face" (@nicislive, Twitter, February 2022). Not all viewers felt as though the characters were relatable: "It honestly feels to me that they took a bunch of 22 y.o.s, had them read the Wiki page about the SATC as the entirety of their research and then had them write this one. Each character is written like what a young person thinks an older person would do/say" (u/BurnedWitch88, Reddit, January 2022). Certainly, lived experiences differ. It seems that the PSRs that viewers have with these characters color their expectations: "They seem determined to keep Carrie the most 'youthful' of the bunch. No kids, no partner, wacky clothes, no real job … she's kind of like an old teenager so far … (u/CommercialStyle4551, Reddit, December 2021). Yet, what may seem "youthful" to one viewer may not be to another.

In a surprising one-episode arc, Carrie's presumed arthritis, which she calls "old lady disease," is actually diagnosed as the congenital disorder hip dysplasia (Robespierre, 2021). She undergoes a procedure and is soon back to her old self, high heels and all. For many viewers, this quick decline and improvement seemed too good to be true. One poster, who was the third generation to be afflicted with this disorder, posted: "As a sufferer and a feminist, I find it disappointing, because it's a very superficial, unrealistic treatment of a situation that was life-altering for me and deepened my disappointment about how women and girls are treated by doctors" (u/molten_suns, Reddit, February 2022). Another poster concurred, stating that it would have been preferable to indicate that the hip disorder was degenerative, not congenital. Meaning, that this type of medical issue would be more in line with normal aging: "[T]hey had to make it clear CARRIE had a ;congenital hip condition' from birth so SHE'S NOT AN OLD LADY, YA'LL! Don't you dare think it! SJP/Carrie is impervious to the harrows of aging and marches of time 😬" (u/CommercialStyle4551, Reddit, December 2021). These comments suggest story arcs inclusive of natural aging processes might be well received by audiences. However, the ability to handle the potential ancillary topics, such as aging female bodies, disparities in healthcare disparities, and ableism, may be beyond the show's depth. As one viewer suggests: "this show isn't super deep.... The show has literally always dealt with big complex things in a simple sentence" (ohnoray, The A.V. Club, January 2022). It may be that *AJLT*, however, might spark some of these conversations which viewers can continue within online communities.

Discussion

Viewers frequently mentioned the length of time that they had been involved with the *SATC/AJLT* characters, which reinforced the work of many scholars who write about the enduring nature of PSRs (Dibble et al., 2016; Hartmann & Goldhoorn, 2011). Demographic data was not collected in this study, but many posters identified themselves as females, and spoke of their relationships with the primary female characters on the program. This seems to reinforce the findings that women form stronger parasocial bonds (Cohen, 2003), and that PSRs with same-gender characters are deeper (Hall, 2019). Posts often referenced various details from a character's history in *SATC* or either of the movies, either using these points as support or criticism of *AJLT* character plots or dialogue. Such posts reinforced the longevity of the PSRs.

Although uncommon in dramatic television, early episodes of *SATC* frequently used direct addresses of the audience by the main character, Carrie Bradshaw. This may explain the deep attachment by many viewers to the characters in the program (Cohen et al., 2019; Dibble et al., 2016). Another common feature in *SATC* was the use of narration (Arthurs, 2003). Again, the main character, Carrie Bradshaw, will often advance the plot, give greater insight into character thoughts and actions, and include sweeping musings about life and love. This is consistent with Semmler et al.'s (2015) findings, that narration is indicative of stronger parasocial engagement with the narrating character. However, since *AJLT* did not have Carrie narrate the episodes, as multiple women mentioned missing in their online comments, this may have contributed to the feeling of distance between the relaunched characters and the audience. One of the functions of the narration is for characters to add insight into their feelings and provide additional background information, and this lack of additional connection was noticed.

The aspect of aging was frequently discussed by fans online. Interestingly, the opinions varied a great deal about the accuracy of these depictions, what physical markers were appropriate for the characters' ages, and how the characters looked. In some cases, it seemed as though even a PSR was not enough to prevent the criticism of the characters appearance, actions, or storyline. Rather, it may be the case that the stronger the PSR, the more likely the audience member is to find displeasure if the character's actions or words displease them. This is likely because PSRs extend the depth of connection to TV shows and characters, so it would make sense to see strong feelings of support or dislike and discussion on personal subjects such as aging, race, sexuality, and gender extended to online communal spaces.

Limitations and Directions for Future Research

One primary limitation of this study is that all of the information gathered in this study was publicly available data on social media sites. The limitation of this approach is that only people who share feelings in these venues were included in the study, and these opinions may differ from those who do not post online. Another limitation is that undoubtedly those who post on these sites also read these sites. Therefore, it is possible that these social media sites can become echo chambers in which opinions grow more similar the more that people spend immersed in these groups. The variety of opinions gathered throughout this study, however, does suggest that this is not the case. Another limitation of the study is that people who have unpopular opinions about the *AJLT* may not post because of fear of retribution from dissenting community members. This is difficult to discern unless other types of audience reception research was undertaken, such as surveys or interviews. Finally, the anonymous nature of the Internet makes it difficult to discern one's identity, determine if they are being truthful, or separate actual attitudes and opinions from trolling behaviors. However, several of the sites were moderated (Reddit and The A.V. Club), but Twitter has less oversight.

Future research may consider using other methods of inquiry as previously mentioned, such as surveys, interviews, or focus groups to more precisely investigate the nature of parasocial relationships and parasocial grief. Unlike other characters, those in *SATC* and *AJLT* had a lengthy gap between iterations of the programs. Thus, it is possible that the PSRs may have waned in the intervening years. Future research may explore whether relationship closeness may ebb and flow throughout the duration of PSRs. Perhaps the freshness of *AJLT* or the long interval since new content was created for the *SATC* universe may have created a honeymoon effect wherein the excitement of the PSR hit higher peaks. The anticipation of the reboot may have also created extraordinarily high expectations on behalf of viewers. Due to the uniqueness of the long hiatus of this program, there is a gap in the literature about parasocial relationships and reboots. However, the recent uptick in the number of rebooted TV programs, such as *The Wonder Years* (2021–2023), *Fuller House* (2016–2020), *Bel-Air* (2022–), *Girl Meets World* (2014–2017), and *BH90210* (2019), among others, indicate a need for further research.

Conclusion

Altogether, comments posted on these media and social media outlets (Twitter, Reddit, and The A.V. Club) support the argument that PSRs exist between the audience and the *AJLT* characters. Viewers seem to feel very protective of the characters with whom they have PSRs, which may lead to very strong opinions about story arcs, character development, and casting decisions. Writers and producers are working in a time in which viewers can easily share these opinions online to wide audiences. Greater pressure, too, exists for the careful representation and inclusion of traditionally underrepresented groups. However, as *AJLT* shows us, efforts that take well known characters too far afield may ring hollow and disingenuous by long-time fans.

Further, the comments also support that parasocial grief has been felt by the audience after experiencing loss of these characters. In some cases, this experience of grief was mingled between the sense of loss of character and the complexity of real-world allegations of criminal behavior. The blurred line between characters and the actors by whom they are embodied may be difficult for some fans to separate. As the characters age, so do the actors playing those roles. The potential for losing these actors increases, which brings increasing risk of parasocial grief. Even when viewers know the reasons behind the character's loss (such as real-world death, retirement, scandal, other roles, etc.), this does not seem to diminish the sense of parasocial grief.

References

Arthurs, J. (2003). *Sex and the City* and consumer culture: Remediating postfeminist drama. *Feminist Media Studies, 3*(1), 83–98. https://doi.org/10.1080/1468077032000080149.

Aurthur, K. (2022). Yep, I'm Che: Sara Ramírez reveals all about 'And Just Like That,' romancing Miranda and TV's buzziest queer character. *Variety.* https://variety.com/2022/tv/features/sara-ramirez-and-just-like-that-che-diaz-miranda-nonbinary-1235281242/.

Auter, P.J. (1992). TV that talks back: An experimental validation of a parasocial interaction scale. *Journal of Broadcasting & Electronic Media, 36*(2), 173–181. https://doi.org/10.1080/08838159209364165.

Auter, P.J., & Davis, D.M. (1991). When characters speak directly to viewers: Breaking the fourth wall in television. *Journalism and Mass Communication Quarterly, 68*(1), 165–171. https://doi.org/10.1177/107769909106800117.

The A.V. Club. (2022). About. https://www.avclub.com/about.

Baldwin, J.A., & Raney, A.A. (2021). Enjoyment of unoriginal characters: Individual differences in nostalgia-proneness and parasocial relationships. *Mass Communication and Society, 24*(5), 748–768. https://doi.org/10.1080/15205436.2021.1916035.

Baldwin, M.W. (1992). Relational schemas and the processing of social information. *Psychological Bulletin, 112*(3), 461–484. https://psycnet.apa.org/doi/10.1037/0033-2909.112.3.461.

Bernhold, Q.S., & Metzger, M. (2020). Older adults' parasocial relationships with favorite television characters and depressive symptoms. *Health Communication, 35*(2), 168–179. https://doi.org/10.1080/10410236.2018.1548336

Blake, M., & McNamara, M. (2021, December 10). How terrible is the 'Sex and the City' reboot? We duke it out. *Los Angeles Times,* 7.

Bostwick, E.N., & Lookadoo, K.L. (2017). The return of the king: How Cleveland reunited with Lebron James after a parasocial breakup. *Communication & Sport, 5*(6), 689–711. https://doi.org/10.1177/2167479516659460.

Braun, V., & Clarke, V. (2022). Conceptual and design thinking for thematic analysis. *Qualitative Psychology, 9*(1), 3–26. https://doi.org/10.1037/qup0000196.

Cohen, J. (2003). Parasocial breakups: Measuring individual differences in responses to the dissolution of parasocial relationships. *Mass Communication and Society, 6*(2), 191–202. https://doi.org/10.1207/S15327825MCS0602_5.

Cohen, J., Oliver, M.B., & Bilandzic, H. (2019). The differential effects of direct address on parasocial experience and identification: Empirical evidence for conceptual difference. *Communication Research Reports, 36*(1), 78–83. https://doi.org/10.1080/08824096.2018.1530977.

Contreras, C. (2022, February 2). *And Just Like That's* original plans for Willie Garson's Standford Blatch revealed. *E! News.* https://www.eonline.com/news/1318379/and-just-like-thats-original-plans-for-willie-garsons-stanford-blatch-revealed?source=twitter-enews&content=organic&medium=-link-post&cmpid=social&fbclid=IwAR2o8UmLTDdUk-QUgS9HlQG0leHKz-a3mRRg847fJVXrDZr5KeaXIQYKWqQ.

DeGroot, J.M., & Leith, A.P. (2018). R.I.P. Kutner: Parasocial grief following the death of a television character. *OMEGA—Journal of Death and Dying, 77*(3), 199–216. https://doi.org/10.1177/0030222815600450.

Dibble, J.L., Hartmann, T., & Rosaen, S.F. (2016). Parasocial interaction and parasocial relationship: Conceptual clarification and a critical assessment of measures. *Human Communication Research, 42*(1), 21–44. https://doi.org/10.1111/hcre.12063.

Eyal, K., & Cohen, J. (2006). When good *Friends* say goodbye: A parasocial breakup study. *Journal of Broadcasting & Electronic Media, 50*(3), 502–523. https://doi.org/10.1207/s15506878jobem5003_9.

Ferchaud, A., Grzeslo, J., Orme, S., & LaGroue, J. (2018). Parasocial attributes and YouTube personalities:

Exploring content trends across the most subscribed YouTube channels. *Computers in Human Behavior, 80,* 88–96. https://doi.org/10.1016/j.chb.2017.10.041.

Ferchaud, A., Yan, Z., & Daniel, E.S. (2022). Binging on the heartbreak: The effect of binge-watching on narrative engagement and parasocial breakups. *Psychology of Popular Media,* 1–11. https://doi.org/10.1037/ppm0000414.

Foss, K.A. (2020). Death of the slow-cooker or #CROCK-POTISINNOCENT? *This Is Us,* parasocial grief, and the Crock-Pot crisis. *Journal of Communication Inquiry, 44*(1), 69–89. https://doi.org/10.1177/0196859919826534.

Freeman, H. (2010, May). The *Sex and the City* films have destroyed the legacy of a funny and fantastic TV show. *The Guardian.* https://www.theguardian.com/film/2010/may/23/sex-and-the-city-film-terrible.

Gardner, W.L., & Knowles, M.L. (2008). Love makes you real: Favorite television characters are perceived as "real" in a social facilitation paradigm. *Social Cognition, 26*(2), 156–168. https://doi.org/10.1521/soco.2008.26.2.156.

Gerhard, J. (2005). *Sex and the City*: Carrie Bradshaw's queer postfeminism. *Feminist Media Studies, 5*(1), 37–49. https://doi.org/10.1080/14680770500058173.

Goss, L. (2021). Revoking the irrevocable: On allyship and performativity. *Journal of Dramatic Theory and Criticism, 35*(2), 99–102. https://doi.org/10.1353/dtc.2021.0027.

Hall, A.E. (2019). Identification and parasocial relationships with characters from *Star Wars: The Force Awakens. Psychology of Popular Media Culture, 8*(1), 88–98. https://doi.org/10.1037/ppm0000160.

Hartmann, T., & Goldhoorn, C. (2011). Horton and Wohl revisited: Exploring viewers' experience of parasocial interaction. *Journal of Communication, 61*(6), 1104–1121. https://doi.org/10.1111/j.1460-2466.2011.01595.x.

Horton, D., & Wohl, R.R. (1956). Mass communication and para-social interaction: Observations on intimacy at a distance. *Psychiatry, 19*(3), 215–229.

Kalina, P. (2020). Performative allyship. *Technium Social Sciences Journal, 11,* 478–481. https://doi.org/10.47577/tssj.v11i1.1518.

Klimmt, C., Hartmann, T., & Schramm, H. (2006). Parasocial interactions and relationships. In J. Bryant & P. Vorderer (Eds.), *Psychology of entertainment* (pp. 291–313). Lawrence Erlbaum & Associates.

Kyewski, E., Szczuka, J.M., & Krämer, N.C. (2018). The protagonist, my Facebook friend: How cross-media extensions are changing the concept of parasocial interaction. *Psychology of Popular Media Culture, 7*(1), 2–17. https://doi.org/10.1037/ppm0000109.

Lacalle, C., Gómez-Morales, B., & Narvaiza, S. (2021). Friends or just fans? Parasocial relationships in online television fiction communities. *Communication & Society, 34*(3), 61–76. https://doi.org/10.15581/003.34.3.61-76.

Lather, J., & Moyer-Guse, E. (2011). How do we react when our favorite characters are taken away? An examination of a temporary parasocial breakup. *Mass Communication and Society, 14*(2), 196–215. https://doi.org/10.1080/15205431003668603.

Leith, A.P. (2021). Parasocial cues: The ubiquity of parasocial relationships on Twitch. *Communication Monographs, 88*(1), 111–129. https://doi.org/10.1080/03637751.2020.1868544.

Longeretta, E. (2021, December 8). 'And Just Like That': Everything we know about the 'Sex and the City' revival. *US Weekly.* https://www.usmagazine.com/entertainment/pictures/sex-and-the-city-revival-what-we-know-about-and-just-like-that/.

Lueck, J.A. (2015). Friend-zone with benefits: The parasocial advertising of Kim Kardashian. *Journal of Marketing Communications, 21*(2), 91–109. https://doi.org/10.1080/13527266.2012.726235.

Lunt, P., & Pantti, M. (2007). Popular culture and the public sphere: Currents of feeling and social control in talk shows and reality TV. In R. Butsch (Ed.), *Media and Public Spheres.* Palgrave Macmillan. https://doi.org/10.1057/9780230206359_13.

Lyles, C.R., López, A., Pasick, R., & Sarkar, U. (2013). "5 mins of uncomfyness is better than dealing with cancer 4 a lifetime": An exploratory qualitative analysis of cervical and breast cancer screening dialogue on twitter. *Journal of Cancer Education, 28*(1), 127–133. https://doi.org/10.1007/s13187-012-0432-2.

Melas, C. (2021, December 23). "And Just Like That..." sends off Willie Garson in emotional goodbye. *CNN.* https://www.cnn.com/2021/12/23/entertainment/and-just-like-that-willie-garson/index.html.

Nahman, E. (2019, June 6). We totally forgot how weird the first episode of *SATC* was. *Repeller.* https://repeller.com/satc-rewatch/.

Noble, H., & Smith, J. (2015). Issues of validity and reliability in qualitative research. *Evidence Based Nursing, 18*(2), 34–35. https://doi.org/10.1136/eb-2015-102054.

Rasmussen, L. (2018). Parasocial interaction in the digital age: An examination of relationship building and the effectiveness of YouTube celebrities. *The Journal of Social Media in Society, 7*(1), 280–294.

Robespierre, G. (Director). (2021, December 30). Tragically hip (No. 5). In *And just like that...* New York. Home Box Office.

Rotten Tomatoes. (2022a). And Just Like That...: *Season 1.* Rottentomatoes.Com. https://www.rottentomatoes.com/tv/and_just_like_that/s01.

Rotten Tomatoes. (2022b). Sex and the City: *Season 6*. Rottentomatoes.Com. https://www.rottentomatoes.com/tv/sex_and_the_city/s06.

Rubin, A.M., Perse, E.M., & Powell, R.A. (1985). Loneliness, parasocial interaction, and local television news viewing. *Human Communication Research, 12*(2), 155–180. https://doi.org/10.1111/j.1468-2958.1985.tb00071.x.

Savage, M.E., & Spence, P.R. (2014). Will you listen? An examination of parasocial interaction and credibility in radio. *Journal of Radio & Audio Media, 21*(1), 3–19. https://doi.org/10.1080/19376529.2014.891214.

Schmid, H., & Klimmt, C. (2011). A magically nice guy: Parasocial relationships with Harry Potter across different cultures. *International Communication Gazette, 73*(3), 252–269. https://doi.org/10.1177/1748048510393658.

Semmler, S.M., Loof, T., & Berke, C. (2015). The influence of audio-only character narration on character and narrative engagement. *Communication Research Reports, 32*(1), 63–72. https://doi.org/10.1080/08824096.2014.989976.

Sharf, Z. (2022, May 5). Kim Cattrall reunites the 'Sex and the City' crew absent from 'And Just Like That.' *Variety*. https://variety.com/2022/tv/news/kim-cattrall-reunites-sex-and-the-city-crew-1235259066/.

Stever, G.S., & Lawson, K. (2013). Twitter as a way for celebrities to communicate with fans: Implications for the study of parasocial interaction. *North American Journal of Psychology, 15*(2), 339–354.

Tian, Q., & Hoffner, C.A. (2010). Parasocial interaction with liked, neutral, and disliked characters on a popular TV series. *Mass Communication and Society, 13*(3), 250–269. https://doi.org/10.1080/15205430903296051.

Tian, Y., & Yoo, J.H. (2015). Connecting with *The Biggest Loser*: An extended model of parasocial interaction and identification in health-related reality tv shows. *Health Communication, 30*(1), 1–7. https://doi.org/10.1080/10410236.2013.836733.

Tolentino, J. (2022, February 16). Candace Bushnell is back in the city. *The New Yorker*, 10.

Tukachinsky, R., & Eyal, K. (2018). The psychology of marathon television viewing: Antecedents and viewer involvement. *Mass Communication and Society, 21*(3), 275–295. https://doi.org/10.1080/15205436.2017.1422765.

Vinney, C., & Vinney, L.A. (2017). That sounds familiar: The relationship between listeners' recognition of celebrity voices, perceptions of vocal pleasantness, and engagement with media. *Journal of Radio & Audio Media, 24*(2), 320–338. https://doi.org/10.1080/19376529.2017.1346659.

Wang, Q., Fink, E.L., & Cai, D.A. (2008). Loneliness, gender, and parasocial interaction: A uses and gratifications approach. *Communication Quarterly, 56*(1), 87–109. https://doi.org/10.1080/01463370701839057.

Warren, S. (2020). Binge-watching as a predictor of narrative transportation using HLM. *Journal of Broadcasting & Electronic Media, 64*(2), 89–110. https://doi.org/10.1080/08838151.2020.1718985.

Wilson, S. (2016). In the living room: Second screens and TV audiences. *Television & New Media, 17*(2), 174–191. https://doi.org/10.1177/1527476415593348.

Wulf, T., & Rieger, D. (2018). Wallowing in media past: Media-induced nostalgia's connection to parasocial relationships. *Communication Research Reports, 35*(2), 178–182. https://doi.org/10.1080/08824096.2017.1383236.

Wulf, T., Schneider, F.M., & Queck, J. (2021). Exploring viewers' experiences of parasocial interactions with videogame streamers on Twitch. *Cyberpsychology, Behavior, and Social Networking, 24*(10), 648–653. https://doi.org/10.1089/cyber.2020.0546.

Zuraikat, L. (2020). The parasocial nature of the podcast. In Hendricks (Ed.), *Radio's second century: Past, present, and future perspectives* (pp. 39–52). Rutgers University Press. https://doi.org/10.36019/9780813598505-005.

Ms. Marvel Beyond Cancel Culture

Multicultural Casting and Mixed Reviews

Farha B. Ternikar

When news was announced online in 2020 that a Ms. Marvel television series was in production, South Asian and Muslim fans in particular expressed their excitement on social media. There were posts on X (formerly Twitter), Instagram and Facebook sharing their anticipation. On December 1, 2020, Salaam Getaway posted on X: "Muslims are increasingly visible in western media eg Ms. Marvel on Disney features a Muslim superhero." On December 12, 2020, Define American tweeted: "Think of all the kids who will grow up watching Ms. Marvel, a 16-year old Pakistani-American superhero." Audiences purportedly had high hopes for the first televised Muslim superhero who would also be female and Pakistani American. Yet, slowly as details were revealed, both about casting choices in terms of ethnicity and religious identity, slight suspicions about the politics of representation took root among online fan groups, even though there was still a strong amount of anticipation from Instagram and X fans. However, once Disney+ aired the first episode in June 2022, audience reception varied. Rotten Tomatoes critical ratings fluctuated between 98 and 99 percent, while the audience score ranged from 50 percent to 79 percent. Historically, superhero and comic book fans have been overwhelmingly male and White, but once the show aired, though there was still very positive feedback from some minority viewers, there was a backlash from many viewers, to include nuanced criticism from some South Asian and Muslim viewers. For example, "Historically, comic books have been a cultural space dominated by White, masculine characters and audiences, leaving narratives for women and minority characters as significantly underrepresented or portrayed in stereotypical contexts" (Hunt, 2018; Davis, 2013; Hall and Lucal, 1999; Singer, 2002). Hunt (2018) explores how though the fanbase is predominantly white and male, there is an increasing portrayal of diversity in comic books and comic-based films.

By taking a closer look at online review sites like IMDb and Metacritic, this essay emphasizes how audience response by building on Stuart Hall's reception theory is shaped by social location, especially race, gender and religion. An intersectional analysis of reader response disrupts the hegemonic discourse around how dominant viewers may react to characters or shows that challenge the status quo. This mode of analysis can offer important frameworks for how to move beyond negative connotations of cancel culture in terms of understanding how patriarchy, White Eurocentrism and xenophobia play out among dominant and oppositional responses.

This essay explores how much influence viewers have, along with how a viewer's response may also reflect xenophobic and patriarchal attitudes of superhero or comic book film and television viewers. Race, gender, immigration, and religion all play an important part in audience reception. By bringing together audience reception theory and intersectionality, we are able to develop a nuanced understanding of both the successes of this show in terms of making strides in representation but also theorize why audience reception has been so uneven. This essay looks to social media to understand how viewers responded to both casting choices and political storylines. Audience reception was also very divisive regarding important sub themes depicted on *Ms. Marvel*, including the history of the partition of India and Pakistan.

This is an important contribution to using audience reception theory in an intersectional analysis but also expands the analysis of diversity in television beyond cancel culture. Cancel culture is a practice by which controversial individuals are targeted by the public in order to "cancel" or remove them from popular culture or social media. In the case of television, we can see how this has played out with actors like Roseanne (Vallette 2022). The character of Ms. Marvel is a Pakistani Muslim girl named Kamala Khan. Khan (played by Iman Vellani) is actually portrayed by an actress of the same background, considered by some critics and viewers as progress in terms of racial, religious and immigrant diversity in television. Additionally, the ongoing nuances of the portrayal of the entire cast, as well as the political storylines, lend itself to further analysis. Even though at times the show might miss the mark in regards to the accurate portrayal of the Pakistani and Muslim characters, it would not necessarily be canceled by minority viewers.

This essay will analyze the character portrayals on *Ms. Marvel*, using Stuart Hall's reception theory to review impacts of online viewer posts from Reddit, Rotten Tomatoes, and IMDb. Examining posts from three review sites reveals problematic gender and racial attitudes of fans. These three sites are the most popular and often cited online review sites, and therefore a cross-section of these sites represents a slice of audience views. An overview of female and Muslim character representation in the Marvel Cinematic Universe and in other fictional spaces like film and television helps frame this analysis.

Female Superheroes: Beyond Marvel's Universe

Ms. Marvel is a character that expands the repertoire of Marvel's female superhero line-up, while also creating implications for superheroes beyond the Marvel Universe. Though Ms. Marvel is not the first female superhero to be on the small or large screen, she is the first Muslim superhero to appear on the small screen. Ms. Marvel (aka Vellani) was cast alongside Captain Marvel (Brie Larson) in the film *The Marvels* (2023). In the much anticipated *The Marvels*, Captain Marvel and Ms. Marvel finally meet. They play opposite Teyonah Parris, who plays Monica Rambeau. These three female actresses together exemplify what is possible in terms of representation changes in superhero films (see Figure 1).

Figure 1. Captain Marvel, Ms. Marvel, and Spectrum. 2022 (Marvel).

The earliest female superheroes can be traced to the small screen with *ISIS* (1975) and *Wonder Woman* (1975), and later on the big screen with *Supergirl* (1984). Though these representations were all very significant especially in terms of early portrayals of female superheroes in television, they were all white and they were all Euro-American White superheroes. *ISIS* debuted in 1975 and was the first American television show to feature a lead with superpowers (*New York Times*, 2021). *The Bionic Woman* debuted in 1976, *Wonder Woman* debuted in 1975 and lasted four seasons until 1979. These three television shows in the 1970s were all ground-breaking for having female-led casts breaking the male mold of superheroes, but they were all White.

Technically *Supergirl* (1984) was the first attempt at a female superhero blockbuster film, but it didn't have the ratings or reviews of *Wonder Woman 1984*. *Elektra* (2005), even though it starred Jennifer Garner, also didn't have high box-office success. In terms of films, *Wonder Woman* (2017) by DC was the first female led superhero/comic book film that became a blockbuster. It is also noteworthy to point out that it was directed by Patty Jenkins, the first female director for a superhero film. Mahji (2017) notes "the comic world is replete with very strong and dynamic female superheroes, but unfortunately, no superhero movie, if *Wonder Woman* excluded, where a woman is found in the leading role could turn out to be a blockbuster one" (p. 5). After *Wonder Woman*'s success, *Captain Marvel* also became a box office hit.

Though there was great success with *Wonder Woman* on the large screen, both *Captain Marvel* and *Ms. Marvel* didn't receive rave reviews initially on social media. This may have more to do with casting choices and story lines, or patriarchy and racism as perceived by some viewers. Taking an intersectional approach, a combination of sexism, racism, and patriarchal norms may help explain audience response and ratings.

Muslims on the Small Screen

Though Ms. Marvel was not the first female superhero on the big or small screen, she is the first Muslim superhero to be televised. I want to frame that in terms of the significance of the show as a portrayal of Muslim women, and in particular against the backdrop of popular culture with the success of Muslim men in Hollywood. Though several Muslim men have had success in American entertainment, we haven't seen the same for women until Iman Vellani. Muslims in popular culture have largely been shaped by patriarchy, heteronormativity and the Western gaze.

In the last 10 years, there's been an increase in the representation of Muslim characters in television. In the past, Muslim portrayals were most often characterized by negative stereotypes, particularly the terrorist trope. Recent Muslim portrayals have moved past this trope, leading to more varied perspectives on Muslim representation. As several scholars have highlighted, especially after 9/11, Arab and Muslim characters were limited to the roles of terrorists in shows like *24* (Selod 2018, Choudhury, 2020). Significant actors in shows include Ramy Youssef, Kumal Nunjani, and Hasan Manaj. These actors have all contributed and helped develop Muslim comedy on the small screen even though they have been critiqued by Muslim and feminist scholars for some of the gendered and overly-stereotypical aspects of their works (Chaudhry 2019).

Ramy Youssef's (2019–2020) show *Ramy* in particular was one of the few portrayals of Muslim American men that rang true for Muslims, particularly Arab American Muslims raised in the United States. Kumal Nunjani, who starred in *Silicon Valley* (2014–2020), portrayed Dinesh, a tech guy, in a very macho environment that also reinforced the misogyny of both tech culture but also the portrayal of Muslim (even secular) actors. Lastly Hasan Minaj challenged some of the stereotypes in his stand-up comedy show *Patriot Act* but was also seen as a breakthrough artist for both Muslim and South Asian American audiences (Chaudhry, 2019). By 2019, the question raised by some critics and viewers was: *where was the portrayal of Muslim women on the small screen?*

Kamala Khan's character is not just a portrayal of a Muslim girl in America. Instead, Khan can be considered a very sophisticated portrayal with attention to details including her wardrobe, music, friends, and hobbies. Miram Kent (2015) writes:

> Kamala's visibility in the mainstream media thus marks a breakthrough for Muslim women's representation in the West. Her conception originates from a completely different ideological space: Kamala is a Pakistani-American with a Muslim background living in New Jersey, who idolizes the Avengers and writes fanfiction. … Unlike Dust, Kamala's introduction served more than shock value, instead seeking to elaborate a genuine contemporary female subjectivity [3].

The *Ms. Marvel* streaming show is based on the comic book of the same name. Some criticism of the comic book accuses Kamala of being an assimilationist character which can also be seen in the audience feedback, especially by Muslim viewers online. In addition, Kent (2015) notes how

> Ms. Marvel's achievements in bringing a female Muslim Pakistani-American subjectivity into the limelight should not be underestimated. Kamala Khan was conceived as a realization of the potentials of the contemporary superhero narrative to resonate the diversity of comic book audiences. That said, examination of the critical reception of the book reveals a need for the character to be relatable to everyone (whoever "everyone" may be). Intersectional feminists still have much work to do until such a character can be appreciated without the need for assimilation [p. 5].

The question about the need for assimilation is something that critics of both the comic book and film equally seem to grapple with. Is Kamala's character assimilationist if she represents the American Muslim experience for Muslim teenagers in the United States?

The First Muslim Superhero?

In addition to HBO's *Sort Of* (2021–2024), the British show *We Are Lady Parts* (2021–present) also offered alternatives to the trope of the Muslim woman as oppressed or the Muslim women as exotic. But the most high-profile representation of Muslim women on the small screen came with Iman Vellani starring as Kamala Khan in *Ms. Marvel*. This representation moves beyond orientalism or the history of objectifying Asian women in popular culture (Said, 1978). Using orientalism as an important foundational theoretical framework which has been used to explore how Muslims and Arabs have been stereotyped as terrorists (i.e., harem girls or "the other" in the history of American film and television), underscores why *Ms. Marvel* is so significant.

Khan's character is noteworthy not only because she's a female superhero, but also because of the significant editorial choices the writers and directors made in how she would be portrayed. Bisha Ali, the head writer and showrunner, made very specific choices in both casting and character development to stay true to her vision of an authentic American Pakistani teenager. NPR (2022) reported how "head writer Bisha K. Ali says Khan's character was informed by her own experiences growing up in England as the child of Pakistani-born parents, as well as the experiences of other second-generation writers" (Briger, 2022, para. 2).

Though there are divergent responses from both South Asian, Pakistani, and Muslim viewers, I will discuss how and why several groups of viewers did not necessarily view the show from a dominant or oppositional lens. They ended up with a negotiated reading of the show. In the next section, two important theoretical frameworks help us further analyze the show with an emphasis on understanding audience reception.

Audience Reception Theory and Intersectionality

This essay applies both Stuart Hall's reception theory and intersectionality to an analysis of the reception of television show, *Ms. Marvel*. Stuart Hall's reception theory is an important framework for analyzing television, especially in the contemporary era. He uses a three-part typology to study audience reception—dominant, negotiated, and oppositional audiences (Hall, 1993). These three audience types are critical to Hall's concepts of encoding/decoding which can challenge dominant readings of text or in this case television. This idea of decoding emphasized that though dominant culture often seeks to maintain the status quo, through the decoding process audience members can disrupt hegemonic understanding of culture. Here it can be acknowledged how race and gender can play an important role in the decoding process. Through social media platforms like X and Instagram, viewers may establish some communication with show writers and directors that can disrupt the decoding process.

Castleberry expands that Hall's concept of encoding or decoding helps us understand the role of the audience. In particular, Castleberry (2016) discusses, "these decoding processes include differentiating between *dominant-hegemonic*, *negotiated*, and *oppositional* readings of texts" (p. 85). According to Garret and Castleberry (2016), "Oppositional positions can be difficult to peg down in television shows. Television is a social institution and an evolving medium, which wields dynamic social, cultural, and political sway. Thus, we can observe that television, in whatever form it assumes, holds a dominant ideological presence" (p. 95). In terms of understanding what the dominant reading of *Ms. Marvel* is—this could be complicated by religion and immigration, in addition to race and gender. Having a Muslim lead with a predominantly Muslim cast and storylines creates some complexity in understanding how the dominant or oppositional readings of *Ms. Marvel* may be received. We can further develop this analysis to explore how political discourse, especially in the contemporary climate shaped by the Trump administration and its aftermath, adds another layer to understanding oppositional or negotiated when it involves viewer response.

Paired with audience reception theory, intersectionality offers an important framework for furthering the analysis of Muslim women in *Ms. Marvel*. Popularized by Kimberlé Crenshaw, intersectionality is an important framework for using race, class, and gender as important interlocking factors to critically examine the status of women in society. I add religion to this intersectional analysis in my previous work that examined Muslim women and modest fashion and media.

Turning to the foundational framework from Kimberlé Crenshaw and Patricia Hills Collins (2011), intersectionality emphasizes the need to go beyond a gender analysis in order to explore how patriarchy and gender inequality work in interaction with race, class, and sexuality as interlocking modes of oppression. Patricia Hills Collins (2015) wrote, "The term intersectionality references the critical insight that race, class, gender, sexuality, ethnicity, nation, ability, and age operate not as unitary, mutually exclusive entities, but as reciprocally constructing phenomena that in turn shape complex inequalities" (p. 2). Contemporary intersectionality is a theoretical paradigm that is ever-changing and often is in conversation with transnational feminism, particularly with non-western understandings of gender and feminism (Narayan, 1997). Purkayashtana (2012) adds a transnational layer to intersectionality:

> Understanding and attending to the complexities of transnationalism—composed of structures within, between and across-nation-states, and virtual spaces—alerts us to look for other axes of domination and the limits of using "women of color" concepts, as we use them now, to look across and within nation-states to understand the impact of transnationalism [p. 613].

When examining Pakistani or Muslim characters in popular culture, it's also important to add religion to this framework.

I also add religion and immigrant status to this framework in my analysis of how social media highlight collective identities in the American context, especially in the current U.S. political climate (Ternikar, 2021). I apply intersectionality to the racialized and gendered "Desi" performance that takes place within immigrant communities. My own research has used intersectionality, race, class, gender, sexuality, and religion to explore how Muslim women are portrayed in social media. Though in many cases we have seen an increase in representation in terms of religion, race, and gender, I emphasize that there are hegemonic representations of women that reinforce racialized, classed, and heterosexist understandings of Muslim women. Similar to television, social media also has a relationship with its viewers and audience reception does create a back and forth between content creators and viewers or audience members. In this essay, I use intersectionality along with audience reception theory to develop a critical analysis of *Ms. Marvel*. Representation matters but there is still much more work to do. The character of Ms. Marvel represents a Muslim American girl in a way that American viewers have never seen before. Yet questions around audience reception help solidify why representation is important but what audience reception reveals about predominantly White male viewers. Anderson et al. (2021) suggested,

> Though not necessarily a new constraint, audiences increasingly make demands of creators and studios to influence content and shape productions. The novelty, and sometimes effectiveness, of such demands, is in part the result of social media platforms that allow for opinions to quickly spread and to then be picked up by news outlets and critics. This symbiotic relationship between creators, audiences, and critics can help boost or sink shows and films [p. 6].

Earlier research on social media platforms and audience response emphasizes the important relationship between creators and viewers.

Audience Reception

In terms of applying audience reception theory, this analysis is complicated by the fact that the cast of *Ms. Marvel* is predominantly South Asian and Muslim with a supporting cast of White characters. For example, Ms. Marvel's character when she is not a superhero is Kamala Khan, a Pakistani American Muslim teenager. Her parents are also Pakistani, and so is her brother. In high school, her best friend is a hijabi Muslim woman and her other close friend is a White male student. However, the cast is predominantly South Asian. However, in the United States context, as well as in the Marvel audience context, viewers have been historically White and male (Hunt, 2018). Therefore, audience reception is affected by this fact: how multiple audiences react is shaped by social factors including race, gender and religion. Therefore, an intersectional analysis is important in addition to applying audience reception theory. How the audience receives and reads the show is shaped by their social location.

Still, since the majority of the writers and producers of *Ms. Marvel* were of South Asian or Muslim background, it can be theorized that the dominant audience response intended to view the show is South Asian and Muslim. Additionally, the oppositional audience can be understood as White American viewers. The negotiated viewers or audience accepted some of the messages and rejected others—this group was represented by both Muslim South Asian and female viewers. In terms of the dominant audience reading, theirs was a very favorable response online in terms of the casting choice of Iman Vellani and also much excitement around a Muslim and female superhero, Kamala Khan. The dominant audience response was positive in terms of casting, however when we do an analysis of online review sites, we find a more complicated picture.

In terms of the casting of Iman Vellani—South Asian and Muslim fans were thrilled that Ms. Marvel was actually being played by a Pakistani Muslim. This mere fact is significant because like the history of casting East Asian, Arab and even Latinx characters, often ambiguously racial actors would be cast for characters that did not accurately represent them. A well-known example of this was when Andy Garcia who is of Cuban-American heritage was cast as an Italian American in *The Godfather* trilogy. Other examples of miscasting especially as it relates to South Asian and Middle-eastern characters include when Jake Gyllenhaal (White) was cast as an Arab prince in *The Prince of Persia* (2010), Benedict Cumberbatch (White) played Khan in *Star Trek Into Darkness* (2013). However, Indian rather than Pakistani actors were cast to play Kamala Khan's characters. This becomes an area of a negotiated response both because of the distinct ethnicities Indians and Pakistanis have but also because of the diverse religious and political histories of Indians and Pakistanis. A negotiated reading of viewer response is necessary to understand the concerns that Pakistani and Muslim viewers had in particular here.

A negotiated reading of the *Ms. Marvel* show largely came from South Asian Muslim women in social media where they applauded the more nuanced and accurate representation of Muslims in the show. Yet, these same viewers had issues with the casting of the parents by Indian actors, and how two political themes were handled—particularly the India/Pakistani partition and the role of the NYPD/FBI. In terms of the casting of the parents of Kamala Khan, a well-known Indian actress was cast to play her mother. Zenobia Shrof (an Indian actress) was cast as her mother. Mohan Kapur was cast as her father and Saagar Shaikh was cast as her brother. Iman Vellani along with the character Kamala Khan are both Pakistani.

Secondly, there was much discussion online on the casting of her family members. In particular, Indian rather than Pakistani actors were cast as her parents which to the dominant viewer may not be of note but because these are distinct ethnic groups with a tumultuous history, there was substantial discussion online. An NPR article titled "Many Pakistanis dig the cultural nods on 'Ms. Marvel' but are mixed on casting" summarizes how Pakistani viewers felt about the casting of Indian actors to play the Pakistani family members. One of the key criticisms of Zenobia Shrof was that she had an Indian rather than Pakistani accent which could perhaps only be detected by South Asian viewers. The scholar Shabana Mir was vocal on X about this when she tweeted: "Indian actors from the Bollywood industry dominate South Asian representation in TV and film. So why did the parents have to be played by Indian actors, we have a ton of great Pakistani actors" (Siddiqui, Zehra, NPR June 29, 2022). In addition, though Ms. Marvel is a Pakistani Muslim female superhero and the show stars Iman Vellani (a Canadian Pakistani Muslim), there were Muslim viewers' concerns over why a non-hijabi was cast. Though her best friend is a hijabi Muslim and played by a Muslim actress, before the show's premiere there was some disapproval of Kamala Khan's character not wearing hijab instead. This might be a minor point for predominantly White and non–Muslim viewers. In going through social media sites, this did strike a chord with certain Muslim viewers. On the one hand, hijab represents modesty for many observant Muslim viewers, but on the other hand, all observant Muslim women do not wear hijab, and there is an array of representation in how Muslim American women display modesty. For example, in the United States many observant Muslim women do not wear hijab but still dress modestly, avoiding baring shoulders or wearing anything above the ankles.

Thirdly, the only significant Black Muslim character in the show was Ms. Marvel's sister-in-law. This was discussed as an oversight but also as a chance for the storyline to have included a substantial discussion on racism within the western Muslim community. Though the global and American Muslim community is multi-racial and incredibly diverse (including Black, South Asian, Middle Eastern/North African, Latinx and even White convert Muslims), there is much inter-ethnic and inter-racial discrimination and prejudice. Though there has been some increase in interracial but more likely interethnic marriage within Muslim communities, second and third generation Muslim immigrants, especially from South Asian backgrounds are often met with disapproval and sometimes hostility from their parents and even communities when they marry outside their racial categories (Ali, 2022; Haqqani, 2022). Since the murder of George Floyd, like many American liberal churches, American mosques and Islamic centers have had forums and discussions on acknowledging and then trying to dismantle racism within their congregations. This was a lost opportunity to discuss anti-racism in the American Muslim community. Instead, it represents an illusion that American Muslims coexist harmoniously even in multi-racial communities. However, in the episode where we meet Kamala's brother and sister in-law and also in the wedding scene, there is no evidence of any discomfort around interracial marriage from her parents or the local mosque community. Amer is Kamala's brother and Tyesha is a Black Muslim woman who wears a hijab. Tyesha is a convert, and when see a clip of her parents in the wedding scene, they are not dressed in Muslim clothing.

Lastly, audience reception was also very divisive regarding two important sub themes of the show—the role of the FBI and NYPD in surveillance of Muslims post–9/11, and the violent partition of India/Pakistan. Both of these storylines received criticism online from American Muslim and South Asian American viewers. Though dominant viewers did not necessarily focus their critical feedback on either of these plots, comic book and Marvel fans were most critical of how the show veered from the original comic book.

Analysis of Social Media Review Sites

An analysis of online review sites gives us evidence from social media of the polarizing audience responses that the show *Ms. Marvel* has received. Though many professional critics rated the show highly after the season finale, many audience reviewers on Metacritic, IMDb, and Rotten Tomatoes were scathing. It's useful to develop an intersectional analysis of how race, gender, and religion may shape audience responses to a historically masculine genre of story-telling.

Metacritic

On Metacritic, there is a clear pattern in terms of how user reviews vary from critical reviews. Metacritic gives *Ms. Marvel* a 78 and 4.1 (July 26, 2022), whereas *Thor: Ragnarok* has a 74 and user score of 7.8, and *Captain Marvel* 64 and 3.0, and *Guardians of the Galaxy* (Guardians) 76 and 8.2, and *Iron Man* (2008) 79 and 8.5 also receive much higher user reviews than *Ms. Marvel*. The quantitative ratings demonstrate that stories (more specifically films) with a female superhero like Ms. Marvel and Captain Marvel have much lower user reviews than the films that have a male lead or an ensemble cast.

The following is a sampling of excerpts of the negative reviews online from Metacritic to provide qualitative evidence of Ms. Marvel from viewers. In the first quote, the reviewer comments on how "the very woke" took away Ms. Marvel's powers: "Very woke took away her real powers for some Aladdin bs. Couldn't finish watching the rest because they kept putting in animations in the background so annoying. Overall will be skipping the rest and the marvels!" This second quote reveals how not just diversity, but politics seem to frame viewer's responses as this comment references, "before the pendulum in this country started to swing back from the left":

> -Garbage. Thank you RogerEbert.com for being the sole voice of reason. This is nothing but pandering **** It seems like it was made before the pendulum in this country started swing back from the left to somewhere sane (before going insane right). Disney seems to be actively trying to kill Marvel and Star Wars. I can't imagine any Muslims being super pscyhed about this, unless they're small children.

This third comment from a viewer rationalizes how negative reviews are wrongly being labeled as racist:

> This is more Disney than Marvel and that is a pity. It is like the TV version of Email spam, another product off the conveyor belt that I could not care less about. But hey if you don't like it your racist, ignorant or something else because of course you have to like brown girls being superhero's and the Muslim religion this show wants to progressively push to the masses because of Disney's diversity agenda.

IMDb

A second online site, IMDb reveals similar patterns from audience responses. As previously mentioned, *Ms. Marvel* has a 6.2/10, *Thor: Ragnarok* has a 7.9, *Captain Marvel* has a 6.8, *Guardians* has a 8.0 and *Iron Man* (2008) has a 7.9. These ratings are also consistent in terms of providing further evidence that female superhero shows are rated lower than those that star male superheroes. Secondly, *Ms. Marvel* has a slightly lower rating than *Captain Marvel*. This could be attributed to the quality of the television show versus the film, but it could also be a response to a Pakistani female lead rather than a White female lead.

A sampling of the negative comments on IMDb shows us how some viewers were frustrated with the aesthetics and plotlines focusing on Kamala Khan's ethnic and religious background. Maxax7774 writes in July 2022:

> but come on—it's supposed to be a Super Hero Show—but instead we spend 85% of the show examining Muslim Culture. It completely misses the point of being fun and full of

action—instead it wants to "woke" and culturally aware! What?!? ITS A SUPER HERO SHOW—jeepers—you're missing the point! Why can't it just be a farfetched super hero show—why can't it just be cute and fun?!? Instead—it's delivering a complete obvious subversive message about Muslim life and culture.

Commenting on both the "woke" aspect of the show and the emphasis on "Muslim culture" this reviewer also negatively reviewed the show at 2/10.

Similarly, eriksheedlo9 also expresses frustration and anger about the diversity aspects of the show: "Bad pacing, poor writing and the things that don't matter to me when reading or watching comic movies like race, gender or religion are pushed to the forefront of this series. I know Disney is trying to involve younger watchers, but why dumb it down so much." This reviewer also rates the show at a 2/10.

spacerat-28280 is a third example of a viewer who found the show's focus on race and religion exasperating:

> I could only make it to episode 3. That's 3 hours of a TV show about a super hero that IN TOTAL contained maybe 20 minutes of action. That's a generous estimate. They spend far more talking about the main characters race and religion. That's cool I guess if we were watching a drama but that's not really what I want my marvel shows to be about.

This viewer also rated the show only 2/10.

These three comments above offer a qualitative sliced of evidence of how there was a negative response to the portrayal of Ms. Marvel (Kamala Khan) as Pakistani, Muslim, and female.

Rotten Tomatoes

Lastly, on Rotten Tomatoes, *Ms. Marvel* received very high ratings from the critics and good overall ratings by audience viewers, though initial reviews by viewers were very low. The critics summary from the site states: "*Ms. Marvel* is a genuinely fresh addition to the MCU—both stylistically and substantively—with Iman Vellani ably powering proceedings with her super-sized charisma" (Rotten Tomatoes). The site gives *Ms. Marvel* an over 90 percent rating, and the viewer rating is at 80 percent. Despite the positive critics rating, many of the viewers wrote negative reviews on the site. One reviewer wrote: "This is the worst Marvel series ever. What did they think? This is so bad I do not even know What they are trying to do. This is sad and cringe as f." A second reviewer explained that they were giving the show a zero rating because of the writing and made a point of saying it wasn't because of the Muslim characters or racial themes:

> I wish I could give it a 0 star. I have no idea why this show has a 98% rating. I created a login just to give this a lower score. THIS SHOW BY FAR IS NOT BETTER THAN STRANGER THINGS! So why is the rating higher. Anyways this show is so corny and it feels rushed and absolutely no character building. The fight scenes are so lame. I have a feeling this show only received a higher review simply because it is Muslim themed. I am not giving it a bad review on the fact that its about Muslims or anything about race. I am simply saying the story is horribly written.

A third reviewer also commented on the "woke" aspect of the show referring to the diversity of the themes:

what bad sleep pill was this. I GET IT religion form other place I DONT CARE in a good or bad way, teen sitcom bs just don't care, quoting millhouse "WHEN ARE THEY GOING TO GET TO THE FIREWORKS FACTORY?!" and brie "the plank" larson its here ... oh greats (not really), can we have a decent show for a change and nota woke fest of nothing burgers? In audience, it's viewership numbers premiered to only 775,000 households compared to 2.5 million with Loki's premiere on television.

Just a survey of online review sites shows the discrepancy between viewer's ratings of *Ms. Marvel* and male or specifically white male led superhero shows. Though when we add race or religion to this analysis, it further complicates our theoretical analysis.

Conclusion

Moving beyond cancel culture is an important aspect of how scholars can better examine television as a reflection of societal attitudes and norms. Audience reception theory and intersectionality provide important frameworks for a more layered analysis of television as an important part of American popular culture. Exploring *Ms. Marvel* as a case study of a diverse portrayal of a superhero on television can help challenge understandings of dominant viewers from a predominantly White and western viewpoint. As U.S. society in particular struggles with polarizing views on race, gender and immigration, television can be a place to further understand and challenge these views. In many ways, shows like *Ms. Marvel* represent the future of television audience demographics but also the overall population as they skew younger and more diverse.

References

Anderson-Lopez, J., Lambert, R.J., & Budaj, A. (2021). Tug of war: Social media, cancel culture, and diversity for *Girls* and *The 100*. KOME - An International Journal of Pure Communication Inquiry, 9(1), 64–84. http://komejournal.com/files/KOME_MS_Girls100.pdf.
Burton, J. (2022, June 10). '*Ms. Marvel*' review bombing called 'racist White replacement nonsense.' Newsweek. https://www.newsweek.com/ms-marvel-mcu-disneyplus-review-bombing-racist-white-nonsense-1714538.
Collins, P H. (2015). Intersectionality's definitional dilemmas. *Annual Review of Sociology*, 41(1), 1–20. https://doi.org/10.1146/annurev-soc-073014-112142.
Goutam, M. (2017). Paradox of gender equality in Hollywood superhero movies. *Arts & Education International Research Journal*, 4(2).
Hall, S. (1993). Encoding/Decoding. In S. During (Ed.), *The cultural studies reader*. Routledge.
Hunt, W. (2019). Negotiating new racism: 'It's not racist or sexist. It's just the way it is.' *Media, Culture & Society*, 41(1), 86–103. https://doi.org/10.1177/0163443718798907.
Seelye, K.Q. (2021, November 10). Joanna Cameron, an early female superhero on TV, is dead at 73. *The New York Times*. https://www.nytimes.com/2021/11/05/arts/television/joanna-cameron-dead.html.
Selod, S. (2018). *Forever suspect*. Choudhury.
Siddiqui, Z. (2022, June 29). *Many Pakistanis dig the cultural nods on 'Ms. Marvel' but are mixed on casting*. NPR. https://www.npr.org/sections/goatsandsoda/2022/06/29/1108279324/many-pakistanis-dig-the-cultural-nods-on-ms-marvel-but-are-mixed-on-casting.

Streaming and Video-on-Demand (SVOD) Has Become the "New Queer Cinema"

Victor D. Evans

Twenty years ago, if a person wanted to watch lesbian, gay, bisexual, transgender and/or queer (LGBTQ) films, the only places to find them were at independent theaters, specialized video stores and film festivals; however, today, thanks to the streaming and video-on-demand services (SVOD), LGBTQ films are so abundant that they can readily be found on the small screen without even leaving home. SVOD is now fulfilling another crucial need because it's on this new platform where the majority of diverse LGBTQ content can be found, and where many queer women and audiences of color can now find representations of themselves.

The television industry has been in a state of immense transformation over the past decade as audiences' media consumption habits change, especially in the last few years during the Covid-19 pandemic, which has only accelerated the industry's evolution. During this time, viewers were actively seeking entertainment to replace the lack of social interaction. This prompted several companies to launch their own streaming platform, thus increasing competition and programming options, so viewers have more choices than ever before. Per *Variety VIP+*, as of 2022, streaming series account for over half (51.5 percent) of all original series in the U.S., a drastic change from just 12.9 percent in 2016 (Bridge, 2022).

The Gay and Lesbian Alliance Against Defamation's (GLAAD) *Where We Are on TV* (*WWATV*) report for 2021–22 has added five new streaming services to its count this year—Apple TV+, Disney+, HBO Max, Paramount+, and Peacock—in addition to its ongoing counts of scripted originals on Amazon, Hulu, and Netflix. On original scripted programming on those eight platforms, GLAAD counted 245 LGBTQ series regular characters and 113 LGBTQ recurring characters, bringing the total to 358 LGBTQ regular and recurring characters, the highest total ever (as seen in Figure 1) since the report began 17 years ago (GLAAD, 2022).

Racial diversity of LGBTQ characters has also increased on streaming services with 49 percent (176) of LGBTQ regular and recurring characters counted as people of color. This marks an increase of two percentage points from the previous year. Considering GLAAD's *WWATV* report analyzed an additional five streaming networks, an increase of only 2 percent is quite negligible (see Figure 2), showing there is still an inadequate amount of media content on the mainstream streaming sites that include

256 Part 3: Streaming Television

LGBTQ characters of color (GLAAD, 2022).

Despite the lack of racial diversity on streaming networks, it's still more diverse than theatrical releases which still fail to include LGBTQ characters of any kind. And even when they do, the roles are often inauthentic, not fully developed, commonly stereotypical and rarely diverse. According to a study by USC's Annenberg Inclusion Initiative, 1,100 popular films from 2007 to 2017 found that only 31 out of 4,403 characters were lesbian, gay, or bisexual, and of those, nearly 68 percent were White. There was only one transgender character in the top 400 films released between 2014 and 2017 (Smith et al., 2018).

There are numerous examples of LGBTQ-themed films in recent years that have failed to accurately portray LGBTQ characters and/or show the diversity within the LGBTQ community. *Bohemian Rhapsody* (2018), which is the highest-grossing LGBTQ film to date, received much criticism for not fully examining Freddy Mercury's sexuality within the film. *Buddy Games* (2020) includes an LGBTQ male character who is coming out and has very stereotypical gay characteristics that are used as comic relief. Even the groundbreaking *Love, Simon* (2018) focused on the coming out of a privileged,

Figure 1. Number of LGBTQ recurring characters.

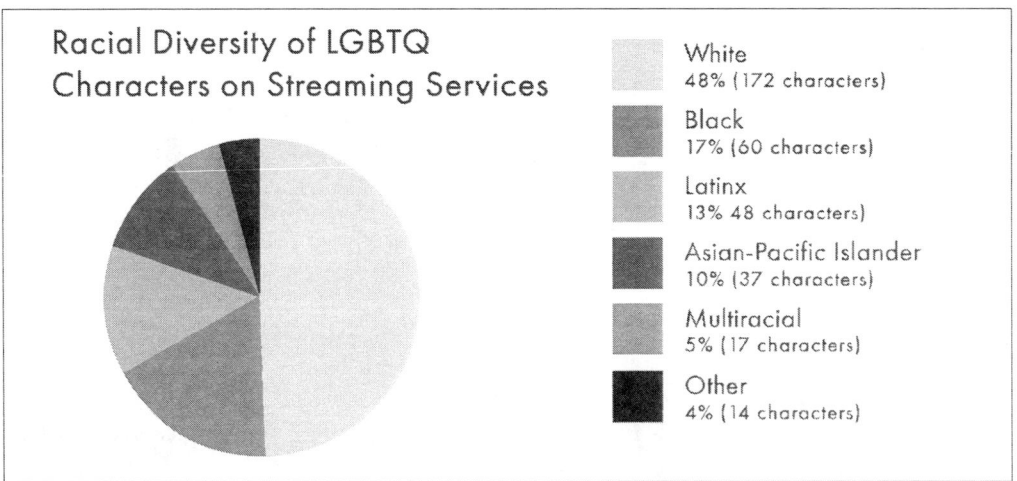

Figure 2. Racial diversity streaming.

White gay teen with LGBTQ cast members of color only included as secondary characters.

In 2021, GLAAD also conducted a survey looking at films, finding that of the 44 films that GLAAD counted from the major studios in 2020, 10 (22.7 percent) contained LGBTQ characters. This is an increase of 4.1 percent, but a decrease of 12 films from 2019's 18.6 (22 out of 118 films). The limited number of movies released theatrically in 2020 is a direct result and consequence of the Covid-19 pandemic, which created a global theater shutdown for large portions of the year (GLAAD, 2021). However, even with the slight increase, there is still a serious lack of LGBTQ characters in mainstream movies, and when looking at the racial diversity of characters in the films (like with Figure 3).

As Figure 4 depicts, gay men still reign supreme with most of the major LGBTQ studio films being focused on them, much like the award-winning LGBTQ films in recent years such as *Call Me by Your Name*, *Moonlight*, and even the first mainstream teen rom-com *Love, Simon*, mentioned earlier.

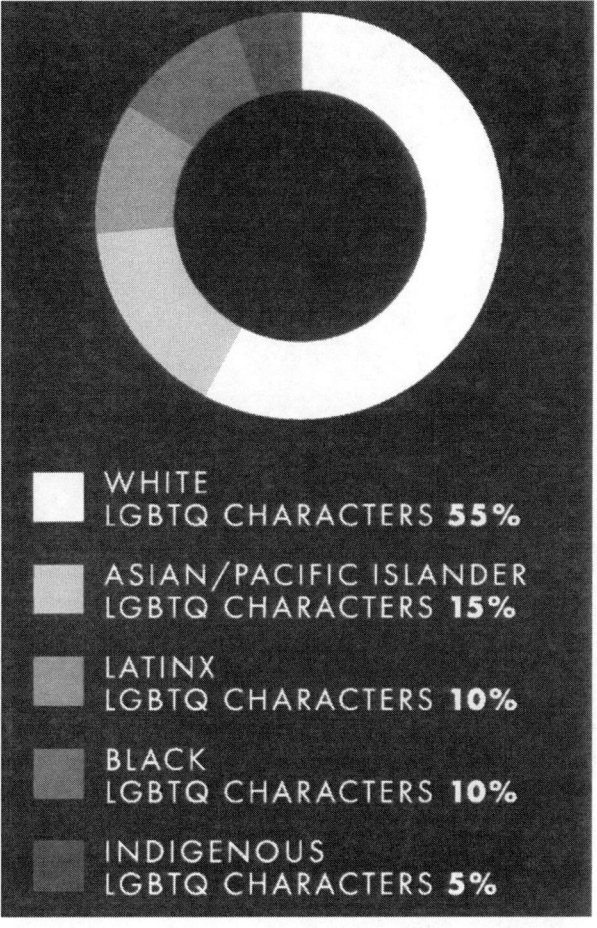

Figure 3. LGBTQ diversity characters film.

This is why viewers looking for LGBTQ content, particularly diverse portrayals, have to venture beyond the major theaters and often have much better luck finding them on the small screen. Nielsen's *Proud & Present* report found that of GLAAD's five tracked streaming platforms, LGBTQ audiences were more likely to have used those services in the past seven days than total population across the board—from 16 to 71 percent more likely based on platform. LGBTQ audiences are also driving buzz, with LGBTQ people reported to be nearly two times more likely to be heavy social media users (Nielsen, 2021).

Queer Cinema—Pre-Streaming

There was a time during the mid to late '90s when LGBTQ films were quite abundant, albeit most were relegated to the art houses, but at least they were relatively

258 Part 3: Streaming Television

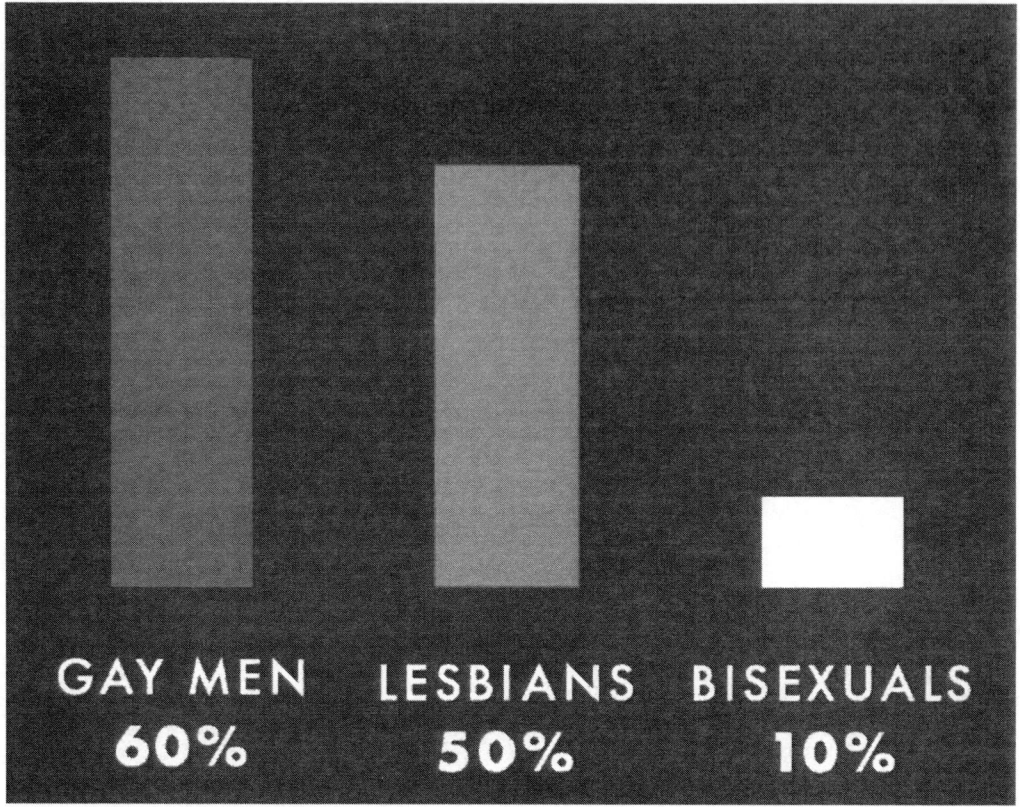

Figure 4. LGBTQ makeup films.

accessible for those who lived near major cities. Dubbed by B. Ruby Rich in 1992 as the "New Queer Cinema," the movement was known for the proliferation of queer-themed independent filmmaking in the early 1990s during which many LGBTQ directors found opportunities to showcase their work during this time period, including Gus Van Sant, Jennie Livingston, Greg Araki, and Angela Robinson.

In fact, some LGBTQ directors, producers, and writers feel that the rise of television actually led to the demise of the new queer cinema movement. Acclaimed LGBTQ director Angela Robinson (2019) of *D.E.B.S.* fame, which came out at the tail end of the movement in 2004, said, "During that time ['90s and early 2000s], you really felt like you were a part of the larger gay community, with each other and the world. It felt really dynamic and cutting edge, an exciting time to be making queer content." But she went on to mention how the queer-themed cable channel Logo and TV in general unintentionally killed the queer cinema boom:

> LOGO launched and they had no money or no vision or commitment to pushing content. Before then, when there weren't TV queer outlets, the mini-majors felt a part of the mission and were pushing to put out queer films. But now we had LOGO, so they didn't feel the need to release them any more.... The first wave of queer cinema died [A. Robinson, personal communication, February 6, 2019].

While television can't completely fill the void left by the demise of the New Queer Cinema movement, SVOD platforms do offer viewers access to a myriad of LGBTQ content, including some of the radical, political, and esoteric queer films reminiscent of those in the '90s. But more importantly, these platforms showcase the diversity of race, gender, class, and gender identity in the LGTBQ communities, much more than mainstream theaters and that even includes most independent venues. Streaming and on-demand services excel at providing content that showcases a larger spectrum of LGBTQ lifestyles and cultures with space for discussion and exploration that cannot be found on traditional media outlets.

In the history of independent LGBTQ filmmaking, distribution has often proved to be one of the most challenging hurdles to overcome. "Failing to find a distributor meant your film would not play outside of local screenings or film festivals. Even films that did secure distribution were often limited to short runs in large cities with active arthouse theaters" (McCracken, 2017, para. 1). SVOD platforms have created avenues for LGBTQ filmmakers, especially those with lower budgets, to connect their films with broader audiences, including worldwide distribution.

This change is quite different from the niche distribution that LGBTQ media was relegated to decades ago. Within the last decade, there has been a significant increase in LGBTQ programming within the mainstream SVOD sites, but in addition to these options, numerous niche LGBTQ-focused media organizations have created their own independent SVOD sites, such as Here TV, Revry, DEKKOO, and a whole host of others, to give LGBTQ audiences even more diversity in their entertainment options.

Mainstream SVOD Sites

Netflix

Netflix is the largest streaming subscription service in the world with over 225 million subscribers, and, as of June 2022, had just over 87 LGBTQ movies and 172 TV shows on its roster. Considering the streamer has over 3,600 movie titles, at first glance, only 87 LGBTQ films seem relatively small, but it is not surprising given Netflix's recent focus from feature films to their own original TV shows. According to Flixable, "In 2010, Netflix had 530 TV shows and 6,755 movies. Today, the number of TV shows has nearly tripled, to 1,569, and the number of movies offered has decreased to 4,010" (Clark, 2018, para. 4).

Netflix only boasts just under 90 LGBTQ-themed films, and of those films, 63 percent of them feature diverse and inclusive content. The quality of queer films is all over the map, ranging from those with star-studded casts, like *The Danish Girl* (2015) and *The Boys in the Band* (2020) to more independent, low-budget films, like *Alaska Is a Drag* (2017). There is also an impressively large selection of international releases such as *Cobalt Blue* (2022). As of late, the network's own original films seem to now be their priority with films such as *Alex Strangelove* (2018), *The Death and Life of Marsha P. Johnson* (2017), and *Straight Up* (2020).

According to GLAAD's *WWATV* report (2022), Netflix continues to consistently top its streaming competitors in LGBTQ inclusivity, with 155 regularly seen or recurring characters on its original comedy and drama series. Inclusive Netflix series include *Heartstopper, Never Have I Ever, Q-Force* and *Sex Education*, but what really puts Netflix leaps and bounds ahead of its mainstream streaming competitors in terms of more diverse LGBTQ portrayals are their foreign-language queer dramas, including *Young Royals* from Sweden, *Rebelde* from Mexico, and *Elite* from Spain.

However, even with the platform's expansive list of diverse titles, one of the most recent criticisms against the international streaming service has been its lack of lesbian-themed titles, especially in comparison to films that feature gay male characters, not unlike mainstream film releases that feature men-centered films rather than those with females. Capon (2018) recounts how

> despite the whole acronym [LGBTQ] being included in the classification, there are a disproportionate number of films focusing on gay men. The conversation trended when Twitter user @dspxna wrote: "Someone let Netflix know that 678 gay men films and 2 lesbian films doesn't make a lgbtq Caponsection [*sic*]" [para. 2–3].

The numbers support this claim, showing that roughly only about one-third of Netflix's LGBTQ movies (as of June 2022) focus on lesbian or even transgender characters. Although, when it comes to its original series, Netflix boasts the majority of shows on a streaming network to feature lesbian characters. Scott (2018) notes, "There have been great shows [on Netflix] such as *Orange is the New Black* which depicts numerous queer women" (para. 25). Other Netflix original shows with lesbian characters include *Ratched* (2020–present), *Trinkets* (2019–2020), and *Teenage Bounty Hunters* (2020).

Hulu

Hulu, the subscription-based streaming company owned by Disney, has recently expanded its repertoire of LGBTQ content. While Hulu's movie library is only a fraction of its competitor Netflix, with just over 1,230 titles, Hulu is more known for its wide array of television shows, close to 1,300 as of June 2022. In fact, the streaming site has the largest selection of classic network and cable shows that include LGBTQ themes and characters, such as *Buffy the Vampire Slayer* (1996–2003) and *My So-Called Life* (1994–1995). However, despite Hulu's smaller movie collection, viewers can still find numerous LGBTQ movies, including *Fire Island* (2022), *Love, Simon* (2018), *Booksmart* (2019), and *Crush* (2022). The site is also known for spearheading some of the first LGBTQ holiday rom-com films such as *Happiest Season* (2020). Like Netflix, Hulu has its own line of original series and many of them include LGBTQ characters in favorites like *Love, Victor* (2020–2022), *The Handmaid's Tale* (2017–2024), and *Conversations with Friends* (2022).

Amazon Prime

Amazon Prime, another subscription-based service, has been expanding its library of LGBTQ films for the past few years, including titles from other studios, so it remains to be seen how the library will expand with the recently completed MGM merger. Numerous LGBTQ-themed movies can be found on the site, including everything from documentaries to dramas and musicals, like *Joe Bell* (2021), *Mayor Pete* (2021), and *Everybody's Talking About Jamie* (2021). Amazon Studios has also produced numerous original LGBTQ films like *Uncle Frank* (2020). The streaming site has long been a frontrunner in transgender representation with the launch of its original series *Transparent* back in 2014. Other noteworthy series with queer characters include *The Boys, Fleabag, One Mississippi,* and *Carnival Row*. Amazon Prime is also known for its international and more diverse titles, which are not nearly as prevalent on other streaming sites like the Israeli film *15 Years* (2019), China's *A Dog Barking at the Moon* (2019), the Latinx's transgender story in *Everybody Changes* (2019), and Korea's *House of Hummingbird* (2018) and *The Handmaiden* (2016).

HBO Max

HBO Max, a subscription video-on-demand service owned by Warner Bros., launched in May 2020, landed in second place in its first appearance in GLAAD's *WWATV* report. According to GLAAD (2022), the service quickly built a reputation for standout LGBTQ-inclusive comedy series with the majority of its 71 LGBTQ characters found in comedies, including the Emmy-winning *Hacks, The Sex Lives of College Girls* and *Euphoria*. The cable streaming company also has a prominent list of just over 30 queer films, including classics like *The Color Purple* (1985), *Gia* (1998) and *Pariah* (2011) to modern films like *Steven Universe: The Movie* (2019) and even their own original films such as *Unpregnant* (2020).

Paramount+

Paramount+, a subscription-based service owned by the ViacomCBS company, has a smaller number of queer titles, but it's the perfect choice for audiences that crave LGBTQ reality television. The site hosts all 12 seasons of *RuPaul's Drag Race* and every season of *RuPaul's Drag Race All Stars*, as well as all the behind-the-scenes *Untucked* episodes. The streaming site also has exclusive rights to all of MTV's *The Real World* series, which began 30 years ago and included a multitude of LGBTQ characters, most notably AIDS activist Pedro Zamora in season 3 and *Queer Eye*'s Karamo Brown in season 15.

Paramount+ also includes some scripted content with LGBTQ content such as the *Star Trek: Discovery* series, which features the first openly gay characters in a *Star Trek* series (incidentally played by openly gay actors Anthony Rapp and Wilson Cruz) and in the later seasons introduces the first non-binary and transgender (trans-species) characters in the franchise. While the site's movie collection is not nearly as robust as Netflix, HBO Max, or Hulu, it does have a few select titles like *Bound* (1996), *Vito* (2011) and *Three Months* (2022).

Peacock

While NBCUniversal's subscription streaming site Peacock's library is only a fraction of Netflix or Hulu's, the newer streamer does include some very impressive titles, especially hit queer movies like *Brokeback Mountain* (2005) and *The Kids Are Alright* (2010). Comedy series with LGBTQ characters like *Modern Family* (2009–2020) and *Superstore* (2015–2021) can be found on Peacock, along with their original shows *Saved by the Bell* (1989–1993), *Girls5Eva* (2021–2022), and the remake of *Queer as Folk* (2022).

Apple TV+

Of all the mainstream subscription-based streaming networks, Apple TV+ and Disney+ have the least LGBTQ content, but it certainly doesn't mean the content they do have is not up to par, and some of it is quite diverse. Apple TV+'s original show *Dickinson* featured biracial Jewish actress Hailee Steinfeld, *Mythic Quest* included Filipino Ashley Burch's lesbian character on the show and Shalini Bathina's lesbian Prisha in *Little Voice*. Apple TV+ also produced a number of LGBTQ-themed docu-series, including *Visible: Out on Television* and *Little America*, in which the season finale tells the story of a gay Syrian refugee and how he dreams of being granted asylum in America so he can live openly as a gay man.

Disney+

Disney+ has even skimpier LGBTQ fare, but the *Loki* (2021–2023) series did confirm that Loki is bisexual, and there is a recurring lesbian character in *Hawkeye* (2021). *Diary of a Future President* (2020–2021), *Big Shot* (2021–2022), and *Doogie Kamealoha, M.D.* (2021–2023) all include LGBTQ characters (GLAAD, 2022). Interestingly, all of the shows previously mentioned, except for *Loki*, contain LGBTQ characters of color.

Tubi

Last, but certainly not least, is Tubi. This lesser-known FOX-owned video-on-demand app burst into the scene in 2014. What sets them apart from all the other mainstream subscription-based streamers previously mentioned is that Tubi is completely free, as long as viewers don't mind sitting through a few ads. The app boasts the largest

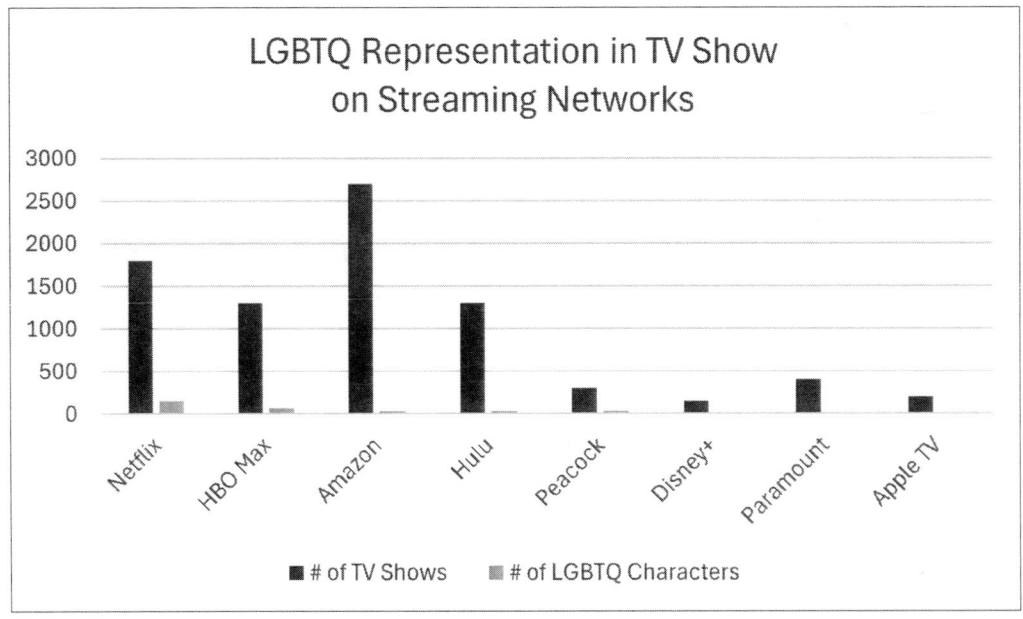

Figure 5. LGBTQ streaming platforms.

library of content with over 40,000 movies and television shows, much more than the other sites combined, and surprisingly, in terms of LGBTQ content, they have a library of more than 2,000 titles, albeit most of them are classics. Titles include *To Wong Foo, Thanks for Everything! Julie Newmar* (1995), *Boys Don't Cry* (1999), and *The Miseducation of Cameron Post* (2018). Also, unlike Netflix, about half of their LGBTQ library focuses on lesbians, and at least 40 percent of the LGBTQ content features diverse characters.

Other than Tubi, the mainstream subscription sites definitely fall short in terms of their overall LGBTQ character count in comparison to the straight counterparts (illustrated in Figure 5), in which roughly on average there is less than one LGBTQ character to every straight character (GLAAD, 2022).

LGBTQ SVOD Sites

The mainstream SVOD sites are not offering an abundance of LGBTQ content, especially in comparison to their heteronormative content. The majority of titles SVOD sites do have are not gender or racially diverse, thus where can viewers turn to find a more robust and inclusive selection? Fortunately, more and more exclusively queer-themed SVOD sites are popping up everywhere, and some have been providing LGBT content for decades.

Wolfe Video

A true pioneer in LGBTQ filmmaking, Wolfe Video began distributing gay-themed titles to the LGBTQ community in 1985. Distributing thousands of queer titles, even today, they are still the largest exclusive distributor of LGBTQ films. Wolfe debuted Wolfe On Demand, its global LGBTQ movie-watching platform, in June 2012 in collaboration with technology partner Distrify, an internet distribution service. Their current film library has just under 180 titles, which lands them ahead of Netflix in terms of LGBTQ film inventory, but while they offer more titles featuring women, with 26 films that feature lesbians of color compared to only 18 films that feature gay males of color, only 25 percent of their entire collection contains titles that feature people of color, well below the diversity found at Netflix. Jenni Olsen, vice president of Wolfe Video's E-Commerce and Consumer Marketing Department, calls this a "gamechanger." "Historically, with people overseas, we couldn't do anything for them, but with WolfeonDemand, we literally have viewers all over the world watching LGBT films" (Moore, 2013, p. 140).

Wolfe's model is also quite innovative because it actively encourages fan-based distribution. When a viewer clicks a title, the website launches a trailer and offers the options to rent or buy. Buttons then pop up eliciting the viewer to "follow" email updates on the film, "share" a link to the film on social media, like Facebook or Twitter, or "embed" the link onto their personal website or blog. Clicking on "share" or "embed" will prompt viewers with an incentive message asking them to promote the movie on their website or blog, earning them 10.0 percent of any sales that come through their referrals. Thus, consumers can earn revenue when their links to films on their personal or social media sites result in an actual rental or purchase from Wolfe.

This innovative marketing strategy tasks the fans with contributing to the site's profitability, which is perfect for promoting material targeted to specific social and/or cultural groups. "For these reasons, it is not surprising that Wolfe would experiment with inviting individual viewers within gay and lesbian communities, not just companies, to be affiliates" (Moore, 2013, p. 141).

Avoiding the frenzied feeds on Twitter and the Facebook clutter, Wolfe also made an interesting choice by deciding to focus the majority of their social media attention on Pinterest, particularly its "LGBT Movie Showcase" board. The board features each of their films in an easily repinnable format, including cover art and a short plot description. By clicking on the film, users are redirected to Wolfe On Demand where they can purchase or rent the film, and they are offered an economic incentive to be part of their team of consumer-distributors. The goal is for the users who find Wolfe films via this method to then return to these same sites to promote the films in their own social networking circles. Therefore, by using this method of user-based advertising, it requires Wolfe to be ever more inclusive with this content by including diverse titles that attract viewers from all facets of the LGBTQ communities. This alone justifies the demand for such content because audiences are proving that they are willing to personally promote these titles, and in the end, it's a win-win for everyone involved, audiences get the content and both the viewers and Wolfe receive monetary gain.

Here TV

Here TV launched in 2004 by Paul Colichman and Stephen P. Jarchow, making it the world's first SVOD LGBTQ+ video service. Here TV reaches millions of viewers each month and has produced Academy Award–winning films in addition to receiving three Daytime Emmy Award nominations. According to their website, "Here TV is the exclusive platform for LGBT filmmakers, artists and performers to showcase award-winning films and series in their original, uncensored form" (Here TV, 2018, para. 1). The subscriber-based site proclaims to have the largest LGBT library featuring over 300 hours of award-winning movies, series, documentaries, and short films, with new material being added every single week. Their video-on-demand section contains just under 200 titles, which is more than both Netflix and Wolfe On Demand. Although, much like Netflix, the majority of their titles feature gay men over lesbians. But the platform does boast 42 percent of titles that are diverse and inclusive, which is not too shabby. "We are passionate about telling stories that entertain while offering the LGBTQ+ audience an opportunity to see their lives reflected on all screens," says Christopher Donaldson, Director of Content at Here TV (PRWeb, 2018, para. 5). The Here TV offering includes countless exclusive originals such as the Here TV GLAAD award-winning film *Shelter*, and a vast and growing library of festival favorites, independent films and beloved documentaries such as *Hidden Kisses, Heartstone, Rift*, and the Here TV exclusive, original, Emmy-nominated *30 Years from Here.*

Revry

Operating under the tagline "Stream. Out. Loud." Revry is a queer-owned and operated subscriber-based, video-on-demand platform, offering "hours upon hours of queer movies and TV to viewers around the world—116 countries total, including China, where even Netflix can't get past censors" (Watercutter, 2018, para. 2). Created by Chief Business Officer, Christopher Rodriguez, and the company's CEO, Damian Pelliccione, Revry bills itself as the first global LGBTQ streaming service and has grown rapidly since its founding in 2015, hosting more than 4,000 hours of films, shows, podcasts and music. Unlike the other LGBTQ on-demand platforms, Revry's mission is to highlight diverse content and spotlight voices and stories that have often been ignored by mainstream media: "Revry was founded to showcase the works that our community wants to see and to highlight stories that are still being overlooked by the mainstream" (Revry, 2018, para. 1).

In an effort to reach even larger audiences, the service is also currently available Hulu-style, supported by ads instead of just subscription fees; therefore, viewers who can't afford to subscribe or would prefer not to have their credit card information associated with an LGBTQ+ streaming service can access the content free just by sitting through a few advertisements. From the start, Revry wanted to create a service that featured programming from a truly diverse lineup of creators and stars, in order to provide queer perspectives beyond the White, cisgender male one, which distinguishes the company from other streaming services with LGBTQ content like Netflix. "They are highly committed to inclusion and creating a space for all voices in the LGBTQ community to be seen and heard," said Jeremy Blacklow, director of entertainment media at GLAAD. "They're off to a great start, and we're excited to see what they're able to achieve" (Watercutter, 2018, para. 9). Revry even streams its content to Iraq, Saudi Arabia, and a number of other countries where homosexuality is rejected, or even illegal, giving queer people in these regions a chance to see themselves reflected in media in a way they might never have before, which was the ultimate goal of the creators. Pelliccione reaffirmed this by saying, "We're a cause-driven company. But it wasn't even just seeing an opportunity in the market, it was seeing an opportunity to reach those audiences who have never seen themselves reflected on television" (as cited in Watercutter, 2018, para. 5).

Based almost entirely on word of mouth, when Revry first launched, it garnered thousands of downloads from over 50 countries. The company's founders credit their wide selection of LGBTQ programming, offering something for everyone to enjoy, to the service's thriving success. The site includes a lesbian web series from India called *The "Other" Love Story*, original programming, such as *Before I Got Famous*, a show following a 21-year-old who moves from China to Hollywood to make it as an actor. This is also known as a docu-series featuring drag queens in Brooklyn, headlined by *RuPaul's Drag Race* Season 10 winner Aquaria, *FML*, a "comedic web series about five millennial friends of color navigating the bullshit called life" (Watercutter, 2018, para. 11).

Revry regularly receives letters from viewers in Iraq, Saudi Arabia, and other countries where homosexuality is not permitted, thanking them for their services and allowing them the ability to see the content for free (Watercutter, 2018). In fact, it was exactly this impact the service was having on viewers from around the world that led Revry's co-founders to move from the subscription model to their more ad-supported one currently being used. And now, like Tubi, by watching a few commercials, viewers can stream the content for free, no login required. According to Rodriguez: "Initially it was only by necessity that we went with the subscription model. But now that we've grown and developed, we were kind of able to actualize this initial inclination to be able to offer our content all over the world for free" (as cited in Watercutter, 2018, para. 15).

DEKKOO

Launched in 2016, DEKKOO is owned by media giant Gaius Media, an entertainment company that has multiple holdings, including their sister company, TLA Releasing, which has been the global leader in LGBTQ entertainment since its inception in 2001. The film distribution company has been devoted to providing the best in independent cinema for LGBTQ audiences. DEKKOO is no different, currently hosting over 600 hours of LGBTQ content, including a mix of feature films and episodic programming, outnumbering the combined LGBTQ content on Netflix and Amazon Prime Video, with a specific focus on smaller lesser-known films. DEKKOO's COO Brian Sokel shared an example of this: "I'm certainly not going to steal market share for the 100 films that Netflix has in their library. But, for a film like *Buddy*, a short film we just acquired and launched from overseas, you're never going to see that anywhere else" (Martens, 2017, para. 14).

Sokel, who is a straight, cisgender male, makes it very clear that they cater specifically to gay men. He states: "We believe every letter of the LGBTQ+ acronym deserves attention. The 'G' just happens to be our specialty" (as cited in Amorosi, 2017, para. 7). Sokel and his team of creators and curators work very diligently to attract new and upcoming filmmakers giving them a platform to showcase their work. DEKKOO wants to become strong partners with filmmakers to make their work available to the public. With almost 50 percent of its titles featuring gay men of color, the platform is fulfilling their mission of giving voice to underrepresented populations. Sokel underscored this when he said, "We believe any content produced for diverse audiences deserves to be seen" (as cited in Schwartz & Hadley, 2017, para. 11).

Logo TV

Owned by Viacom Media, Logo Television launched in 2005, originally targeting LGBTQ audiences. However, in a controversial decision in 2012, the network announced that it was shifting its focus away from queer programming toward more general cultural and lifestyle programming. This decision was fueled by low ratings and the lack of buzzworthy shows, other than *RuPaul's Drag Race*, but with the show's recent move to VH1, outside of occasional reruns, Logo has been increasingly airing classic TV shows and movies. Although even with the channel's change to more mainstream fare, Logo's General Manager Chris McCarthy said Logo will always have an alliance with the LGBTQ community: "We are a channel that is born and bred from gay culture, and now that subculture is driving mass culture. So, we are about a sensibility and a mindset. That is our unique calling card. We certainly don't tell anyone else they can't join us, but we are gay in our core" (as cited in Hod, 2013 para. 8). Logo mostly uses its internet presence to solicit additional viewers to access its network via cable providers. Logo's website offers viewers the ability to stream programs and featured films, mostly documentaries, online for free rather than using a pay model. While the website does offer programming, its library is minimal when compared to the previously mentioned SVOD sites. Like most other television networks, Logo only uploads a handful of episodes of any particular series and only a sprinkling of films in order to entice potential viewers to watch the actual channel.

However, even with its meager offerings, where Logo shines is its commitment to diversity and highlighting the diverse populations of the LGBTQ community, especially within their original documentaries and reality series like *Logo30, Finding Prince Charming,* and *Fire Island*. All of the network's series include LGBTQ Black, Indigenous and people of color (BIPOC) men, women, and transgender representation. Logo is also the only place audiences can watch free episodes of *Noah's Arc*, one of the first LGBTQ series that features an entire Black/Latino cast.

Like Wolfe On Demand, Logo does include options for viewers to share links to videos on multiple social media sites. However, where the network soars is with their app. Downloading the Logo app allows users to interact with one another, and most importantly, feel "at home" wherever they are by providing them with recommendations for local gay businesses, travel tips, bars, museums, retail shops, restaurants and other "gay hot spots" from coast to coast and around the world.

WOW Presents Plus

The newcomer to the bunch is WOW Presents Plus, which launched in 2018 as the streaming service for LGBTQ titles from the production company originally behind *RuPaul's Drag Race*. WOW sets itself apart from the other streamers by focusing on anything and everything "drag." When viewers grow tired of the U.S. seasons of *RuPaul's Drag Race* on Paramount+, they can view all of the international seasons of the franchise on the streamer with spinoffs hosted in Canada, Australia, Spain, Holland, United Kingdom, and Thailand. The series, which began in 2009, is known for its racially diverse selection of contestants, and although they are primarily cisgender men, transgender competitors have increased dramatically over the past few years. The WOW Presents Plus catalog also features interesting LGBTQ documentaries like *The Eyes of Tammy Faye*, and shows from *Drag Race* alumni, including *Painted with Raven*, and *UNHhhh*, a talk show with Trixie Mattel and Katya.

Race/Gender Specific LGBTQ SVODs

There are a few LGBTQ SVODs whose missions are to specifically cater to more marginalized audiences or at least host content that features them. These streamers provide a one-stop shop for those viewers who want to see specific representation and often have titles that most of the others do not.

Tello Films

Tello Films is a production company and streaming service that focuses on queer women content. Their original movies include *Season of Love* and *I Hate New Years*, which were reportedly the first lesbian holiday movies to be made and distributed outside the traditional mainstream channels. All of their original content includes racially diverse casts, and its small but growing film selection has a moderate number of films that feature BIPOC protagonists. For viewers in search of more queer content focused on queer women, Tello Films is the place to start.

TysonPlus

TysonPlus is an LGBTQ streaming service that produces people-of-color-inclusive content. The site includes original series in numerous genres like drama, horror, coming of age, and boundary-breaking stories, exploring emotional narratives for people of color in the LGBTQ+ community. A few of its well-known series are *Boys Hurt Too, Miseducated* and *I Can Tell You Anything.* TysonPlus allows LGBTQ+ writers to work with other LGBTQ+ creatives and turn their stories into streamable content. As Kevin Anthony (2021), a writer at TysonPlus puts it: "I mainly love working on sets with members of the LGBTQ community and hearing them express how my set is a place where they can let their guards down and feel accepted" (Madwar, 2021, Section 3).

Fearless

If viewers want to discover new, independent, and inclusive content, Fearless should be their first choice. The independent media company, founded by Canadian filmmakers Deanna Widmeyer and Matkai Burmaster in 2017, offers viewers access to inclusive content from *all* under-represented groups. They make sure BIPOC, LGBTQ+, disabled, and female creators are being heard and can share their stories with the world. Founder Burmaster is passionate about making media more diverse and inclusive. He explained, "Hollywood systematically excludes queer, BIPOC, disabled and other minority voices, so we believe it our duty to ensure that these stories are given a space to truly thrive" (Pomegranate Platform Inc., 2021, para. 4).

This is why over 95 percent of the content on Fearless isn't available on Netflix, Disney+, Hulu, or other major services. Therefore, Fearless offers an array of content categorized by 16 genres with over 40 filters to make sure that people can see themselves represented on screen. Titles include *Two Brothers*, a series featuring a BIPOC-led cast; *Desert Migration*, a series focusing on HIV-positive men moving to Palm Springs; and a documentary focusing on famed drag artist from *RuPaul Drag Race,* Jinkx Monsoon. Like TysonPlus, Fearless also offers opportunities for filmmakers devoted to creating inclusive content to get their work seen and monetized. The site works with independent filmmakers, giving them a platform to reach more viewers in an attempt to level the playing field among Hollywood studios with bigger budgets.

Lesflicks

The UK-based Lesflicks VOD, founded by Naomi Bennett, is an online space for women who love women. The site proclaims to host the world's largest collection of authentic sapphic stories on screen despite only launching in 2019. Focusing mainly on lesbian, bisexual, and some transgender movies, shorts, and TV series, Lesflicks brings viewers content they couldn't find on traditional (and even LGBTQ+) streaming services. The library is filled with both classic and new titles, and many are quite diverse, including *The Watermelon Woman* (1997), *Pariah* (2011), *Rafiki* (2018) and *Saving Face* (2004). The site even has a mature women category, numerous anime titles, and a section that is free for all to access.

Like so many of the other LGBTQ niche sites, Lesflicks works with investors and content creators to assist with the creation and distribution of diverse content. According to founder Bennett, Lesflicks is also a social enterprise, committed to paying filmmakers a fair rate, while educating the audience on the value of film and being completely transparent in their running costs. "We are disrupting a broken model and the values we have in place have really helped in our success" (Leonard, 2022, para. 6). In fact, it is the site's loyal community whose recommendations keep the platform bustling.

Uscreen

Lesflicks, Fearless, and TysonPlus are all hosted by Uscreen, a leading turn-key video content monetization platform that allows creators from across industries and various interest groups, like the LGBTQ community, to sell their videos online. Created by CEO and founder PJ Taei in 2015, the video monetization and distribution platform has over 25,000 creators sharing content with over 8.5 million end-users in over 95 countries. "The direction of our product development is determined by what our clients tell us they need to run a successful video business, paired with data that illuminates the path" (Uscreen, 2022, para. 5). This must be working for them because their revenue continues to grow over 100 percent every year, and they are making it possible for lower-budget niche creators and distributors like the streamers mentioned above to share more racially, sexually, and gender representative content with the world.

GagaOOLala

LGBTQ Asian characters are rarely seen on both the big and small screens. But thanks to GagaOOLala, viewers have a site where they can find uncensored content that specifically centers on people of Asian descent. the Taiwan–based Portico Media worldwide subscription VOD service, homes a large collection of queer Asian stories from across the continent. Their library includes K-queer films, drama series, animations and even a free section. Portico Media's CEO Jay Lin discussed the platform's global mission:

> Of course there are LGBT-focused services in Europe and the U.S., but they're almost exclusively Western. There are very few Asian titles, and if there are, they're more Asian American, or from a U.S.-centric or Western-centric point of view. This is the first time where an OTT service is available globally with such a high concentration of Asian content [Davis, 2020, para. 4].

Now in its sixth year, GagaOOLala has begun producing its own originals. These include the Taiwanese film *The Teacher* (2019), which won Winnie Chang a Golden

Horse Award last year for best-supporting actress, *Handsome Stewardess* (2019), the first Singaporean series to star a lesbian couple, and *Sodom's Cat* (2016), one of the first Asian queer films to depict a same-sex orgy.

Interestingly, much of the site's traffic can be attributed to its yaoi fandom (also called "boys' love" or BL) offerings—gay male love stories for straight female audiences, mostly teenage girls and young women. Dr. Rebecca Copeland, a professor of Japanese language and literature, discussed how such movies are the "ultimate chick flick" in Japan where BL stores have been popular with Japanese women for decades:

> … Japanese women are attracted to stories of male homosexuality because it's the only place in their society where they can see images of men in a loving, caring relationship where both partners are considered to be equals. It's the kind of relationship that Japanese women crave for themselves but rarely find within the confines of traditional Japanese society [Everding, 2006, para. 6].

Relevance of Niche LGBTQ Streaming Services

Ultimately, all these niche LGBTQ streamers are setting themselves apart by doing something that none of the mainstream SVODs are doing and that is giving opportunities to LGBTQ BIPOC and women filmmakers to hone their craft and showcase their work. These sites are grooming such creators to break down the doors of Hollywood and infiltrate the powers that be to advocate for stories about people whose voices are rarely heard because that is the only way to bring about real change in the film and television industry.

This is evident when looking at successful LGBTQ creators directors, producers and writers, like Greg Berlanti (*Love, Simon, Supergirl,* and *Black Lightning*), Shonda Rhimes (*Bridgerton, Scandal,* and *Grey's Anatomy*), Ryan Murphy (*American Horror Story, Boys in the Band,* and *The Prom*) and Ron Carlivati (*Days of Our Lives*) who are sexual and/or racial/gender minorities that have each created financially viable, high-rated television shows and films, portraying multi-dimensional racial and sexual minorities who all have integral parts in their projects. This invariably proves that having more BIPOC and LGBTQ content creators behind the scenes equates to films and series with more diverse content.

YouTube: The King of All Social Media and SVOD Sites

While in a league all its own, YouTube is another online destination where viewers can find LGBTQ content, including queer shorts and full-length feature films. Because the offerings on the site vary day to day, it is impossible to determine exactly how much content is available on the site, but just doing a cursory search for LGBT content brings up hundreds, if not thousands, of titles. Since the content is user-generated, the quality of the films varies from amateur to professional; however, the diversity offered is probably the most found at any one site. High-profile LGBTQ YouTubers such as Todrick Hall, Lilly Singh, Anna Akana, and so many more, regularly produce content highlighting the experiences of LGBTQ people of color.

Unfortunately, YouTube's relationship with the gay community, as of late, has been strained, causing the video-sharing site to put out a Twitter statement in June 2018 stating how they have let the community down. It all started when many of the YouTube creators noticed anti–LGBTQ ads (mostly those created by the Alliance Defending Freedom and *AskDrBrown* Ministries) were running against their content—especially those who identified as and spoke openly about LGBTQ issues. The demonetization of LGBTQ content has also been a major concern for creators, especially after the experiment by YouTuber Chase Ross in 2018, which proved that whenever he included the words "transgender" in his title his content was instantly demonetized. (Hills, 2018, paras. 4, 8). YouTube (2018) responded with the following statement on Twitter:

> We've taken action on the ads that violate our policies, and we are tightening our enforcement. And when we hear concerns about how we're implementing our monetization policy, we take them seriously and make improvements if needed. It's critical to us that the LGBTQ community feels safe, welcome, equal, and supported on YouTube. Your work is incredibly powerful and we are committed to working with you to get this right.

This is not the first time YouTube has encountered hurdles with the LGBTQ community. In 2017, creators noticed their LGBTQ content was being hidden in "restricted mode," even though it didn't contain mature content. Restricted mode was originally created to give public institutions like libraries and schools the ability to prevent people from watching mature content like porn or graphic violence on their computers. CEO Susan Wojcicki admitted the system also filtered out innocuous LGBTQ content, and examples she gave included "kissing at weddings, personal accounts of difficult events, and speaking out against discrimination" (as cited in Shu, 2017, para. 3).

This filtering hiccup was extremely problematic for two primary reasons. The filter prohibited gay youth from being able to access the content, thus isolating them from finding a community during a time in their lives when such support can be critical in preventing emotional distress and even suicides. YouTuber Rowan Ellis, an author and speaker known for her educational online content and advocacy work in the LGBTQ+ community, noted: "The platform is 'one of the only places that queer and trans youth, gay youth, bisexual youth, pansexual youth, asexual youth, any of these kids, have a way into community, have a way into knowledge, have a way of feeling that they are not alone'" (as cited in Shu, 2017, para. 4).

The second reason affected monetization. Some YouTube creators claimed the platform's algorithms not only impacted their view counts, but also greatly affected their income because many of them saw their ad revenue drop as several major advertisers boycotted the platform, citing that the videos contained extremist content. According to Wojcicki, the organization has taken steps to correct these issues. In April, YouTube said it corrected an engineering problem that was wrongly filtering LGBTQ videos. They also rewrote guidelines seeking to clarify its position by specifically allowing personal accounts from victims of discrimination or violent hate crimes, as long as they don't contain graphic language or content. Wojcicki also said they added new content to its Creator Academy, or resources for video makers, to help them create videos that won't be blocked in restricted mode. She also asked people to submit videos they thought were wrongly restricted and promised that YouTube would review each one (Shu, 2017, para. 5–6).

YouTube has taken steps to remove some of the obstacles the LGBTQ community has encountered with the video-sharing platform, so hopefully, this will create a better experience for YouTube creators and viewers alike. Being a social media platform, YouTube also allows viewers to connect with one another by creating, discussing, and commenting on their preferred content. Much like B. Ruby Rich (2002) described LGBTQ film festivals as "gather[ing] queer communities together in a statement of identity and solidarity" (p. 1), YouTube in some ways appears to be filling that void.

Conclusion

Streaming services play a pivotal role in reshaping the landscape of cultural production by providing a platform that responds directly to the diverse needs and preferences of marginalized groups. Unlike traditional media channels, streaming services can leverage data analytics to understand and cater to the specific tastes of their audience. This personalized approach enables a more accurate representation of various cultures and identities, fostering a sense of inclusivity.

With consumers currently abandoning their home video collections and, in many cases, even their cable subscriptions, the mainstream streaming sites, the LGBTQ and niche LGBTQ SVOD companies, as well as YouTube have allowed those craving queer content a sacred space to explore their identity and feel a connection with the community in the comfort of their own homes. LGBTQ-plus representation has significantly increased on streaming platforms, allowing for more nuanced and authentic storytelling that resonates with the queer community. This responsiveness to diverse audiences challenges traditional reception theory, which posits that media consumption is a passive process. Instead, streaming services engage viewers as active participants, acknowledging and incorporating their feedback into content creation.

SVOD has also allowed longtime LGBTQ distributors like Wolfe to maintain visibility and profitability in this new media economy. And most importantly, where so many of the streaming platforms appear to fall short is with diverse content, especially the mainstream streamers, so the exclusive LGBTQ and specialty queer streamers have stepped up to provide viewers access to more gender and racially inclusive LGBTQ content, with the latter even finding ways to financially support up-and-coming LGBTQ BIPOC and female content creators. This exemplifies how the democratization of cultural production is amplified through streaming services, as they provide a platform for underrepresented voices to reach a global audience. Independent creators from marginalized groups can now produce content without the same gatekeeping mechanisms present in traditional media. This shift in power dynamics challenges the hegemony of mainstream narratives and allows for a more democratic exchange of ideas. By offering a stage for a multitude of voices, streaming services contribute to the decentralization of cultural production, breaking down barriers and enabling a richer tapestry of stories and perspectives. In this way, streaming services become not just distributors of content but catalysts for social change by democratizing the creation and consumption of cultural products.

Ultimately, LGBTQ viewers can rest assured that whichever streaming site they decide to access out of the ones discussed in this essay will more than likely have more diverse and inclusive LGBTQ options than what is being offered at mainstream movie theaters.

References

Amorosi, A.D. (2017). Dekkoo, a new gay-focused TV/film streaming service, launches in Philly. *Metro.* https://www.metro.us/news/local-news/philadelphia/dekkoo-new-gay-focused-tvfilm-streaming-service-launches-philly.

Bridge, G. (2022, January 4). Fading ratings: A special report on TV's shrinking audiences. *Variety.* https://variety.com/vip-special-reports/fading-ratings-a-special-report-on-tvs-shrinking-audiences-1235142986/.

Capon, T. (2018). *Netflix's LGBTQ Film section is mostly gay men and people aren't happy.* Gay Star News. https://www.gaystarnews.com/article/netflix-gay-films-lgbt-lesbian/#gs.UDodaoY.

Clark, T. (2018, February 20). *New data shows Netflix's number of movies has gone down by thousands of titles since 2010—but its TV catalog size has soared.* Business Insider. https://www.businessinsider.com/netflix-movie-catalog-size-has-gone-down-since-2010-2018-2.

Davis, R. (2020, May 15). Taiwan's LGBTQ streamer GagaOOLala launches worldwide. *Variety.* https://variety.com/2020/film/news/gagaoolala-portico-media-taiwan-gay-marriage-boys-love-1234608357/.

Everding, G. (2006, March 1). *'Brokeback Mountain' might be ultimate 'chick flick' in Japan, says literature expert.* The Source. https://source.wustl.edu/2006/03/brokeback-mountain-might-be-ultimate-chick-flick-in-japan-says-literature-expert/.

GLAAD. (2021). *Studio responsibility index.* https://www.glaad.org/sri/2021/.

GLAAD. (2022). *Where we are on TV.* https://www.glaad.org/sites/default/files/GLAAD%20202122%20WWATV.pdf.

Here TV. (2018). Retrieved at https://www.heretv.com/.

Hod, I. (2015, April 8). *LOGO chief Chris McCarthy on how the network returned to its gay roots; Why Bravo is not competition.* The Wrap. https://www.thewrap.com/logo-chief-chris-mccarthy-on-how-the-network-returned-to-its-gay-roots-why-bravo-is-not-its-competition/.

Hills, M.C. (2018, June 30). YouTube 'let the LGBTQ community down,' it says in a Twitter statement. *Forbes.* https://www.forbes.com/sites/meganhills1/2018/06/30/youtube-lgbt-community/#10d4202a99d0.

Leonard, M. (2022). *No paying audience: How Lesflicks brings films to fans who don't exist.* Canon. https://www.canon-europe.com/view/no-paying-audience-lesflicks-lesbian-film/.

Martens, J. (2017, February 7). Streaming gay culture. *Rage Monthly.* http://www.ragemonthly.com/2017/02/07/dekkoo/.

McCracken, C. (2017, October 2). *An LGBTQ Netflix: Productive? Restricting? Lasting?* Flow Journal. https://www.flowjournal.org/2017/10/an-lgbtq-netflix.

Moore, C. (2013, Fall). Distribution is queen. LGBTQ media on demand. *Cinema Journal, 53*(1), 137–144.

Nielsen. (2021). *Proud and present: LGBTQ audiences and content take center stage.* https://www.nielsen.com/us/en/insights/article/2021/proud-present-lgbtq-audiences-content-take-center-stage/.

Pomegranate Platform Inc. (2021, June 10). *Inclusive streaming service, Fearless, goes global.* PR Newswire. https://www.prnewswire.com/news-releases/inclusive-streaming-service-fearless-goes-global-301310544.html.

PRWeb. (2018, September 18). *Here TV expands its award-winning programming to satellite provider DISH.* https://www.prweb.com/releases/here_tv_expands_its_award_winning_programming_to_satellite_provider_dish/prweb15769520.htm.

Revry. (2018). https://revry.tv/.

Rich, B.R. (2002, March 26). Vision quest. *Village Voice.*

Schwartz, D.H., & Hadley, C. (2017, October 24). *DEKKOO: Video entertainment for gay audiences.* Huffington Post. https://www.huffingtonpost.com/entry/dekkoo-video-entertainment-for-gay-audiences_us_59ef9d39e4b04809c05011ca.

Scott, C. (2018, April 14). *Lesbians are not being properly represented in Hollywood.* Study Breaks. https://studybreaks.com/tvfilm/lesbian-representation/.

Shu, C. (2017, June 20). *YouTube updates its policies after LGBTQ videos were blocked in restricted mode.* TechCrunch. https://techcrunch.com/2017/06/19/youtube-updates-its-policies-after-lgbtq-videos-were-blocked-in-restricted-mode/.

Smith, S.L., Choueiti, M., Pieper, K., Case, A. & Choi, A. (2018, July). Inequality in 1,100 popular films: Examining portrayals of gender, race/ethnicity, LGBT & disability from 2007 to 2017. *USC Annenberg Inclusion Initiative.* http://assets.uscannenberg.org/docs/inequality-in-1100-popular-films.pdf.

Uscreen. (2022). *About us.* https://www.uscreen.tv/about-us/.

Watercutter, A. (2018, September 19). Revry: The streaming service trying to take queer content global. *Wired.* https://www.wired.com/story/revry-streaming/.

YouTube. [@youtube]. (2018, June 30). *We've taken action on the ads that violate our policies, and we are tightening our enforcement. And when we hear* [Tweet]. Twitter. https://twitter.com/YouTube/status/1013104844364763136.

Conclusion

JONINA ANDERSON-LOPEZ *and* ALLISON CHRISTINA BUDAJ

In pulling this essay collection together, the editors were unsure of the direction this project would take. Understanding audience reception and television is full of nuance, as the various essays analyzed. Each year, networks and streaming services update their show offerings, perhaps in response to the changing demographics and wider acceptance of diverse characters. When we were first drafting our television research in 2020, we approached it by reviewing a show that had ended (*Girls*) and an ongoing show (*The 100*). Now, at the time of publication for this essay collection, both *Girls* and *The 100* have ended, and thus the editors contend their impacts can be assessed as early indicators for the intersections of online audience reception, cancel culture, and diversity surrounding contemporary television.

With online audience reception, television audiences are making meaning of the narratives. As some of the essays have noted, the viral capabilities of certain audience sentiment can elevate issues or result in seeming cancellations of characters, plotlines, or shows. As Stuart Hall (1973) notes, "the 'object' of production practices and structures in television is the production of a message" (p. 1). The message audiences perceive versus what a creator intended will vary. Leo Tolstoy (1899) shares "this capacity of man to receive another man's expression of feeling, and experience those feelings himself, that the activity of art is based" (p. 41). However, audiences can attribute their own feelings and interpretations to perceive works. Through these sentiments, they can inscribe meaning to a text, but that meaning is not "as a solid be-all and end-all. Rather, it is the result of an inevitable operation of transmutation triggered and sustained by the necessity to cope with the experience of the imaginary" (Iser, 1993, p. 18). Based on Wolfgang Iser's work, audiences could be building the meaning of television narratives (i.e., texts) to diffuse the tension of the unknown. In this pursuit of meaning-making, audiences have easier and far wider-reaching opportunities to share their sentiments.

Concerning cancel culture, there are many different types, like online harassment or call-outs as mentioned by Camille S. Alexander. There are also types of political and economic cancel culture. This work chose to focus on the economic associations of cancel culture in television. Yet, economic forms of cancel culture may not have been as prevalent as more recent high-profile case studies of a political nature. Nearly five years ago, senator Al Franken was "canceled" due to sexual misconduct allegations. Yet, in the current political climate, congressman like Matt Gaetz can weather a similar (if not worse) sexual misconduct storm in the public eye. Comparatively, economic cancel culture has seen a swift evolution in the past five years, leading to firings and shakeups at networks and production companies. Though the firings or production decisions are made by people in power, sometimes the ideas behind them are motivated by people with little power (i.e., #BuryYourGays or #MeToo movement). Due to the popularity of online fan forums and other forms of online fan criticism, networks have seemingly applied more scrutiny to how their employees are publicly perceived. These perceptions have, at times, coincided with production decisions or firings. Networks consistently look to customer and stakeholder input as one factor measured against creative and economic decisions. Yet, the colloquial use of "cancel culture" is also an all-encompassing term that can shield businesses like Bravo, CBS, and other networks from intense scrutiny for what is ultimately a business decision. At times, these decisions are made quickly, and the companies can hide behind ideas like "cancel culture" or "solving racism" rather than approaching a complex decision with patience and empathy.

This project has illuminated (for the editors) how the opportunity for diverse characterization has always existed. It's only in the last decade that it has been popularized in U.S. media spaces on a wider scale than previous decades. Non-White, non-heteronormative actors (and creators) have always been available. They have not always been afforded equitable opportunities. Instead, White heteronormative casts have often taken precedence. More recently, television and streaming shows have highlighted how storytelling is an opportunity in and of itself to revert expectations. For instance, *Vikings: Valhalla* is a show with historical expectations, with these expectations diverging among critics and fans. Paul Csillag's analysis of *Vikings: Valhalla* and audience reception showed how a television show is a work of fiction, and the creators can decide how best to depict the surrounding world and reflect said creation back to the audience. This may generate pushback of imagined notions of "authenticity," but it can be argued that in a fictional world, nothing is authentic except as set forth by the standards of the characters and worldbuilding. When television and streaming creators decide to create a new narrative, they can assess what came before (with all the historical, literary, and media representations that may or may not be associated with their narrative) and reshape any exclusionary storytelling tactics. An example similar to *Valhalla: Vikings* approach to diverse characterization is the 2022 Amazon series *The Lord of the Rings: The Rings of Power* (or *LoTR: The Rings of Power*). Similar to *Valhalla: Vikings*, *LoTR: The Rings of Power* is set in a medieval past, or what viewers might perceive to be a White homogeneous past. In the lived imagination of some viewers, a medieval past (even a fantastical medieval past) would negate diverse representation as a matter of principle because as this *LoTR* Reddit fan posted "they'd better NOT be turning is PC by mixing races where Tolkien didn't, it'll ruin it for all long-time Tolkien fans" (u/No-Mastodon-7187, 2022).

A similar sentiment followed after casting was announced for *GoT* prequel *House of the Dragon* (2022–present). As mentioned in the essay "Tug of War: Social Media, Cancel Culture, and Diversity for *Girls* and *The 100*," Whoopi Goldberg discussed these developments on *The View*. Her words echoed much of the research reflected in this work: the relationship between fans and creator decisions. Goldberg was critical of the fan backlash involving casting and her words are worth repeating:

Conclusion (Anderson-Lopez & Budaj) 277

Figure 1. Film and TV casts (from top): *LoTR* 1999, *The Hobbit* 2012, and *LoTR: The Rings of Power* 2022 (New Line Cinema and Amazon Prime Video).

> They [… dragons, hobbits …] don't exist in the real world, [...] You know that? There are no dragons. There are no hobbits. Are you telling me Black people can't be fake people too? Is that what you're telling me? I don't know if there's like a hobbit club, I don't know if there are gonna be protests, but people! What is wrong with y'all? [as cited in Sharf, 2022].

This quote epitomizes the dichotomy between fictional worlds and fan demands for what they consider to be authentic. Despite the otherworldly settings and characters intrinsic to fantasy stories, some fans may insist on an imagined historical narrative (as outlined by Csillag).

For fantasy film and television projects ten and twenty years ago, diversity may have been rarer among casts and creators than by recent standards. The film franchises of *LoTR* (1999–2003) and *The Hobbit* (2012–2014) lacked diverse casts (see Figure 1). Thus, it was a change to see the casting for *LoTR: The Rings of Power* feature several women and BIPOC as co-stars, including characters like Míriel (played by Black actor Cynthia Addai-Robinson), Bronwyn (played by Iranian actor Nazanian Boniadi), Arondir (played by Puerto Rican actor Ismael Enrique Cruz Córdova), Princess Disa (played by Black actor Sophia Nomvete), and Sadac Burrows (played by Black actor Lenny Henry). Brenzican and Robinson noted (2022), "When Amazon released photos of its multicultural cast, even without character names or plot details, the studio endured a reflexive attack from trolls—the anonymous online kind" (para. 34). *LoTR: The Rings of Power* producers and cast members defended the new direction a Tolkien adaptation had taken with a BIPOC cast. Lindsey Weber, executive producer of the series stated, "Tolkien is for everyone. His stories are about his fictional races doing their best work when they leave the isolation of their own cultures and come together" (as cited in Brenzican & Robinson, 2022, para. 35). Television and streaming networks are increasingly illustrating how stories are a way to promote the ever-expanding multi-racial and multi-everything populace of the U.S. Though these sorts of decisions (i.e., diverse casting) are not altogether altruistic, nonetheless, their inclusion by network and streaming platforms can positively impact audiences.

More than anything else, this essay collection has demonstrated how audience participation is opening casting and showrunner opportunities. As Brenzican and Robinson (2022) mentioned, there is a "Great Global Streaming War" taking place (para. 22), which may shape the format and delivery of content in the following decades. The pressure to be the most popular network or streaming service is coinciding with the rise of online audience participation. With social media as an expanding tool, audience expectations can now evolve more rapidly and be heard by networks just as quickly.

References

Breznican, A., & Robinson, J. (2022, February 10). Amazon's *Lord of the Rings* series rises: Inside *The Rings of Power*. *Vanity Fair*. https://www.vanityfair.com/hollywood/2022/02/amazon-the-rings-of-power-series-first-look.

Hall, S. (1973). *Encoding and decoding in the television discourse*. ePapers Repository. http://epapers.bham.ac.uk/2962/

Iser, W. (1993). *The fictive and the imaginary: Charting literary anthropology*. Johns Hopkins University Press.

Sharf, Z. (2022, September 6). Whoopi Goldberg rails against racist 'Rings of Power' and 'House of the Dragon' fans: 'What is wrong with y'all?' *Variety*. https://variety.com/2022/tv/news/whoopi-goldberg-racist-rings-of-power-house-of-the-dragon-fans-1235361828/.

Tolstoy, L. (1899). *What is art?* (Aylmer Maude, Trans.). Thomas Y. Crowell.

u/No-Mastodon-7187. (2022). r/SelfAwarewolves page, *Reddit*. https://www.reddit.com/r/SelfAwarewolves/comments/stnt7s/regarding_lotr_casting_poc/.

About the Contributors

Camille S. **Alexander** is an assistant professor of English at Tuskegee University. She earned a PhD in English at the University of Kent, where her research focused on Caribbean female migratory literature. Her research interests include Caribbean studies and literature, Black British literature, film, African American literature, and third-wave feminism.

Jonina **Anderson-Lopez** teaches at institutions like the University of South Florida (USF) and Joyce University of Nursing and Health Sciences. She earned a PhD in interdisciplinary studies from Union Institute & University (UI&U). She served as lead editor for the UI&U interdisciplinary journal *Penumbra* and her research has resulted in awards and fellowships.

Chandrama **Basu** is a doctoral student in the English Department of Presidency University, Kolkata, India, and a faculty member of the Department of English, Prasanta Chandra Mahalanobis Mahavidyalaya, Kolkata. Her articles have been published in various national and international journals and her research interests center on Victorian culture, reception history, gender studies, and popular culture.

Allison Christina **Budaj** is an administrator for the General Education Department at Joyce University of Nursing and Health Sciences. She earned a PhD in interdisciplinary studies from Union Institute & University. Her research has primarily focused on popular culture and visual narratives. Her academic history includes teaching humanities, communication, and interdisciplinary studies courses.

Saleema Mustafa **Campbell** is the director of the Adolescent Literacy Project at Kentucky State University. She earned her doctorate in pan–African studies and postcolonial literature from the University of Louisville in 2020 after teaching in both secondary and post-secondary institutions for more than a decade. She has worked in educational training and diversity recruitment.

Anna **Caterino** is pursuing a PhD in linguistics, literary, and intercultural studies at the University of Milan. She holds a BA and MA in foreign languages and literatures. In 2023, she won the Alexei Kondratiev Award (student paper) for her essay "Hell on His Mind: Dean Winchester's Journey to Hell and Back."

Paul **Csillag** studies Europe, the Mediterranean, and the Orient as portrayed by the historical novel of the nineteenth century at the European University Institute. He studied history and European ethnology at the universities of Innsbruck, Jean-Jaurès (Toulouse), and Yeditepe (Istanbul), earning degrees in both fields with papers on the reception of history in pop-cultural fiction.

Victor D. **Evans** is an assistant professor of communication at Seattle University where he teaches journalism and mass communication courses. His research focuses on how LGBTQ media images affect gay youth as they come to terms with their sexuality. He has also authored a middle-grade LGBTQ series, the Evan Sinclair Mysteries.

Ragan **Fox** is a professor of communication at California State University, Long Beach. In the summer of 2010, he was a contestant on the 12th season of CBS's *Big Brother*. He is the author of two poetry collections and *Inside Reality TV: Producing Race, Gender, and Sexuality on "Big Brother"* (Routledge, 2018).

About the Contributors

Chris **Galloway** teaches public relations on the Auckland, New Zealand, campus of Massey University. His research encompasses crisis communication, reputation management, and the impacts of technologies such as artificial intelligence on the promotional industries, and he combines diverse senior professional experience with his academic achievements.

Erin E. **Gilles** is an associate professor of advertising and public relations at the University of Southern Indiana. She is also the director of the Master of Arts in communication program and serves as the editor of the *Kentucky Journal of Communication*. Her research interests include social justice, health communication, and popular culture.

Rosemarie **Jones** works in diversity, equity, and inclusion at Washington University in St. Louis. Her research includes the intersection of gender and policy, with specialization in intimate partner violence. She is an adjunct instructor at area institutions. Her courses are interdisciplinary in nature, crossing between women and gender studies, sociology, philosophy, and law.

Dean **Kruckeberg**, APR, Fellow PRSA, is a professor in the Department of Communication Studies at the University of North Carolina at Charlotte. He is the co-author of several books on public relations and has won prestigious awards for his teaching of public relations. His areas of interest include global public relations and public relations ethics.

R.J. **Lambert** is an associate professor at the Medical University of South Carolina. He holds national service positions for the Council for Programs in Technical and Scientific Communication and the National Communication Association Health Communication Division. He has published on student safety and healthy risks in writing pedagogy and crisis response failures after the Gulf of Mexico oil spill.

Arien **Rozelle** spent more than a decade working in marketing and public relations before joining the Department of Media and Communication at St. John Fisher College in Rochester, New York. She is an award-winning professor and practitioner, and her research interests include the role of public relations in activism, public relations pedagogy, and diversity in public relations.

Ronen **Shay** is an assistant professor at the Gabelli School of Business at Fordham University. His research addresses contemporary challenges in media management, strategic communication, and technology diffusion. He has published articles in *Journalism & Mass Communication Quarterly*, *Games and Culture*, and *International Journal on Media Management*.

Lukasz **Swiatek** lectures in the School of the Arts and Media at the University of New South Wales (UNSW) in Sydney, Australia. He mainly undertakes research in media and communication, cultural studies, and higher education. He has taught courses in media studies, communication, and international and global studies at universities in Australia and New Zealand.

Juanita "Tico" **Tenorio** is a faculty member of the English Department at Guam Community College, where she teaches courses in English, gender studies, and critical thinking for civic engagement. After teaching in English departments for more than twenty years, she earned a PhD in interdisciplinary studies from Union Institute and University.

Farha B. **Ternikar** is an associate professor at Le Moyne College, where she teaches gender and society, social inequality and gender and feminist theory. She has published several articles in the *Journal of Ethnic Studies*, *International Journal of Contemporary Sociology*, and *Sociology Compass* as well as books on Muslim women and consumption.

Marina **Vujnovic** is a professor in the Department of Communication at Monmouth University in New Jersey. Her work explores intersections between journalism and public relations, looking at issues of participation, activism, transparency, and ethics. She is the author of *Forging the Bubikopf Nation: Journalism, Gender and Modernity in Interwar Yugoslavia* (Peter Lang, 2009).

Christina S. **Walker**, Esq., J.D., is a licensed attorney pursuing a PhD in communication at the University of Kentucky, College of Communication and Information. She is an intercultural communication scholar with recent publications focusing on audience perceptions of race, gender, and sexual orientation in response to media portrayals of intimate partner violence.

Index

ABC (American Broadcasting Company) 5, 113, 115, 130–132, 136–137, 142, 211–214, 216, 220–223, 238
ableism 10, 223, 238
abortion 210–212
Academy Award 264
Ackles, Jensen 148–149, 156, 160, 163–165
active shooter 216
Adam 172
Addai-Robinson, Cynthia 278
Aden (*The 100*) 183
after school special 211–212
age 19, 38, 64, 65, 81, 97, 131–133, 138, 142, 154, 181, 196, 236–238, 240, 248, 282
ageism 225, 234
aging 223, 228, 233, 236–238
Aiossa, Elizabeth 182
Akana, Anna 270
Aladdin 252
Alaska Is a Drag 259
alcoholism 57, 218
Alex Strangelove 259
Alexis (*Schitt's Creek*) 175–180
Ali, Bisha 247
Ali, Muhammad 138
All American 214, 218
All in the Family 211
Alliance Defending Freedom 271
Alston, Bernice 183
Amazon 95, 211–214, 217, 220–222, 255, 260–262, 266, 276–278
Amazon Studios 260, 278
AMC 123
Amer (*Ms. Marvel*) 251
American Broadcasting Company *see* ABC
American Horror Story 270
And Just Like That... 10, 12, 223–225, 228–236, 238–239
Anne Boleyn 193
Anthony, Kevin 268
Apple TV+ 255, 262
April (*Supernatural*) 161
Araki, Greg 258

archetype 17, 135, 153–154
Archie (*All in the Family*) 211
Aristotle 201
Arondir (*LoTR: The Rings of Power*) 278
asexuality 271
Asian 18, 20, 23, 25, 75, 122, 243, 246–247, 249–251, 269–270
AskDrBrown Ministries 271
The Assistant 213
Atwood, Margaret 105
audience reception 1, 2, 10–12, 36, 64, 67–68, 72–73, 77, 96–99, 101, 103, 106, 108, 115–116, 133, 136–137, 140, 144, 150–151, 160, 165, 172, 181, 228, 239, 243–244, 247–249, 251, 275–276
audience reception theory 133, 244, 247–249
authenticity 58, 70, 132, 143, 193–196, 198–199, 203, 208, 276
The A.V. Club 136–137, 143, 223, 228, 230–231, 233, 235, 238–239

Baker, Jack 172, 174
Baker, Lily 184
Balaban, Liane 162
Barry 214, 219
Bathina, Shalini 262
Beaver, Jim 160
Before I Got Famous 265
Beharie, Nicole 5
Bel-Air 239
Below Deck 66
Benedict, Rob 148
Bennett, Naomi 268
Berens, Robert 160–161, 166
Berlanti, Greg 270
BET 46
BH901210 239
Big (*Sex and the City*) 230, 231
The Big Bang Theory 214, 218–219
Big Shot 262
Big Sky 164

Billions 8
binge watching 182, 227
biological sex 176
The Bionic Woman 245
biphobia 164
BIPOC 29, 145, 267–268, 270, 272, 278
bisexuality 111, 175–176, 184–185, 224, 255–256, 262, 269, 271
Black, Carol 131
Black America 126, 128, 131, 133, 210
Black Lightning 270
Black Lives Matter (BLM) 29–31, 35, 42, 55, 61–62, 65, 72–73, 75–76, 210, 213
The Blacklist 214, 218
Blacklow, Jeremy 265
Blackstone, Amy M. 177
blasphemy 215
Blatch, Stanford 173, 230–231, 235
blindness 217
blogging 130
Bohemian Rhapsody 256
Boniadi, Nazanin 278
Booksmart 260
Bosch Legacy 214, 217
Bound 261
boycott 35, 46, 70, 72, 76, 78, 85, 106, 162, 271
The Boys 214, 217, 261
Boys Don't Cry 263
Boys Hurt Too 268
The Boys in the Band 259, 270
boy's love 270
Bradbury, Charlie 162
Bradshaw, Carrie 173, 223, 229–232, 234, 236–238
Braff, Zack 9
Brando, Marlon 154
Bravo 53–56, 58–62, 64–77, 276
Brewer, Patrick 173, 175–181, 183, 185
Bridgerton 270
Brittany (*Glee*) 173
Brokeback Mountain 261

283

Bronwyn (*LoTR: The Rings of Power*) 278
Brookliyn Nine-Nine 214
Brown, Kamaro 261
Buddy 266
Buddy Games 256
Buffy the Vampire Slayer 182, 184, 260
bullying 29, 58, 136, 215, 228
Burch, Ashley 262
Burmaster, Mitkai 268
Burrows, Sadac (*The Lord of the Rings: The Rings of Power*) 278
#BuryYourGays 102–103, 105, 107, 109, 111, 151, 159, 161, 163, 182, 184, 185, 276
Bushnell, Candace 224
Butler, Judith 174

Cady (*Mean Girls*) 173
Call Me by Your Name 257
Calzo, Jerel P. 186
Cam (*Modern Family*) 173
cancel culture 1, 2, 6, 10–12, 36, 43, 45–49, 53, 55–57, 59, 62, 63, 77, 95–97, 103–106, 109, 114–116, 150, 152, 160, 166, 243–244, 254, 275–276
Candy 214, 219
capitalism 25, 31, 77, 151, 166, 207
Captain Marvel (character) 244–245, 252
Captain Marvel (film) 245, 252
Carlivati, Ron 270
Carlton (*Fresh Prince of Bel-Air*) 210
Carnival Row 261
Carter, Kenneth E. 179
Carver, Jeremy 155–156, 163
Castiel 148, 151–152, 155–163
Castleberry 248
Cattrall, Kim 224, 230
CBS 17–23, 25–26, 29–31, 36–39, 41–50, 87–88, 109, 213, 214, 218, 219, 220–222, 261, 276
Chang, Winnie 269
Change.org 31
Chapelle, Dave 11
Charlotte (*Sex and the City*) 229–230, 232–233, 235–236
Cheadle, Don 132, 138
child abuse 212
Choudhury, Sarita 232
cisgender 39, 42, 54, 59, 265–267
Civil Rights era 131, 135, 138
Civil Rights movements 143
class 248–249, 259
Clexa 103, 110–111, 116, 181–183, 185
Clinton, Bill 174
CNN 8, 100
Cobalt Blue 259

Cohan, Lauren 150
Colichman, Paul 264
Collins, Misha 148, 155, 161–163, 166
Collins, Patricia Hill 248
The Color Purple 261
colorblindness 75, 126
comedy 138
The Conners 5
conspiracy theory 215–216
Conversations with Friends 260
Copeland, Rebecca 270
Córdova, Ismael Enrique Cruz 278
counterculture movement 131
COVID-19 58, 65, 69–70, 75, 88, 255, 257
Crenshaw, Kimberlé 248
Criminal Minds 214, 218–219
Cristina (*Grey's Anatomy*) 211
cross-sex 178
Cruise, Tom 206
Crush 155, 260
Cruz, Wilson 261
cultivation theory 186
cultural expectations 139
cultural misappropriation 130
cultural norms 130
Cumberbach, Benedict 250
The CW 148, 150, 160, 162–164, 213, 214, 217–218, 220, 221

Dabb, Andrew 148, 152, 156, 162–163
Damian (*Mean Girls*) 173
Daniels, Lee 132–133
The Danish Girl 259
Darwinism 201; *see also* Social Darwinism
Davis, Kristin 236
Days of Our Lives 270
DC 245
Dean, James 154
The Death and Life of Marsha P. Johnson 259
Debnam-Carey, Alycia 98, 181
D.E.B.S. 258
decoding 4, 133–135, 143, 145, 247–248; *see also* encoding
DeGeneres, Ellen 172
de Groot, Jerome 195
DEI 221
DEKKOO 259, 266
Delphine (*Orphan Black*) 184
Denise (*The Walking Dead*) 182
Desert Migration 268
Desi 248
Designing Women 212
Destiel 148–149, 155, 158, 160, 163, 165
Deviant Media 86
Diary of a Future President 262
Diaz, Che 230, 234–235
Dickinson 262

Diff'rent Strokes 212
disability 163, 237, 268
discrimination 8, 22, 35, 43, 55, 62, 76, 138, 175, 186, 251, 271
Disney 105, 142, 221, 243, 252–253, 260
Disney+ 12, 213–214, 219–222, 243, 255, 262, 268
Distrify 263
diversity 1–2, 4, 6–12, 18–19, 30, 35–36, 38, 41–44, 46, 49–50, 54–55, 58–59, 68, 71, 73, 75–77, 95–101, 103, 105, 107–111, 113–116, 120–123, 125–127, 130, 132, 135–137, 141, 143, 145–146, 150, 163, 165, 204, 207, 221, 224, 232, 244, 252–253, 255–257, 259, 263–265, 267–268, 270, 272, 275–276, 278
Doctor Strange: Multiverse of Madness 5
A Dog Barking at the Moon 261
domestic terrorism 216
Domingo, Coleman 128
Donaldson, Christopher 264
Doogie Kamealoha, M.D. 262
drag 267–268
drug 122–124, 126, 212; abuse 217; addict 123; use 114
Dry, Judy 173
Dryer, Richard 173
Due, Tananarive 124

E! News 231
Earthsea 193
Echo Chamberlin 194, 196, 200–201, 203–207
Edith (*All in the Family*) 211
electron fraud 216
Elektra 245
Eliot (*The Magicians*) 173
Elite 260
Ellis, Rowan 271
Ellen 172
Emmy Award 212, 224, 229, 261, 264
emoji 228
encoding 4, 133–134, 143–145, 247–248; *see also* decoding
equity 35, 55, 61, 73, 75, 77, 145–146, 221
ER 212
ethnic 18, 39, 42–43, 46, 49, 100, 122, 125, 127, 130, 135–137, 143, 145, 193, 196, 205–206, 243, 248, 250, 252
Euphoria 172, 261
Everybody Changes 261
Everybody's Talking About Jamie 260
The Eyes of Tammy Faye 267

Facebook 45, 65–67, 72, 99, 104, 227, 243, 263, 264

Family Guy 214, 216–217
Family Ties 212
fatherhood 154
FBI 151, 174, 250–251
Fear the Walking Dead 12, 120–123, 125–128
fearless 268–269
Federal Communications Commission 131
feminism 6, 18, 65, 100–101, 103, 139, 150, 224, 237, 246, 248
15 Years 261
Finding Prince Charming 267
Findlay, Maude 211
Finn (*The 100*) 182
Fire Island 260, 267
Flach, Kate L. 131, 141
The Flash 214, 218
Fleabag 261
Fleischer, Richard 194
Floyd, George 29, 55, 57, 64, 68, 109, 210, 251
FML 265
Foucault, Michael 108–109
FOX 213–214, 216–217, 220–222, 262
Fox News 69
Franken, Al 275
Fresh Prince of Bel-Air 210
Friends 97, 106, 115, 227
Full House 132, 212
Fuller House 239

Gaetz, Matt 275
GagaOOLala 269
Gaius Media 266
Gamble, Sera 152, 157
Game of Thrones 95–97, 148, 214, 219, 276
Gandhi, Mahatma 206
Garcia, Andy 250
Garner, Jennifer 245
Garson, Willie 230, 231
gaslighting 159
gay 21–23, 115, 153–154, 156, 158–160, 162, 164, 173, 175–176, 179, 181, 186, 230, 234–235, 256–258, 261–264, 266–267, 270–271
Gay and Lesbian Alliance Against Defamation (GLAAD) 172, 255, 257, 259, 261, 265
gender 2, 38–39, 41, 44, 48–49, 65, 77, 97–98, 100, 102, 108, 132 135 153, 157, 166, 173–174, 176, 178–179, 183, 193, 196, 223, 225, 235, 238, 243–244, 246–249, 251, 253–254, 259, 263, 267, 269, 270, 272
George (*My Best Friend's Wedding*) 173
Gerbner, George 186
Gia 261

Gilmore Girls 7
Ginsberg, Alan 153
Girl Meets World 239
Girls 1, 7, 10–11, 96, 275, 276
Girls5Eva 261
GLAAD *see* Gay and Lesbian Alliance Against Defamation
GLB 186
Glee 173
Global Citizen 86–87
Gloria (*All in the Family*) 211
Glover, Donald 98, 106, 110
The Godfather 250
Goldberg, Whoopi 96, 276
The Golden Girls 212
Golden Globe 224
Golden Horse Award 269, 270
The Good Fight 1, 11
Google 90
Grey's Anatomy 211, 214, 216, 270
Griffin, Clarke 98, 102–103, 107, 111, 173, 181–184
Gross, Larry 186
Grounder clan 181
Guardians of the Galaxy 252
gun control 217
gun violence 212
Gunn, James 105
Gyllenhaal, Jake 250

Haakon, Jarl 193–195, 197–198, 200, 202–203, 205, 207
Hacks 261
Hall, Stuart 3–4, 10, 39, 133–136, 143–145, 243–244, 247–248, 275
Hall, Toderick 270
Hallahan, James 173
Halperin, David 173
Hampshire, Emily 176
The Handmaiden 261
The Handmaid's Tale 210, 219, 260
Handsome Stewardess 270
Happiest Season 260
Hastag 5, 10, 72, 74, 99, 104, 107, 111, 162
hate crimes 216
Hawkeye 262
HBO (Network) 2, 8–9, 95, 112–114, 212–213, 223, 233, 247
HBO Max 148, 210–211, 213–214, 219–222, 255, 261–262
hearing loss 216
Heartstone 264
Heartstopper 260
hegemony 19, 36, 38–40, 43–49, 134–136, 150, 154, 159, 243, 247–249, 272
Héloïse (*Portrait of a Lady on Fire*) 173
Henderson, Caroline 193, 197–203, 205–206

Henry, Larry 278
Here TV 259, 264
Hernriksen, Victor 151, 165
Heteronormativity 158–159, 165, 246, 276
heterosexuality 17, 21, 25–26, 102, 150, 153–155, 157, 161–162, 172–174, 178, 185, 187, 249
Hidden Kisses 264
Hill, Dulé 132
Hinter Gittern 184
historical fiction 193–194, 196–197, 199–208
HistorySpark 194, 196, 203, 205–207
HIV/AIDS 155, 186, 212, 261, 268
Hobbes, Miranda 223, 229–230, 232–237
The Hobbit 277–278
Homoerotica 149, 153, 155–156
homophobia 21–23, 25, 31, 55, 65, 68, 73, 77, 149, 151–152, 156, 160–166, 174, 177, 179, 184, 186
homosexuality 151, 154, 162, 165–166, 172–175, 177, 179–180, 183–187, 265, 270
homosocial 155
Hoover, J. Edgar 174
House 214, 216–217
House of Cards 215
House of Hummingbird 261
House of the Dragons 95–96, 276
How I Met Your Mother 100
Hulan, Haley 185
Hulu 12, 141, 210, 212–214, 216, 218–222, 255, 260, 261–262, 265, 268
human extinction 215
human trafficking 215, 217
hypermasculinity 153–154

I Can Tell You Anything 268
I Hate New Years 267
identity 8–9, 60, 65, 77, 95, 100, 111, 134–135, 149, 151, 166, 174–178, 180, 186, 194, 197, 203–207, 223, 234–235, 239, 243, 259, 272
IMDb 132–133, 136–137, 214, 243–244, 251–252
IMDb MOVIEmeter 214
immigration 7–8, 100, 122, 213, 217, 244, 248, 251, 254
implicit bias 211, 222
inclusivity 29, 50, 130, 150, 159, 163, 180, 200, 203–204, 206, 208, 237–238, 259, 261, 263–264, 268, 272–273
Indian 232, 250
Instagram 65–66, 69, 72, 75–76, 214, 243, 248

286 Index

intersectionality 234, 244, 247–249, 254
intertextuality 155
Iron Man 252
Iser, Wolfgag 2, 3, 9–10, 96, 106, 275
ISIS 245
Israeli 161

Jake (*Schitt's Creek*) 176
James, Lennie 121
Jane the Virgin 111, 184
Janice (*Mean Girls*) 173
January 6 217
Japanese 270
Jarchow, Stephen P. 264
Jenkins, Henry 1, 82–83, 150
Jenkins, Patty 245
Joe Bell 260
John (*Sex and the City*) see Big
Johnny (*Schitt's Creek*) 175–176
Jones, Majorie 173
Jones, Samantha 224, 229–231
Jordan, Michael B. 109
Jules (*My Best Friend's Wedding*) 173

Kang, Angela 127
Kapur, Mohan 250
Kariuki, Laura 132
Katya (*UNHhhh*) 267
Khan (*Star Trek Into Darkness*) 250
Khan, Kamala 244, 246–247, 249–253
The Kids Are Alright 261
Killing Eve 184
King, Martin Luther 206
King, Michael Patrick 224, 231, 234–235
King, Stephen 108
Knight, Tracy 173
Krasinski, John 5
Kripke, Eric 149–150, 152–156, 165
Krohg, Christian 202

Lafitte, Benny 162
Larsen, Katherine 151
Larson, Brie 244, 254
The Last Airbender 193
Latinx 8, 21, 25, 54, 75, 122, 235, 250–251, 261, 267
Layla (*Supernatural*) 154
Leahy, Eileen 162
Lee, Spike 9
legalization of marijuana 216
lesbian 103, 107, 111, 113, 173–176, 185, 224, 255–256, 260, 262–265, 268–270
Lesflicks 268–269
Levy, Dan 173, 175, 180
Levy, Eugene 175

Lexa (*The 100*) 98, 101–103, 105, 107, 111, 173, 181–185
LGBTQ 38, 40–41, 98, 102, 103, 107, 111, 151, 155, 160–162, 164, 172, 174–175, 178, 180, 183–186, 212, 216, 220, 223, 255–260, 262–273
liberalism 196, 203–204
Lin, Jay 269
The Lincoln Lawyer 214–216
Lisa (*Supernatural*) 157–158
Little America 262
Little Voice 262
Livingston, Jennie 258
Ljufvina 200
Logo 258, 266–267
Logo30 267
Loki 254, 262
The Lord of the Rings: The Rings of Power 95–96, 276–278
Love, Death, & Robots 214–216
Love, Simon 256–257, 260, 270
Love, Victor 260
Lucifer 214

Madi (*The 100*) 183
MAGA 22, 74
The Magicians 111
Magnum, P.I. 83, 132
Manaj, Hasan 246
The Mandalorian 1, 214, 219
Māori 122, 126
Marentino, Anthony 173, 231, 235
marginalization 18–19, 21–22, 37–38, 50, 56, 61, 70, 86, 107, 145, 178, 186, 225, 267, 272
Marianne (*Portrait of a Lady on Fire*) 173
Marlboro Man 153
Marlens, Neal 131
marriage 172–173, 179, 184
Marvel Cinematic Universe 244, 249, 251–253
The Marvels 244, 252
Mary Jo (*Designing Women*) 212
masculinity 54, 124, 126, 150, 153–154, 165, 198
Mattel, Trixie 267
Maude 211
Max *see* HBO Max
Maya (*Pretty Little Liars*) 184
Mayor Pete 260
McConnell, Michael 172, 174
Mean Girls 173
Meg (*Supernatural*) 156
mental health 174, 179, 186, 212, 218
Mercury, Freddie 256
Meredith (*Grey's Anatomy*) 211
Merigold, Triss 193
metacritic 243, 251–252

Metatron 194, 196, 198–200, 202–207
#MeToo 31, 213, 276
Mexican 21, 234
Michael (*My Best Friend's Wedding*) 173
microaggressions 65, 72, 74, 139, 141, 225
Microsoft 90
migration theory 199–200
Mike (*All in the Family*) 211
Milligan, Dustin Wallace 179
Miner, Rachel 156
minorities 7–8, 17, 21, 22, 29, 36, 38, 40–42, 53–54, 57, 59, 62, 101, 109–110, 113–115, 120–121, 140, 151, 163, 243–244, 268, 270
Mir, Shabana 250
Miriel (*The Lord of the Rings: The Rings of Power*) 278
Miseducated 268
The Miseducation of Cameron Post 263
misogyny 151–152, 156, 164, 236, 246
Mison, Tom 5
Mitch (*Modern Family*) 173
Modern Family 173, 214, 216, 220, 261
Moira (*Schitt's Creek*) 175–176
Monsoon, Jinkx 268
Moonlight 257
Moore, Spence II 132
Morarity, Dean 152, 157
Morgan, Jeffrey Dean 154, 182
Ms. Marvel (character) 244–246, 249–253
Ms. Marvel (series) 10, 12, 214, 220, 243–254
MTV 261
Muhammad 213
Murphy, Ryan 270
Muslim 243–253
My Best Friend's Wedding 173
My So-Called Life 260
Mythic Quest 262

NAACP 35, 42, 50
Naomi (*Supernatural*) 157
NBC 210, 212–214, 218, 220–222, 261
NCIS 214, 218–219
Negan (*The Walking Dead*) 182
nepotism 110
Netflix 8, 9, 11, 95, 105, 205–207, 210–211, 213–216, 220–222, 255, 259, 260–266, 268
neurodiversity 232
Never Have I Ever 260
New Line Cinema 277
New Queer Cinema 258
The Nielsen Company 64
Night Sky 214, 217

9/11 150, 154, 165, 246, 251
Nixon, Cynthia 235
Noah's Arc 267
nonbinary 8, 143, 176, 178–179, 187, 232, 234–235, 261
Nonvete, Sophia 278
nostalgia 97, 132–133, 140–141, 145
Nostalglia Critic 193
Noth, Christopher 230
nuclear family 143
Nunjani, Kumal 246
NYPD 250–251

Obama, Barack 174
Obi-Wan 214, 220
The Office 214, 218
Olsen, Jenni 263
Olsson, Ty 162
On the Road 153, 165
The 100 1, 10–11, 97, 172–173, 181–183, 275–276
One Mississippi 261
opioid addiction 217
Orange Is the New Black 212, 260
Orientalism 247
Orphan Black 184
The Orville 214, 219
The "Other" Love Story 265

Padalecki, Jared 148, 160, 164–165
Painting with Raven 267
Pakistani 243–244, 246–250, 252, 253
pansexuality 176, 181, 271
Paradise, Sal 157
Paramount+ 255, 261–262, 267
parasocial 166, 223, 225–231, 234, 237–240
paratext 149, 163–164, 166
Pariah 261, 269
Parker, Nicole Ari 232
Parker, Sarah Jessica 224, 237
Parris, Teyonah 244
participatory culture 82–83
Patel, Seema 232–234
patriarchy 18, 73, 77, 139, 174, 244–246, 248
Patriot Act 246
Patterson, Saladin K. 132–133
Peacock 255, 261
pedophilia 164
Pelliccione, Damian 265
performativity 20, 158–159, 164
petition 1, 3, 29
Pittman, Karen 232–233
plausibility 198–200, 202
POC 232–234
police misconduct 215
political discourse 248
The Politician 172

Portico Media 269
Portrait of a Lady on Fire 172
Pose 172
positivism 194–195, 200, 202, 205, 207
poverty 212
power dynamics 234
prejudice 138
Pretty Little Liars 184
Pride Month 174, 184
The Prince of Persia 250
Princess Disa (*LoTR: The Rings of Power*) 278
Prisha (*Little Voice*) 262
The Prom 270
protagonist 152, 160, 227
Purgatory Convention 160

Q-Force 260
queer 6, 8, 22, 56, 59, 62, 98, 102, 105, 108, 111–113, 143, 150–152, 155–159, 162–165, 173, 183–185, 235, 255, 257–263, 265–266, 268–272
Queer as Folk 261
queer-coding 155, 161
Queer Eye 261
queerbaiting 10, 102, 148, 150–151, 153, 155, 164–165
queerphobic 154
Queliot 184
Quentin (*The Magicians*) 173, 184

race 181, 196–197, 206, 212, 223, 232–233, 238, 243–244, 247–249, 251, 253–254, 267, 276
race-swapping 145, 193, 197, 203, 205, 207
race theory 35, 44, 47, 195
racism 2, 17–32, 35–36, 38–43, 46–49, 53–59, 61–62, 64–65, 68, 70–77, 121, 123, 126, 131, 140–141, 194, 205–207, 210, 232, 244, 249, 252–253, 255–257, 263, 267–270, 272, 276
Rafiki 269
Rambeau, Monica 244
Ramirez, Sara 234–235
Ramy 246
Rapp, Anthony 261
Ratched 260
The Real World 261
Rebelde 260
reception theory 244
Red Scare 56
Reddit 5, 66–67, 74, 96, 136–137, 223, 228–229, 231–239, 244, 276
Redditor 136–137, 223, 228–229, 231–238
Reid, Noah 173, 175
religion 19, 44, 49, 71, 243–244, 248–249, 251–254

representation 244, 246, 249, 251, 267, 276
Resident Evil 83
Revry 259, 264–265
Rhimes, Shonda 5, 270
Rich, B. Ruby 258, 272
Richardson, Amelia 162
Rift 264
Robinson, Angela 258
Robinson, Sean 183
Rodriguez, Christopher 265
Roe vs. Wade 210
RogerEbert.com 252
The Rookie 214, 216
Rose (*Jane the Virgin*) 184
Rose (*The Golden Girls*) 212
Rose, David 173, 175–181, 183, 185
Roseanne (actor) 244
Roseanne 5, 97, 105, 132, 212
Ross, Chase 271
Rothenberg, Jason 101, 103, 107, 111, 181–183
Rotten Tomatoes 224, 243–244, 251, 253
RuPaul's Drag Race 261, 265–268
RuPaul's Drag Race All Stars 261
Ryfe Scale of Psychological Well Being 176

same-sex 163, 172, 174–178, 182, 183, 185–186, 234, 270
Sampson, Cindy 157
San Diego Comic-Con 148
Sandilands, Neil 181
Santana (*Glee*) 173
Saturday Night Live 95
Savage, Fred 132, 140
Saved by the Bell 261
Saving Face 269
Saxton, Laura 196
Scandal 99, 115, 270
Schitt's Creek 10, 172–173, 175, 178–181, 185
Seasons of Love 267
Segura, Tom 105–106
Seifert, Colleen M. 179
Sengbloh, Saycon 132
Sense8 8
September 11 see 9/11
Seven Seconds 213
Sex and the City (film) 224
Sex and the City (series) 97, 223–224, 229–230, 232–234, 236–239
Sex and the City 2 173, 224, 232
Sex Education 260
The Sex Lives of College Girls 261
sexism 68. 73, 114, 210, 212, 234, 245
sexual abuse 212

Index

sexual fluidity 224
sexual harassment 185
sexual identity 174, 176–177, 184, 234
sexual minorities 17, 21–22, 270
sexual misconduct 275–276
sexual orientation 19, 177–178, 185
sexuality 12, 18, 65, 75, 77, 102, 108, 153–157, 159, 163–164, 166, 174, 183, 238, 248–249, 256
Shaikh, Saagar 250
Shelter 264
Shoresy 214, 219
Showtime 8
Shroff, Zenobia 250
Siken, Richard 155
Silicon Valley 246
Singer, Bobby 160
Singh, Lilly 270
Sleepy Hollow 5, 97
Smith, Justin 159
Smith, Will 210
Socarides, Charles W. 174
social cause 213–222
social construction 135, 177
Social Darwinism 195; see also Darwinism
social issue 211–212, 214–221
social media 1, 3–5, 9–12, 18, 20–21, 31–32, 35, 40, 43–45, 49–50, 53–69, 71–72, 75–76, 78, 81–84, 87, 90, 95–99, 101, 103–106, 109–110, 112, 114, 130, 135–136, 145, 148–152, 162, 164, 165, 182, 184, 223, 226–231, 234, 239, 244, 245, 248–251, 257, 263–264, 267, 270, 272, 276, 278
social movement 213–214, 220–221
social structure 65, 174, 187
socio-cultural 133–134, 173, 185–186
Sodom's Cat 270
Sokel, Brian 266
Sort Of 247
Soul 220
South Park 213
Spectrum 245
The Staircare 214, 219
Star Trek: Discovery 261
Star Trek Into Darkness 250
Star Trek: The Next Generation 1, 97
Star Wars 252
Steinfeld, Hailee 262
stereotype 5, 18, 27, 38–39, 42, 54, 65, 123, 126–127, 135, 160–161, 172–174, 178, 181, 185–186, 235–236, , 243, 246–247, 256
Stern, Danielle 140
Stern, Shosannah 162

Steve (*Sex and the City*) 234, 236–237
Steven Universe: The Movie 261
Stevie (*Schitt's Creek*) 176
Stone, Sharon 230
Stonewall Movement 174
The Stonewall Uprising 174
Straight Up 259
Stranger Things 132, 214–216, 253
streaming and video-on-demand (SVOD) 255, 258–259, 263, 264, 267, 270, 272
streaming platform 7–9, 12, 73, 211, 255, 257, 272, 278
streaming video 214–215, 217–219, 226
Sue Anne (*Supernatural*) 154
suicide 159, 184, 186–187, 212, 271
Supergirl 245, 270
superhero 243–247, 249–250, 252, 254
Supernanny 7
Supernatural 10, 148–166, 184, 214, 218
Superstore 261
SVOD *see* streaming and video-on-demand
symbiotic relationship 2, 96, 108, 150, 249

Taei, PJ 269
Talbot, Bela 150, 165
Tara (*Buffy the Vampire Slayer*) 182, 184
Tara (*The Walking Dead*) 182, 184
Taylor, Breonna 29, 57
Taylor, Eliza 98, 181
The Teacher 269
Ted (*Schitt's Creek*) 179, 180
Teenage Bounty Hunters 260
Tello Films 267–268
Terhune, Cindy 178
terrorists 247
30 Years from Here 264
This Is Us 210, 214, 218
Thompson, Robbie 155
Thor: Ragnarok 252
Three Months 261
TikTok 73, 231
Titus (*The 100*) 181
To Wong Foo, Thanks for Everything! Julie Newmar 263
Tokenism 137, 166, 185–186, 232
Tolkien (*The Lord of the Rings*) 276, 278
Tolstoy, Leo 275
tomatometer 224
toxic masculinity 153–154
transgender 38, 185, 232, 234, 255, 260–261, 267, 269, 271

Transmedia 60–61, 163, 166
transnationalism 248
Transparent 261
transphobia 232, 235
trans-species 261
The Trevor Project 107
Trinkets 260
Trump, Donald 35, 43, 68–70
Tubi 262, 263, 265
Tukey's HSD Test 220
Tumblr 96, 153, 159, 164–165
Tweet 1, 5, 10, 26, 30, 57, 62–63, 65–66, 68, 70, 72, 74, 76, 90, 99–104, 115, 136–137, 161, 163, 228–230, 243, 250
24 246
Twin Peaks 97
Twitter *see* X
Two Broke Girls 100
Two Brothers 268
Tyesha (*Ms. Marvel*) 251
TysonPlus 268–269

Ugly Betty 8
Uncle Frank 260
UNHhhh 267
universal healthcase 216
Unpregnant 261
Uscreen 269
Uses and Gratifications Theory 36, 40–41

Van Sant, Gus 258
Vellani, Iman 244, 246–247, 249, 253
VH1 266
Vietnam 138, 154
The View 96, 276
Viking 193–196, 198–201, 20–208
The Vikings 194
Vikings: Valhalla 193–194, 196–199, 202–203, 205–208, 276
Villanelle (*Killing Eve*) 184
Visible: Out on Television 262
Vito 261
VOD 268–269

Walker 164
The Walking Dead 111, 120–121, 123–125, 127–128, 182, 184
Wallace, Nya 232–234
Walter (*Maude*) 211
Ward, L. Monique 186
Warner Bros. 261
Warner TV 162
Washington, Denzel 206
The Watermelon Women 269
We Are Lady Parts 247
Weber, Lindsey 278
weird relativism 204, 208
Wexley, Lisa Todd 232–234
White, Hayden 204
White Eurocentrism 244

Whitfield, Charles Malik 151
Widmeyer, Diana 268
Wikipedia 214
Wilde, Oscar 154
Williams, Bill 132
Williams, Bruce 132, 138–139
Williams, Dean 132, 137–139, 141
Williams, Elisha 132
Williams, Kim 132
Williams, Lillian 132, 139–140, 144
Winchester, Dean 148–150, 152–162
Winchester, John 154
Winchester, Sam 149, 152, 154, 162
Winchester brothers 165
The Winchesters 149

The Wire 212
The Witcher 193
Wojcicki, Susan 271
Woke 44–45, 48–49, 63, 70, 74, 203–207, 232, 252–254
Wolfe On Demand 263–264, 267
Wolfe Video 263–264, 272
womanhood 154
Wonder Woman (1975) 245
Wonder Woman (2007) 245
The Wonder Years (1988) 131–132
The Wonder Years (2021) 10, 12, 130–133, 136–137, 141, 143–146, 239
Workin' Moms 210
Wow Presents Plus 267

X 4, 136–137, 148, 152, 159–160, 162–165, 175, 214, 228–234, 237, 239, 243, 248, 250, 263–264, 271
The X-Files 214, 216–217
Xenophobia 244

Young, Helen 197
Young Royals 260
Younger 1, 11
Youssef, Ramy 246
YouTube 9–10, 18, 20, 23, 45, 70, 158, 164, 177, 193–200, 202–208, 214, 270–272

Zamora, Pedro 261